# RECORDING HISTORY

# RECORDING HISTORY

*Jews, Muslims, and Music
across Twentieth-Century North Africa*

———

CHRISTOPHER SILVER

Stanford University Press
Stanford, California

STANFORD UNIVERSITY PRESS
Stanford, California

Printed in the United States of America on acid-free, archival-quality paper

Library of Congress Cataloging-in-Publication Data

Names: Silver, Christopher (Christopher Benno), author.

Title: Recording history : Jews, Muslims, and music across twentieth-century North Africa / Christopher Silver.

Description: Stanford, California : Stanford University Press, 2022. | Includes bibliographical references and index.

Identifiers: LCCN 2022004427 (print) | LCCN 2022004428 (ebook) | ISBN 9781503630567 (cloth) | ISBN 9781503631687 (paperback) | ISBN 9781503631694 (ebook)

Subjects: LCSH: Popular music—Africa, North —History and criticism. | Sound recording industry —Africa, North —History —20th century. | Jews —Africa, North —Music —History and criticism. | Arabs —Africa, North —Music —History and criticism. | Africa, North —Ethnic relations —History —20th century.

Classification: LCC ML3502.5 .S55 2022 (print) | LCC ML3502.5 (ebook) | DDC 781.63096 —dc23

LC record available at https://lccn.loc.gov/2022004427

LC ebook record available at https://lccn.loc.gov/2022004428

Cover design: Derek Thornton | Notch

Cover art: (photo) Algerian Jewish and Muslim musicians in the studio at Radio Alger, c. early 1930s. From the personal collection of Gilberte Kalfon and Brigitte Kalfon. Record and sleeve: Mike_shots | Shutterstock

Typeset by Newgen North America in 10.25/15 Adobe Caslon Pro

*To Emily, Roy, and Elias,*
*for me helping me hear the world anew*

# CONTENTS

# MAP AND FIGURES

# NOTE ON TRANSLITERATION
# AND TRANSLATION

In general, song lyrics are best heard rather than read. It is in listening that one begins to apprehend the staggering diversity of pronunciation, embellishment, stress, and accent of voices past, as well as the difficulty in rendering it clearly on the printed page. Still, there is tremendous value in transcription, transliteration, and translation. I have endeavored to reflect as best as possible the very rhythm and musicality of songs which so often moved effortlessly between linguistic registers and, in certain cases, multiple languages. This book follows modified versions of the Arabic and Hebrew transliteration systems specified by the *International Journal of Middle East Studies* (IJMES) and the Library of Congress respectively. For transliteration of words from Arabic, for example, I have omitted all diacritics except for ayn (ʻ) and hamza (ʼ). For Hebrew, I have omitted most diacritical marks as well. Names with an established English or French spelling have been preserved as such (for example, Samy Elmaghribi, not Sami al-Maghribi). The goal here, as elsewhere, is to make further research as straightforward as possible. Song titles are given first in Arabic or Hebrew transliteration and then in English translation in parenthesis. When French or English lyrics appear in otherwise Arabic language songs, I keep their original spelling for ease of reading. If available, I have used existing English translations of non-English texts. All other quotations from Arabic, Hebrew, and French are my translations, although many people listened with me along the way and are given their due credit in the acknowledgments. Given the mélange of languages and dialects gleaned from well-loved and well-worn records, there may be inconsistencies of transliteration in the pages that follow. All errors are mine alone.

# ACKNOWLEDGMENTS

For scholarship to really sing it requires the collaboration of many. This book was made possible by a chorus of mentors and allies who have long provided me with both the call-and-response and deep listening necessary for a project like this one. Liner notes will never be able to do their voices justice but here is a start.

The genesis of this book is owed to many people and places. More than a decade and half ago at UC Berkeley, Emily Benichou Gottreich nimbly guided me toward the study of her own area of expertise: Moroccan and Moroccan Jewish history. That push, which turned into its own pull, brought me to Morocco for the first time in 2005 and then again in 2008 and 2009. While there in 2009, I happened upon a record store in Casablanca which changed the course of my life. In Le Comptoir marocain de distribution de disques, I was first introduced to many of the musicians who occupy the pages that follow. Since then, I have been collecting records that not only inspired this book but which continue to inspire me as well. Musicians, who do so much for so long for so many others, deserve some of the first acknowledgments here.

From my father Roy Silver, who passed away in 2003 and whose own illustrious career in the American music business I hope to someday chronicle, I learned that stars are made, not born. With this in mind, I persisted in attempting to tease out the mechanics of the North African recording industry by looking beyond the more traditional sources. Ever the producer, my father's hand can be felt throughout this entire project.

From the moment I first spoke by phone to Sarah Abrevaya Stein at the end of 2011, she has served as a constant source of inspiration and proved the most steadfast of supporters. I came into UCLA not sure which story I wanted to tell but, as usual and with unmatched deftness, Sarah guided me in the right direction and taught me to write from the heart. For years now, Sarah has given of her time to shape my work in untold ways. Simply put, this book would not have been possible without her and her encouragement. I am forever grateful for her mentorship and friendship. Alongside Sarah, Aomar Boum, whom I had known even before arriving at UCLA, has long motivated me and my work. Possessing boundless insight, Aomar has also been a faithful guide to the borderland joining history and anthropology, archival research and ethnography, and memory and nostalgia. At UCLA, Jim Gelvin not only indelibly enriched my knowledge of the modern Middle East but also coached me in the fine art of concision (which I practice on occasion). David Myers, in addition to giving me the firmest grounding in modern Jewish history that I could have ever hoped for, offered me and others advice that I have long sought to follow: if historians do nothing else, they should surprise their readers. I hope I have accomplished that here. Finally, Edwin Seroussi, as knowledgeable as he is generous, has been an indefatigable partner on this project. It is a privilege to count him as a teacher and a friend.

There are additional scholars and mentors that deserve special mention. Jonathan Glasser has served as a model of scholarship and generosity since, anxious to read his dissertation, I first reached out to him many years ago. Jonathan was also one of a handful of individuals that read this manuscript in its entirety, and his remarkable ability to hear between the notes made this book that much better. Hadj Miliani (1951–2021), who died too young and had so much more to give, was one of the most faithful guides to Algerian culture and history that I have ever encountered. Whether strolling with him in Oran or breaking bread in Cassis, he was the best intellectual companion, encyclopedic in his knowledge but also possessing an infectious sense of humor, and I miss him dearly. Finally, I have had the great honor of sitting with

Susan Gilson Miller and Susan Slyomovics in a number of settings over the years, and their expertise has strengthened this project.

Thanks is very much due to a handful of people who gave of their time and ears to listen to some of the music discussed in this book and to offer their thoughts. Above all, I am indebted to Ouail Labassi, my *cheikh*, whose expertise in and passion for the sounds of Algeria's past are helping to keep the memory of musicians alive and relevant. Labassi hears things in music that few others do and I feel fortunate to merely be in his orbit. I also want to give much deserved credit to Wafa Ben Hassine, Lamia Benyoussef, and Rania Said for enabling me understand the words of Louisa Tounsia in ways I could have never imagined. To be in such company is a privilege.

To the families of some of the musicians discussed in this book, I extend my deepest gratitude. Vered Amar, Yolande Amzallag, Freha Amzallag, Lucien Attoun, Raphaël Chenuil-Hazan, Paulette Habib, Roger Hazan, Gilberte Kalfon, David Kornblum, Etty Lassman, Brigitte Martel (née Kalfon), and Karen Zrihen helped me get to know their loved ones as they once did and made me feel part of their families as well.

For sharing materials, works in progress, wise counsel, or general expertise, I thank Hisham Aidi, Farah Atoui, Reem Bailony, Wissam Batran, Joshua Cole, Raph Cormack, Morgan Corriou, Kasper Janse, Ethan Katz, Erica Lehrer, Margarida Machado, Jessica Marglin, Katie Mullen, Yigal Nizri, Malika Rahal, Dwight Reynolds, Jessica Roda, Ted Swedenburg, Stephanie Tara Schwartz, Jonas Sibony, Malcolm Théoleyre, and Naïma Yahi.

This project has afforded me the opportunity to travel, figuratively and literally, with an extraordinary group of people. For sharing this journey with me in some shape or form, I thank Murielle Abitbol-Levy, Samuel Anderson, Bachir Aguerguan, Arthur Asseraf, Leila Ben-Gacem, Ilan Bieber, Amir Cohen, Neta Elkayam, Adam Eilath, Sami Everett, Philippe Gemgembre, Amit Hai Cohen, Alma Heckman, Thomas Henry, Elad Levi, Fred Kramer, Sam Keeley, Pauline Lewis, Yoann Morvan, Sara Nacer, Winter Schneider, Aaron Shulman, Jonathan Ward, Uri Wertheim, and Dor Zlekha Levy.

For their invaluable feedback and friendship over the years, I am especially thankful to Sara Rahnama, David Stenner, and Murat Yıldız.

I have derived tremendous benefit from trying out writing and thinking aloud at a series of workshops over the years. I thank the organizers and participants of the American Institute for Maghrib Studies Workshop (UC Berkeley), Minorities in the Islamic World Workshop (Stockholm University), the California Working Group on Jews in the Maghrib and the Middle East (UC Berkeley, USC, and UCLA), the Maghrib Studies Workshop and the Spain–North Africa Project (UC Santa Cruz), the Digital Diaspora: New Approaches in Sephardi and North African Jewish Studies Workshop (UC Santa Cruz), the very vibrant meetings of the Dynamic Maghrebi Jewish-Muslim Interaction across the Performing Arts, 1920–2020 group (University of Cambridge and Camargo Foundation in Cassis), and the Jewish Contributions to Middle Eastern Music Workshop (University of Arkansas).

For their unparalleled professionalism I also offer my thanks to the directors and staff at the various centers, archives, and libraries I have had the good fortune of visiting over the years: in Algeria: Archives nationales d'Algérie and Archives de la wilaya d'Alger; in France: Archives de l'Alliance israélite universelle; Archives nationales; Archives nationales d'outre mer; Archives de la Préfecture de Police; Bibliothèque nationale de France; Centre des archives diplomatiques de Nantes; Centre de recherche en ethnomusicologie (CREM-Paris); and Institut européen des musiques juives; in Israel: Central Zionist Archives and National Library of Israel; and in Tunisia: Archives nationales de Tunisie (ANT); and Bibliothèque nationale de Tunisie (BNT).

Deserving particular thanks are Robert Parks, Karim Ouaras, and Nassim Balla at the Centre d'études maghrébines en Algérie (CEMA), Laryssa Chomiak at Le Centre d'études maghrébines à Tunis (CEMAT), Anas Ghrab at Le Centre des musiques arabes et méditerranéennes (CMAM), Yacine Touati at the Conservatoire municipal d'Alger, Joanna Hughes at the EMI Archive Trust, Valerie Cottet at Les Archives de la Société des auteurs, compositeurs et éditeurs de musique, and Agnès Kaloun-Chibani and Matthieu Moulin at the Warner Music Archives (France).

Research requires all manner of sustenance, including financial. My work was sustained by the following organizations, foundations, and departments. At UCLA, thanks is very much due to the Maurice Amado Program, fellowships from the Roter and Monkarsh families, the Graduate Student Research Mentorship Award (GSRM), the History Department, the Center for Jewish Studies (CJS), and the Sady Kahn Trust. Similarly, the American

Institute for Maghrib Studies (AIMS), the American Academy of Jewish Research (AAJR), and the Posen Society of Fellows provided me with generous funding. At McGill, I have benefited a great deal from the support of the Segal family, a Start-Up Grant, funding from the Arts Student Employment Fund, a Paper Presentation Grant, and an Internal Social Sciences and Humanities Development Grant. Portions of the McGill funding have enabled me to work with a number of outstanding graduate and undergraduate research assistants. I thank Emma Chittleburgh, Andreas Koch, Yasmine Mossiman, Roi Ofer Ziv, Roy Shukrun, and Sophie Weiler for all of their efforts.

For her unmatched insight, support for this book from the start, and dedication to making music heard, I thank Kate Wahl. My gratitude extends as well to the entire team at Stanford University Press, especially Caroline McKusick. I also wish to recognize Susan Olin for her awe-inspiring copyediting. For the poignant and precise comments of my anonymous reviewers, I am also grateful.

Finally, for their steadfast belief in me, words can only begin to express my appreciation for my mother Linda, my sister Molly, my late grandparents Geraldine and Merrill, and my in-laws Marian and Martin. The love and support of my partner Emily have made this project and our life project possible. I am thankful to her for always encouraging me to follow my passions. With every passing day, my children Roy and Elias make my heart sing in ways that I could have never dreamed of. For that and so much more, I thank them.

# RECORDING HISTORY

# INTRODUCTION

Sometime in 1959, in the midst of the Algerian War (the bloody, anticolonial struggle which resulted in Algerian independence after more than 130 years of French rule), the famed Algerian Jewish musician Lili Labassi (né Elie Moyal) walked through the doors of RCA in Algiers to record the era's last shellac discs. For five decades, that brittle, heavy, and yet durable technological medium, which contained approximately three minutes of music per side, had held. As it did for Labassi, it made innumerable artists popular and made countless songs ubiquitous in the lives of North Africans. It also furnished a heritage. Indeed, the recently opened flagship store and studio of RCA (Recording Corporation of America), in a prime location on rue Dumont d'Urville, was very much a newcomer to a region with a long history of recording. Labassi, whom RCA believed to be critical to the success of its North African catalog, had been making records in the country since the 1920s. And the North African recording industry could trace its origins to the last years of the nineteenth century, to a place not far from where RCA now stood. It was there and then, in Algiers' lower Casbah, that the pioneering Edmond Nathan Yafil, another Algerian Jew, began to gather the tremendous Jewish and Muslim musical talent in his midst before a large phonograph horn, in order to funnel their sounds, with the aid of a cutting stylus, first onto wax cylinders and then onto shellac records.

In many ways, Labassi's RCA releases served as an embodiment of the continuity of the recording industry's past and near present and the resilience of the shellac record. The introduction that opened each disc, spoken just before the artist bowed his violin, adhered to roughly the same formula as it did in the 1890s when recordings were being released on cylinder: "RCA Records presents the famed singer Lili Labassi and his ensemble." Much as he had apprenticed with his father Joseph before him, now Labassi's ensemble included his disciple and son Robert Moyal. The young Moyal (soon to act under the French name of Castel, with which he would gain tremendous celebrity) plucked away at the 'ud, accompanying his famous father who held his signature instrument upright on his knee. "For me, it was solemn," Castel later wrote of the recording sessions which produced records even he himself no longer possessed.[1] "I thought that these records had been etched for eternity," he would lament, "the luth," his 'ud, languishing "in the grooves of the song Ezhiro [Azhiru]." Labassi's "Azhiru" (The beauty) proved another link. In addition to interpreting and ornamenting the various genres associated with the Andalusian repertoire, the Jewish musician had composed and recorded hundreds of songs like "Azhiru," helping give voice to a genre known as *sha'bi* (popular).

The RCA catalog was, indeed, popular, pulsating, and sometimes political, even if scholars have tended to focus on the persistence of the high prestige, classical, and reserved Andalusian tradition (*al-musiqa al-andalussiya, la musique andalouse*).[2] Cheikh Djilali Ain-Tedelès (né Djilali Belkaouis), a Muslim musician who must have passed Labassi in the studio hallway, recorded the Bedouin repertoire from the Oran region that would serve as the basis for the emerging and electric sounds of *raï*.[3] Nadjet Tounsia (née Fortunée Zeitoun), a Tunisian Jewish vocalist who appeared regularly on Radio Alger and in the press, recorded a much-sought-after modern Tunisian music, which took many of its cues from the Egyptian scene. In addition to "Azhiru," Labassi's anthems, dedicated to Algeria's principal cities of Algiers, Oran, and Constantine, were profound lyrical acts. As the Algerian National Liberation Front (FLN) and the French government and military engaged in a fierce battle over the fate of Algeria, Arabic-language music valorizing contested capitals was no small matter.

At mid-twentieth century, Lili Labassi and Nadjet Tounsia were among many, interconnected Jewish recording artists of their stature to move across North Africa (*al-Maghrib*). In 1952, Tounsia toured for the second time in as many years with the rising Moroccan Jewish star Samy Elmaghribi, doing so "in Casablanca and in all of the cities of the interior, Tangier, and all of the cities of Spanish Morocco," and with a contract-mandated minimum of four costume changes per engagement.[4] In turn, Elmaghribi, whose mere appearance in public drew large crowds of adoring fans, often credited Labassi as an inspiration.[5] At venues like Le Bristol, Dancing Vox, and Le Boléro in Casablanca, all of these musicians crossed paths and rubbed shoulders with the legendary Salim Halali. Having recorded with the Pathé label since 1939 and survived World War II while hidden in the Grand Mosque of Paris, this Algerian Jewish musician reemerged after the war with a new repertoire that enthralled admirers from metropolitan France to Morocco and across North Africa. He was considered to have "the most beautiful Arab male voice of the postwar era."[6] He had also become the best-selling North African recording artist of all time.[7]

The popular songs of Halali and Elmaghribi, performed live before thousands of Muslims and Jews and released on shellac records also in the thousands, skillfully blended Latin rhythms, swing, and other styles with vernacular Arabic to express decidedly modern takes on life, love, and the nation. Both artists were regulars at the royal palace and vocal supporters of the increasingly defiant Sultan Mohammed ben Youssef. The soundtrack for the Moroccan drive for independence was largely provided by Elmaghribi, whose political repertoire, released on his independent record label Samyphone, attracted attention from major anticolonial nationalist parties like the Istiqlal, French intelligence agents, and most importantly, ordinary Moroccans, as well as Algerians. Whether in concert, on radio, by way of record, or merely hummed in marketplaces, the sounds of Halali and Elmaghribi were everywhere. Their secular melodies were quickly rendered sacred by vaunted figures like Rabbi David Bouzaglo, who incorporated them into the synagogue service in an attempt to attract members of his community to Jewish prayer through Arab music.[8] Reflecting on the profane and the holy, Labassi's son Castel would later describe "Arab music" as his "second religion."[9]

Halali, Elmaghribi, Tounsia, and Labassi were among the most audible and influential cultural figures of an era of profound change and critical importance, one in which Morocco, Tunisia, and Algeria began to chart their own political futures in the absence of French colonial rule. The records of these and other artists set the tone for the period in question. Yet most histories of mid-twentieth century North Africa mention Jews only in passing and usually in reference to their departures. And music, if discussed at all, might get little more than a nod or a note. Tens of thousands of Jews did leave Morocco and Tunisia for France, Israel, and North America between Israel's establishment in 1948 and Moroccan and Tunisian independence in 1956. The vast majority of Algerian Jews, French citizens since 1870, would wait until just before and after Algerian independence in 1962 to restart their lives in France as "repatriates" of a country that most had never visited. Halali, Elmaghribi, Tounsia, and Labassi resisted as long as possible, but they, too, eventually succumbed and departed. But departure alone does not explain the silencing of the sounds of mid-twentieth century North Africa nor of the many years leading up to it. For a fuller explanation, we must return to the shellac record.

In 1959, as RCA began operations in North Africa, it became the last major label in the region ever to press new music on the old format of shellac. Since its introduction in 1948, the "unbreakable" vinyl record, which was quicker to produce, easier to store, and held far more music, had steadily displaced the technology of the past five decades. By 1959, there was no looking back as far as the recording industry was concerned. Some, like RCA, released shellac and vinyl simultaneously. But most shellac records would never make the transition to vinyl nor be preserved with an eye for perpetuity. As a result of their seeming obsolescence, an untold number of discs were discarded or otherwise disappeared. With them went the sounds of a half century.

Given all I describe, it is entirely reasonable that Labassi's son Castel would lament the lost "Azhiru," that record that captured his young self on 'ud alongside his famous father. He believed the last remaining copy of this disc—and with it, a world of North African music—was forever gone. How delighted I am to have proved him otherwise.

In 2011, more than fifty years after it was first produced for RCA, I had the spectacular fortune of happening upon an original, pristine copy of the

FIGURE 1. Lost and found: Lili Labassi's "Azhiru," RCA F 88.037,
1959—in its original sleeve. Personal collection of author.

Labassi record in question. Packed with care and then brought to Israel by a
Moroccan or Algerian migrant sometime after 1959—perhaps via France—it
sat unplayed in an apartment crawlspace in a remote development town before making its way to an Ebay seller just outside Tel Aviv, who placed it for
sale online. I bought it and it journeyed once more. What follows is a story
which could not have been written without the surfacing of that disc and
hundreds of others like it. Tracing an arc along the trajectory of a technology,
this book excavates the sounds embedded in the grooves of a forgotten musical medium. My goal is to render audible a Jewish-Muslim past which has
been quieted for far too long.

## A Deep Prelude and a Modern One

In the late 1890s, Edmond Nathan Yafil, an Algerian Jewish twenty-something raised on the music which enveloped his working-class neighborhood, began putting the infrastructure in place to revive a musical tradition—his tradition—which he referred to variously but perhaps most significantly as "the words of al-Andalus" (*kalam al-andalus*).[10] As others were beginning to do, he identified "the words of al-Andalus," in part, with the multimodal repertoire known around the capital Algiers and to the west in Tlemcen as "ghernata" (*gharnati*, from Granada), inherited from the "old Moors of the eighth and ninth centuries."[11] Yafil was motioning to what Jonathan H. Shannon and Carl Davila have referred to as the emerging "standard narrative" of Andalusian music, whose modern iteration he was also very much in the process of shaping.[12]

That standard narrative begins around the year 822, when the Baghdadi musician Ziryab (born Abu 1-Hasan ibn Nafi) arrived in Cordoba via Qayrawan (in present-day Tunisia) at the court of the newly crowned Umayyad caliph Abd al-Rahman II. Chaperoning him on his journey from North Africa to al-Andalus was the influential Umayyad court musician whose name has been left to us simply as Mansur al-Yahudi (Mansur the Jew).[13] Even in its purported origins, the seeds of a rather remarkable Muslim-Jewish tale had been planted. At the caliphal court Ziryab ushered in "the splendid era of Arab music in Spain."[14] Among his many activities, he "founded the first school of music, added a fifth string to the *'ud*, taught a corpus of several thousand songs, and developed distinct music structures, including the rudiments of the *nawba* (or *nuba*, "suite") form, common in contemporary Andalusian musical traditions."[15] Central to the developing nuba (pl. *nubat*) was *muwashshah* (pl. *muwashshahat*), a strophic (or verse-repeating) poetic form which gained preeminence alike in Arabic and Hebrew and which was particularly well suited to music. Therein lay its attraction which, in addition to its subject matter, included "union with the beloved, separation, desire, wine, and the natural world as embodied in the garden."[16]

But even if the "rudiments" of the North African suite music known as the nuba were already present in al-Andalus, scholars now agree that it did not move out of the Iberian Peninsula as a whole or finished product with the fall of Granada in 1492. In fact, what became identified as the nuba in early modern North Africa was markedly different from Ziryab's music in both melody and rhythm. In the cities of Saʿdi and then ʿAlawi Morocco and the Ottoman regencies of Algiers and Tunis, many of the song texts performed by Jewish and Muslim musicians were based on muwashshah of post-Andalusian provenance.[17] In other words, terms like nuba were applied to a varied North African art music which looked back to al-Andalus but whose meaning and substance were being shaped and reshaped in-house. Shared terminology reminds us that the standard narrative of the nuba, even if revised, is often used to stand in for the totality of music in North Africa over half a millennium and therefore necessarily falls short in capturing its diversity. *Stambeli*, for instance, a trance music developed and practiced in Tunisia by the descendants of enslaved sub-Saharan men and women, also employs the word nuba but in reference to particular tunes (not suites), imbuing it with an import all its own.[18] Likewise, the word *diwan*, which refers to a collection of song texts when applied to "the words of al-Andalus," figures in multiple traditions, including as the name for a nocturnal healing ritual among the Bilaliyya order in Algeria.[19]

In the eighteenth and nineteenth centuries, songbook compilations in manuscript form began to explicitly link and refer to the nuba as it was performed in North Africa as "Andalusian" (*Andalusi*). Among them was the foundational *kunnash* (notebook) of the Moroccan jurist Muhammad Ibn al-Husayn al-Haʾik, which likely appeared sometime after 1788.[20] This is when we might begin to date the relatively recent consolidation of a music identified as Andalusian into a heritage known as "Andalusian music," although its practitioners would be the first to admit that it was never practiced as a single tradition. If for Yafil Andalusian music was gharnati, as it was for those in a geographic area extending to the Moroccan-Algerian border, it was *al-ala* for the inhabitants of northern Morocco and *maʾluf* for Jews and Muslims dwelling between eastern Algeria, Tunisia, and Tripoli, Libya. Whatever it was named, Yafil feared it at risk of disappearing due to the elapse of time and to the failure of manuscript holders to get with the times by committing their collections to the modern medium of print. Moving from print to recording, he dedicated his life to reversing a trend that had accelerated since France had led a violent conquest of Algeria more than half a century earlier.

In the French imagination, Yafil, as an Algerian Jew, was supposed to have distanced himself from this "native art" (*l'art indigène*), as it was reified and debased in colonial parlance, by the 1890s. The combined effects of the French conquest of Ottoman Algiers in 1830, the annexation of Algeria to the metropole in 1848, the 1870 Crémieux Decree, which legally transformed arabophone northern Algerian Jews into French citizens, and the ongoing "civilizing mission," were to have steered Yafil and his coreligionists away from all things native, including Muslims (who remained subjects of empire), and toward acculturation into France.[21] Much of this was also true in Tunisia and Morocco, which were made French protectorates in 1881 and 1912, respectively. While Tunisian and Moroccan Jews were not naturalized en masse, Crémieux being regarded as a mistake by colonial officials, members of this non-Muslim minority group were deemed, in the words of Tunisian Jewish writer Albert Memmi, "candidates for assimilation."[22] In advance of French occupation, in fact, French Jews thought similarly. Through schooling, the Franco-Jewish educational system of the Alliance israélite universelle (AIU), founded in 1860 by, among others, the same Adolphe Crémieux whose name was attached to the Algerian decree, pushed forward a "regenerative" program to modernize and make French their brothers and sisters in North Africa. The first ever AIU school opened its doors in Tetouan, Morocco, in 1862. By 1878, it had moved into Tunisia as well. Dozens of others would follow. By the eve of World War I, the AIU could count some thousands of French-speaking graduates, many of whom now filled important and intermediate positions in the colonial economy.

Most accounts of twentieth-century North African Jewish history trace a line along that path to assimilation in what Memmi has described of his fellow travelers as "their efforts to forget the past, to change collective habits, and their enthusiastic adoption of Western language, culture and customs."[23] This is not one of them. Indeed, for that story to work, we must ignore figures like Yafil. In similar fashion, most historical accounts of North African music during that same period—of Jewish emancipation and then dislocation— extend the standard narrative of Andalusian music forward. But telling the story along that model, I contend, is to get lost in Yafil's words and/or to ignore what he and his successors recorded.

## Toward a History Written in Grooves

Some 120 years ago, the recording industry was born in North Africa. The leading figure behind it was our very own Yafil.[24] Ever the impresario, he had already put to use the major technology of the day to record the most renowned musicians of his generation on cylinder and then disc even before international labels like Gramophone, Odeon, and Pathé arrived on the scene in Algiers, Tunis, and elsewhere in North Africa. In quick succession, those companies recruited him to represent their interests and to serve as their artistic director. Thanks to Yafil, the pages of early twentieth-century North African record catalogs were filled with Jewish vocalists and instrumentalists, alongside a minority of Muslims. Their output, increasingly dedicated to all styles popular, topical, and comedic then emerging, as well as to the Andalusian repertoire, was initially labeled by the major companies as "Arab music" but then increasingly packaged in national terms as either "Algerian," "Moroccan," or "Tunisian," depending on the context. Such was the nature of rendering music commercial.

Immediately before and after World War I, additional labels moved into North Africa as homegrown ones developed too. Again, their representatives and concessionaires were for the most part Jews who served as talent scouts, producers, and distributors. Their products, shellac records ranging from 10 to 11½ inches in diameter (sometimes bigger) and which spun, in general, at 78 rotations per minute (rpm), reproduced approximately three minutes of music per side; they were recorded locally and then pressed in places like Germany and France before being made available for purchase in cities all across North Africa. Records were sold to individual Jews and Muslims and as well to a network of Jewish and Muslim middlemen who then resold them to the far reaches of Morocco, Algeria, and Tunisia and across colonial and imperial borders. Consumed in cafés, bars, restaurants, cabarets, theaters, and even brothels as well as in private homes, record sales exploded in the interwar period. In part, this was thanks to the advent of electrical recording via the microphone, which allowed for a greater range of sounds to be captured on disc.

Radio emerged. So did stars and superstars. At the forefront of that celebrity and notoriety was a coterie of young Jewish women who recorded words both Arabic and French, salacious and subversive. They rose against a backdrop of popular melodies crafted by Jewish composers and drawn from the foxtrot, inspired by the Charleston, and indebted to a robust music scene in Egypt. In the concert halls where these "modern girls" reigned, new ideas about love, marriage, the role of women, and the nation were communicated at full volume to Jews and Muslims of diverse classes, who managed to gather in large numbers and listen collectively despite a French colonial system designed to keep them apart.[25]

So Jewish was Arab music across North Africa between the two world wars that it begged constant comment from contemporaneous observers. Algeria proves a particularly illuminating case study. Some, like writer Gabriel Audisio, son of the director of the Algiers Opera, saw fit to acknowledge in a 1930 review of the Parlophone label's entrance to the Algerian market that "the native professionals of Algiers are for the most part, as elsewhere, the Jews of the country." He added, "this is a point that one should not neglect in the study of this music."[26] To French colonial officials, Jewish fidelity to their "native" language and music seemed to betray their status as citizens and as heirs to a civilizing mission more than five decades in the making. That some of their recorded music was also nationalist and anticolonial, even pan-Arabist, confused and angered intelligence agents and bureaucrats who noted with growing trepidation the role played by Jewish "auxiliaries" in spreading what Rebecca Scales has referred to as "subversive sound."[27]

Muslim elites were sometimes none too pleased themselves. At the very moment that Audisio made his remarks, Mahieddine Bachetarzi, Yafil's Muslim disciple and successor, was confronted with "a widespread grievance" then current in Algiers. The novelist and critic Abdelkader Hadj Hammou delivered the message to the tenor known as the "Caruso of the Desert": El Moutribia, the acclaimed Algerian orchestra founded by Yafil and whose direction he had inherited, was too Jewish, its repertoire not faithful enough to al-Andalus, and its sound too popular. Bachetarzi responded at first by defending Yafil, then by describing his own failed efforts to recruit Muslims to his orchestra. He lamented, "it is extremely unfortunate that an artistic effort has aroused confessional conflict. Good relations would have done much more to aid the development of Arab music."[28] He meant the admixture of Muslim musicians to the Jewish base of pioneering musicians, like early recording artists and founding members of El Moutribia Eliaou "Laho" Seror and Saül "Mouzino" Durand, who had transformed Arab music since just before the turn of the twentieth century. After all, Bachetarzi reminded, "Jews, Yafil, Laho Seror, Mouzino had been the first to spread it." Despite their confession, this was not "Jewish music" (*la musique juive*), he argued against a charge that must have been leveled, but "Arab music" (*la musique arabe*), shared by Algerians of both faiths.

The "widespread grievance" communicated to Bachetarzi—that his Algerian orchestra was not Algerian enough—pointed to the growth of an interwar mass politics which increasingly defined the nation in Arab and Muslim terms. Across North Africa and in metropolitan France as well, nationalist political parties demanding reform and rights but not yet independence attracted considerable membership as well as negative attention from French authorities. Music, disseminated on records, proved pivotal to that process. That movement was further accelerated by World War II, which for many North Africans commenced with the fall of France's Third Republic and the concomitant rise of the Vichy regime in 1940.[29] While music was far from silenced in Morocco, Algeria, and Tunisia under Vichy rule between June 1940 and November 1942, Jewish musicians certainly were. That was also the case for those North African Jews who found themselves living in the German Occupied Zone of France during that same period and until the liberation of Paris in 1944. Under Chief of State Marshal Philippe Pétain, Vichy applied a series of anti-Jewish race laws (*statut des juifs*) to the Unoccupied Zone of southern France and North Africa beginning in October 1940. This legislation, similar to that in Germany, extended to domains like radio and public performance, which meant that the Jewish musicians largely synonymous with the recording industry and concert scene of just a few years prior were increasingly difficult to hear across the Mediterranean. This was not true for their Muslim counterparts, including Bachetarzi, who continued to perform under and for Vichy, replacing their former Jewish collaborators and competitors on the airwaves and on stage in the process.

But as the reappearance of Halali, the debut of Elmaghribi, and the continued popularity of Labassi postwar remind us, our narrative does not end at midcentury, as many others have, with either the establishment of Israel in 1948, the start of the Algerian War in 1954, or Moroccan and Tunisian independence in 1956 and Algerian independence in 1962. The music of Elmaghribi, for example, first recorded for Pathé in 1948, provided the Moroccan march to liberation with its rhythm. It also lifted the spirits of Algerians. Even after the Jewish musician departed Morocco in 1959 for Paris, he recorded music to comfort his compatriots after a catastrophic earthquake leveled the Moroccan coastal city of Agadir, toured Algeria in the midst of the National Liberation Front's (FLN) struggle for independence from France, and maintained a centrally located record store in Casablanca that bore his name until 1965. During that period and for long afterward, a number of his iconic songs were reprised and reinterpreted by Muslim artists in North Africa. While he was not forgotten, much of his nationalist repertoire was. If "the incontestable Jewish element in this profoundly North African musical tradition stakes perhaps the strongest claim in Muslims' collective memory of Jews," as Emily Benichou Gottreich and Daniel Schroeter have written, echoing Hadj Miliani, still missing is the breadth, scope, and impact of their sounds.[30] Given all of this, it is time to finally listen for them.

Why was Arab music so Jewish for so long across twentieth-century North Africa? Ethnomusicologists have proposed at least one answer: that the vexed nature of music and certain musical instruments in Islam created a space for Jewish instrumentalists, as well as Jewish vocalists, who used the instrument-free space of the synagogue to hone their craft. But such a conclusion, as many of the same scholars readily admit, satisfies only in the broadest of strokes, especially when considering Islamic legal theory as separate from the rich tradition of Muslim musical praxis.[31] As research for this book progressed, other questions, less obvious and more intriguing, came to feel more pressing. What did Jewish participation in this all-important cultural realm in such large numbers say about their (changing) place in twentieth-century North Africa? How might we understand the nature of their musical contributions? Who were their audiences and what was the meaning of music to them? Finally, what might music reveal about the region and about the Jewish-Muslim relationship that other sources could not?

*Recording History* serves as a wake-up call. Situated at the nexus of Middle Eastern and North African (MENA) and Jewish history but so too studies of popular culture, it is first and foremost an acknowledgment that music is of consequence. In this way, I contend that listening to the past provides twentieth-century North Africa with a soundscape that dramatically alters its historiographical landscape. Or, put differently: this book demonstrates that music remembers much of what history has forgotten.[32] In this first-of-its-kind study, an investigation of the origins of recording across North Africa and its largely Jewish infrastructure provides for a rewriting of the not-too-distant past in Morocco, Algeria, and Tunisia. By attuning our focus to music as a process, involving impresarios and intermediaries as much as it did instrumentalists and vocalists, it locates North Africa as an integral nodal point in a global industry—still little understood—which supported among the most monumental technological innovations of the last century and half: the phonograph and the record.[33]

Although *Recording History* deals mainly in the popular and commercial, the Andalusian repertoire gets the attention it deserves. In part, this is because popular melodies sometimes drew inspiration from the high art tradition. In fact, musicians like Labassi and Elmaghribi often moved back and forth between the two registers over the course of their careers. Despite this, the very legitimacy of popular music has long been bound up with the undeniable prestige of al-Andalus and its musical legacy. Not coincidentally, the recasting of Andalusian music at the turn of the twentieth century as the one and only national tradition, whether in Morocco, Algeria, or Tunisia, was a reaction, to a considerable degree, to the popularity of Thomas Edison's 1877 invention (the phonograph), Emile Berliner's 1887 modification (the disc instead of the cylinder), and the spread of mass culture. As others have done in connecting the growth of Andalusian music associations and orchestras under colonialism to the formation of nationalism, this book centers the story of nation building on the commercial recording of popular music as well.[34]

By following composers and lyricists, artistic directors and distributors, critics and audiences, in addition to the star musicians themselves, *Recording History* likewise contributes to a growing literature on mass culture and mass politics in MENA, notably but not exclusively in Egypt.[35] Similarly, by immersing itself for the most part in popular music, which proved to provide the content for the best-selling records of the time, this book locates colonial modernity both locally and regionally, a modernity that was expressed in various forms of vernacular Arabic, including those morseled with French.[36] The orientation away from both metropolitan France and elite-centered high culture surfaces notable absences from the normative narrative of twentieth-century North Africa. In *Recording History*, for example, female musicians take center stage as among the most articulate voices of the nation and nationalism.

The pursuit of music in this book, whether in following artists who toured and settled between capitals, the unfettered flow of records across borders, or styles incubated in geographical borderlands, makes the case not only for the utility of a regional approach to North Africa but for its necessity as well. Pushing back against a "colony-metropole perspective [ . . . ] severed from the Maghreb and its many histories," Julia Clancy-Smith has proposed "a horizontal axis to investigate the problematic of identity and physical displacements." *Recording History* therefore moves beyond the nation-state by operating along a "horizontal axis." In so doing, it links parallel, inter-connected, and inseparable processes across Morocco, Algeria, and Tunisia (and farther afield in Egypt) while resisting the *telos* of fitting a transnational story into national boundaries.

Finally, in mapping the prominence of a Jewish minority who produced and popularized a modern Arab music that indelibly shaped the culture of the Muslim majority, this book joins recent scholarship which has come to view Jews and Muslims in the wider MENA region through lenses of entanglement and enmeshment rather than of power relations as seem-ingly self-evident as "majority-minority."[37] As *Recording History* illustrates, the Jewish-Muslim relationship in Morocco, Algeria, and Tunisia was often intimate, improvised, and unpredictable. In a way, this was not unlike the music itself.

## Sourcing Music

Given its political, cultural, sensorial, and emotional importance, the general silence of historians on music surprises. As Edwin Seroussi has pointed out, "comprehensive textbooks on Jewish culture of recent publication do not in-clude the word 'music' in their index."[38] The same is true for their analogues in MENA studies, although this is changing.[39] In a different context, Richard Cullen Rath has traced this reticence to the "belief that, unlike a document, sound is ephemeral, going out of existence even as it happens."[40] Compli-menting Rath, Seroussi has suggested that "one could add to this perception of inaccessibility the poor public relations that music has among nonmusic scholars in the modern and postmodern eras of mechanical reproduction."[41] Expressed differently, too many have operated for too long with the understanding that music is at best intangible and, at worst, the domain of someone else.

*Recording History* recovers a world of physical, visual, and audible musical documents, making clear that sourcing music in the first half of the twentieth century is not only possible but of considerable benefit to scholars moving forward. This has meant that alongside a more conventional source base used by historians of North Africa, like the press, the colonial paper trail dotting Morocco, Algeria, Tunisia, and France, the literature of the period, and memoirs—all of which teem with sounds—this book has employed a novel and hitherto untapped primary resource: the Arabic-language records themselves. Gathering discs one by one, in some cases more than a century old, has brought me into spaces not typically associated with historical monographs—like flea markets and bric-a-brac shops—a process which has allowed me to build a new type of archive filled with old media from the bottom up.

As physical objects, shellac records hold considerable data: the names of record companies, song titles, musicians and composers, as well as issue and matrix numbers indicating the order and dates of release, sometimes identifying the sound engineer, and much more. As aural objects, recordings provide a wealth of information, in addition to the powerful music itself: the branding and copyright inherent to the spoken announcement of record company, performer, and often the performer's epithet before the start of the music, words, pronunciation, and instruments that have fallen out of use, the identification of a musician not listed on the printed label but whose name might be invoked by others after a particularly expert execution of improvised vocals or instrumentals, and the contours of the recording facility (cavernous or not) and its proximity to the street (evidenced by the sound of a passing vehicle). Meanwhile, worn grooves and hand-fashioned repairs made to chipped or broken records bear witness, both physically and aurally, to their repeated play over time.

There are also the ephemera: the multilingual record catalogs, branch details printed on paper sleeves, and import stamps and store stickers affixed to discs, all of which permit us to map a pioneering industry and the movement of its history-making sounds. Together with newspapers, documents of French policy and bureaucratic concern, radio transcripts, production sheets from pressing plants, concert posters, family papers, and personal letters, these fragile, well-loved discs allow us to hear that which our historical actors once heard in order to better understand them and their society.

That records have survived outside of more traditional archives is remarkable. Musicians themselves do not always hold on to their own creations. To begin with, music is a difficult business. At the best of times, it forces our greatest artists to travel lightly. Many of those discussed in this book endured war, turmoil, and dislocation, sometimes at the height of their success. Their discs, of awkward size and weight, made of the most inelastic of material, vulnerable to mishandling or the application of the wrong playback equipment, and containing just a few minutes of aging music per side, could not have been expected to survive, whether in their possession or not. But survive the records did. In a testament to the significance of music, individual Moroccans, Algerians, and Tunisians grasped discs carefully over great distances and many years hoping to hear them again.

Answering the unspoken call of these caretakers and stewards, I have collected hundreds of records from locales expected and unexpected for well over a decade. Thanks to handwritten inscriptions and address labels provided by their one-time owners, we can begin to follow their direct and sometimes meandering paths: of a Salim Halali record gifted in Tunis on May 20, 1949, and then brought to Paris sometime after; of a certain Moïse Benayoun's collection of interwar Algerian discs transported to Los Angeles's San Fernando Valley; or of the last surviving copy of Tunisian Jewish superstar Habiba Messika's "Inti suriya biladi" (You are Syria, my country), once cherished by the Ottoman Syria-born Saleeh Farroh in his adoptive Detroit and which somehow made its way to an online seller in Kansas before arriving at my doorstep (in New York at the time).

These precious materials, ably cared for by individuals who acted as archivists and preservationists in all but name, passed through many hands and between many ears long before I ever encountered them. Turning knobs, pressing buttons, and making other adjustments on amplifiers, equalizers, and record players, I placed needles of various shapes and sizes on discs in order to surface sounds buried deep in their grooves. In this way, I was not only able to reproduce the product of an original recording session but also to commune with those previous to me. Indeed, Benayoun, Farroh, and I were all privileged to hear the exact same recordings, albeit at different times and in different places.

I have collected these discs for one reason: to return them to the soundscape, to repatriate them to those who once delighted in their sounds and to others who might yet do so. To accomplish this goal, I have been digitizing them for years, making them available to anyone with an internet connection through an online, trans–North African archive I have called "Gharamophone," a portmanteau of the Arabic "*gharam*" (love or passion) and the English "gramophone."[42] After decades of dormancy, the records uploaded thus far, many of which feature in this book and represent but a fraction of my overall collection, have been listened to more than 200,000 times and counting.

Among those who have found their way to the online archive have been the children and grandchildren of the music makers and purveyors in question. Initial connections have developed into lasting relationships. Eventually, we would sit together in their homes. Once, Gilberte Kalfon (née Kespi), the nonagenarian daughter of El Moutribia's famed interwar conductor Joseph "Cheb" Kespi, placed herself at the piano and tapped out a piece of music learned from her father in Algiers. On another occasion, a similarly aged Roger Hazan reminisced about his father's record store Bembaron et Hazan in Morocco. During yet a different meeting, Paulette Habib, the octogenarian daughter of recording artist and artistic director Messaoud Habib, provided insight into the Tunisian female stars of yesteryear. Always, grandsons and granddaughters and their children would bring out a box filled with photos, handwritten letters, and other documents found nowhere else. I then pressed play on the computer and together we would marvel as the soaring voices of their loved ones filled the room. As one grandson remarked:

> It is just unbelievable for me to listen to the grandfather that I never knew[.]
> We only had one poor quality recording[.] All the discs have disappeared[.]
> I am his grandson and I bear his name.[43]

The discs may have not yet completely disappeared, but we are on the precipice of a last chance to gather them. Given that, *Recording History* bears a responsibility to amplify their sounds again for the future.

### Fidelity to the Past

> "The first rule must always be: if you can't hear it, be suspicious."

> —R. Murray Schafer,
> *The Soundscape: The Tuning of the World*[44]

This book understands music to be both inherently political and inseparable from history. This idea is a not a new one, but it has sometimes been slow to gain ground depending on the context. Writing in 1963 in a very different setting but about a not dissimilar cultural domain, C. L. R. James suggested that a history of the sport of cricket was the history of his native West Indies itself. An important advocate for Trinidadian independence, a lifelong activist, and a passionate cricketer, he observed in his pathbreaking *Beyond a Boundary* that "cricket had plunged me into politics long before I was aware of it. When I did turn to politics I did not have much to learn." For James, a history of elite pursuits and individuals, that which "filled space in print but not in minds," was little reflective of the collective past.[45] It was sports that mattered. In our case, it is music. Either way, the proof is in the audience.

*Recording History*, therefore, approaches North African music much as its audiences once did rather than through the use of highly technical language. As Alex Ross has written, "at a performance, listeners experience a new work collectively, at the same rate and approximately from the same distance. They cannot stop to consider the implications of a half-lovely chord or concealed waltz rhythm. They are a crowd and crowds tend to align themselves as one mind." Whether in the concert hall or in the café, in public or in private, "ultimately, all music acts on its audience through the same physics of sound, shaking the air and arousing curious sensations."[46] In much the same multi-sensorial fashion, music acts on society as a whole. Simply put, modern North African history is also a history of music, those who embodied it, and the many others that lived it. As best the printed page can, this book records that past in high fidelity.

# CHAPTER 1

# THE BIRTH OF THE RECORDING
# INDUSTRY IN NORTH AFRICA

On November 5, 1924, Mahieddine Bachetarzi entered a makeshift recording studio in a hotel ballroom in Algiers. By now a five-year veteran of the music business, the Muslim tenor knew well how to position himself in front of the phonograph horn, operated in this instance by English sound engineer George Walter Dillnutt for the Gramophone Company.[1] The same familiarity and expertise certainly held true for the other musicians there that day: the flutist Driss, the alto violinist Jacob Ladjimi, and the mandolinist Edmond Nathan Yafil.[2] Indeed, for all involved, it was their second such session with Gramophone in that year alone.

In fall 1924, Bachetarzi recorded one side in particular that stood out from the others. While he drew upon the melody of "Qum yassir lana al-qata'an" (Pass round to us the cups of wine), a song text belonging to the five-suite, multimodal Andalusian musical tradition, the composition and words were nonetheless his own.[3] With religious-like devotion, he sang the following in the refrain.

Ah! O master! O master!
Ah! O master! O master!
Ah! O master! O master!

Ya la la la
Ya la la la

Ya la la la

Ya la la lan.[4]

For the initiated, both the "Ah!" that punctuated the above lines and the vocables "ya la lan" which followed would have signaled a longing for the glories of "the lost paradise": *al-firdaws al-mafqud*, al-Andalus, medieval Islamic Spain.[5] In a way, given the skill of the Muslim and Jewish performers, the splendor of that centuries-old experiment in Jewish-Muslim symbiosis, including the pride of place given to poetry and music, was in the room again that day. But for many other listeners, this was not the past. It was the future, or at least the present. In fact, the "master" invoked by Bachetarzi was sitting just behind him. The song title printed in French characters at the center of the Gramophone record that resulted from the session revealed his identity: "Ah! Ya! Meaâlim Yafil!" (Ah! O! Master Yafil). In more ways than one, Yafil's name was all over that double-sided disc. Hardly just a session mandolinist, the Algerian Jew had served as the in-country artistic director for the Gramophone enterprise since 1908.[6] He was also the individual almost entirely responsible for establishing the recording industry in Algeria and across North Africa at the beginning of the twentieth century.

To date, the scholarship on Yafil has focused on a set of activities read in light of an extended early twentieth-century moment of Andalusian musical revival.[7] This frame is not without merit. Consider his ambition. Then consider his truly remarkable accomplishments. At the end of the nineteenth century, the twenty-something, born in the lower Casbah of Algiers in 1874, embarked on a mission to save the soul of his musical heritage, one that he believed in danger of loss and one that he referred to, alternately, as "Arab," "Moorish," or "Muslim," but, perhaps most importantly, "Andalusian."[8] In 1904 alone, he released multiple print publications related to this work of research and rescue. This included a series of sheet-music pieces for piano as well as his magnum opus, the *Majmu' al-aghani wa-l-alhan min kalam al-andalus* (Collection of songs and melodies from the words of al-Andalus).[9] Weighing in at just under four hundred pages of at-risk and never-before-published song texts gathered directly by Yafil from manuscripts and musicians, the *Majmu'*, as it became known, was with just cause heralded as the

FIGURE 2.  Mahieddine Bachetarzi, "Ah! Ya! Meaâlim Yafil,"
Gramophone K 2655, 1924. Personal collection of author.

authoritative work on the Andalusian musical corpus—despite some mistakes of grammar and orthography.[10]

In the years following publication of the *Majmuʿ*, Yafil founded a free music school in Algiers which by 1912 he had transformed into El Moutribia, the first modern Andalusian orchestra not just in Algeria but in all of North Africa. El Moutribia would soon tour the region and eventually Europe, doing so before large audiences for the next two and half decades. By the time that Bachetarzi sang his master's praises on the 1924 recording, Yafil had also taken on the task of serving as the first chair of Arab (Andalusian) music at the Algiers Conservatory.[11]

As Jonathan Glasser has demonstrated, Yafil's authority and that of the *Majmu'* have held strong among "Andalusi musical practitioners" for well over a century. Still, "while his importance has been widely acknowledged," Glasser has also argued that "Yafil is an ambiguous figure whose enigmatic status is compounded by a dearth of relevant source materials."[12] Put differently, aficionados and academics alike, working with little more than the *Majmu'* and the sheet music, some coverage in the French-language press of the time, mentions in a couple of contemporaneous Arabic-language publications, and a scattering of nods in the colonial archives, have found Yafil difficult to locate within a genealogy of Andalusian musical transmission stretching from the nineteenth century until the present.[13] The reluctance to integrate Yafil, which derives in part from his iconoclasm, commercialism, and two high-profile critiques leveled at him by Europeans, has often rendered him a mere "interlocutor" despite his achievements.[14]

But what if his ambiguity owes to a certain flattening of his biography along constrictive Andalusian lines? Could his enigmatic quality derive from the persistent use of a *paper* trail that is by definition too thin and whose materiality is too narrowly constructed? In other words, where do his activities with Gramophone, alluded to in the scholarship but hardly elucidated, fit into the story?[15] What might other types of materials, like the Bachetarzi record, which bore Yafil's name and imprint, offer? As this chapter reveals, the turn to such new (old) sources not only speak, sometimes quite literally as we will soon see, to Yafil's centrality to Algerian music beyond the Andalusian tradition, but also enable the excavation of the origins of the recording industry in North Africa, which has until now remained largely unknown.[16]

The pages that follow come to a focus on "Master Yafil" and the music empire he built from the ground up at the turn of the twentieth century. Also surveyed are the contemporaneous and overlapping efforts of the brothers Joseph and Aurelio Bembaron in Tunisia and Algeria and Raoul Hazan (Joseph's nephew) in Morocco. As we will learn, Yafil's success, enshrined on that Gramophone record, owed much to his working-class background and arabophone upbringing. The same was true for Bembaron's most important employee in Tunisia: the pianist Messaoud Habib, who would work closely with Yafil's successor Bachetarzi.

As this chapter also makes clear, the attention given to the divergent legal and social statuses of Jews and Muslims under French rule, which was at its most extreme in Algeria, has long obscured the enduring importance of class in cementing relationships between Jewish and Muslim musical collaborators. If the story of Jews and Muslims across nineteenth- and twentieth-century North Africa is usually told separately or in relation to France, the turn to music reveals the continued and productive entanglement of the two communities at the horizontal level well into the interwar period. In the process, music as it was once known was now largely redefined through a number of projects to record.

## Print

Edmond Nathan Yafil tried his hand at a smattering of ventures before coming to the phonograph. During the initial years of the twentieth century, publishing music was chief among them. Of course, the inspiration for such an undertaking owed to an earlier moment as well as his milieu. Born in the lower Casbah of Algiers in 1874, the young Algerian Jew had grown up mere steps from a number of cafés that provided stages for the capital's leading musicians of the Andalusian repertoire. From his perch at his father's kosher restaurant Chez Maklouf (also known as Makhlouf Loubia for its famed bean dish), Yafil was nourished on the sounds of the era's undisputed master: Shaykh Mohammed Ben Ali Sfindja.[17] Through the 1890s, the Muslim vocalist and virtuoso of the *kwitra* (a type of 'ud) performed regularly at Qahwat Malakoff, the café—still in existence—which sat diagonally opposite the elder Yafil's greasy spoon, where he was also known to dine.[18] Yafil the son also ventured to the establishment across the way which, as opposed to some of the other cafés in the immediate area frequented by "older music lovers," as later recalled by Bachetarzi, "was composed of younger music lovers and Jews."[19] As in the personage of Yafil, sometimes the two groups overlapped. In fact, he was more than just a young music lover or even a musician. Bachetarzi, the vocalist and actor whose fame would in time surpass that of his teacher, described him not only as a patron of the aging Sfindja but one with a vision for preserving his voice into the future.[20]

To Yafil, Sfindja, born in 1844, just fourteen years after the landing of the French army at Sidi Fredj, seemed to be the last of his generation. With him, it was thought, would go his music. While a feeling of imminent loss had long infused the Andalusian musical repertoire in particular, as Glasser has shown, the sentiment was amplified and diffused beyond music and throughout Algeria with increasing ferocity over the nineteenth century. From its outset, French imperial rule had wrought major physical and social changes across the former Ottoman territory. Famine and epidemic accompanied conquest, as did violence.[21] Already by 1834, for example, the Algerian population of the capital had fallen from 30,000–40,000 to 12,000.[22] Those remaining found a city reordered to accommodate the growing number of European settlers. And 1834 was also the year that the Emir Abdelkader challenged French rule by declaring an independent state in western Algeria. It held until 1847.[23] The following year, Algeria was absorbed into France as the French expanded their conquest to the Algerian interior. Securing land and offering protection for the expanding settler colony once again meant famine, epidemic, and violence for Algerians. The 1871 Kabyle insurrection, also known as the Muqrani Revolt, would be the last major act of rebellion until the end of World War II. That uprising was met with the full force of the French military and its settler auxiliaries in the form of executions, land confiscation, and expulsion.[24] The cumulative result of four decades of French occupation was that by 1872 the Algerian population stood at 2 million, roughly half of its total number in 1830.[25]

During that period, the French had also restructured Jewish life as well as the Jewish-Muslim relationship, at least legally. As Joshua Schreier has detailed, the 1842 "Report on the Moral and Political State of the Israelites of Algeria, and the Means of Ameliorating It," written by French Jewish communal leaders Joseph Cohen and Jacques-Isaac Altaras and commissioned by the French Ministry of War, concluded that Algerian Jews "need us to initiate [them] into the principles of civilization [ . . . ] and that we develop, in a word, their intelligence for the journey toward political and moral progress."[26] Colonial officials adopted the report's recommendations, pairing the civilizing mission with the imposition of a consistory, a structure developed under Napoleon which represented Jews to the government, regulated the appointment of rabbis and synagogues, and surveilled the actions and speech of the Jewish community.[27] In its Algerian guise, the consistory was made subservient to that of France and was tasked with instilling allegiance to a country most had never been to and of which most were not citizens.[28] That last point was to be remedied by the promulgation of the Crémieux Decree of October 24, 1870, which stipulated that "the indigenous Israelites of the departments of Algeria are declared French citizens. In consequence, their real status and their personal status will be registered from the promulgation of the present decree, by French law; all rights acquired up to this day shall remain inviolable."[29]

Muslims, meanwhile, retained their subject status, which as of 1881 also meant their subjugation under an arbitrary but consistently punitive *indigénat* regime.[30] Someone like Sfindja also suddenly found himself in a position of inferiority vis-à-vis his Jewish neighbors. Of course, like Makhlouf and Edmond Nathan Yafil, the vast majority of Algeria's 35,000 Jews did not cease to be embedded in a Muslim milieu nor did they stop speaking Arabic with the change of legal status. For a great many, including colonial officials like Charles du Bouzet, former prefect of Oran in western Algeria, the newly emancipated remained "Arabs of the Jewish faith" despite the changes that were to accrue with their citizenship and as beneficiaries of the civilizing mission.[31]

For Algerian Jews, the first two decades after the enactment of the Crémieux Decree carried with them grave consequences alongside social advancement. Like metropolitan France, Algeria had emerged as a locus of anti-Semitism. Between the 1894 show trial of French Jewish army captain Alfred Dreyfus, who was falsely accused of espionage, and the 1898 libel trial of French novelist Émile Zola, whose high-profile letter in support of Dreyfus turned the twin episodes into an affair, waves of violent anti-Semitism were unleashed across Algerian cities. The perpetrators were European settlers of many backgrounds, including the Spaniards and Italians who had been newly naturalized in 1889 through legislation similar in form to the Crémieux Decree.[32] In January 1898, immediately following the publication of Zola's open letter "J'accuse!" on the front page of the French daily *L'Aurore*, anti-Semitic marauders tore through the lower Casbah and other Jewish areas in central Algiers. In addition to one death and many injuries recorded by Algerian Jews, synagogues and Jewish-owned businesses came under attack.[33] Among

those damaged properties was Chez Maklouf.[34] Edmond Nathan Yafil and
Shaykh Mohammed Ben Ali Sfindja, whose bond seemed little affected by
their legal segregation, were direct witnesses to this, as to so much else.

On May 31, 1898, five months after Chez Maklouf was vandalized, Edmond Nathan Yafil and Matthilde Yafil (né Seban) gave birth to their first
son: Martial Maklouf. It was around that time that the new father, listed on
his son's birth certificate as "without profession," invented one all his own.[35]
That year, Yafil began the process of compiling and transcribing Andalusian
song texts with the aid of the master Sfindja and his Jewish disciple Eliaou
"Laho" Seror.[36] This was no easy task. Musicians were especially loath to hand
over the unique manuscripts in their possession and on which their liveli-
hoods depended. Nonetheless, through an "obstinate perseverance," as Yafil
later described their efforts, the three made significant progress.[37] In the esti-
mation of Bachetarzi, the team collected dozens of unique pieces from across
Algiers.[38] Yafil began composing short selections from them for that most
un-Andalusian of instruments, the piano. Ultimately, he endeavored to pub-
lish his compositions in Western notation and make them available for sale.

On November 4, 1903, Yafil hired a non-Jewish French journalist and
emerging musicologist by the name of Jules Rouanet to assist him in his
efforts.[39] Born in Saint-Pons in the south of France in 1858, Rouanet soon
after settled in Algiers with his family.[40] In Algiers, the Frenchman built a
reputation for himself as a savant. By the 1880s, he served as editor of the ag-
ricultural journal *La Gazette du Colon* and, toward the end of the century, he
assumed the role of director of the École de musique du Petit Athénée.[41] Perhaps most importantly for Yafil, his European hire was also a gifted pianist
with knowledge of staff notation. Over the next few months, Sfindja, Seror,
and their students performed Yafil's compositions for Rouanet, who in turn
transcribed them for piano.[42] Less than a year after their initial collaboration,
Yafil and Rouanet published the first installments of a set of sheet music entitled *Répertoire de musique arabe et maure*.[43] For Rouanet, at least, the *Répertoire*
represented the pinnacle of saving from "oblivion" Yafil and Sfindja's musical
heritage.[44] For Yafil, it was a step along a career path in recording.

The mauresque covers of the *Répertoire* reveal a vexed relationship between Rouanet and Yafil despite the fact that both were French citizens.
While Rouanet was a salaried employee of Yafil, the *Répertoire* was presented

as though the Algerian Jew had been the charge of the European. That reversal of the actual power dynamic may have stemmed from the discomfort that Rouanet felt toward the Frenchness of his Algerian Jewish colleagues, what Sophie B. Roberts has referred to as the "status anxieties" of the settler population, and which often manifested in anti-Semitism.[45] Similarly, it may have been an attempt to assuage a European target audience that the *Répertoire* was really produced by a Frenchman like Rouanet rather than a "native," as the Algerian Jewish Seror was referred to in the publication.[46] Whatever the case, Yafil still managed to maintain the upper hand. Even as the *Répertoire* was described as being "under the direction of Mr. Jules Rouanet," the pages that followed clearly branded the effort as part of what Yafil called "Collection Yafil."[47] Over the course of the next decade, that brand graced all of his recording endeavors in some shape or form. This was as true of the *Répertoire* as it was for his other 1904 master work: the *Majmuʿ al-aghani wa-l-alhan min kalam al-andalus* (Collection of songs and melodies from the words of al-Andalus), on whose spine and early pages were appropriately marked "Collection Yafil."[48]

Tellingly, Yafil's magnum opus was actually two compilations printed in parallel: the *Majmuʿ*, in Arabic, and the *Diwan al-aghani min kalam al-Andalus* (*Treasury of songs from the words of al-Andalus*) in Judeo-Arabic (Arabic in Hebrew characters).[49] The *Diwan's* very existence owed to the fact that more than three decades after the promulgation of the Crémieux Decree, Jewish musicians, like so many of their coreligionists, continued to read, speak, and sing in their native tongue. For the twin publications, as Yafil announced in the *Majmuʿ*, he had worked tirelessly to gather the dispersed and hoarded manuscripts of "Arab and Jewish singers" in order to reconstitute the core movements of the Andalusian tradition from its scattered pieces.[50] To do so, he also organized the song texts by musical suite (nuba) and melody before reproducing them in type.[51] While there were differences between the volumes—the *Majmuʿ*, for example, contained a French-language preface, whereas the *Diwan* contained no language other than Arabic in Hebrew characters—the approximately four hundred pages of musical material in each was identical.

More than just his most important works to date and more than the reconstitution of a classical tradition feared lost, the latest installations of

Collection Yafil changed the rules of the music game in Algeria—and Yafil was now moving toward its center. Few of the song texts presented in the *Majmuʿ* and the *Diwan* had ever been published before and certainly not in the form of readily accessible print compilations geared toward multiple audiences. Yafil's effort, however, was no abstract intellectual exercise. It was a commercial venture. By selling the *Majmuʿ* and the *Diwan* from his home office in the lower Casbah and making the former available in the Muslim upper Casbah at outfits like the Roudoussi brothers' print shop, he had guaranteed its placement in the hands of capable and budding musicians, both Jewish and Muslim.[52]

With just cause, the local and international music communities heralded Yafil's publications, especially the *Majmuʿ* and by extension the *Diwan*. Despite its tremendous value, a small chorus of orientalists and French colonial officials lashed out at the thirty-year-old Yafil. Joseph Desparmet, a French Arabist based in Blida, southwest of Algiers, who had recently published his own similar volume, inveighed against his competitor for not having corrected the original manuscripts for misspellings and meter before typing them up and printing. Desparmet wrote disparagingly of Yafil, who, "lacking any criterion for the establishment of his texts—was reduced to simply publishing the notebooks of the native singer and those of his colleagues."[53] By insinuation, he blamed the volume's errors on Yafil's Jewishness, citing his supposed "ignorance of standard Arabic."[54] Yafil, in fact, possessed a diploma in "standard Arabic" from the prestigious Lycée d'Alger, an important detail Desparmet likely knew but ignored.[55]

Of course, such criticism resonated little with Muslim and Jewish musicians who found the *Majmuʿ* and the *Diwan*, respectively, of tremendous utility. Most extant copies, including both those in libraries and those in the hands of individuals, show signs of considerable use by their owners, with flowing notes tucked into pages or penciled into margins.[56] And today, over a century after its initial publication, the Algerian government has made what it now calls *The Yafil Treasury* (*Diwan Yafil*) available again "in print." In 2019, the Ministry of Culture posted a scanned version to an official website dedicated to "Algerian Cultural Patrimony."[57] As a testament to the reach of the *Majmuʿ*, the copy in question once belonged to Ghouti Bouali, an Algerian Muslim schoolteacher whose life had, at least for a time, closely tracked that of Yafil. An amateur musician, Bouali had studied with the legendary Algerian Jewish vocalist Ichoua "Maqshish" Medioni and in 1906 had himself published a work on Andalusian music.[58]

## Records

On January 1, 1901, the French subsidiary of the London-based Gramophone Company published a thirty-five page general catalog of wax phonograph cylinders.[59] But as was well known, Emile Berliner's domain was not cylinders but discs.[60] Typical of the recording industry at the turn of the twentieth century, in which the cylinder and disc continued to compete through the early aughts, Gramophone saw fit to sell the products of a rival.[61] In this case, the competitor was France's premier record label Pathé. The Pathé cylinders on offer, which spun at roughly 160 rpm for a total output of about two minutes, contained mostly military marches, anthems, and light operas. Also listed, however, were thirty cylinders of Andalusian music and the various genres associated with it, recorded no later than 1900 by a certain "Mouzino of Hammam Bou Hadjar." Whoever he was, the Algerian musician from the Oran region had drawn on the nickname and repertoire of Yafil's colleague, close collaborator, and coreligionist Saül "Mouzino" Durand in order to elevate his own profile. Remarkably, it was this aspirational Mouzino who was almost certainly the first North African ever to record commercially for the phonograph.

Given the competition from Pathé, Gramophone quickly moved to register its trademark in Algeria and Tunisia.[62] After formally establishing itself in North Africa in 1902, two of Gramophone's subsidiaries—the French Gramophone Company and the Italian Gramophone Company—moved to carve up the Mediterranean market along imperial lines.[63] On September 19, 1902, Alfred Michealis, the head of Italian Gramophone, wrote to Theodore Birnbaum, managing director of Gramophone's London headquarters, noting that Alfred Clark, the director of French Gramophone, had agreed to "divide the Mediterranean with me so that the whole Western part which, starting from France, means Spain, Marocco [sic], Algiers and Tunis be worked by him, and the Eastern part, viz: Tripoli, Egypt, Asia Minor and Greece be worked by me."[64] Italian Gramophone had taken control of the record trade in Libya, even before the Italians laid siege to Tripoli in 1911. The same was true of French Gramophone in Morocco, which had staked a claim on the Sharifian Empire a decade in advance of the establishment of the French protectorate there in 1912.

Despite its early entry, Gramophone's initial showing in Algeria and Tunisia was disappointing at best. In both territories, the company had stagnated under its local representative, a European in Algiers by the name of De Simone. In April 1906, a frustrated Alfred Clark called on De Simone "to reinvigorate the Algerian market."[65] He was especially concerned that increased competition from German labels like Odeon would further marginalize Gramophone in North Africa.[66] Some months later, Clark dispatched American sound engineer Charles Scheuplin to Algeria and Tunisia in an attempt to remedy the situation. Beginning in Algiers and then traveling overland to Tunis, Scheuplin recorded a number of artists on 216 single-sided discs, including for the first time the real Mouzino: Saül Durand.[67] The wax masters from those sessions were then sent to Gramophone's main European pressing plant in Hannover, Germany. One hundred of the "best sides" were subsequently transformed into fifty double-sided discs.[68] Those records represented the backbone of Gramophone's new catalog for the region. As a first run, only twenty-four copies of each record were shipped back to Algeria and Tunisia for sale.[69] To be sure, the output was rather meager. Nonetheless, Gramophone continued to see great potential in North Africa. As executives like Clark were beginning to understand, however, the company possessed neither the right access nor representation. If it hoped to make a stronger showing, Gramophone needed to find someone whose hand was on the pulse of the local music scene.

In September 1908, Clark traveled to Algeria to investigate for himself Gramophone's position there. In Algiers, he quickly connected to the two most important entities dealing in phonographs (also referred to as "disc talking machines" or merely "talking machines") and records: the P. Colin Company and Edmond Nathan Yafil. On September 9, 1908, Clark wrote to Theodore Birnbaum, managing director in London, with an update: "I found that in Algiers itself there were two people who dealt considerably in Talking Machines, i.e., Colin (Erard's agent), who possesses a fine music saloon, with six travelers, and a Mr. Yafil, an Algerian Jew, who has an establishment in the native town."[70] While P. Colin, established in Algeria since 1903, represented French phonograph manufacturers like Erard in a well-adorned showroom and counted six employees in its operation, Yafil was the one who was more difficult to ignore. "Before the advent of the disc talking machine," Clark added, "Yafil made phonograph records [on cylinders] and obtained the exclusive services of the best Arabian and Moorish artistes, holding them under contract." Indeed, beginning in 1905 and likely earlier, advertisements for "Arab cylinders" as part of Collection Yafil—and featuring the aforementioned Mouzino and Laho Seror—ran in the twice-weekly newspaper *Le Radical: Politique, littéraire, social.*[71] Yafil was already recording in Algeria before the major labels had even found their footing.

The encounter with Yafil made evident to Clark that Gramophone had entrusted its Algerian representation to the wrong individual. Clark observed, for example, that "all the good trade in the place goes to Colin; all the native trade to Yafil."[72] De Simone, for his part, was hardly a player at all. That the so-called native trade went to Yafil owed to the fact that he operated much as North African Jewish merchants had in the previous century with regard to imported goods.[73] Clark noted, for instance, that "the position in Algeria is that everything is sold on the installment plan and to be able to do this in Algeria with any safety, one must be a native of the place." As his coreligionists had done in the immediate past, Yafil was extending credit to his Muslim and Jewish clients, but now to purchase records. Not to be outdone, P. Colin soon followed suit. De Simone did not. Instead he "quarreled" with P. Colin but especially Yafil, the latter over access to artists. "The result of all this has been that de Simone has for nearly two years, the worst records on the market," Clark reported. Sardonically, he wrote, "it is quite obvious that de Simone is practically starving and is worth nothing." P. Colin and Yafil, on the other hand, understood well their own value. Beginning in 1905, the two competitors turned their sights on the world of recording beyond Gramophone. Clark informed Birnbaum that "Colin and Yafil being anxious to do business, invited Odeon and Pathé to come down to Algeria and make records, which they did at a later date to us."

While P. Colin largely catered to a bourgeois European record-buying public, Yafil held the advantage with Algerian Jews and Muslims. Quite literally, he spoke the language of Jewish and Muslim musicians and those most interested in purchasing their discs. Furthermore, his working-class Jewish background, which placed him and his business operations in the "native town" (the Casbah of Algiers), meant he operated out of their neighborhood. In addition to building upon a network of trust and class, his Jewishness may have also lent him an advantage over non-Jewish French competitors like P. Colin. Time and again, Yafil found himself dealing directly with his co-religionists in the global recording industry. "One of the Ullmanns himself," Clark wrote of the Jewish brothers who directed the French subsidiary of the German Odeon label, "fixed the deal with Yafil, and obtained the services exclusively of the artistes mentioned."[74]

Through Yafil, Odeon "obtained the services" of the two most important artists of early twentieth-century Algeria: Sfindja, who was ushered into a recording studio in Algiers three years before his death in 1908, and Mouzino. That same year, in 1905, during a public demonstration of "Arab Music" at the International Orientalist Congress in Algiers, Jules Rouanet introduced Mouzino as a talented instrumentalist and vocalist, "who had recently been bestowed the honor of the phonograph."[75] Those honors were entirely thanks to Yafil. As with his print compilations, he was once again transforming Algerian music, this time etching its sounds onto cylinders and discs that might be preserved for posterity.[76] In the meantime, he showed little sign of slowing down. When the French Eden label and French subsidiary of Germany's Anker-Record moved into Algeria sometime between 1906 and 1908, Yafil was once again employed as a consultant.[77]

Given what he saw and heard in the course of his 1908 visit to Algeria, Clark easily concluded that the recording giant needed Yafil.[78] Yafil, himself a recording giant in the making, agreed. Enthusiastically, Clark announced to Birnbaum that "we then fixed up Yafil to represent us in his own sphere of business; further to give us the services of all his tied up artistes. I fixed up a new catalogue, and arranged to make the records on 12″ plates. I finally left Yafil highly delighted and a keen Gramophone man."[79] As for Tunisia, also a source of concern for Gramophone, Clark transferred representation from De Simone to Jacques (Joseph) and Aurelio Bembaron, Tunisian Jewish brothers of Livornese origin and the major purveyors of Arabic- and Hebrew-language records in Tunisia and soon in Algeria and Morocco as well.

Within a year of the first international recording sessions in Algeria, Yafil had become synonymous with the emergent industry itself. Odeon records,

FIGURE 3. Meaalma Yamina, "Frag Ghezali," Disque Yafil
(Odeon) 36979, ca. 1908. Personal collection of author.

for example, initially branded for the Algerian market as "Disque Odeon,"
much as they were in metropolitan France, soon appeared under the name of
"Disque Yafil." Disque Yafil records not only carried the name of Yafil on the
printed labels that adorned their center but also depicted the Islamic symbols
of crescent, hand of Fatima, and five-pointed star.[80] As for Pathé, the French
label for whom "North Africa was almost a home market," as Pekka Gronow
has written, Yafil marked nearly all of its Algerian releases before the First
World War by providing spoken introductions to the music that followed.[81]
He first announced the title of the song performed and then the name of
the performer before pronouncing the record a product of Collection Yafil.[82]
When Yafil released his last major print publication, his 1907 *Majmu' zahw*

*al-anis al-mukhtas bi-l-tabasi wa-l-qawadis* (Collection of the companion's splendor specializing in discs and cylinders), the song texts he included were paired with Odeon and Pathé matrix numbers, all of which represented records that either bore his name or comprised Collection Yafil.[83] Thanks to the cylinder and the disc—and unlike Western notation—musicians could now model their music on what they heard, much as had been done in the past.

## Artists, Repertoire, and Copyright

So whom did Yafil record? Mostly other Jews. In Algiers, almost all were in earshot of the impresario's headquarters, first at 16 rue Bab-El-Oued (formerly rue Bruce) and then at 24 rue Bab-El-Oued in the lower Casbah. Laho Seror, for example, among the first Algerians to record, shared Yafil's home office. Alfred "Sassi" Lebrati, another of the earliest Algerian recording artists, lived around the corner from Yafil at 25 rue Socgemaah. Moïse Bensiano, who recorded for Pathé as part of an ensemble called the "Association of El Moutribia" (*Jama'iyya al-Mutribiyya, Choeurs de La Moutribia*), could be found down the street from Yafil at 36 rue Bab-El-Oued. In fact, as Malcolm Théoleyre has carefully documented, the vast majority of the members of what would eventually become simply El Moutribia, Yafil's expanded and renowned Andalusian orchestra established in 1912, lived within two hundred square meters of one another in what was ostensibly the Jewish quarter of Algiers.[84]

Although Jews from the lower Casbah could sometimes stand in for the near totality of artists featured in the debut Algerian record catalogs, Muslims from the same compact quarter were represented as well—albeit in smaller numbers. Among them, Sfindja featured prominently. So did Yamina, the premier Algerian female artist of the era. With her gifted voice, she maintained the most prominent place in Pathé's 1912 Algerian catalog—her records being the first listed and running for several pages—while also being the only non-Jewish artist on offer performing selections from the Andalusian repertoire.[85]

While the Jewishness of early twentieth-century recording in Algeria—or Tunisia or Morocco, for that matter—is perhaps best understood as a question of degree rather than kind, class was an important part of the equation. Yafil, we will recall, was not just a Jew but also the son of a restaurateur. Seror,

Sassi, and Sfindja were cobblers by trade. The Muslim vocalist Abderrahmane Saïdi, who recorded in duet with Seror, earned his living as a stevedore among other jobs. This turn to class suggests that while recording tended to favor Jews, the industry also remained an intimately Jewish-Muslim affair of a certain social status from its outset.

With Yafil acting as guide to the lower Casbah and its surrounds, record companies captured an impressive range of music and spoken-word dialogue in the period prior to and immediately after World War I. The vast urban Andalusian repertoire and its associated forms—especially the popular, colloquial *hawzi* and *'arubi*—were but one piece of a larger whole. *Piyyut* (pl. *piyyutim*), the Hebrew paraliturgical tradition which also employed Andalusian modes and melodies, albeit in a Jewish idiom, featured prominently in the multilingual catalogs of Gramophone and Pathé as well. So did Bedouin music, rural Kabyle song, and all styles popular, topical, and comedic then emerging. The varied genres, repertoires, and languages were hardly dissonant. After all, it was sales that counted. In Algeria, all discs were therefore quickly classed, marketed, and sold as "Algerian," a category that included, for example, the vast Hebrew offerings recorded by rabbis, cantors, and the *paytanim* (executors of piyyut) who congregated daily in the synagogues of the lower Casbah.[86] Thanks to Yafil, mass commercial culture was contributing to the notion of an "Algerian music"—one which had the potential to help consolidate new and inclusive forms of national identification.

As expansive as recording was, there were limits. The very range of music that could be recorded was circumscribed by what technology at the time could offer. The process of acoustic recording, which required musicians to crowd around a phonograph horn, favored only the highest audio frequencies.[87] By contrast, deeper voices and lower-pitched instruments had the potential to dislodge the cutting stylus connected to the horn's diaphragm from the very grooves of the master record it was tasked with etching. At the same time, the size and speed of records, which in the case of those bound for Algeria, Tunisia, and Morocco ranged from 10 to 14 inches in diameter and spun at various speeds of approximately 78 to 90 rpm, constrained recording to an average of three or so minutes of music per side. In theory, this rendered all forms of music in North Africa, for which such constraints of time did not exist, incompatible with the format. Yafil, however, found a way around the technological impasse, much as other recording pioneers did around the world.[88] In the process, he produced a novel type of sound. Under his tutelage and employing his arrangements, musicians began to truncate and transform lengthy pieces that would have previously unfolded over the course of an evening (and sometimes into the morning) into up-tempo compositions of about three or six minutes in length, the duration of one or two sides of a record.[89]

On April 11, 1914, armed with a catalog of arrangements and compositions, Yafil applied for admission to the *Société des auteurs, compositeurs et éditeurs de musique* (SACEM) in Paris.[90] Shortly thereafter, he became the first North African to gain admission to the powerful French society dedicated to protecting authors, composers, and publishers of music, including their rights to royalties. As a newly minted member of SACEM, he also came to serve as the Algerian representative for the French *Société générale internationale de l'édition phonographique et cinématographique*, entitling him to additional mechanical rights related to the reproduction of his arrangements and compositions on discs and cylinders and for piano rolls and music boxes.[91] In entering two of the most hallowed musical societies in the world, Yafil was now a formidable presence on the international recording scene. That his arrival there was facilitated by his humble upbringing in the lower Casbah infuriated his detractors, as we will soon see.

## Record Stores, Record Labels, and Commercialization

Yafil sold the very records he played such a critical role in producing from his home office on rue Bab-El-Oued in the lower Casbah. By 1908, Mouzino also sold records, including his own, from a storefront at 3 rue de la Lyre, a stone's throw away from Yafil.[92] The vast majority of records, however, were first distributed through much larger establishments. This included branches of French record stores, like that of P. Colin, but also a great number of North African Jewish-owned commercial enterprises, which, in at least one prominent case, operated transnationally across the region. Perhaps surprisingly, it was in the midst of World War I, at the very moment in which the European recording industry experienced a downturn, that the firm of J. & A. Bembaron expanded its business from Tunisia into Morocco.

J. & A. Bembaron was founded by Livornese Jewish brothers Jacques (born Joseph, also known as "Pippo") and Aurelio Bembaron in Tunis around 1903. Like its counterparts elsewhere around the world, it was born primarily as a store dedicated to musical instruments and sheet music. But contemporaneous to its establishment, the firm began to stock phonographs and records as well. Alongside holding exclusive concession in Tunisia for French piano makers like Erard and Pleyel, Bembaron also represented record companies based in metropolitan France. As we may recall, French Gramophone had already transferred its Tunisian representation to Bembaron at the time of their "discovery" of Yafil in Algeria in 1908.

In 1916, as Bembaron branches in Tunisia steadily increased in number, Jacques Bembaron dispatched his son-in-law Raoul Hazan to Morocco. Despite the fact that the recording industry had been slower to take off in the French protectorate, there was significant opportunity there as well. Odeon had recognized this potential when it held its first recording expedition in Morocco in 1905.[93] Whether Yafil was connected to this effort or those of the first Gramophone sessions conducted there at the end of 1913 remains unclear but seems likely.[94] Whatever the case, Hazan would provide an outlet for the Algerian's merchandise and that of others.

In many ways, Hazan was a curious choice to lead the expansion of Bembaron into Morocco. Most intriguingly, the individual tasked with setting up a music business there was almost completely deaf. His political orientation also had the potential to bring him unwanted attention from the French protectorate authorities: Hazan was an active socialist.[95] But within months of his arrival, Hazan triumphed. In 1916, he established Bembaron in the *mellah* (Jewish quarter) of the cultural capital of Casablanca. Appropriately, he named his enterprise "Bembaron et Hazan." In time, Bembaron et Hazan would decamp for a larger and tonier location at 86 rue de Bouskoura (later renamed rue Blaise Pascal) in the rapidly expanding *ville nouvelle* (new city).[96]

By the 1920s, Bembaron et Hazan had grown further still, operating at least ten branches in Morocco in major urban centers from Casablanca to Oujda and south to Marrakesh while dotting smaller cities in both the French and Spanish protectorates.[97] It was thus within a few short years of his installation in Casablanca that the Tunisian Hazan could lay claim as one

FIGURE 4. Polyphon record sleeves listing Bembaron store locations
in Algeria and Tunisia. Personal collection of author.

of the most important retail outlets for records in Morocco and, in particular,
as the largest distributor of Arabic- and Hebrew-language discs there as well.

While Hazan developed the family business in Morocco, Bembaron in
Tunisia likewise flourished. In the first decade after World War I, Bembaron
spread its record empire across the country to the cities of Bizerte, Sfax,
Sousse, Gabès, Nabeul, Béja, Le Kef, Mateur, and Mahdia.[98] The company
boasted seven locations in Tunis alone.[99] Bembaron was also established in

Algeria at this time. Their flagship store in Algiers was well situated, located on rue Dumont d'Urville like Yafil's rival P. Colin. In short order, Bembaron in Algeria opened stores of varying size in Oran, Bône, Souk Ahras, Djidjelli, Sétif, and Constantine.[100]

The Bembarons and their employees served to identify the talent that helped propel the trade in records across North Africa. Messaoud Habib, for example, the general manager of the Bembaron location at rue de Constantine in Tunis, played a role akin to Yafil not only in discovering and recording some of the era's most iconic artists—some of whom we will meet in the next chapter—but in his capacity as representative of the era's major labels as well.[101] An accomplished pianist himself, Habib, born in Tunis in 1889, began his recording activities on paper, as had Yafil. During the 1910s, for instance, he released fifty rolls of Andalusian and popular music for the player-piano as part of "Collection Bembaron."[102] By the 1920s, in addition to his operation of a record store, he assumed the position of artistic director for Pathé and Gramophone in Tunisia.[103] Mahieddine Bachetarzi, who had sung Yafil's praises in "Ah! Ya! Meaâlim Yafil!" in 1924, became Gramophone's artistic director for all of North Africa in 1929 and would later even go so far as to describe Habib as an "all powerful" figure. The description was meant to be disparaging and stemmed from Bachetarzi's anger over Habib's attempt to prevent other Tunisian musicians from joining the French organization SACEM, which would entitle them to rights and royalties. Dissatisfied with the direction of Gramophone in Tunisia, the Algerian tenor replaced Habib with another Tunisian Jewish musician, Jacob "Kiki" Attal.[104]

## Distribution and Expansion

Without a doubt, Bembaron (and Bembaron et Hazan) helped develop the taste for records among Jews and Muslims in North Africa. It did so, in part, by providing the necessary infrastructure to move records between France, where most Moroccan, Algerian, and Tunisian discs were mastered after having been recorded locally, and North Africa, where they were consumed. It then sent them horizontally across Morocco, Algeria, and Tunisia as well. The distribution network and talent scouting operations pioneered by firms like Bembaron allowed for the entrance of additional record labels to North

Africa between the two world wars. French colonial authorities in Morocco, Algeria, and Tunisia encouraged such an expansion, believing that recorded music, at least of the Andalusian variety, served as a distraction from a set of burgeoning anticolonial nationalist politics.[105] In 1922, Baidaphon, a Middle Eastern label established by the Baida cousins in Beirut around 1906 but which had long been headquartered in Berlin, was invited into Tunisia by the French protectorate authorities to record ma'luf, the variant of the Andalusian repertoire which straddles eastern Algeria and Tunisia.[106] To oversee their activities in North Africa, the Baidas dispatched Théodore Khayat, a young relative from Syria, who settled in Casablanca. Khayat did so with official permission and encouragement. In due time, Baidaphon's representative partnered with Bembaron et Hazan to distribute the label's ever-expanding catalog of North African records.[107] By decade's end, a host of other international record companies moved in, including but not limited to Columbia, Parlophone, and Polyphon. In most of these cases, Jews served as their representatives and were, like Messaoud Habib, sometimes themselves high-profile recording artists. Such was the case with Parlophone, where Algerian Jewish artist Lili Labassi took on the role of artistic director.[108]

This flurry of activity in the mid-to-late 1920s, inspired in no small part by the advent of electrical recording in 1925, prompted another development: the rise of the independent record label in North Africa.[109] While some Muslims now joined the fray, it was again a largely Jewish affair. In Tunis, the Muslim impresario Bechir Rsaissi, who had previously worked for the Italian-owned record store Triumpho, a branch of P. Colin, and finally, Baidaphon, launched two of his own labels by decade's end: Oum-El-Hassen and B. Rsaissi.[110] Not to be outdone, Bembaron began to release records on its own imprint Bembarophone. In Algeria, the Jewish artistic director Mardoché Léon Sasportas, who had worked with Gramophone in Algeria and represented Polyphon there as well, established Algeriaphone in 1930.[111] In Morocco, al-Sawt al-Maghrib (La Voix du Maghreb, the Voice of Morocco) appeared on the scene, its discs pressed in-country at the Electra Company factory in Casablanca.[112] In the meantime, the more established companies redoubled their efforts. On August 28, 1928, a recommendation was made to Gramophone's executive committee to dispatch ten permanent sound engineers to record in North Africa.[113] It was further suggested that the recorder, or recorders, appointed to a branch should remain in the services of that branch as long as possible, it being highly important that the recorder should come under the influence of the manager for whom he is working, acquire a working knowledge of the language and make the acquaintance of the various artists, conductors, and members of the branch staff.

The recording industry was there to stay.

By the end of the 1920s, hundreds of thousands of acoustically and electrically made records were circulating across North Africa. In 1929 alone, French labels sent an estimated 122,000 discs to Morocco, 125,000 to Tunisia, and 330,000 to Algeria. In 1930, German labels exported an additional 14,622 records to Morocco, 67,671 to Tunisia, and an unknown but no doubt much higher number to the larger Algeria. That same year, the number of records bound for Algeria from France increased to half a million.[114] As for how many of them were Arabic—or Hebrew, Chleuh, or Kabyle for that matter—is difficult to ascertain given that these figures included records aimed at the European population. Still a great many were meant for arabophone Jews and Muslims. Bachetarzi, for example, estimated that sales for Gramophone's North African offerings had quadrupled between 1928 and 1929.[115] In 1928, Gramophone also reported that it was shipping tenfold more Arabic- and Spanish-language records to Bembaron et Hazan in Morocco than it was French discs.[116] Unfortunately, how many Baidaphon, Algeriaphone, Bembarophone, or B. Rsaissi records were sold is impossible to determine. But that these records existed in significant quantities, were passed around, and listened to in communal settings speaks to a burgeoning trade across Morocco, Algeria, and Tunisia that the extant numbers only begin to capture.

## Controversy

Clearly, the success of the recording industry across North Africa was owed to many but perhaps none more than Yafil. In his time, his centrality was regularly acknowledged in the press, which tended to credit him with having a hand in making two thousand individual recordings by the mid-1920s.[117] If later scholars have little commented on this aspect of his career, we end by revisiting a related episode which has garnered attention: the sudden and

very public denunciation of Yafil's recording activities by his early collaborator Jules Rouanet.[118]

On September 25, 1927, Rouanet penned a scathing, unprovoked attack
on Yafil in the prominent daily *La Dépêche algérienne*. He did so without ever
mentioning the Algerian's name. The European began with a perceived slight.
"Many of my friends," Rouanet wrote in the pages of the paper where he had
once served as editor, "among them Muslim notables, have expressed their
shock at not seeing my name mentioned during the recent concerts of Arab
musicians in Algiers."[119] He reminded readers (or more likely, alerted them
for the first time) that two decades earlier he had coauthored the *Répertoire
de musique arabe et maure*, the Western notation project dedicated to preserving the music of "our natives." But after casting the spotlight on himself,
he sought to "reassure" his audience that he was "not the victim of a guilty
oversight, because it is I who desired this oversight." He contended that for
several years he had "formally requested that my person be in no ways impli-
cated in a commercial enterprise that would aim to monopolize, for material
ends, a domain that constitutes part of the Muslim folklore."[120] Supposedly,
he took issue with the "exploitation of music that belongs to everyone due to
its anonymity and great age." He concluded:

> I did not wish to shout from the rooftops that I had composed Andalusi songs
> from the ninth century or from other distant epochs. I did not agree to call
> myself a great and illustrious composer in order to secure rights to melodies
> that are older than our "Au Clair de la Lune" or tunes that Mohammed Ben
> Ali Sfindja, Ben Farachou, and other masters of genuine fame had dictated
> to their students just as they had received them from their predecessors.[121]

To denigrate Yafil publicly, Rouanet had summoned the public domain of a
French song of unclear provenance: "Au Clair de la Lune." In typical orientalist fashion, he had also attributed a near-timeless quality to Andalusian
music while ignoring the contributions of individual musicians like Sfindja
who had innovated well into Rouanet's time.

Within days of the letter's appearance, Yafil responded. He described it as
his "duty" to do so.[122] If Rouanet's friends, including unidentified Muslim notables, had "expressed their shock" at having not seen his personage attached

to recent concerts of which he had little to do with, Yafil countered that "in the world of musicians who are interested in Arab music, as well as among all Muslims, notable or not, the letter of Mr. Rouanet caused the deepest astonishment." With just a few words—"all Muslims, notable or not"—Yafil had exposed the classist nature of Rouanet's screed. To further right the historical record, Yafil turned to his own archival documents (which have since disappeared). Digging up an employee contract, he noted that "before the date of November 4, 1903, Mr. Rouanet knew nothing of Arab music." He announced:

> It was on this date that, while it had been a long time since I started imagining collecting the Arab melodies which were disappearing into oblivion for lack of musical notation, I hired Mr. Rouanet for a weekly salary which was fixed for the duration of the contract related to the Arab melodies that I had collected and selected or composed, and that I or my students, or the master Arab musicians who had granted me a monopoly on their repertoire, would come sing before him.

He proceeded to describe Rouanet as a mere "mechanical recorder of music," a phonograph, a device that meant little if not placed in capable and knowledgeable hands.[123] Put differently, "for Yafil," as Glasser has written, "the technological apparatus is dead, while it is the genealogically situated musician who is alive and deserves the protection of copyright law."[124] As for the claim that the Frenchman from the metropole had abstained from or even objected to the realm of the commercial, Yafil described this as "one of the most audacious untruths." He argued that Rouanet's myriad public-speaking engagements, paid writing assignments, and acceptance of awards and honors related to a music not his own were the essence of commercial exploitation. According to Yafil, it was in the course of this overstepping by Rouanet that he "invited him to cease his services." With his signature, Yafil's accomplishments stood for themselves:

Edmond NATHAN YAFIL
Professor at the Municipal Conservatory of Algiers, Publisher, Composer of
    Arab music,
Member of the Society of Authors

For Rouanet, hardly preoccupied with the provenance of intangible heritage or questions of copyright, it was Yafil's Jewishness and the fact that he had transcended his social class that bothered him so. In his final letter to the editor and the last word on the matter in *La Dépêche algérienne*, Rouanet, who finally acknowledged Yafil, refused to refer to him as Edmond or Edmond Nathan and instead insisted on calling him "E. Nathan," emphasizing his Jewish name over his French one.[125] He denigrated Yafil's résumé, claiming that he had "always been known as an illiterate musician, although he believes himself to be a famous composer, teacher, publisher, etc., extending this undeniable prerogative to literary texts." Time and again, he questioned Yafil's fluency in French, which Rouanet claimed was learned from "the kitchen boys of his dignified and honorable father, Mr. Makhlouf, the well-known restaurateur on Bruce Street." That dignity and honor, as sarcastic as Rouanet's remarks were, apparently accrued from the fact that Makhlouf Yafil knew his place—and it was at Chez Maklouf in the lower Casbah rather than with Europeans like Rouanet. Recalling the injury inflicted by that line above all else, Bachetarzi shot back decades later, "and if his father ran a restaurant in the Bazar Malakoff, it was very fortunate for Arab music, because it was precisely the clients of 'Makhlouf Loubia' who paid for, unknowingly, the publications of 'Hawazas,' 'Zendanis,' and 'Noubas'"—of the Andalusian tradition and other repertoires associated to it. "For all of his 'trafficking,'" Bachetarzi wrote of the supposed riches that had accrued to his master, "Edmond Yafil could have died of hunger!"[126]

———

Within a year of Rouanet's smear, Edmond Nathan Yafil had died but not of hunger. Instead, it was a rather sudden passing at the age of fifty-four. Coming as it did but recently after the deaths of famed recording artist (and Yafil's close collaborator) Saül "Mouzino" Durand and Muhammed Boukandoura, the Hanafi mufti of Algiers who oversaw Quranic recitation in the capital's mosques, *L'Écho d'Alger* declared that "Arab Music Is in Mourning."[127] For its part, *L'Afrique du nord illustrée* reported that Yafil's passing had caused "painful emotions among the Jewish and Muslim populations" of Algiers, ordinary and elite alike.[128]

Yafil's funeral procession began appropriately where his life had begun: in the lower Casbah. From there it slowly weaved its way to the St. Eugène Cemetery close to the sea, where he was laid to rest among "a large crowd of friends and personalities from the music world."[129] Among those bidding him final farewell was a representative of Pierre-Louis Bordes, governor general of Algeria; a representative for the mayor of Algiers; Hadj Moussa, imam of the Grand Mosque; a delegation of "Arab musicians"; members of El Moutribia; and "figures from the worlds of industry and commerce." Whichever Muslim notables Rouanet had referenced as his allies in his letter to *La Dépêche algérienne*, those in attendance at Yafil's burial were not among them. After a number of stirring eulogies, including from Algeria's chief rabbi Léon Fridman, Bachetarzi, Yafil's heir apparent, spoke "in a voice broken by sobs." Bachetarzi addressed Yafil directly: "Your life's work, my dear master, will not have been in vain, for I hereby make a solemn oath to pursue the aim of your efforts [ . . . ] and will, inspired by your example, endeavor to spread this music that you have loved so much and to which you have given the best of yourself." Bachetarzi then turned to El Moutribia, which he had presided over since 1923, and, finally, to Yafil's family to offer his condolences. Amid the chanting of passages from the Hebrew Bible and the recitation of the Kaddish, the Aramaic prayer exalting God, Yafil was laid to rest. In his relatively short life, he had built the recording industry in North Africa from the bottom up. That effort was indebted to his class and the Jewish-Muslim milieu from which he emerged more than to his legal status. As we will see in the next chapter, that infrastructure paved the way for the emergence of a star system of recording artists, many of them women and by and large Jewish, who rose to fame as tastemakers across North Africa between the two world wars.

# CHAPTER 2

# THE ARAB FOXTROT
# AND THE CHARLESTON

Their takes on this particular "Arab foxtrot," in which an unmarried man implored his female lover to keep their relationship a secret, were all slightly different but equally salacious. For her recording of "Mamak" (Don't tell your mother) for Pathé in 1930, the Moroccan Jewish artist Cheikha Aicha "La Hebrea" (the Jewess) set the story in Oran, Algeria, assumed the male part, and using language that invoked a crucial prewedding ritual, entreated her mistress: "Don't tell your mother why you skipped the henna."[1] That same year and for the same label, the Marrakesh-based Jewish duo Simon Ohayon and Hazar Cohen recorded another version in which the euphemism of leap-frogging the henna ceremony for the postnuptial consummation was made explicit, albeit in another geographical context: "In Mogador [ . . . ] on top of the ramparts, we'll make love."[2] Brilliantly, Ohayon and Cohen had rhymed *Mogador*, the Portuguese name for the Moroccan coastal city of Essaouria, with both *fawq al-sur*, the Arabic for "on top of the ramparts," and *na'mal l'amour*, the turn of phrase which ended in a French word that had little need for translation. Between 1930 and 1932, alongside the Moroccan releases, no fewer than six records entitled "Mamak"—or something similar—were also made by Algerian artists for four different labels.[3] This included the original on Columbia, written, composed, and performed by the Algerian Jewish musician Lili Labassi.[4] By the mid-1930s, thousands of copies of the "Mamak" record, in one interpretation or another by figures with names like Madame

Louisa "Al-Isra'iliyya" (the Jewess) and Madame Ghazala, circulated across North Africa, in metropolitan France, and possibly in Spain, where Cheikha Aicha La Hebrea had long made her career as a flamenco artist.[5]

Between the two world wars, a coterie of Jewish recording artists, many of them women, rose to fame as tastemakers across Morocco, Algeria, and Tunisia with a new type of song. Their popular music, almost always penned by a cohort of male Jewish composers who emerged out of the theater and were sometimes deeply connected to the synagogue, captured a certain working-class encounter with colonial modernity that was as true for the urban Jewish masses as it was for their Muslim counterparts.[6] It did so in the colloquial Arabic and local idiom of everyday people, which, like "Mamak," included a smattering of French and other European languages. Of the hundreds of record titles released in the 1920s and 1930s, many of them explored and shaped new ideas about sex, love, marriage, and the role of women in society. To accomplish that feat, lyrics were set to styles like the foxtrot and the Charleston, while also employing in-demand Egyptian musical modes.

The era's female stars explicitly identified themselves as "modern girls" or even flappers (al-garsun, la garçonne).[7] With music that was both revelatory and ribald and by playing the male lead or wearing their hair short, these "new women" challenged traditional gender roles at the very moment that a feminist agenda emerged across the Middle East, most famously in Egypt but throughout North Africa as well.[8] Much as Susan A. Glenn has demonstrated in her study of female theatrical performers in the early twentieth-century American context, the feminism pronounced on the North African stage and on popular records was "less a coherent movement than a set of principles and goals. These included the belief in the social, political, and economic equality of the sexes, and the idea that although men and women were biologically different, gender roles were not 'predestined by God or nature' but shaped by socialization."[9]

As part of those principles and goals, artists demanded "greater freedom to express their sexuality" and "individualism."[10] This was certainly evident in "Mamak." And while it is true that performers "exercised a degree of freedom that was rarely available to women in public," it is also clear that the large and diverse concertgoing public which gathered around them sought out that changing sound of modernity.

"Mamak" and its analogues were no passing phenomenon. In the years after World War II, that song in particular could still be heard across Morocco
and Algeria, irking a vocal minority. In April and May 1946, as Malcolm
Théoleyre has shown, Gontran Dessagnes, director of the Algiers Conservatory, lambasted "the foreign influence" of "new songs," from "modern dances"
to "jazz" and with "mixed French and Arabic lyrics" in the Algerian press.[11]
Among the worst offenders, according to Dessagnes, was still "the foxtrot
Mamak," despite its having been released more than a decade and half earlier.[12] In 1947, the composer Léo-Louis Barbès, writing in *Documents algériens*,
an official publication of the Government General of Algeria (GGA), saw fit
to condemn "the immense success of numbers like Mamak (Ma tqoulech a
l'mamak!), this foxtrot that not a shoeshine boy from Souk Ahras [in Alge-
ria] to Oujda [in Morocco] did not know by heart and sing daily during a
certain period."[13] For Barbès, the song, "trotted out all night long in the cafés
of the countryside" for the "easy to please," was not deserving of the title of
"Arab music." He preferred another word: "decadence."[14]

Notwithstanding the decades-long popularity of "Mamak," the many
songs like it that emerged on records during the interwar years have received
scant treatment in the historiographical literature on North African music
in the early twentieth century.[15] In part that is due to the criticism of figures
like Dessagnes and Barbès, which has loomed at times explicit and implicit
in a scholarship focused largely on the Andalusian traditions and its mostly
male performers.[16] The unbridled attack on the song by the two composers stemmed from the perceived threat it posed to the colonial-era push by
European reformers and local elites to render the high-art Andalusian repertoire in North Africa a "classical" tradition on a par with European music.[17]
Such projects received official sanction and included the establishment of the
Conservatory of Moroccan Music in Rabat in 1930, the formation of the all-
Muslim orchestra El Djazaïria in Algiers in that same year, and the founding
of the orchestra La Rachidia in Tunis in 1934.[18] In the years after Moroccan
and Tunisian independence in 1956 and that of Algeria in 1962, North African governments elevated the Andalusian repertoire to the status of a national music, promoting festivals and supporting publications, among other
activities.[19] Starting in the 1960s and continuing through the 1980s, scholars
picked up where an earlier generation had left off but now operated within a

decidedly nationalist framework.[20] Alongside a program of valorization, the degradation of popular music and songs like "Mamak" persisted.

At the beginning of the twenty-first century, as Ruth F. Davis has revealed, some still saw fit to refer to the interwar musical scene as "the age of decadence."[21] The record industry was blamed for that state of affairs. Its central figures were castigated as "a class of opportunists whose depraved behaviour and financial greed dragged the art of music and the status of the musician into a deplorable situation."[22] One result is that the music that propelled an era has been effectively removed from scholarly conversation.

This chapter puts songs like "Mamak" and the figures behind them back into circulation. To do so, it highlights the lives and music of four Tunisian women: the era's first bona fide superstar, Habiba Messika, and her heiresses Ratiba Chamia, Louisa Tounsia, and Dalila Taliana. It also delves into the biographies of some of the male composers behind these female icons, like Gaston Bsiri and Acher Mizrahi. In each case, the musicians and their popular sounds transcended the national, even while shaping a Tunisian national culture in the making. Their records, for example, moved across North Africa and inspired local imitators. Their touring schedule brought them before sold-out crowds from Casablanca, Morocco, to Benghazi, Libya. But even before we arrive at that particular moment, we must turn back once again to Edmond Nathan Yafil, his orchestra El Moutribia, and, for the first time, to the world of theater across the region.

## Setting the Stage

In its original incarnation in the first decade of the twentieth century, El Moutribia strongly resembled its immediate nineteenth-century musical predecessors. The ensemble, for example, initially featured the six to seven musicians of a traditional Andalusian orchestra (*jawq*). In similar fashion, an early studio photo of El Moutribia captures a physical arrangement that would have been familiar to connoisseurs of the high-prestige repertoire at the time: the master musician (the *shaykh* or *m'allim*) seated at center, in this instance represented by Yafil, flanked by a half-dozen instrumentalists who also doubled as vocalists. The individual musicians in the photo, associated with Yafil's Free School of Arab Music of Algiers, can be seen grasping the instruments which had by then become typical: the kwitra (the Andalusian

Orchestre de la Moutribia en 1919. Au milieu le professeur E. Yafil

FIGURE 5. El Moutribia with Yafil at center (on violin), 1919. Source: *Ici-Alger: Revue mensuelle des émissions en langues arabe et kabyle de Radio-Algérie*, August 1959, no. 4, 20. Reprinted with permission of the Bibliothèque nationale de France (BNF).

'ud), the mandolin, the *mandole* (an elongated mandolin), and the *darbuka* (a type of goblet drum).

By 1910, however, El Moutribia had already undertaken considerable changes. That year, it became the first Andalusian orchestra in North Africa to record for the phonograph under its own name (others had recorded anonymously). It did so as *Jam'iyyat al-Mutribiyya* (El Moutribia Association) on a handful of 14-inch, double-sided discs for Pathé, the label where Yafil also acted as artistic director.[23] The recordings were just the beginning for the orchestra. On July 4, 1912, Yafil filed paperwork with the prefecture of Algiers to transform El Moutribia and the all-Jewish alumni of the Free School of Arab Music into a single, officially recognized association.[24] On July 31, 1912, its letters of incorporation were approved.[25]

El Moutribia's newly formed administrative council alone was more than double the size of the original orchestra. Among its fourteen administrators were now a handful of Muslim personalities. The involvement of figures like Ahmed Ben Mohammed Hadj Moussa, the imam of the Sidi Abderrahman mosque and shrine, helped it arrive at the goals it outlined in its by-laws including the charge to "save from oblivion" and "propagate" Andalusian music.[26] Like Yafil, the orchestra was as invested in executing music as it was in spreading it.

From its formal inception, El Moutribia vowed to "allow young natives to learn Arab and Moorish song free of charge." Given the demographics of its membership, Yafil clearly understood the "young natives" to include Jews, who despite their legal status as French citizens did not always enjoy the socioeconomic privileges that were supposed to accrue to it. In fact, the Jewish musicians of El Moutribia would be required to wear a modern symbol atop their heads that looked east rather than north to metropolitan France. Dutifully, El Moutribia's performers soon donned the *chechia*, the fez favored by a modernizing coterie of nationalist reformers across North Africa and the Middle East.[27]

In the years immediately following its establishment as a formal association, El Moutribia added dozens of instrumentalists to its core as it moved to bigger, more public venues. On October 19, 1912, the association held its first concert at the Hotel Excelsior in Algiers, a relatively short walk from the Casbah but also a world apart.[28] Approximately six hundred were in attendance, including a considerable number of women and girls, some of whom now counted among the 120 members of El Moutribia. If large audiences, mixed in gender, were turning up in more bourgeois spaces, the orchestra's regular outdoor concerts at the centrally located Square de la Republique and Square Bresson attracted similar numbers of working-class Jews and Muslims in addition to "curious Europeans."[29] As Omar Carlier has observed, the growth of El Moutribia and other such "cultural initiatives, novel in their very nature and manner of functioning, burst upon the scene from the medina (the historic city) [ . . . ] bearing witness to a new social dynamic that not only stretched the framework of daily life but also reshaped the desire for different ways of coming together."[30] In other words, Yafil's orchestra was contributing to the formation of a new urban public in Algeria, what Carlier has referred to as "the emergence of Muslim civil society."[31] It did so, in part, by diversifying its repertoire.

Following World War I, El Moutribia transformed its ostensibly Andalusian concerts into what the press described as "Moorish festivals" (*fêtes mauresques*). Intriguingly, it was Yafil's recruitment and retention of Mahieddine Bachetarzi, the Muslim tenor, that helped push El Moutribia into the realm of the music hall. Given that Bachetarzi previously served as chief Quranic reciter (*bash-hazzab)* at the New Mosque (*Jami ʿ jadid, Mosquée de la pêcherie*), close to the lower Casbah, the new direction he inspired was curious. Nonetheless, El Moutribia's "musical repertoire became highly mixed during this period as well, with Bachetarzi performing songs from the *nūba* tradition alongside arias from Italian opera, original compositions combining Arabic and French, and popular songs from Tin Pan Alley translated into colloquial Arabic."[32] Belly dancing was added too.[33] So was theater, including that performed by visiting acts from Tunisia and Egypt.

While theater emerged out of the music scene established by El Moutribia in Algeria, in neighboring Tunisia it was theater that provided a bridge to the emergent music and recording industry. Much like in Egypt, host to a modern theatrical tradition that dated to the nineteenth century and which drew on European and Arab forms alike, there was also a nationalist quality to it.[34] In Tunisia, under French control since 1881, that nationalism was reform-oriented rather than anticolonial per se. In similar fashion to the Algerian case discussed in chapter 1, the French invasion of Tunisia, along with the official support given to the growing settler population, had reconfigured the capital Tunis and led to the displacement and impoverishment of rural Tunisians.[35] The French initially applied what Mary Dewhurst Lewis has referred to as "divided rule," in which "sovereignty was split" between the protectorate government and the Husaynid beys, the former Ottoman dynastic power.[36] Still, as Lewis has also made clear, even within this configuration the bey may have reigned but he did not rule. In order to extend its authority in light of this arrangement, the protectorate promoted a policy of "political assimilation to France" for Tunisian elites.[37] It was perhaps best embodied by the establishment of Franco-Arab schools, which aimed to groom a minority of Muslims for service in colonial governance.[38] In the early years of the twentieth century, a group known as the Young Tunisians, themselves graduates of the French educational system in one form or another and inspired by their Young Turk analogues in the Ottoman Empire, had begun speaking the language of French liberalism absorbed at school. The Young Tunisians were now also channeling their discontent through protests of various sorts.[39] Their main demand was for increased rights for Tunisians, whose honor, they argued, had been impugned by the failure of the protectorate to live up to its promise to set the nation on a path to self-government. To articulate their grievances, Young Tunisian leaders like Abd al-Aziz Thaalbi and Hassan Guellaty turned to petitions and the press as well as to the stage.

At least a half-dozen theatrical companies formed in Tunis in the years just before World War I.[40] Their connections to the nationalist reform movement are not difficult to detect. Several representatives of Young Tunisia, including Thaalbi and Guellaty, served on the administrative council of the troupe El Adab (Arab Belles-Lettres), founded in 1911.[41] Likewise, Chahama Arabia (Arab Pride), established in 1912 by Mohamed Bourguiba—the older brother of future Tunisian president Habib Bourguiba—exalted the Arab, Muslim, and, by extension, national past by staging historical dramas related to the eighth-century conquest of al-Andalus or to Saladin's liberation of Jerusalem in the twelfth century.[42] Tunisian Jews participated as well. Like Chahama Arabia, al-Tarraqi (the Jewish Progress Troupe), created in 1913 by David Hagège, also presented *Saladin* (*Salah ad-Din*), the same aforementioned piece of musical theater about the eponymous hero's encounter with Richard I (the Lionheart) during the Third Crusade.[43] In all cases, plays were accompanied by concerts, which increasingly featured an emerging genre of popular music known in Tunisia as *ughniyya* (literally, "song").

Al-Tarraqi's founder Hagège, while remarkable for his talent, was also representative of an era which witnessed considerable movement between theatrical performance, concert making, and the recording industry. In addition to his stage work, Hagège was among the first artists to record for the Gramophone label in Tunisia.[44] The record companies, for their part, saw fit to highlight such connections. In an early Pathé catalog, the female vocalist Aïcha Bent Bezzoul was identified as "the artist from the theatrical society El Adab," while her contemporary Leïla Sfez was promoted as "the famous singer of the café-concerts of Tunis," the popular venues in which small-scale review theater was likewise performed.[45] Alongside his theater and recording activities, Hagège served as the voice teacher for the Alliance israélite universelle (AIU), the modernizing and westernizing Franco-Jewish school system that had operated in Tunisia since 1878. His business card listed his professional affiliation with the gallicizing institution and his role as director of an Arabic theatrical outfit side by side with seemingly little issue.[46]

Like the Franco-Arab schools which targeted Tunisian Muslims for assimilation after 1881, the AIU promoted a similar civilizing mission vis-à-vis Tunisian Jews and other Jewish communities in North Africa, the Middle East, and the Balkans at about the same time. The French and British Jewish political figures and professionals who established the educational network in 1860, including Adolphe Crémieux (from whence the Crémieux Decree had taken its name), were first and foremost concerned with the legal status and "moral progress" of their coreligionists in the Islamic world.[47] Motivated by a host of factors, including their own status anxieties as recently enfranchised Jews, extraordinary events in the region like the Damascus Affair of 1840, and European orientalism, the personalities behind the AIU pushed forward a program of "regeneration" for their brethren as the first step toward emancipation.[48]

But as Alma Heckman has written, "'regeneration' also meant deracination."[49] Given that the AIU leadership blamed the supposed degeneration of Jews on their cultural proximity to Muslims, itself believed to be a result of their status as dhimmis (non-Muslims who are "protected" and yet tributary under Islamic law), the AIU attempted to orient its students away from their actual milieu and toward France. This feat was accomplished through the erection of schools—five alone in Tunisia between 1878 and 1910—and through a curriculum which emphasized French language, French history, and French geography.[50] Following the considerable pushback from parents and traditional educators, the AIU began providing lessons in Jewish history and religion and Hebrew as well. While the AIU did indeed graduate thousands of francophone students across the region by the interwar period, its success has long been read through the missives of its foreign-born and French-acculturated directors and educators. It should be remembered, however, that not all attended (as was especially true of girls), that some attended traditional schools simultaneously, that many dropped out, and that even those closely associated with it sometimes embraced a different type of modernity than the one envisioned by the institution.[51]

In Tunis, in fact, the AIU was not only connected to the Arab stage through individuals like Hagège but also remained a space for the Arab music that populated it. In 1922, for example, Kiki Guetta, a Tunisian Jewish recording artist famous for skewering the trappings of modern life in Arabic, headlined their annual gala.[52] The same event, itself a fundraiser, also featured an "Egyptian concert." Among the audience (and possibly the orchestra) for that particular celebration was another AIU employee who moonlighted with al-Tarraqi: Gaston Bsiri. Born in Tunis in 1888 to Ottoman Jewish parents of humble origins from the Anatolian port city of Izmir, Haim "Gaston" Bsiri served as a Hebrew and music teacher at the AIU's Hafsia Boys School in Tunis throughout the 1920s.[53] During that same period, he became a fixture of the nearby and recently erected New Synagogue (*Slat al-jadid*). There, as one of his Judeo-Arabic songbooks noted, he taught Zionist folk music (accompanied by his own translation of modern Hebrew into Arabic) and piyyut on Friday evenings.[54]

As with Hagège, Bsiri maintained a prominent position in Jewish communal affairs while also contributing to the creation of a modern national and even transnational culture. Most of his other songbooks, for instance, sold from his record store at 56 rue d'Alfa, contained the lyrics to popular Tunisian and Egyptian music recorded by himself and others for companies like Gramophone and Pathé.[55] In order to ensure the integrity of a wide, coalescing audience of Jews and Muslims who clamored for such sounds, his publications tended toward the trilingual—Arabic in Arabic characters,

Arabic in Hebrew characters, and Arabic in Latin characters—with Arabic
in Arabic often serving as the language of his most important announce-
ments.[56] Equally important, Bsiri, together with Acher Mizrahi (whom we
will soon meet), was also one of a handful of Jewish composers who were
responsible for crafting the most popular sounds of the interwar period for
an emerging set of mostly Jewish female recording artists.

## A Star Is Born

God, the voice of Habiba,
In the heart its effect is more powerful than the arrows of
    her eyes
What is the ʿud worth if not in the palm of her hands
God humbles it, as she lowers her eyelids
        —A poet who yearns for *tarab* (ecstasy)[57]

The anonymous poem, above, was printed just below a headshot of Habiba
Messika in a 1928 Baidaphon record catalog largely dedicated to her output.
In just two short couplets, the unknown poet had perfectly articulated the
very qualities that had distinguished the Tunisian Jewish superstar since her
professional start: her voice, her look, and her ability through her music to
summon a state of tarab among her dedicated fans.[58] But if she drew on an
older concept of musical rapture, her photographed image captured something else. With her cropped hair and strapless dresses, Messika embodied
a certain colonial modernity then coming to the fore. As much as she was a
novelty, she was also a harbinger of changes taking place for Jewish and Muslim women across North Africa that were intimately tied to the consumption
of objects like records.

    As is true for so many musicians of her era and class, Messika's rapid
rise to stardom has made the fashioning of a biography separate from her
onstage persona difficult. So has her tragic, premature death, which meant
that, among other things, she was never afforded the opportunity to write
her memoirs. Yet by turning to novel types of sources, including fiction, records, and ephemera like record catalogs, some pre-limelight details can be
pieced together. Marguerite "Habiba" Messika was born in 1903 to Daïdou
and Maïha Messika in the working-class neighborhood of Bab Souika in the

Tunisian capital.[59] Both her father Daïdou and her paternal uncle Khailou Esseghir were musicians. So was her maternal aunt Leïla Sfez. The latter two were well-known concert performers and recording artists, with their careers spanning decades.[60] As Richard Jankowsky has shown, Daïdou, proficient on 'ud as well as *mizwid* (a type of bagpipe), first made a series of ethnographic recordings in Tunis in 1903 and then again in 1904 in Berlin for the German musicologist Paul Träger.[61] Just a few years later, Daïdou pulled his very young daughters Habiba and Ninette (b. 1904?) into a makeshift studio for the Anker-Record label.[62] "The Messika Children" (*Awlad Messika*), as the artists were credited, made at least four lively sides complete with mizwid.[63] As in the case of Yafil in Algeria, the recording industry across North Africa was an intimate and sometimes family affair.

Like many other Jewish girls of her generation, Habiba Messika did not attend the AIU.[64] While she may have been enrolled at her local French public school, it is also quite possible that she did not have any formal schooling at all.[65] At the same time, she received a rigorous education in music first from her father and mother and then from her aunt and uncle. In Jeanne Faivre d'Arcier's work of historical fiction *Habiba Messika: La brûlure du péché*, for example, it is Sfez, her aunt, who introduces Messika to her future career by treating her to a performance of *Saladin* staged by El Adab at Tunis's Municipal Theater.[66] According to Hamadi Ben Halima, Sfez also taught her niece to play the piano.[67] In Faivre d'Arcier's telling, Messika had begun giving performances at private gatherings and family functions by the age of twelve, doing so under the tutelage of and with instrumental accompaniment by her uncle Khailou Esseghir and the orchestral leader and composer Maurice Attoun. As with others of her generation, she seemed to learn her craft from the phonograph as well.[68] Even if some of the particulars here are merely representative, her first published biographical sketch, a short text printed on the cover of a 1925 Pathé record catalog bound for Tunisia, corroborates much of it, albeit in broader strokes.

Habiba Messika, born in Tunis, was from her youth raised on Tunisian and Egyptian music. Her parents were well-known musicians who inculcated in her a sound education which today positions her as one of the leading Tunisian stars.

Her beginnings date back to 1918 to the many concerts where she could be heard.[69]

In this version of her story, no doubt supplied by Messika herself, she was all of fifteen years old when she ascended the stage.

In 1920, Messika joined Mohamed Bourguiba's legendary troupe Chahama Arabia. Her first major role, as predestined in Faivre d'Arcier's novel, was as Richard the Lionheart's sister Julie in a staging of *Saladin*. Here she played the love interest of William (the standard bearer of England), taken up by Egyptian actor, recording artist, and long-time Tunisian resident Hassan Bannan. In July 1921, she performed as another female lead, this time as Desdemona in *The Moroccan Commander* (*Al-Qaʾid al-Maghribi*), an adaption of Shakespeare's *Othello*.[70]

As in an earlier moment, the theater remained close to a rapidly evolving nationalist movement.[71] Recently coalesced around the Dustur (*al-Hizb al-Hurr al-Dusturi al-Tunisi*, the Tunisian Liberal Constitutional Party), the movement, as its name suggested, advocated for a constitution among other demands. Like its predecessor the Young Tunisians, it worked through street protests and strikes as well as on stage. As far as the performing arts were concerned, the French protectorate authorities, acting through the police, responded by surveilling actors and shutting down performances, often with little warning.[72] In mid-1921, for instance, the French police first recorded Messika's association with nationalist elements, both near and far.[73] According to one informant, the Jewish actress had developed ties to at least one member of the Egyptian royal family who in turn provided her with considerable financial support.[74] Since the 1919 revolution there, which united Egyptians against the British (who had occupied the country since 1882) and wrung major concessions from them, any connection to Egypt or the Egyptian leadership was of particular concern to the French.[75] On December 28, 1921, Messika herself wrote to the protectorate's secretary general, calling out the last-minute cancellation of one of her shows at the Municipal Theater "under the pretext that the municipality had repairs to do in the basement of the building."[76] When her troupe attempted to solve the problem by moving to the nearby Palmarium, the police intervened again, citing a piece of legislation which prevented that venue from competing with the

Municipal Theater. Messika demanded answers. She also made clear that the show should go on. As will become evident, her confrontation and dissatisfaction with the French authorities, even when couched in pleasantries, were previews of what was to come.

Over the next few years, Messika assumed a number of roles in adaptations of Shakespeare, Hugo, and Verdi.[77] Much as "on Cairo's stages," as Raphael Cormack has written, in Tunisia and across North Africa, "every play became a musical and every actor a singer."[78] This was especially true for Messika, who not only sang and danced between acts—and sometimes in the midst of them—but also appeared frequently in concert at venues like the Municipal Theater and the Palmarium in Tunis or at the Kursaal in Algiers, where she regularly drew crowds in the thousands.[79] With nearly every appearance, Messika left a lasting impression. While she did have her conservative detractors in the press, she also had her "soldiers of the night" (askar al-layl), her devoted male fans who offered her their unwavering protection.[80]

In multiple memoirs, well-placed male admirers vividly recall encounters with Messika that almost certainly went unnoticed by the star. Habib Bourguiba, who served as the first president of Tunisia between 1957 and 1987, remembered skipping school twice weekly in 1921 to see Messika perform the role of Dolorès in Shuhada al-watan (Martyrs of the nation), an adaptation, with obvious nationalist overtones, of Victorien Sardou's Patrie (Fatherland) about the sixteenth- and seventeenth-century Dutch revolt against Hapsburg Spain. In the years that followed, Bourguiba would again cut class— French this time—in order to catch his preferred actress on stage. Acting alongside her in an adaptation of Hugo's Lucrèce Borgia, a melodrama about the early modern Spanish-Italian noblewoman and governor Dona Lucrezia, Bourguiba even "demanded" that Messika kiss him "romantically," despite the fact that he was playing the role of her son.[81] In Algeria, Bachetarzi dated his transition from "tenor to impresario" to the moment when he persuaded Messika to perform with El Moutribia.[82] The first visit of the Tunisian to Algiers in 1923, he emphasized, "had a real importance" in pushing forward Algerian theater. Her "universality," he concluded—her ability to move effortlessly between song, dance, and drama, a quality shared by the great "Arab artists of that era"—was the future of his craft, métier, and industry.

Between 1924 and 1930, Messika recorded close to one hundred records for Pathé, Gramophone, and Baidaphon, for which she secured royalties.[83] She was the first North African female recording artist to be in such control of her voice. That voice, the supreme instrument of tarab, adorned and ornamented Egyptian songs, both art music and the latest compositions by Sayyid Darwish and Zaki Murad, as well as pieces from the Tunisian Andalusian repertoire, popular creations, and even selections from the trance-healing tradition known as *rebaybiyya*.[84] Her lilt, pace, and amorous subject matter invited her listeners in and then held them there, awaiting her next utterance. Typical was "Habibi al-awwal" (My first love), first recorded for Pathé in 1926.[85]

> O night, o my eyes
> My first love, Lord, I will never forget him
> My first love, for my life, I will never forget him
> My first love is dear to my heart
> Why try, Lord, I will never forget him.[86]

Within each verse, she repeated and embellished single strophes. But the song's conceit was more than that. In addition to her "first love," Messika proceeded to enumerate five additional lovers that she would "never forget."

The sexuality and individuality embodied by Messika in "Habibi al-awwal" coincided with an emerging feminist movement in Tunisia, which itself ran parallel to that of Egypt. In 1924, a young Tunisian Muslim woman by the name of Manubiya Wartani spoke unveiled at the French literary circle *L'Essor* in Tunis and "advocated for the removal of the veil, a recognition of women's rights, and improvements in female education."[87] That same year, Messika, who was already referred to as both a "superstar" and the "star of the theaters," began demanding and receiving the unheard-of sum of 500 francs per role.[88] On her concert posters and handbills, meanwhile, she was crowned the "queen of tarab" (*malikat al-tarab*).[89] That epithet in particular was shared with two of her contemporaries in Egypt known for being in control of their business affairs: Um Kulthum, considered the greatest Arab female vocalist of the twentieth century, and Mounira al-Mahdiyya, the recording artist, actress, and impresario.[90] As Messika's star rose over the next few years, a debate raged in the Tunisian press, both in Arabic and French, on questions related to women, feminism, and the veil. Tahar Haddad, scholar of Islamic law, notary ('udul), one-time member of the Dustur, and the best known contributor to that debate, tied the status of women to that of the debased state of the country under French rule. Their emancipation, he argued, would lead to the emancipation of Tunisia. In his book *Imra'tuna fi al-shari'a wa-l-mujtama'* (Our women in sharia and society), he therefore called for an end to "polygamy, repudiation, and the veil (which he likened to a muzzle)," as Julia Clancy-Smith has written, and for the advancement of certain rights, like education.[91]

Messika, of course, asserted her right to act in leading roles, female *or* male. In 1924, she thrilled and shocked as Romeo in a staging of *Shuhada al-gharam* (Shakespeare's *Romeo and Juliet*) at the Municipal Theater of Tunis.[92] For that, she immediately earned comparison to Sarah Bernhardt, the French Jewish woman who ruled every stage she graced at the end of the nineteenth and beginning of the twentieth century.[93] The link to Bernhardt made sense and not only because she had also thrilled and shocked as Romeo. Like her cross-dressing analogue, known for her appearance as much as for her sound and her ecstatic effect, Messika's beauty, body type, and daring sartorial choices constituted a notable departure from the artists of a generation prior.

Her famous aunt Leïla Sfez, for example, had been associated with a different French Jewish *belle epoque* figure: the corpulent Jeanne Bloch. While Sfez's weight was mocked at the time by satirical artists like Kiki Guetta (who was the highlight of the AIU annual gala in 1922), her figure was much closer to that of the ideal Tunisian Jewish or Muslim bride at the turn of the century.[94] The few surviving photos of Messika, on the other hand, preserve images of a svelte woman looking not to the immediate past but to the future. At the same time, Messika's slight stature, while symbolic of her youth and unmarried status, belied her tremendous presence. Her professional photos tended to focus on her round face, which was framed by her finger-wave bob and accentuated by her bee-stung lips. In at least one instance, Messika invoked an iconic photo of Bernhardt. In her studio portrait, Messika sat, wearing an off-the-shoulder white gown, low cut at the back, and tilting her head to the camera in imitation of Nadar's 1865 series with the French actress.[95] In

HABIBA  MESSIKA

dans ses Danses et Chants d'Egypte à " L'ORIENTA "
Rue  Halévy  -  NICE

FIGURE 6.  Habiba Messika graces the cover of *L'Éclaireur du dimanche*,
February 3, 1929. Source: Gallica BNF, Collection numérique: Fonds régional:
Provence-Alpes-Côte d'Azur, https://gallica.bnf.fr/ark:/12148/bpt6k9802556g.

another image, Messika stares directly into the camera, donning a cloche hat
festooned with jewels and draping pearls.[96] In still another, Messika looks
into the distance, sporting a strapless dress, with her hair wrapped in a glit-
tery headband and her neck adorned with the silver, oval-shaped beads—
possibly a family heirloom—typical of much of North African jewelry.[97]

For its part, the record label Pathé nimbly marketed an already popular Messika to an ever wider audience through her modern image. Their 1925 Tunisian record catalog featured a stunning headshot of Messika—round face, bobbed hair, and barely visible gown—on its cover.[98] The use of an artist's photo to sell records was a first not just for Pathé in Tunisia but for any record company operating in North Africa. Her likeness was put to use in two other novel ways in the coming year: first, with the publishing of the label's supplementary photo spread of its Tunisian artists; and second, with photo stickers affixed to her records. At the center of that photo spread was an encircled portrait of Messika—curls and cupid's-bow lips and all. That same circled image was then printed as a sticker and adhered to the labels on her 1926 Pathé releases.[99] In this way, generic, imageless labels were turned into image-focused tools for promotion. Again, the photo stickers were a first for a North African performer and rare for European artists as well. Among the few to earn that honor was the world's highest paid female entertainer of the early twentieth century: French singer-actress Mistinguett of Moulin Rouge fame.

At a profound moment of change, Messika's image, music, and presence transfixed North African women as much as it did men. Decades after the fact, Haydée Tamzali (née Chikly), Tunisia's first screen actress, could still describe with stunning vividness a private performance by Messika she witnessed in 1927.

> Suddenly the lute player began a prelude that silenced the chatterboxes, for it was the tune of a famous dance from Habiba. The artist stood up, with a graceful gesture she untied her thick black hair which enveloped her like a sumptuous cloak, then her hands rose towards the sky in a gesture of prayer. Calm, her eyelids lowered, her parted lips revealing a subdued smile, she took very small, imperceptible steps, while on her almost motionless legs, her hips undulated, rolled, oscillated. [ . . . ] There was a surprising contrast between this deeply sensual movement of the hips and the chaste expression on that beautiful face. Then the rhythm picked up and Habiba continued her extraordinary dance, sometimes sensual, sometimes pure, almost religious, sometimes primitive, sometimes deep and mysterious.[100]

Like the anonymous poet in the Baidaphon catalog, Tamzali was cast into a state of ecstasy as Messika lowered her eyelids.

## "Mawt Habiba Messika" (Death of Habiba Messika)

On February 19, 1930, Messika made an appearance at a prewedding henna party at the Lumbroso residence on rue d'Isly in the capital. With the star out for the evening, a trespasser entered her apartment building at 22 rue Durand-Claye.[101] The individual in question was Eliaou Mimouni, a seventy-seven-year-old Jewish merchant from the nearby city of Testour. It was not his pilgrimage to her domicile that was out of the ordinary for a fan but rather the hour and what he held on his person.[102] According to neighbors, including Tamzali, he arrived with an oil canister in hand.[103] Sometime thereafter, Messika returned home from what must have been an exhausting evening.

From what police could later gather from witnesses, Mimouni reentered Messika's building between 8:00 and 8:30 in the morning on February 20, 1930. Moments later, her apartment went up in flames. Soon her anguished screams were heard throughout the neighborhood.[104] When police officers and firefighters arrived on the scene, Messika was found burned alive. An ambulance rushed her first to Dr. Jacques Guez and then transferred her to a Dr. Ganem. From her hospital bed, Messika identified Mimouni (whom she recognized) as the assailant. Others did as well. He had lit her bed on fire, she told police. He had held her down so that she could not escape. But while the press offered fantastical, misogynistic ideas about the circumstances of the attack, Messika herself stated, in some of her last words, "I have no idea what could have pushed him to commit this act." Through it, Mimouni was injured as well. He fled to a nearby hotel, where he attempted to hang himself but was soon apprehended.[105] On February 21, 1930, Habiba Messika succumbed to her injuries. At twenty-seven, North Africa's first superstar was dead. Less than a month later, her assassin was as well.[106]

In addition to the obituaries which appeared in Europe, North Africa, Egypt, and Palestine, her impact can be measured by the staggering amount of music, much of it printed in songbooks or recorded to disc, that took up the subject of her life in the immediate aftermath of her tragic death.[107] As Yosef Tobi and Tsivia Tobi have shown, dirges such as "Qinat al-artist Habiba" (Lament of the Artist Habiba), written by the Tunisian Jewish writer and publisher Maklouf Nadjar, not only narrated with painful detail her final moments, much of it lining up with the press accounts at the time, but also spoke to the ecumenical outpouring of "Jews, Christians, and Muslims" (*al-yahud, al-nasara, wa-l-muslimin*) that followed.[108] To reach such audiences, Nadjar printed the cover of his text in three Arabic linguistic registers: Arabic, Judeo-Arabic, and French transliteration. Furthermore, while Nadjar approached Messika as "a saintly figure" throughout the lament, he was hardly oblivious to the multiple spaces, sacred and profane, where the mourning over her took place.[109]

> Who will comfort her mourning relatives
> Over her untimely death?
> Who will comfort the 'ud and the playing band
> Over the actress who'd intoxicate a man's senses?
> Who will comfort the men of the pub
> Over the singer who'd drive them mad?
> And who will comfort even me,
> Save you, O Lord of all flesh![110]

Acher Mizrahi, the individual most responsible for cementing the memory of Messika in song, was a figure who transcended those various places of mourning. Born in Jerusalem in 1890 to Ladino-speaking parents originally from the island of Rhodes, Mizrahi had first made his way to Tunisia in the course of the Balkan Wars of 1912–13.[111] Already a known musician in Ottoman Palestine, the twenty-something found work as a cantor at Tunis's New Synagogue, the same institution that would host Gaston Bsiri.[112] After World War I, Mizrahi returned to Jerusalem. He remained there until the mid-1920s before settling again in the Tunisian capital, where he established himself as a recording artist and composer, while also serving as music teacher and cantor at the École Franco-Hebraïque "Or-Thora."

Mizrahi's "Qissat Habiba Messika" (Tale of Habiba Messika), recorded for the Parlophone label and narrated, devastatingly, from the perspective of Messika herself, was released with varying titles by at least two other artists for two other companies: the up-and-coming Tunisian Jewish recording star Ratiba Chamia on Baidaphon and her aunt, the artist and dancer Flifla Chamia on Gramophone.[113] By 1935, Flifla's "Mawt Habiba Messika" (Death of Habiba Messika) had sold more than 3,800 copies, making it one of the best-selling North African records of the interwar period.[114] Given that it

was listened to in communal settings like cafés and that the song would appear decades later in Morocco as a lullaby, one can only begin to gesture at
its ubiquity.[115]

Still other records dedicated to Messika were made at the time. In 1931,
the Libyan-born Tunisian Muslim Bachir Fahmy recorded "Habiba matit"
(Habiba died) for the Baidaphon label.[116] Bichi Slama, a Tunisian Jewish
recording artist, released "Surat Habiba Messika" (Sura of Habiba Messika), which rendered her story as though it were a chapter recited from the
Quran.[117] Hardly just a national tragedy, the Algerian Muslim artist Redouane Bensari, scion of the Tlemcen-based Andalusian master musician
Larbi Bensari, recorded a song entitled simply "Habiba Messika" for Gramophone, while in Morocco original dirges about Messika were printed and
circulated.[118]

## Messika's Heiresses

In the shadow of Habiba Messika, other artists stepped in with material
inspired by the fallen star and the current moment. At least a segment of
Tunisians was ready for it. Writing in the journal *La Revue des études islamiques* in 1932, a certain L. V. found that "the native Tunisian public" was
embracing what he called "Arab vaudeville-operettas." While claiming that
"the emancipation of women, already advanced on the banks of the Bospho-
rus and even on the banks of the Nile, had progressed only slowly in Tunisia," he suggested that Tunisians were now catching up to their Turkish and
Egyptian counterparts. He pointed to a certain type of music and musician
as proof. "Concerts of Arab music," L. V. wrote, "interspersed with lyrical, satirical, or simply light-hearted songs, are very much flourishing in Tunis and
bring together every night, in one or another of the city's theaters (Ben Slama,
Mondial Alhambra, Idéal, and various music halls), a native public very fond
of this sort of entertainment."[119] One of those at its helm was "the star Ratiba
Chamia," whom he argued even "seems superior to her brilliant companions."

As the stage name Ratiba Chamia (Ratiba the Levantine) implies, the
Jewish artist was not born in Tunisia. But according to L. V., she hailed not
from Greater Syria but from Morocco. Like Messika, but to a far greater
degree, early and even later biographical details are difficult to come by for
Chamia. Her maternal uncle Rafoul Roffi, possibly also Moroccan, was

likewise a musician, and first brought her to Tunisia. Roffi's wife, the recording artist and dancer Bahia Chamia, was the one who bestowed Ratiba with her stage name. Sometime in the late 1920s, the Morocco-born Chamia first began recording in Tunis for Bembaron's in-house label Bembarophone.[120] Over the coming years, she would make dozens of records for Baidaphon, Rsaissi, and its sister label Oum-El-Hassen under a number of names including Ratiba El Maghrabia (Ratiba the Moroccan) and Ratiba Tounsia (Ratiba the Tunisian). According to L. V., it was Chamia's "charming physique" and "perfect diction" that helped her sell out concerts and sell records. "All phonograph fans have Ratiba's records," he announced before elucidating the many types:

> Taqtuqas, qasidas, etc. [ . . . ], Egyptian, Tripolitanian, Tunisian, Algerian, and Moroccan songs of the classical Arabic genre, and other still amusing or charming songs, of a new genre, I mean mixed up with French and Arabic: "Le voyage de noces," "Oh! mon chéri," etc.[121]

Alongside her look and sound, then, it was that "new genre" which dealt in honeymoons and love interests that was catapulting her and other mostly Jewish singers into stardom.

"Popular songs," as Frédéric Lagrange has written of the Egyptian music of the era but which applies equally to Tunisia and elsewhere across North Africa, "began to express the questions and anxiety of a changing society, dealing with conflicting perceptions on modernity and the colonial age."[122] Indeed, female artists like Chamia gave voice to the urgent issues of the day for Jews and Muslims on records that were pressed in the thousands. That it was a commercial venture meant that vocalists, together with their music, had to appeal to a wide audience—"to fathers and daughters alike"—in order to be successful.[123] Time and again, it worked. "Her admirers assure," L. V. reported of Ratiba Chamia, "perhaps with some exaggeration, that she will one day be the equal of the famous Egyptian singer Oum Kolthoum, the musical star of the Orient." And, in many ways, she was.[124]

If Chamia compared favorably to Um Kulthum, Louisa Tounsia was in a league of her own. Born Louisa Saadoun in Tunis in 1905, the Jewish artist began her professional career in music in the mid-1920s. Her earliest recording sessions appear to have been with the Columbia label toward the end of

FIGURE 7. Ratiba Chamia concert poster, Ramadan
1934. Personal collection of author.

the decade. Shortly thereafter, she graced the cover of their 1930 Tunisian
catalog.[125] Like Messika, her popularity enabled her to record for multiple labels at once, despite the preference of artistic directors for exclusive contracts.
By 1931, the Columbia Records cover girl, for instance, was also recording for
Pathé and would soon add Baidaphon, Perfectaphone, Polyphon, Gramophone, and Philips to her roster. That same year, Bembaron publicity began to
refer to her as a "superstar," the designation earlier earned by Messika.[126] After
her 1931 tour of Morocco, "a triumph of unprecedented proportions," which
included stops in Casablanca, Rabat, and Fez and a private performance for a
young Sultan Mohammed ben Youssef, the Algerian daily *L'Écho d'Alger* announced that "the reputation of Louisa Ettounsia has for a longtime reached
us, and the public has been charged with a current of curiosity."[127] Over the
following two years, she added annual stops at the Royal Miramare Theater
in Benghazi, Libya, to her touring schedule.[128] As she performed between
North African capitals and Paris, she enthralled her fans.

Like Messika, her very look at once anticipated and reflected a changing society. In 1930, for example, when Tounsia appeared on the cover of the Columbia Records catalog in Tunisia, she did so in an unfurled haik, the traditional covering worn by Jewish and Muslim women and intended to veil the head and body in a single cloak.[129] Having extended it to her full wingspan, she was quite literally unveiling as she grasped castanets at the garment's edges. Facing the camera, a whisp of bangs peeking out from under a headband, her neck draped in waist-length pearls, she revealed a modern costume adorned with local elements: sleeveless blouse, harem pants, and high heels. In still other publicity materials, with her hair cut at her jawline and bare shoulders, she would accomplish much the same effect.

Thus at the moment that Tunisian men were debating the place of women and especially the veil in the press, Tunisian women, like Manubiya Wartani, were already insisting on their individuality and the right to unveil. By the 1930s, as Julia Clancy-Smith has shown, a generation, albeit small, of Tunisian Muslim women had graduated from French schools only to continue on with their studies in the metropole. While "French feminists and North African nationalists alike condemned the colonial educational system as a signal failure due to high illiteracy rates, especially among Muslim girls," it nonetheless produced figures like Tawhida Ben Shaykh, who in 1936 became "the first North African Muslim woman to earn a French medical diploma." During that same period, women not only came to play critical roles in nationalist politics, including with the breakaway Neo-Dustur, established by Habib Bourguiba in 1934, but formed their own associations as well.[130] In 1936, as Ben Shaykh became a doctor, Bchira Ben Mourad established the *Union des Femmes Musulmanes de Tunisie* (Tunisian Muslim Women's Union), "whose official aim was to make Muslim women understand their rights and duties." That same year, Mahmoud Zarrouk founded *Leïla*, the first Tunisian magazine which stood, in its own words, "in defense of the Tunisian woman, for her social and intellectual evolution, against old, unjustified traditions which render marriages expensive and difficult, torment youth and worry families."[131]

In the pages of *Leïla*, women who resembled Tounsia appeared frequently. In fact, as Nadia Mamelouk has illustrated, the magazine's vision for the new

FIGURE 8. Louisa Tounsia on the cover of Columbia Records' Tunisian catalog, 1930. Source: Collection phonographique du CNRS—Musée de l'Homme, Le Centre de Recherche en Ethnomusicologie (CREM).

"Tunisian woman" not only included illustrious figures like Dr. Ben Shaykh but Tounsia's predecessor Habiba Messika and other Jewish artists.[132] Music was an important component of *Leïla's* messaging. To that end, it featured regular columns on upcoming concerts and recently released records written by pseudonymous authors who adopted titles like "the music lover" (*le mélomane*), "the enthusiast" (*l'amateur*), and "the listener" (*l'auditeur*).[133] Furthermore, advertisements for concerts, records, and radios targeted women directly, employing slogans like "LADIES!!! Buy the best wireless radio," a recognition of their increasing financial independence.[134]

While at present many of the archival sources usually preferred by historians elude treatment of Tounsia and her impact, her records reveal a great deal about the message that she brought to her audiences, sometimes even in advance of outlets like *Leïla*. "Please allow me (to speak), friends, men, and all of (you) women," she began on "Hukm al-niswan" (Control of women), released on Pathé about 1931.[135] She continued:

> This world is not safe anymore
> In my mind, I had no [bad] intentions
>
> This is the end of the world
> Maybe now I have some regrets
>
> The girls are cutting their hair [short]
> even married women are doing it
>
> Everything has a sign
> I won't hide anything from you
>
> Only what women say goes
> And their men say nothing.[136]

Accompanied by Khailou Esseghir on violin and Messaoud Habib on piano, two longtime musical collaborators of Messika, Tounsia was in many ways leading a conversation about an interwar reality—"the end of the world," as she joked—in which women were adopting a new look, increasingly in control of their own finances, and asserting themselves inside and outside of the home.

Unlike in the French-language *Leïla*, Tounsia articulated the "questions and anxiety of a changing society" in (mostly) Arabic-language lyrics accessible to the vast middle and lower classes of Tunisian society. She did so as a figure she invoked on the second side of "Hukm al-niswan": the "modern girl" (*al-garsun*, la *garçonne*), the epitome of individualism and sexuality, who was wont to dance "the Charleston" (*al-Sharlistun*). She was not the only one to call attention to the appearance of the modern girl in North Africa or her preferred dance. Men got into the act as well. On "Hadha takhir al-zaman" (End of the world), recorded for Gramophone, Lili Labassi, the Algerian composer behind "Mamak," sang of the "modern girl" with her "short hair" and her predilection for "the Charleston."[137] Already in 1925, Judeo-Arabic lyrics for a "Modern Charleston" (*Sharlistun mudirn*) circulated in Tunis. By decade's end, the Algerian Jewish musician Joseph "Sosso" Cherki recorded "The Charleston" (*al-Sharlistun*)—or rather a song set to the tune of Lee Morse's "Yes Sir, That's My Baby"—for Columbia Records.[138]

If on "Hukm al-niswan" Tounsia ironically decried "the end of the world" (much like Labassi), on most other records she heralded her new position in it. On "Ma fish flus" (If there's no money), written and composed by Maurice Benaïs and recorded for the Polyphon label in 1935, she announced that *if* she was going to get married, she would do so on her terms.[139] She informed her potential suitors, for instance, that money still talked but it now answered to the would-be bride, not to a male guardian negotiating the dowry.

> If there's no money
> Then we don't have any words
> Get out of here, love
> Goodbye
>
> But if you're well-to-do, light of my eyes
> You'll be loved by everyone
> Even a rich girl
> Will tell you to come over
> Really!
>
> And if you've got a bundle of money
> You'll always be living free
> Your wife will accept you taking a second wife
> And there'll be no fighting, no quarrelling[140]

If the notion of "taking a second wife" was exaggerated here, it proved the point all the same.

Tounsia asserted her newfound place as a modern girl in other ways. On "Viens chez moi" ("Ta ʻala ʻandi," Come over to my place), also written and composed by Benaïs and released on Polyphon, it was she who assumed the part of a man lusting for and then seducing an unmarried woman. Given the inversion of male and female roles and the lyrics themselves, the record was downright indecent. With music based on the Moulin Rouge hit foxtrot "Je cherche après Titine" (I'm looking for Titine), it was also extremely popular.[141]

> Darling, how much I love you
> I am seriously speaking to you
> My love, how much I love you
> When [I see] you leave the hammam
>
> . . . . . . . . . . . . . . . . . . . .
>
> Come over to my place for a moment
> I'm alone in the house
> You will see how
> We will quench that fire
> I will forget all my suffering
> In your big eyes[142]

On a great number of other interwar records, women also played the role of the male lead. Such was the case with "Où vous étiez mademoiselle" (Where were you, mademoiselle), first recorded for the Gramophone label in 1931 by Dalila Taliana (the Italian). While her last name is unknown, her stage name seems to have signaled her descent from the Italian Catholic community of Tunis, although she is often remembered as Jewish.[143] Taliana made her first public appearance as a performer at the age of ten, debuting in March 1922 at the Rossini Theater on Avenue Jules Ferry in the capital, alongside Gaston Bsiri and others.[144] Sometime in the late 1920s, she cut her first records for Pathé. By 1930, French Jewish modernist composer Darius Milhaud hailed the young Tunisian in the pages of the journal *Art et déco-ration* as "a star of this very moving music" and the rightful heir to Habiba Messika.[145] In addition to recording some of the repertoire made famous by Messika, Taliana somewhat resembled the late superstar. The proximity to Messika can be seen in a 1931 Pathé catalog produced for the French Colonial Exhibition held in Paris that year.[146] In her photo, Taliana was captured in profile, her face framed by a finger-wave bob and her neck adorned in a choker of pearls.

"Où vous étiez mademoiselle" was composed by Acher Mizrahi, the same music teacher and cantor at the École Franco-Hebraïque "Or-Thora" who had written and recorded a popular lament about Messika. Journeying as he did from Ottoman Jerusalem to French-controlled Tunisia and inhabiting both religious and secular spheres, Mizrahi was well placed to produce music that moved among multiple registers. With lyrics that alternated between French and Levantine Arabic, "Où vous étiez mademoiselle" was no exception. And Taliana, who similarly operated among many domains, executed it exquisitely.

Where were you, mademoiselle
Every day I ask about you
I love you, my beauty
I go crazy in your arms
My word as a man, mademoiselle

. . . . . . . . . . . . . . . . . . . .

Where have you been, not asking about me?
Not knowing that I love you
Every day, I wait a little bit [for you]
You'd think a crazy man was next door
My word as a man, mademoiselle

. . . . . . . . . . . . . . . . . . . .

We will have a date
Look for a nice place
May God be with you, love is sweet
You are the only lady in my life
My word as a man, mademoiselle[147]

If tamer than Tounsia, Taliana's recording was still bold. In the first verse, after asking why her lover never asked about her—in a line that began in French and ended in Arabic—she flirted with her listeners as she chirped, "not knowing that I love you" (*mish ʿarifti illi habbitik*). In fact, even if the language was softer, she was still a woman assuming the male lead—one who presided over a choir of men who repeated after her in unison.

## A Modern Public Emerges

By the end of 1935, Taliana's "Où vous étiez mademoiselle" had sold close to 4,500 copies across North Africa and in metropolitan France.[148] That impressive figure meant that it had displaced Flifla Chamia's ode to Messika as the best-selling North African record of its time. By contrast, most other records released on Gramophone in the 1930s, especially those featuring selections from the Andalusian repertoire, could be expected to sell no more than a third of that number.[149] Given that "Où vous étiez mademoiselle" was also recorded by Louisa Tounsia, Ratiba Chamia, and others, it would be no exaggeration to gesture toward some 10,000 physical copies of the song circulating by the mid-1930s.[150] Not only had it become a standard in Tunisia at that point, it was well on its way to achieving similar status in Morocco and Algeria as well.

In July 1933, Taliana arrived in Algiers for her first series of concerts in the country. Appearing in Square Bresson, she drew a crowd of eight thousand.[151] *L'Écho d'Alger* declared her tour a "colossal success." As to what she performed, the newspaper reported that her concerts included her "Egyptian and Tunisian repertoires and her most popular dance numbers in Tunisia, for which she has found success in the United States of America." Although "Où vous étiez mademoiselle" may have not crossed the Atlantic, it had landed in Algeria, even before Taliana did. In *Tout l'inconnu de la Casbah d'Alger*, for instance, published the same year as Taliana's Algerian tour, the European writer Lucienne Favre gave the song mention in the course of her exploration of what she called the "nocturnal Casbah." Observing a cabaret favored by dockworkers at the entrance to the lower Casbah, she wrote, "The phonograph is large and has an excellent sound. Tunisian music resonates on it with a vigor, which together with anisette, raises the morale of men for a while." As for the music in question, she noted that "the phonograph sings gaily.... Ah ... Mademoi ... z ... è ... è ... lle."[152] It was, in her rendering, as if Algiers itself breathed the song born of Tunis and penned by a composer with roots farther east.

Six months after her initial visit to the Algerian capital, Taliana returned for an encore performance at the Algiers Opera. The occasion was Laylat al-Qadr, the Ramadan evening which commemorates the revelation of the Quran to the Prophet Muhammad and which was typically marked by musical celebration. For the concert, she was joined by Bachetarzi's El Moutribia, including its major star Labassi. Lucienne Jean-Darrouy, the music critic for *l'Écho d'Alger*, was suitably impressed by nearly every facet of the evening: from the entrance and execution of the instrumentalists and choir of El Moutribia to the solo performances by Labassi and Alfred "Sassi" Lebrati to the diversity of Bachetarzi's repertoire.[153] As for Bachetarzi, she reported, "he brings along varied songs, some of pure oriental inspiration, others adapted to Western tastes, the most popular of which, as we know, have a large Arab clientele." One of those songs "adapted to Western tastes" caught her attention. Perhaps it was because she understood every other line. Or maybe it was because those assembled could hardly contain their excitement. It was "a mixed song, where, in a blending of the Arabic and French languages, a romantic vows to love a woman, giving her his 'word of honor' [*parole d'honneur*]." While she may have misheard the word "man" (*d'un homme*) for "honor" (*d'honneur*)—or more probably it was merely sung with the changed lyric—the song was without a doubt "Où vous étiez mademoiselle." It was likely performed twice that night given that the evening ended with Taliana and her "Arab music hall" numbers. It was "Où vous étiez mademoiselle," in particular, that Jean-Darrouy credited with having a "positive effect on the 'modern public' of Muslim music" in Algeria.

What did that "modern public" seeking out the "Muslim music" of Taliana and Mizrahi look like? Jean-Darrouy observed an overflow crowd. Among them were many women, who while "generally veiled," were not entirely so. She explained:

> Independent of the musical value of these performances, it is a matter of
> interest to note the evolution of taste in theater under the influence of the

"El Moutribia" company. The young musicians wear their tuxedos effortlessly, sporting or not the chechia; and, more and more, the practice of families going to concerts is spreading. The women, generally veiled, attend in large numbers, sitting next to their husbands. It should be remarked that with this female presence, the appearance of the concert hall always improves considerably.[154]

For another glimpse of an emerging modern public in North Africa born of its female artists and their popular music, we head back to Tunisia. "It is in the grand hall of the Palmarium," visiting French writer Pierre Mac Orlan (né Dumarchey) wrote of a Louisa Tounsia concert, "so full that the parquet floor and ceiling buckle under the weight of a marvelous, colorful crowd, that Tunis offers me, for 10 francs a ticket, a spectacle that I could only dream of."[155] He too made note of the men and women among "the colorful crowd" but more importantly captured the diversity of the Jews and Muslims assembled:

> In a complete fusion of all of the native social classes of Tunis who have come together to applaud Louisa Tounsia, one can see heavy-set Jewish old maids in long, baggy trousers, held up at their waists, with gold-embroidered bolero jackets; Muslim women in white, faces covered by black veils; veiled Muslim women, but dressed a bit European; in-the-know Tunisian women dressed according to the dictates of the most recent fashion catalogs; musicians of the Beylical guard dressed all in red with bolero jackets decorated in the yellow wool of military trim; the "tramway workers"; the well-dressed in pearl gray, donning the fez made of astrakhan or red cloth; the fortunate-to-be-born-on-Friday, and for that reason, wear the green turban; the hunchbacked topped with the red fez; the thoroughly maimed and crippled; the young zouaves of a Semitic type; the baharias, the native seamen who have replaced their red-tasseled sailor caps with the national fez; the little girls already anxious to please; the bleary-eyed children; the young men without hats and with square shoulder pads and loose-fitting pants; the audacious and troublesome ragabouches, the aggressive dwarfs.[156]

"When the curtain is raised," Mac Orlan wrote, "one takes in the orchestra on stage: a virtuoso pianist, lute and cymbal players, a violinist, a darbuka player, and a young man who rattles iron castanets. This group resembles, with its hint of solemnity, a council of ministers."[157] But "when Louisa appears, the entire concert hall cheers for her; the clapping of hands never ceases." The thunderous, rolling applause for Tounsia ended only when "the little brunette singer, graceful yet soft around the edges, wearing an apple-green silk dress ornamented with scarlet roses, signaled for silence."[158]

After the artist, wrapped in sensual fabric, calmed the crowd, "the orchestra struck up and the sultry voice of this mischievous, risqué young woman projected Arabic lyrics full of sexual and romantic innuendo to the farthest reaches of this immense hall." *This* was the modern girl and her music, in an Arabic blended with French, indecent, and above all, popular, for which the "complete fusion of all of the native social classes of Tunis" was coming together. Meanwhile, her performance of the high art, Andalusian repertoire, which occupied the "rest of the week," was confined "to intimate settings in the homes of rich men who invite some of their friends to come and listen." "Louisa's real place," Mac Orlan concluded, "is in front of her people, on the grand stage of the Palmarium." "Louisa Tounsia," he proclaimed, "is the idol of her city."[159] The Andalusian tradition might have been the ideal of the elite, but Tounsia made music for the masses.

## The Afterlife of "Où vous étiez mademoiselle"

In 1951, the "General Catalog of Arabic Records" of EMI Pathé Marconi, the conglomeration of Pathé, Gramophone, and Columbia formed in 1936, still listed Dalila Taliana's "Où vous étiez mademoiselle" for sale. Two decades after its release, the interwar song composed and written by Acher Mizrahi had outlasted the Gramophone Company itself.[160] In his memoir, Bachetarzi claimed that the song was the top-selling North African record of the first half of the twentieth century.[161] In all likelihood, he was right.

In the aftermath of World War II, a legal challenge to the song's copyright emerged from an unlikely corner. Farid Ghosn, a well-known Egyptian musician, claimed ownership of the composition which was by then unknown in his native Egypt.[162] His petition to the French music society SACEM to wrest control of "Où vous étiez mademoiselle" from Mizrahi must have been driven by the record's success. Nonetheless, a SACEM investigation found in Ghosn's favor and awarded him the rights, alongside Bachetarzi. In this fashion, a song closely associated with Tunisian artists (including one born in Palestine) was now credited to an Egyptian and an Algerian. When Lili Labassi's protégé Blond Blond (né Albert Rouimi) released his postwar version of the song on a 45 rpm vinyl record for the Dounia label—complete with electric guitar and the addition of Spanish lyrics—Ghosn, not Mizrahi, was listed as both composer and lyricist.[163]

Mizrahi himself may have not objected much to the erasure. Twenty years hence, the pillar of Jewish religious life in Tunis had distanced himself from the suggestive tune and the secular stage. Still, for anyone with the original Taliana recording, this was a moot point. Two minutes into the second side of the record, the modern girl can be heard calling out to the individual she held responsible for the song and its success: "Well done, Acher Mizrahi!" (*Allah 'alayk ya Asher Mizrahi*). Copyright or not, Mizrahi's name was still all over "Où vous étiez mademoiselle."

In 1981, the provenance of the song was once again challenged but this time from someone who wanted nothing to do with it. "Among the most imminent dangers to Tunisian music," wrote Tunisian musician and musicologist Salah El Mahdi, "was the rise of a small group of artists and cultural figures who mixed Arabic lyrics with French lyrics, as with, 'Où vous étiez mademoiselle' — '!' — 'Kul yawm asal 'alayki."[164] El Mahdi's exclamation mark put a fine point on the disdain with which the composer and reformer, who came of age after "Où vous étiez mademoiselle" had become a standard, regarded the popular music of the interwar years. "It is no secret," he claimed, "that the most prominent Tunisian cultural figures considered this insolence to be the gravest danger to Arab song." If "the most prominent Tunisian cultural figures" felt this way, the people did not. Nor did the very prominent Tunisian cultural figures who crafted this repertoire in the first place. But for El Mahdi it mattered little. He slammed what he called the "pretenders to the art, such as: Gaston Bsiri, Maurice Benaïs," who "composed at a tasteless level" through "the spread of trivial words in songs and in addition, phrases and intimations with vile words."[165]

But these "pretenders to the art" were, in fact, important tastemakers who reflected, anticipated, and gave voice to a changing society, much as their literary counterparts did. Their words, hardly "trivial" or "vile," explored and shaped modern ideas, especially about the place of women, in conversation with a coalescing, transnational audience of Jews and Muslims. In fact, in drawing attention to the music of a half century earlier in order to silence it, El Mahdi merely reminds us of the staying power of the Arab foxtrot, the Charleston, "Où vous étiez mademoiselle," and the pioneering female artists behind them. Alongside their daring coiffures and clothing, figures like Dalila Taliana, Louisa Tounsia, Ratiba Chamia, and Habiba Messika offered North Africans a soundtrack for the day, one which captured the spirit of the interwar moment through the bold sounds presented by the modern girl. As we will see in the next chapter, some of their songs also embodied the essence of an emergent politics of nationalism.

# CHAPTER 3

# NATIONALIST RECORDS

The February 1930 murder of twenty-seven-year-old superstar Habiba Messika stunned her native Tunis and sent shock waves across North Africa. It also set the region on edge. In her death, as in her life, Messika had brought Jews and Muslims together. That fact alone was not necessarily cause for alarm for the French protectorate authorities in Tunisia then preparing for her public funeral. But the ways in which the two communities had coalesced around the increasingly nationalist tenor of her music was.

On February 23, 1930, the office of Resident General of Tunisia François Manceron sent a hurried note to the director of public security regarding Messika's impending funeral.[1] Manceron's plenipotentiary minister had gleaned from the morning papers that the burial on February 24, 1930, just a few days before the end of Ramadan, would be a decidedly Jewish-Muslim affair. "The funeral of the Jewish singer Habiba Messika," he reported, "has been moved to 2:30 p.m. at the request of the Muslims of Tunis who are eager to attend" and who preferred fasting at home before joining the cortege in the afternoon. Not mentioned in the press, however, was the more actionable piece of intelligence. Manceron's minister spelled it out in no uncertain terms: "Habiba Messika has been in the service of the Destourians for the last few years." Given that her most recent recordings for the Baidaphon label had celebrated Egyptian independence,[2] the Great Syrian Revolt,[3] the Iraqi king,[4] and the Tunisian Bey[5]—and that security services were already

having difficulty impeding the flow of her discs supporting Arab independence and uprisings—the director of public security was likely aware of her
political proclivities. That Messika had found common cause with the nationalist Dustur, whose protests for major reform had successfully led to the
dismissal of the resident general immediately previous to Manceron, justified
the call to conduct "the most serious observation of what was to take place
at the funeral."[6]

On February 24, 1930—the day of Messika's funeral—the director of public security reported back to Manceron.[7] By midday, the funeral procession had
ballooned beyond expectation—five thousand according to one estimate[8]—
"growing minute by minute" as it made its way eastward out of the capital's
Jewish quarters toward the Bourgel Cemetery.[9] "The crowd," cosmopolitan
in its ethnoreligious and social diversity, "was composed of Jewish, European,
and Muslim elements belonging to all classes of the population."[10] As the
mass of mourners arrived at the city's principal Jewish cemetery, the director
of public security underlined the fact that Dustur supporters were among the
procession but had been careful not to congregate so as not to arouse suspicion. Clearly, it did not work. Given the multiconfessional, cross-class, and
high-profile nature of the funerary ceremonies, it was with little exaggeration
that the director of public security drew the conclusion that "never before
in Tunisia has a funeral taken place among such a vast gathering of people."

Within weeks of Messika's funeral, the French residents general in Tunisia and Morocco and the governor general in Algeria found themselves with
another problem on their hands. While Messika was gone, her voice, whether
invoking Egypt or Syria, was everywhere. In Morocco especially, her death
had contributed to a surge in the spread of her nationalist records, which like
"Inti suriya biladi" (You are Syria, my country) spoke of "pride" (*shahama*) in
national terms, and projected the defeat of foreign "enemies" (ʿ*adu*, pl. *a ʿda*ʾ),
at the very moment that a Moroccan nationalist movement, similar in its
aims to the Dustur, was emerging.[11] That swell in sales was facilitated by the
commercial collaboration of North African Jews and Muslims who worked
hand in hand to distribute her discs across the region. As a result, French pa-
tience with an industry that had once had their support wore thin. Adding to
their frustration was the subsequent release of other nationalist records—or
records understood to threaten French control—by Algerian Jewish veteran

FIGURE 9. Habiba Messika's record in support of the Great Syrian
Revolt, released on Baidaphon in 1928. Personal collection of author.

recording artist Lili Labassi and newcomer Salim Halali. To stop the potent
sounds of Messika, Labassi, and Halali, draconian censorship policies targeting records were established by the French in Morocco, as well as in Algeria
and Tunisia, throughout the 1930s. Many such laws remained in place until
the end of the colonial period at mid-twentieth century, targeting records
which now gave voice to aspirations of independence, rather than just reform.

Scholars have long acknowledged a particular sonic experience as central
to the growth of Moroccan nationalism in the interwar years: the countrywide public performance of the Muslim communal prayer known as the *latif*
in the aftermath of the promulgation of the Berber *dahir* (edict) on May 16,
1930.[12] The dahir, which attempted to segregate Berbers from Arabs through

the erection of a dual legal system, was seen by many as a violation of Islamic law. It also set off months of protests punctuated by the repurposed latif, which had been "customarily reserved for occasions of public calamity such as earthquakes, droughts, visitations of locusts and the like."[13] Now, however, the latif was not the only such sound to which nationalists turned for inspiration. Nor were the sounds that inspired a pride in nation among a wide cross-section of the Moroccan public voiced exclusively by Muslims.

In the pages that follow, we will trace the distribution in Morocco of three interwar records made by Tunisian and Algerian Jewish artists in order to think about how nationalism spoke across borders in North Africa while also considering for whom that message resonated. These discs, recorded respectively by Messika, Labassi, and Halali, were all deemed nationalist by a host of North African actors and French officials, the latter of which subsequently subjected them to censorship. This trio of musical episodes reveals as much about the practice of nationalism among ordinary Muslims and Jews in North Africa as it does about the Jewish-Muslim relationship.[14] While treatment of nationalism in the region has tended to render Jews, Muslims, and their relations as static, if not opposed, music and its movement make clear the frenetic energy with which Jewish and Muslim musicians, alongside purveyors of music and their customers, actively participated in and shaped emerging nationalist forms. To make these arguments, this chapter follows music rather than borders. In other words, the story of three censored North African records necessitates narrating at the level of the horizontal rather than looking northward to metropolitan France.[15] What happened in Tunis played out in Morocco while taking inspiration from farther afield in Egypt and elsewhere. Such was the case with Habiba Messika and her recording of an Egyptian anthem, the first of our three case studies.

## Habiba Messika and "Al-Nashid al-watani al-misri" (The Egyptian national anthem)

On February 24, 1930, the Tunisian theatrical luminary Bechir Methenni delivered an eloquent eulogy for Messika, the Tunisian Jewish leading light of stage and song now fallen. The prominent Muslim personality did so before a diverse and overflowing Jewish, Muslim, and European crowd in the capital's expansive Jewish cemetery. As the director of public security informed French Resident General Manceron, members of the Dustur were there as well. The Dustur (meaning "constitution"), founded in 1920, was the direct heir to the reform program advocated by the Young Tunisians (discussed in chap. 2).[16] Its emergence also owed to the Paris Peace Conference of 1919, which, in an echo of American President Woodrow Wilson's "Fourteen Points," promised "self-determination" for peoples around the globe, as well as to the Egyptian Revolution of 1919.[17] In both cases but especially the latter, the Dustur drew inspiration from a revolution which rallied Egyptians around Wafd party leader Saad Zaghlul and curbed the power of the British.[18] As its name suggested, the Dustur's agenda rested on the demand for a constitution that would guarantee the rights of Tunisians but within the framework of the protectorate. In order to achieve its objective of "the emancipation of the Tunisian country from the bonds of slavery," it also called for a representative parliament, suffrage, and the establishment of an Arabic-language primary school system. Throughout the 1920s, the Dustur's membership grew by thousands, just as labor unions like the Confédération Générale des Travailleurs Tunisiens (CGTT) formed. By mid-decade, protests and strikes, whether coordinated by the Dustur, the CGTT, or both, were endemic.[19] The French colonial government, prone to view challenges to their authority as menacing even when merely reformist, clamped down on nationalist activity through arrests, forced exile, and press censorship.

Still, for the French to intercede with Messika's funeral would have been to overplay their hand. The slain Jewish artist was a national icon. Like the rest of Tunis, Methenni, director of *l'Avenir théâtral* (*al-Mustaqbal al-masrahi*, the Theatrical Future), the theater troupe in which Messika had starred, was devastated by the loss of the woman who had earned the title of "queen of tarab" (*malikat al-tarab*).[20] In his elegiac remarks, Methenni highlighted Messika's extraordinary contribution to Tunisia. She was at once *the* embodiment of an artist "in the eyes of the Tunisian population," he reminded the assembled, and, at the same time, no less than a "second Sarah Bernhardt"—the turn-of-the-century French Jewish actress to which she was frequently compared and the highest compliment in the world of theater at the time. He concluded by speaking to Messika directly:

Alas, dear friend, your voice will no longer be heard, but rest assured that its memory will remain engraved in our imaginations, and when our children listen to your records, it will be with tears in our eyes that we will tell them about your life, about your generous spirit, and that we will instill in them the idea that no one was ever the equal of your genius.

Farewell Habiba, rest in peace, sister, you have earned it.[21]

Methenni's words no doubt reverberated among the mourners. As many already knew, however, Messika's records hardly had to wait a generation to be passed down and around. Within months of her death, her discs proliferated across North Africa. For the French protectorate authorities in Morocco in particular, a problem had emerged. As the civil controller of Morocco's Doukkala region cautioned in a report to his superior in Rabat, one record of hers in particular, "'El Nachid El Mousri' ([Al-Nashid al-watani al-misri], The Egyptian national anthem) 'record number B 86.520')"—Messika's rendition of a song composed in the wake of the Egyptian Revolution of 1919 and set to the tune of "Salam Afandina," Egypt's de facto national anthem, was "prone to provoke unrest in the Muslim milieu."[22]

In 1928, a decade after the launch of her illustrious musical and theatrical career, Messika had traveled beyond French control to record with the Baidaphon label in Germany. It would be her first and last trip, given her death less than two years later. Baidaphon had commenced operations in North Africa perhaps as early as 1922 but had only begun to record commercial artists there—or, more accurately, from there—in 1928.[23] Rather than meeting North African musicians where they were, as was common practice at the time among other record labels, Baidaphon brought them to Berlin. In doing so, the company accomplished two aims. First, it guaranteed artists access to new technologies like electrical recording, which through the use of a microphone rather than a phonograph horn permitted larger orchestras and a wider range of frequencies to be captured on disc than ever before.[24] Second, the label provided a space for musicians to record the very nationalist material that audiences were beginning to clamor for.

As Messika herself noted, she was very pleased with her Baidaphon sessions. In a letter penned to company executives on April 21, 1928—and reproduced in the label's first Tunisian record catalog—she thanked the company

FIGURE 10. Habiba Messika poses with one of her records. Source: *Ad-Dunya al-Musawarra*. Digitale Sammlungen der Universitäts- und Landesbibliothek Bonn. Digitalisierungsprojekt "Translatio." https://digitale -sammlungen.ulb.uni-bonn.de/ulbbni0a/periodical/pageview/7285738.

for "the fine electrical recordings" of her voice.[25] "More than exceptional," she added of her discs, "these are the best that I have recorded to date." They included selections from the Andalusian repertoire, along with popular songs from Tunisia and Egypt, much like her past sessions with the Pathé and Gramophone labels. But in Berlin, Messika veered headlong into the politically subversive as well. For Baidaphon, the Jewish artist made records extolling Tunisia as well as Syria, Iraq, and Egypt, the latter of which served especially as a potent symbol for Arab nationalists across the greater Middle East.[26]

If it could have been concluded, however, that Messika was merely singing about elsewhere, the queen of tarab quickly laid that to rest by adding geographically specific verses to certain songs and by recording unambiguously nationalist dialogue in the midst of others. On "Baladi ya baladi" (My country, O my country), for example, Messika sang mostly of Egypt, "my distant country" (*baladi ba'ida*), but also added a powerful couplet about her "Tunisian land" (*baladi tunsiyya*).[27] It included an emphatic, almost straining, assertive statement that contrasted her own feeling of liberation—"AND *I* live in freedom" (*w-ana 'aisha fi l-hurriyya*)—with the state of the country. That sentiment was met with the approving shout of "Lord!" (*Allah*), captured clearly on the recording itself. On still other Egyptian-themed records, such as "Marsh jalalat al-Malik Fuad" (His Majesty King Fuad's march), the pianist Mohammed Kadri can be heard yelling, "Long live the King" (*ya 'ish al-malik*) and "Long live Fuad, King of Egypt" (*ya 'ish Fuad ya 'ish malik misr*) as Messika and her orchestra, identifying with one such symbol of Egyptian sovereignty, erupted in thunderous applause.[28] For that matter, her recording of an Egyptian national anthem for Baidaphon was much more than just a foreign hymn. Here, Messika gave voice to powerful words that were sure to resonate in North Africa, even as she invoked the Egyptian leader Saad Zaghlul, hero of the 1919 Revolution.

> To a death that has become sweet as long as justice is our heaven
> Love of homeland is a matter of faith and the Spirit of God calls us
> Justice is ours, and the hand of the Lord runs over our hands
> If independence did not bring us together, then in Paradise we will meet
> Let the people's anger descend upon those who oppose patriotism

Long live Egypt's independence, and long live patriotism

And long live the people, strengthened by the young men and the fellah of the
village

And long live Saad and those with him, and long live the victims of the battle
for liberty.[29]

For Tunisian or Moroccan fans of the Jewish artist, an Egyptian anthem hailing liberty in these terms could easily be imagined as a Tunisian or Moroccan one as well.

In early May 1930, just a few months past Messika's death, Baidaphon sent a large shipment of records from Germany to Bembaron et Hazan, the record stores run by Raoul Hazan, in Morocco.[30] It was business as usual as far as the two companies were concerned. The French security services, however, were still acclimating to an evolving nationalist reality in their midst. "Hidden in a bundle of records of Arabo-Andalusian music," the civil controller of Morocco's Oued Zem region wrote on May 16, 1930, to civil control headquarters in Rabat, was a disc entitled "The National Anthem of Moroccan Youth" (*L'Hymne national des jeunes marocains*) recorded by Thami Ben Aomar, a musician and cobbler from the administrative capital of Rabat.[31] Civil Control headquarters, however, was already well aware of

FIGURE 11. Bembaron et Hazan's flagship store in Casablanca. At far
left, a poster of the Egyptian star Um Kulthum can be seen. Source:
Edouard Sarrat, *Le Maroc en 1932; ou 20 ans de Protectorat français
au Maroc* (Algiers: Imprimerie Fontana Frères, 1932), 275.

the Ben Aomar record. Since Bembaron et Hazan had begun selling it in its ten-plus branches, reports on the nationalist hymn—apparently penned by Baidaphon's Khayat—had been flooding the main office of Civil Control.[32] By May 16, 1930, the day when the French residency promulgated what became known as the Berber dahir, the stakes had been raised considerably.

The Berber dahir attempted to deploy different legal systems for Morocco's Muslim population along Berber-Arab lines. According to the text, "Berber law," a customary law, was to be applied to the country's Berber majority while Islamic law was to be reserved for Arabs. "Had it been fully implemented," as John P. Halstead has written, "the new policy would have subordinated to the French courts in Morocco roughly half the population classified officially as 'de coutume berbère.'" Given that the two groups in question were both Muslim, a group of Moroccan reformers also "condemned it as a violation of the Islamic religion."[33] Among them were two leaders from Fez who had asserted control of the nationalist movement in the making: Allal al-Fasi and Mohammed Lyazidi.

The promulgation of the Berber dahir coincided with the inflammatory centenary celebrations of the French occupation of Algeria and an equally provocative Catholic congress held in Tunisia.[34] Seizing on the outrage and the moment, al-Fasi, Lyazidi, and others moved forward with "repurposing" the communal latif prayer—traditionally reserved for natural disasters—to include explicit reference to the indivisibility of the Moroccan nation: "O Savior (*Ya Latif*) protect us from ill treatment by fate and allow nothing to divide us from our brothers, the Berbers."[35] Between June and August 1930, the weekly intonation of the now nationalist-tinged latif brought together thousands across the country. Rightly, Jonathan Wyrtzen has pointed out the theatrical quality of the protests, invoking what he has referred to as the "mise-en-scène of the latif performance."[36] It is no coincidence that Muhammad Lyazidi had a background in theater nor that there was a musical aspect to the spectacle. In the period leading up to the Berber dahir and the repurposed latif, for example, the weekly meetings of the Moroccan nationalist cell in Tetouan (in Spanish Morocco), led by Abdesselam Bennouna and Mohammed Daoud, "consisted of mint tea before dinner, a session of music after dinner and finally, a discussion."[37] Already at an early juncture, music and nationalism went hand in hand.

When the civil controller of Oued Zem informed his superiors of Ben Aomar's Baidaphon record on that fateful day of May 16, 1930, he referred to it as no less than a "Moroccan Marseillaise."[38] Given the climate, civil controllers across Morocco redoubled their efforts to seize copies of the disc before it could do further harm. But even at its outset, the search quickly shifted away from Ben Aomar and toward Habiba Messika, whose 1928 recording of an Egyptian anthem proved enduringly popular among ordinary Moroccans. In the hunt for Ben Aomar's music, security officials, intelligence officers, and police instead found the Jewish artist's records time and again. On May 5, 1930, hot on the trail of the "Moroccan Marseillaise," security service agents in al-Fasi and Lyazidi's Fez zeroed in on a merchant by the name of Mustapha Lemcharfi.[39] Operating out of the medina, Lemcharfi was found to be renting phonographs for the sum of ten to fifteen francs per day. That price included a stack of approximately twenty records, a number of which, according to the author of the unsigned intelligence report, had the effect of "stir[ring] up Arab feelings." An informant passed on a sample list of the records included with a rental from Lemcharfi. On it were three titles. Each was by Messika and included the Egyptian national anthem. In other words, two years after the release of her Baidaphon records and more than two months after her death, it was the Jewish Messika who was still "stirring up Arab feelings" in an important urban center in Morocco at what proved to be just weeks before the historic latif protests. And it was a small-scale Muslim merchant who enabled the reach of her nationalist message from beyond the grave.

On May 30, 1930, yet another civil controller sent an urgent message on the subject of "foreign propaganda on records" to Civil Control headquarters in Rabat.[40] "It has been signaled to me," the civil controller of Doukkala wrote, "that a record label in Berlin has sent phonograph records to Morocco reproducing, in the Arabic language, songs in favor of Egyptian independence which are prone to provoke unrest in the Muslim milieu." The civil controller identified the main culprit as Messika's Egyptian national anthem. But the characterization of her records as "prone" to wreak havoc was too little, too late. According to the same report, Messika's nationalist record was already "a huge success among the natives of Mazagan," a "Muslim milieu" within the Doukkala region that held a sizable Jewish minority. Residents of Mazagan

(El Jadida) were "excited by the rousing music and words hailing liberty," he reported. "They sing it in groups, full of energy, in sync with the phonograph, and accompany themselves on guitar ['ud] and mandolin." Given the scale of the Messika problem—Radio Maroc had reportedly broadcast her anthem on at least one occasion—the authorities concluded that Baidaphon would need reining in.[41] But the label was only part of the problem.

"It is relatively easy to control the importation of records made by the large and medium-sized firms," wrote the director general of the Military Cabinet in Morocco to the Bureau of Native Affairs and to the protectorate's secretary general on February 27, 1931.[42] False confidence aside, his concern at that moment was the mushrooming of small record labels of unknown origin that had suddenly appeared on the Moroccan market. "It is more difficult," he emphasized, "to prevent the clandestine fabrication [of records] which is within reach of individuals." Arabic Record, one of those secretly fabricated independent labels and which curiously carried an English-language name, proved particularly vexing for the Military Cabinet. So too did it confound Lieutenant Colonel Margot, head of the Muslim Press Service and director of *Es-saâda*, the official Arabic-language journal of the protectorate. Some of the releases on Arabic Record, according to Margot, had "whet the appetite of our Moroccans," by which he meant (paternalistically) their taste for nationalism.[43] Among the Arabic Record titles causing a stir were those that listed the performer on the label simply as "*malikat al-tarab*." Using her sobriquet in place of her real name, Arabic Record was bootlegging Messika's Baidaphon records. Or perhaps Arabic Record was Baidaphon itself. Either way, the fact that a label of unclear origin could sell the Jewish artist's records in the years after her murder, without inscribing her actual name anywhere on the disc, signaled at once the enduring popularity of Messika and, at the same time, the scale of the nationalist problem, which could join Moroccan Jews and Muslims together via a Tunisian Jewish voice heralding Egyptian independence.

While regional civil controllers chased Habiba Messika records, the resident general, the head of the military, and the director of the Bureau of Native Affairs simultaneously considered a more robust response to the nationalist record problem. On May 1, 1930, the protectorate's secretary general wrote to the directors general of the Military Cabinet and the Bureau of

FIGURE 12. An Arabic Record release featuring Habiba Messika (malikat al-tarab) and Ahmad Boliman (al-mutahajib al-shahir), ca. 1930. Personal collection of author.

Native Affairs on the subject of "the introduction to and sale of phonograph records in Morocco."[44] The secretary general proposed that a committee be established to explore control mechanisms for records of a "seditious character." He suggested that entry points for record shipments be restricted to Casablanca and Oujda, and that French translation be appended to a file for every record arriving in Morocco. On May 6, 1930, Resident General Charles Noguès wrote back to the secretary general.[45] He was on board.

Six months later, Noguès wrote again to the secretary general.[46] The phonograph record problem was growing worse. "I have been told that many natives record on blank discs, in the course of private concerts, analogous hymns [to those of Habiba Messika] and sometimes [even more] subversive ones." The resident general continued, "instituting control over phonograph record production is [now] therefore necessary." On January 26, 1931, following a gathering of government representatives from Morocco, Algeria, and Tunisia at the sixth annual North African Conference, the director of general security in Algeria wrote energetically to his director of native affairs.[47] When it came to control of records, he reported, Morocco should serve as a guide.

Between 1931 and 1932, a legislative committee attached to the Residence General of Morocco met three times in an attempt to decide the fate of phonograph records there. If successful, the legislation would be turned into a dahir. That Moroccan decree would await approval for several years as bureaucrats jostled over how best to handle the problem that spanned North Africa. Meanwhile, other nationalist records, this time made by Algerian Jews, were again sounding the alarm in Morocco.

## Lili Labassi and "Lillah ya-l-ghadi li-l-sahra"
## (By God, O you who are going to the Sahara)

On October 26, 1937, Allal al-Fasi was imprisoned by order of Resident General Noguès.[48] In recent years, he had become ever more emboldened and more organized. Buoyed by the latif protests of 1930, an inner circle of activists known as the "Zawiya," which included al-Fasi and Mohammed Lyazidi, and a larger, outer circle known as the "Ta'ifa," had by 1933 birthed the Comité d'action marocaine (CAM or the *Kutlat al-amal al-watani*), which pushed forward a reform program for Moroccans. The CAM articulated its agenda through a Paris-based journal called *La Voix du Maroc*—the same name as the country's first independent record label—while also making its presence felt through protests and strikes, especially in urban centers. There were other important symbolic actions taken as well. As Susan Gilson Miller has written, "even the subject of personal demeanor became an arena for nationalist expression." The same tarboosh worn by members of El Moutribia in Algeria, for example, "became the national costume for men" in Morocco. Meanwhile, Sultan Mohammed ben Youssef, who had ascended to the throne in 1927, was made a central and emblematic figure by the nationalists. Among the activities they organized was the first "Festival of the Throne" in 1933.[49]

By 1937, as the CAM grew to thousands of members, al-Fasi transformed the organization into *al-Hizb al-watani li-tahqiq al-matalib* (The National Party for Realizing Our Rights). In September of that year, as a confrontation over water rights came to a head in the city of Meknes, al-Hizb al-Watani, as it was known, helped lead a protest movement that bore the appearance of a "general uprising."[50] Within a month, French security officers arrested al-Fasi and shuttled him to the Saharan desert. In early November 1937, al-Fasi was transferred still farther into the Sahara along with other leading members of his nationalist circle including Lyazidi. From the Sahara, al-Fasi was taken by plane to Gabon in Central Africa, where he spent the next decade as a political exile.[51] Protectorate officials were attempting to quiet al-Fasi and his clique.

On October 27, 1938, nearly a year to the day after al-Fasi's arrest, Yves Sicot, director of Political Affairs in Rabat, sent a confidential letter to the heads of Civil Control and to the highest ranking generals across Morocco, warning of a new musical menace—a "subversive phonograph record related to Allal El-Fassi"—that threatened to undo the temporary silencing of the nationalist movement by protectorate officials.[52] In his letter, Sicot wrote, "it has been reported to me that an Arabic song containing very obvious allusions to the exile of Allal El Fassi has been recorded to disc—a certain number of which have recently been distributed in the medinas." He asked political and military heads to investigate the origins of the al-Fasi-themed record and the mechanics of its distribution. Days later, the reports started pouring in.

On November 2, 1938, the civil controller of Rabat sent word back to Sicot that he had identified the record championing al-Fasi's cause as "'By God, O you who are going to the Sahara' [ . . . ] recorded in Algeria around a year ago and sung by Mealem [Master] Lili Labassi."[53]

O you who are going to the land of the gazelles
If you find my love
Tell him, tell him he's still, he's still [alive]
No one can replace him for me
By God, O you who are going to the Sahara
find my love.[54]

**Bembaron et Hazan record stores in Morocco; Bembaron record stores in Algeria and Tunisia, c. 1930**

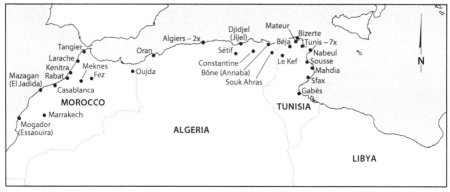

**Louisa Tounsia concert locations by city, 1931-1933**

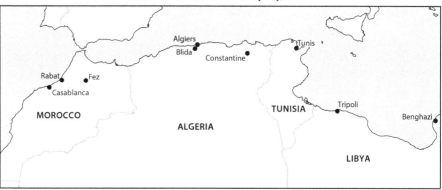

**Cities where French authorities discovered Lili Labassi's "subversive phonograph record related to Allal El-Fassi," 1937-1944**

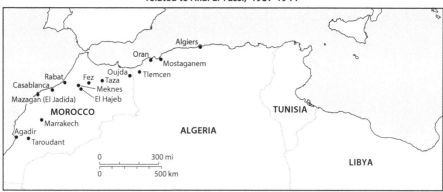

MAP. Records, record stores, and a concert tour across North Africa.

Mealem Lili Labassi, of course, was the same Labassi that we first met as he recorded for RCA in 1959. Born to Moroccan Jewish parents in Marseille in 1897, Elie Moyal settled with his family in the western Algerian city of Sidi Bel Abbès (Sidi bi-l'abbas) shortly thereafter.[55] It was there that he learned music from his father Joseph Moyal, a musician by night and a lantern maker by trade. It was also from there that he earned his stage name of Labassi, which would grace records like the runaway success "Mamak" and many others for years to come. For that hit and similar ones, Columbia Records had boasted that "Western influence can clearly be detected in the interpretations of Mr. LILI LAABASSI, who is incorporating French words into his songs."[56] The celebration of Western influence was ironic given that Labassi was not only born in France but was a French citizen, as were the majority of Algerian Jews since the Crémieux Decree of 1870. Certainly by the 1930s, he was already supposed to be Western, French-speaking, and even sympathetic to the French colonial project. It was thus that much more jarring when French security services in Morocco discovered that Labassi's "Lillah ya-l-ghadi li-l-sahra" seemed to make allusion to the deportation of the nationalist al-Fasi, a figure who had, in fact, been known to make anti-Jewish statements.[57]

In that same letter, the civil controller outlined the path of the Labassi release on Polyphon as it fanned out across the protectorate. It did not look good. The record about a beloved exile in the Sahara had been imported into Casablanca by Polyphon concessionaire Jules Toledano, distributed in the hundreds to Jewish-owned record stores in the country's major cities, and then passed around by a network of Jewish and Muslim middlemen. As with Messika, Jews and Muslims were once again collaborating to facilitate the spread of a nationalist record by a Jewish artist. In many ways, its success could be measured by the fact that Labassi's "Lillah ya-l-ghadi li-l-sahra" had even found its way into the hands of the wife of exiled nationalist Mohammed Lyazidi. She had apparently picked up two copies of the disc after "finding in the song an allusion to her husband's exile in Tafilalt [in the Sahara]."[58] No longer just a problem of the French imagination, those Moroccan Muslims most involved with the nationalist movement believed that an Algerian Jew was best giving voice to their aspirations.[59]

In reality, Labassi's "Lillah ya-l-ghadi li-l-sahra" was not intended to be nationalist. Here, Messika and Labassi differed. To begin with, the record, as evidenced by a faint mechanical stamp in the dead wax at the disc's center, was produced in 1937 but just prior to al-Fasi's exile. In addition, the recording itself was not explicitly political. The unambiguous dialogue found on Messika's records, for example, was nowhere to be heard. Instead, Labassi was merely, if expertly, interpreting an older *qasida*, a song text belonging to the Algerian hawzi genre, itself intimately connected to the Andalusian repertoire.[60] Given its stature, "Mamak" this was not. On November 2, 1938, a deputy officer in the Regional Bureau of Fez accurately described the Labassi release of a record about a Saharan exile at the same time as the exile of al-Fasi to the Sahara as "coincidence."[61] Nonetheless, the officer understood that coincidence or not, the record "could very well be put to use by the leaders of the nationalist movement." Lyazidi's wife had already done just that. Yet if the intent was different from Messika's Egyptian national anthem, then Moroccans heard much the same nationalist message in Labassi's recording of a music considered at once classical and, at the same time, national.

On November 19, 1938, the brigadier general of the Meknes region further laid bare the scale of the problem, alerting Sicot that "we have evaluated around one thousand records made by Maalem Lili Labassi—of Jewish origin it is said—in relation to the exile of Allal El Fassi. It seems difficult, due to the high number of records, to withdraw it from circulation.'"[62] The assessment was correct. In Mogador that same month, Regional Security found "Lillah ya-l-ghadi li-l-sahra" in the possession of a great many Jewish merchants including Moise Kedouchim, who managed the store of a certain Mr. Brami, and David Kakon.[63] Under interrogation, Kedouchim reported that he had purchased three or four copies of the disc after first seeing it in a Polyphon record catalog distributed by Jules Toledano.[64] Kakon declared that he had purchased the record from Bembaron et Hazan in Casablanca, by which he meant Art et Industries, the latest venture of Raoul Hazan.[65] In the case of Kedouchim, the commissioner of Regional Security believed his informant little. "In fact, it seems like," he remarked, "the order was of a much greater number than indicated."[66] The evidence could be found in the important detail that "many natives of Mogador own a copy of this record, notably spice merchants, which they play from their stores."[67] Hardly confined to Meknes or Mogador, "in Casablanca, the same record is similarly broadcast in the native milieu."

Security officials found the record by the "Jewish cheikh," as one civil controller rightly designated Labassi, in nearly a dozen Moroccan cities.[68] No copies were found in the Sahara itself.[69] Despite the difficulty of withdrawing the record from circulation, officials attempted to do just that through ongoing search-and-seizure operations. Those pinpoint raids were conducted not in the homes of known nationalists but in other places where nationalism was expressed: in the markets of the medina and the mellah. When the hunt for "Lillah ya-l-ghadi li-l-sahra" moved to Agadir in November 1938, for instance, the record was seized mostly from Jews like J. Hayoun, Maurice Sebag, Haim Lusqui, Émile Bensimon, and David "Baba" ben Haim Amar, among whom were again spice merchants but also tailors, bakers, and truck drivers.[70] Many of those caught with the musical contraband seemed to understand the stakes. Roughly half of those questioned refused to incriminate either the store (usually Art et Industrie) or the individuals (often Hazan and Toledano) from whence their records had been purchased.[71]

## Auxiliaries

The Labassi and Messika records made the rounds in Algeria as well. Messika, in particular, proved an irritant to the French intelligence and security services there. As Rebecca Scales has shown, "fears of imported Arabic records inciting political subversion in North Africa spread quickly through the French colonial bureaucracy during 1935–1936, when Bachagha Smati, an Algerian agent working for the Bureau of Native Affairs, produced a detailed study of Arabic-language records and Algerian listening habits and distributed his findings in a training course for French officers."[72] In a February 1937 address to his fellow officers, the same Smati teased out a history of commercial recording in North Africa, identifying the post–World War I years as marking the industry's "first period of prosperity, attended by a veritable and sudden invasion of the native milieu by the record."[73] This would not have been a problem in and of itself, he argued, if not for the "flooding of the market with Middle Eastern records," especially "Tunisian, Egyptian, and Syrian discs." Labels like Baidaphon, he informed his audience, were responsible for the release of

> the official or unofficial songs of the different Muslim countries: Cherifien hymns, Tunisian, Egyptian, Lebanese, Syrian, Iraqi, etc. [ . . . ] [and] while

this might appear anodyne, in fact they inculcate in the native the idea that
there exist in the world peoples having his faith [ . . . ] who have kept more
or less the façade of Arab states and who proclaim their desire for liberty in
their maternal language and not in that of a foreign Marseillaise.[74]

For Smati, emblematic was Messika's "Nashid jalalat al-Malik Faysal" (His
Majesty King Faysal's anthem), likewise recorded for Baidaphon, despite the
fact that he never mentioned the artist by name.[75]

As for the "invasion" and "flooding of the market," the Algerian agent
blamed his conationals but not his coreligionists. "It is, in particular, Jewish elements," Smati announced, "who were the artisans of this vogue for
records." He continued:

> Operating generally in their capacity as agent-resellers of the large labels:
> Gramophone, Pathé, Columbia, Odeon, Polyphon, etc. [ . . . ] they have been
> responsible for, in just a few years, thanks to their well-known business acu-
> men, creating in the country a complete network of retailers, who offer their
> merchandise at lower and lower prices, with increasingly elaborate payment
> schemes. Thanks as well to their knowledge of native languages, they have re-
> corded, locally or in studios in the metropole, a considerable repertoire today
> in which new compositions are added without stop.[76]

Their "well-known business acumen" aside, he made clear the consequences
to those assembled:

> In effect, after this period, Jewish merchants, under the double pressure of
> their own competitiveness and the new demands of their native clientele
> more and more partial to foreign music, became auxiliaries, most of the time
> unwittingly, of a form of anti-French propaganda, which is all the more dan-
> gerous in that it is exercised in a new terrain and by insidious means; I mean
> propaganda by way of the disc, in favor of nationalist and pan-Arabist ideas,
> of Middle Eastern importation.[77]

But that Jewish music makers or purveyors themselves were "unwittingly"
acting as "auxiliaries [ . . . ] in favor of nationalist and pan-Arabist ideas,"
as Smati claimed, is not quite borne out by the evidence, Labassi perhaps
excepted. As we have seen, Messika herself was well aware of the message

she was broadcasting, as were those around her. In addition, between 1938 and 1940, despite repeated raids on their stores in Casablanca, Toledano and Hazan continued to stock her records alongside Labassi's "subversive disc related to Allal al-Fasi"—as a thick file in the office of the director of Political Affairs in Rabat was labeled.[78] Over those same years, individual Moroccan Jews, alongside Muslims, in cities like Mazagan, Mogador, and Agadir endured perpetual harassment by French officials, confiscation of their goods, and worse, all in the pursuit of "rousing music and words hailing liberty." Put differently, their fidelity to certain records and their persistence in acquiring them despite the risks reveal a certain sympathy for nationalist aspirations, if not for nationalism itself.

Enforcement notwithstanding, the Labassi problem hardly abated, among either Jews or Muslims. In spring 1940, as France fell to Germany, the French military in Morocco focused at least some of its energy on the disruptive record by the Algerian Jewish veteran artist. On May 30, 1940, Secretary General of the French Residency in Morocco Jean Morize finally banned "Lillah ya-l-ghadi li-l-sahra" given that it had "the nature to cause disorder."[79] In this case, Labassi's chance nationalism was legally silenced. As late as 1944, the military continued its operations against the record. It found that Moroccans were still listening to "Lillah ya-l-ghadi li-l-sahra," despite its supposed exile.

As for Messika, other actors filled the void left by French censorship. In 1939, Nazi Germany began broadcasting the Jewish musician's nationalist records into North Africa as part of a radio war aimed at undermining French control in the region (and which will be discussed in greater detail in the next chapter).[80] Even if the Germans were aware of her Jewishness, it was the message that mattered above all.

### Salim Halali and "Arja' l-biladak" (Return to your country)

> Return to your country, man.
> Why do you remain estranged?[81]

In 1939, as French authorities in Morocco hunted Labassi's "Lillah ya-l-ghadi li-l-sahra" and Messika's Baidaphon and Arabic Record releases, a nineteen-year-old Algerian Jew by the name of Simon "Salim" Halali launched his recording career in France. Born to a family of modest means in Bône (Annaba) in eastern Algeria in 1920, Halali arrived in Paris alone in the early 1930s, having apparently stowed away on a cargo ship.[82] In the French capital he was soon joined by his parents and siblings. Together, the Halalis rented an apartment in the Marais, a largely Ashkenazi area where North African Jewish migrants had begun to settle between the wars.[83] Their installation in the *Pletzl* (as it was referred to in Yiddish) also placed them within earshot of a number of North African Jewish cafés and restaurants. At one of those venues, Au Petit Marsellais, the young Halali and his mother Chelbia began to sing Algerian and Tunisian popular songs for the patrons-turned-audience.[84]

In time, the teenager also ventured out of the fourth arrondissement and into the infamous Pigalle district. By 1938, he could be spotted at a cabaret there known as Le Club, where he sang in Spanish and adopted a Latin persona. The act was convincing. One evening there, a visiting Mahieddine Bachetarzi caught what he perceived to be a Spaniard in concert. When Halali introduced himself to the tenor and fellow Algerian as a fan (presumably in Arabic), his compatriot quickly comprehended that "my Spanish singer was no more Spanish than I."[85] By Bachetarzi's side that fateful evening was Mohamed El Kamal, an actor affiliated with El Moutribia and a recording artist associated with the Pathé label who experimented with jazz, along with a host of Latin genres that had gone global.[86] The two began a collaboration with Mohamed Iguerbouchène, the London- and Vienna-educated world-renowned composer originally from Algeria's Kabyle region.[87]

In March 1939, Halali entered Pathé studios in Paris with El Kamal and Iguerbouchène by his side. The very first record the three cut together differed considerably from the paso-doble and tango that would immediately follow and which would come to define Halali's sound. Indeed, "Arja' l-biladak" (Return to your country) was exactly the type of "propaganda by way of the disc, in favor of nationalist and pan-Arabist ideas" that Smati had most feared. While Messika had invoked another country and Labassi had reinterpreted an older song text, Halali gave voice to an original composition that seemed to speak directly and unambiguously to an emerging North African demographic in interwar Paris.

Between the two world wars, tens of thousands of Algerian Muslims, mostly men, had settled in Paris in search of work. The Third Republic soon

forced separate services and institutions upon them, while also implement-
ing laws restricting their movement and their ability to gather. In both cases,
the intent was to control a population it feared was gravitating toward the
nationalism of movements like the Étoile nord africaine (ENA), established
in the French capital in 1926 by Messali Hadj, and which initially maintained
strong links to the French Communist Party. Even the erection of the Grand
Mosque of Paris, inaugurated in the same year that the ENA was founded
and ostensibly a "gesture of appreciation" for the Muslim contribution to
the French war effort during World War I, operated as such a site of surveillance.[88] When in 1939 Halali recorded the lines "Return to your country,
man. Why do you remain estranged?" he appeared to be speaking to his now
100,000 compatriots laboring far from home.

Within weeks of recording "Arja' l-biladak," hundreds of copies circulated between France, Morocco, Tunisia, and Algeria.[89] On May 26, 1939, it
came to the attention of the subprefect of Mostaganem, Algeria. While the
subprefect was unfamiliar with Halali, the Algerian Bureau of Native Affairs made clear to him the danger that the Jewish singer and his nationalist
record posed. Since the spread of Messika's and Labassi's songs and of other
records deemed seditious, a 1938 censorship order in Algeria had mandated
translation for all imported discs "in any 'foreign' language (including Arabic)
other than French."[90] Halali's was no exception. The translation noted that
significant wear to the copy obtained by the Bureau of Native Affairs rendered some of his words difficult to understand. Presumably this was from
repeated play. Nonetheless, the Jewish artist's lyrics, which not only included
the titular call on Algerian laborers in France to return to their country but
also implored a pride in nation—"Say: I am an Arab Muslim" (*qul ana 'arabi
muslim*)—made him quickly known to the subprefect.[91] In short order, the
official declared the record to be nationalist propaganda and ordered that its
distribution be prevented.[92]

For two years, the demonstrably nationalist "Arja' l-biladak" was played
in Morocco as well, but either it eluded the authorities during that period or
the chase for Messika and Labassi, coupled with the fall of France's Third
Republic, slowed efforts to suppress a new subversive disc. Almost suddenly
then, on July 1, 1942, some two years into Vichy rule in Morocco, "Arja'
l-biladak" was banned by official decree in much the same way Labassi's

record had been. This time, however, an additional line was appended to the order: "Copies of the record, which are found at businesses (like music stores, record stores, etc.) and in public places (like cafés, etc.), will be withdrawn from circulation and destroyed."[93] Halali's voice had permeated public space and public consciousness alike.

———

Throughout the interwar period, the Jewish-Muslim relationship was sometimes at its most energetic when it came to the production and consumption of nationalist records. High-profile Jewish musicians, like the Tunisian Habiba Messika and the Algerian Salim Halali, partnered with their Muslim colleagues to craft, record, and perform a repertoire of nationalist songs that delighted mixed Jewish-Muslim audiences of various social classes, frustrating French authorities in the process. Beyond the musicians, Jews and Muslims collaborated to import and then distribute these records to the farthest reaches of North Africa through a Jewish-Muslim network of merchants and peddlers. In this manner, ordinary Jewish and Muslim North Africans played a vital role in providing nationalism with a soundtrack drawn from many sources. Of course, the passing around of nationalist records was done at great risk. Nonetheless, when caught with musical contraband, its Jewish and Muslim purveyors were seldom deterred and frequently recalcitrant.

Even when not deliberately nationalist, as with Lili Labassi's record, an inner circle of Moroccan nationalists could still hear the articulation of a powerful message in the music recorded by North African Jews. But many of those voices were soon to be silenced with the onset of Nazi and Vichy rule in the course of World War II.

# CHAPTER 4

# LISTENING FOR WORLD WAR II

On August 25, 1944, Mahieddine Bachetarzi hosted a Ramadan concert featuring a constellation of Algerian, Tunisian, and Libyan stars then at the
height of their fame.[1] That it coincided with the liberation of Paris was coincidence. The cause for celebration was not German surrender but rather
the relocation of Chez Mahieddine, Bachetarzi's wartime cabaret, from 7 rue
Lezard in the lower Casbah to a much larger space overlooking the sea.

Given the holiday and the lineup, the change of venue would have been
necessary to accommodate the crowd. Opening night included the pianist
Abdelhamid Ababsa, the jazzman Aziz, and the dancer Djamila.[2] The "pro-
digious little Aouaoueche," known as the "Arab Shirley Temple," made an appearance, as did Lili Boniche, seemingly the lone Jewish musician to appear
among the otherwise Muslim talent.[3] In the midst of all the fanfare, however,
one individual was notably absent: the high-profile Algerian Jewish recording artist Salim Halali. In the course of announcing Bachetarzi's concert,
*L'Écho d'Alger* had, in fact, presumed Halali not missing but dead.[4] Making
reference to the pedigree of the aforementioned Aziz, the newspaper noted
that during a stint in Paris the jazzman had led Mohamed El Kamal's orchestra, which was featured "on all of the recordings of the late Salim Hilali."

The "late" Salim Halali was one of the many prominent North African
Jewish musicians who had established themselves in the French capital in the
years just before World War II. Like the veteran Tunisian Jewish composer

Gaston Bsiri, the music teacher at the AIU whom we met in chapter 2, he had been little heard from since the start of the German occupation of Paris in June 1940. Back in North Africa, others would go quiet as well. The orchestra El Moutribia, the occupant of 7 rue Lezard prior to Chez Mahieddine, was among them. With southern France and North Africa under the control of the collaborationist and anti-Semitic Vichy regime, the predominantly Jewish group founded by Edmond Nathan Yafil had been disbanded. For the next three years, El Moutribia appeared neither on radio nor in public concert. In French colonial territories, as in the metropole, anti-Jewish race laws had become the new order of the day.

Joining a growing body of literature on North Africa, World War II, and the Holocaust, this chapter demonstrates that the war had a decided impact on the North African soundscape, determining what and who could be heard for years to come.[5] To capture that embodied, sonic experience of the war, we will listen in on radio broadcasts and concerts, follow the release of records and published songbooks, and attend to the forced silencing of musicians like Halali and Bsiri. We will also turn our attention to the amplification of voices like that of Bachetarzi, who, to the astonishment of many, began singing in praise of Vichy and much worse. Indeed, whether careers blossomed, withered, or were cut tragically short often followed Muslim-Jewish confessional lines. The quieting of Jewish musicians, who had largely dominated the North African recording industry and concert scene until World War II, created openings, opportunities, and new realities for their Muslim peers which would carry into the postwar period. But even before we arrive at that reconfigured musical world at war's end, or consider the ultimate fate of Halali, we must tune into an earlier moment and an earlier war carried out over radio.

## Radio Tunis, the War of the Airwaves, and the Hebrew Hour

Radio Tunis was founded on October 14, 1938.[6] Headquartered at 1 Place de l'École Israélite, adjacent to the AIU school where Gaston Bsiri had once taught, it was the third state-owned station to be established in North Africa and followed the inauguration of Radio Maroc in 1928 and Radio Alger in 1929. In all three cases, the promoters behind the mass medium hoped at once to connect the European population to the metropole and, at the same time, "to advance a spiritual conquest of Arab hearts and minds" through programming aimed at the Muslim subjects of French empire.[7] But among colonial officials, expectations for what was ostensibly to be national radio—what Morgan Corriou has referred to as "the national challenge" in the midst of an ascendant Tunisian nationalism—differed.[8] As Rebecca Scales has shown in the Algerian context, "colonial civil servants in Algeria judged metropolitan fantasies for creating a mass of docile native listeners to be woefully impractical and politically naïve."[9] If, from a power perspective, Radio Alger was in actuality "the voice of France in Algeria," as Frantz Fanon put it, while "Radio-Tunis appeared to be less the voice of Tunisia than the voice of France in Tunisia," as Corriou has written, there were also limits to that control.[10] Thanks to the wireless quality of radio broadcasting, Muslim announcers and audiences of both Muslims and Jews were able to subvert a French hegemony far better calibrated to what could be seen than to what could be heard.

In addition to marking a decade of colonial infrastructure, the establishment of Radio Tunis owed its existence to the "war of the airwaves" (in French, *la guerre des ondes*), a sonic harbinger of a world war in the making. Since 1934, fascist Italy, which long had designs on Tunisia, had targeted Tunisian Muslims with a daily Arabic-language broadcast emitted from Radio Bari.[11] The station's powerful twenty-kilowatt range, in fact, guaranteed that Bari Arabic Radio (*Radio Araba di Bari*) reached across French-controlled North Africa as well. Italian radio's hostile attitude toward "the Muslim politics of France," as one French intelligence report on the spread of radio among Muslims and Jews in Algeria framed it, first galvanized France's Third Republic into defensive action.[12] While many reports suggested that countering Radio Bari and its agenda required Radio Maroc and Radio Alger to improve their Arabic programming and expand their musical offerings, the French instead opted for monitoring radio dials and jamming radio signals.[13] By 1936, the nationalist and Francoist Radio Sevilla had joined the fray with Arabic programming that extended across the Spanish and French protectorates of Morocco and into Algeria.[14] Even as France launched Radio Tunis in October 1938 as a countermeasure in the war, the erection of Radio Tripoli in Italian-controlled Libya in December 1938 would further hem it in.[15] The start of Arabic broadcasting by Radio Berlin in 1939 did not portend well for the French either.[16]

But while North African audiences tuned into a variety of stations, including French-controlled ones, Italian radio dominated until 1940, when a series of decrees made listening to foreign stations ever more difficult.[17] The supremacy of Radio Bari owed to the fact that it played music that was rarely heard on Radio Tunis, Radio Alger, and Radio Maroc, due either to their sparse discotheques, outright censorship, or both.[18] The popular records of the Tunisian Jewish female stars Louisa Tounsia and Ratiba Chamia, for example, were regularly featured on Radio Bari but less so on French radio in North Africa.[19] This is all the more remarkable given that by 1938, Jewish musicians and composers had been officially removed from Italian radio.[20] As the war of the airwaves intensified, such irony abounded. Nazi Germany's Radio Berlin, as we saw earlier, broadcast a long-banned Habiba Messika record in praise of Iraq's King Faysal on July 9, 1939.[21] Interspersed with the music was fascist and Nazi discourse laden with anti-Semitism and pandering to emerging nationalist sensibilities. Whether listeners paid much attention to the incoherent message was unlikely. But that those with their fingers on the dial could hear a war playing out on the airwaves was certain. Fully one quarter of Tunisian "natives" owned radio sets by 1939, gathering an even higher number around them.[22]

Shortly after the launch of Radio Tunis and well into the war of the airwaves—sometime toward the end of 1938 or perhaps at the beginning of 1939—the Tunisian Jewish journalist Félix Allouche approached Philippe Soupault, the secretary general of Radio Tunis, with a well-crafted, if curious, idea. Much as he had done throughout his career, Allouche, a revisionist Zionist from the coastal city of Sfax and the founder of the newspaper *Le Réveil juif* (1924–34), aimed high.[23] He proposed the creation of what he called "a Hebrew Hour" (*une heure hébraïque*) for Tunisian radio. In his pitch to Soupault, Allouche spoke the language that French administrators were wont to hear. He described the nascent and limited state-owned radio station as no less than "an imperial station," much as its supporters intended. But given their ambitions and the expansion of the war of the airwaves to the Middle East, he argued, it "must be able to reach all of the Mediterranean population groups, at the same time to appeal to all of the listeners in the Oriental countries." In particular, he cited the importance of "the Jewish populations of Egypt, Syria, Palestine, Tripolitania [Libya], Greece, Iraq, and Turkey." He reminded Soupault: "It is a moral duty of imperial French radio to make itself heard, to put itself within reach so as to make them able to hear, if need be, the Voice of France."[24]

Of course, the question of language complicated matters significantly. To begin with, the "Voice of France"—generally expressed *in French*—was not necessarily well understood by all of the various Jewish communities Allouche invoked. Even in his native Tunisia, with a Jewish population of about 95,000, many outside of the elite classes hardly spoke the language fluently despite both half a century of AIU schooling and French colonial rule.[25] But French was only part of the linguistic equation. In fact, the program Allouche envisioned for "a Hebrew hour" was a Zionist one, at least culturally, and would indeed include the modern Hebrew largely born of the nineteenth century, a language even fewer of his coreligionists recognized.

Allouche, however, acknowledged that the broadcast would need to include Arabic if it wanted to reach a Tunisian Jewish audience. He also therefore complicated Radio Tunis's standard practice of French-Arabic division, in which the "French broadcast" was necessarily counterposed to the "Arab broadcast." For potential Jewish listeners in Libya, meanwhile, he suggested dedicating five minutes of every program to reportage in Italian that "should skillfully discuss and focus on the <u>happy goings-on</u> of Jewish life in Tunisia, Algeria, and Morocco. Drawing attention to, if need be, the racist bullying of Rome <u>through the form of news</u>."[26] Once again he reiterated that the proposed hour would serve as an important part of the French arsenal in its radiophonic battle with fascist Italy.

According to the plan, the program, in addition to Jewish news and interest stories, was to dedicate one-third of its airtime to music.[27] While some of that time was reserved for a "modern Hebrew choir" devoted to the emerging Zionist canon, most of it was allocated to "traditional Tunisian music," by which Allouche meant a mix of Hebrew piyyut and Arabic song on Jewish themes (some of quite recent vintage). He likened all of it to "Soulemeya," the liturgical praise poetry of the eponymous Sufi brotherhood based in the coastal city of Nabeul. The comparison was apt in more ways than one. The brotherhood's imam, Sidi Mohamed Buôuina, had recently employed the other major sound technology of the day, the phonograph, to make a number of recordings as part of the ensemble "Soulamia de Nabeul" for the

Gramophone label.[28] Allouche made other references to Muslim practice in order to justify his programmatic choices. In advocating for the inclusion of Biblical chanting during the proposed hour, he compared it favorably to Quranic recitation. Finally, despite his commitment to a maximalist Zionism, one which among its Eastern European base demanded a Jewish homeland on "both banks of the Jordan," Allouche assured Soupault that "the news will summarize the events of the week related to Judaism (with the exclusion of Palestine—this to avoid irritating Muslim listeners)." In this way, Allouche imagined that "a Hebrew hour" might find a Muslim audience alongside a Jewish one.

*The Hebrew Hour*, as it became known, debuted on the Arab broadcast of Radio Tunis on Saturday, April 1, 1939, at 8 p.m., just after the close of the Sabbath and two days before the start of the Passover holiday.[29] A triumph in and of itself, Allouche had launched the first Jewish radio program in North Africa. In addition to his own role as anchor, he assembled some of the greatest musical talent in the Tunisian capital to fill out the hour, including the respected paytanim (executors of piyyut) Joseph "Babi" Bismuth and Fragi Senouf.[30] While the *Hebrew Hour* was quickly hailed by the Jewish community, the musical portion in particular proved a source of immediate tension. This was not a question of the merits of Bismuth and Senouf but one of who was missing, largely as a result of Allouche's preferences for modern Hebrew music and Central and Eastern European cantorial records. Within weeks of its first broadcast, listeners unanimously began demanding the addition of Acher Mizrahi, the Palestine-born composer behind "Où vous étiez mademoiselle," to the lineup.

On April 21, 1939, Jacques Tebeka, director of the École Franco-Hebraïque "Or-Thora" and Mizrahi's employer, wrote to Philippe Soupault, the secretary general of Radio Tunis, strongly suggesting the addition of "one or two broadcasts per month with Or-Thora students and their master teacher Acher Mizrahi, the well-known artist composer."[31] With Mizrahi, Tebeka guaranteed that Tunisian listeners and those spread from Morocco to Egypt would enjoy listening with the "utmost satisfaction." One week later, the president of the Société Talmud Thora of Nabeul made two requests of the director of Radio Tunis. First, he asked that the *Hebrew Hour* include the performance of a piyyut dedicated to the sainted Rabbi Yacoub Slama, whose tomb was the object of an upcoming pilgrimage for the holiday of Shavuot. Second, he suggested that it should be chanted by "Acher Mizrahi who is the author of the poem."[32] On May 16, 1939, Moise Berdah of Ariana, just northeast of the capital, sent a letter to Soupault that strongly echoed those already received. "In my humble opinion," Berdah wrote, "the source of musicality and instruction of the Hebrew choir is missing our dear cantor Mr. Achir Mezrahi. Can we count on your impartial intervention to facilitate the formal introduction of our popular Achir?" He continued, "with this gesture, Jewish listeners will be satisfied beyond measure."[33]

While Tunisian Jews anxiously awaited the potential addition of Mizrahi to the *Hebrew Hour*, its audience grew even as it continued to make demands on programming. On May 17, 1939, the patriarch of the Fellous family in Tunis thanked Soupault "for the wonderful initiative he has taken in favor of the Jews of Tunisia."[34] He reported that he, his wife, and their children gathered together every Saturday evening to tune into the program, of which the "musical education" it provided was "the most interesting" part. This growing audience also made requests which would pull the program in directions possibly not envisioned by Allouche; if the broadcaster had hoped to use the *Hebrew Hour* as an instrument to disseminate a cultural Zionism, listeners had other ideas about what a Jewish broadcast should sound like. Time and again, there were demands for Arabic and liturgical, not modern, Hebrew. In the weeks leading up to Shavuot, for example, there were multiple requests for Mizrahi's song in honor of Rabbi Yacoub Slama.[35] Its performance on May 13, 1939, did not diminish continued interest. Two days later, a "Muslim Tunisian listener" from Grombalia, southeast of Tunis, announced that he "was delighted to hear the song chanted in honor of Rabbi Jacob Slama (of Nabeul). Please let us hear this song again."[36] On May 26, 1939, Mrs. Elie Fargeon of the town of Béja sent a follow-up to Allouche entreating the program to play a *ta'lil* (an Arabic-language praise song) in honor of her son Mouchi's bar mitzvah.[37] In a postscript, she also included a request to play the recordings of the Muslim popular artist Fadhila Khetmi. It was made on behalf of a certain "Mrs. F. Mimi," who was almost certainly Mrs. Fargeon herself. Finally, on June 7, 1939, Joseph Bijaoui, editor of the journal al-Yahudi (The Jew), offered to join the broadcast and read the news in "Judeo-Arabic" so that it could be "well received by the country's Jews."[38]

On June 17, 1939, Mizrahi at long last made his debut on the *Hebrew Hour*.[39] Allouche had listened to his constituents. In this way, as Elena Razlogova has illustrated in the American context, "broadcasters did not conjure up their listening public with a throw of a switch. The public participated in its own making."[40] Mizrahi did not disappoint that public. Accompanying himself on ʿud and joined by the Or-Thora children's choir, Mizrahi began the program by performing "Salam al-Bey" (the Beylical hymn) in honor of Tunisia's Husaynid monarch. Throughout the hour, he sang popular Egyptian songs, as well as piyyutim set to Egyptian melodies including the medieval Spanish Hebrew poet Yehuda Halevi's "Yafe nof meshut tevel" (To Jerusalem).[41] In addition, an eleven-year-old David Riahi, protégé of Mizrahi and later to become a hazzan and paytan of considerable repute first in Tunis and then at the central Sephardic synagogue in Netanya, Israel, also made his entrance on that mid-June broadcast, alongside an equally young singer by the name of Yaïche.[42] Given how much music was performed and played that Saturday night, it is unclear when Allouche would have had time to report on Jewish life or read news headlines from the Jewish world. In addition to the *Hebrew Hour* regulars Bismuth and Senouf, two records were played on June 17, 1939: the German cantor Hermann Fleishmann's "Kaddich" and French Jewish composer Darius Milhaud's "La Séparation, Chanson populaire hébraique," a rendition of "Hamavdil," a piyyut marking the end of the Sabbath.[43]

On September 23, 1939, the *Hebrew Hour* aired a special program for Yom Kippur. No music was heard that evening. Instead, Allouche addressed his audience at length. Knowing that his Jewish listeners would have just emerged from Yom Kippur services as the broadcast went live, Allouche asked, rhetorically, whether there was much he could add since the rabbis had already covered the "solemnity" of the occasion in their sermons.[44] But given that World War II was now three weeks in the making, Allouche felt compelled to provide a different, complimentary perspective. "You have never stopped praying for peace," he reminded his listeners, but "now you are praying for Victory." That prayed-for victory was an Allied one over the Axis powers of Germany and Italy. Allouche suggested that the upcoming Sukkot holiday, which marked the four decades in which the ancient Israelites, guided by their faith in God, dwelled in the Sinai desert after their exodus from Egypt, would act as their "symbol" moving forward. While the original transcript is torn at its edge, most of Allouche's powerful conclusion can be pieced together. The final line read, "After the judgment, forgiveness [ . . . ] we prostrate ourselves before God sanctifying [ . . . ] the triumph [of good] over evil."

Just two short weeks later, Allouche used another Jewish holiday, that of Simhat Torah, to again call for "resounding Victory." "You will excuse me," he said half-apologetically on October 7, 1939, "for bringing everything back to the tragic circumstances of today." He continued with a question that demanded no response: "Are we not in the midst of war—the most ardent fight for a better Humanity, a happier life for Man??" He ended by calling on "the Most High" to protect "the country where we live happily and peacefully, its military and civilian leaders, as well as the Sovereign of this Tunisian country [the Bey], a link in the great French imperial chain!"[45]

As war in Europe raged over the next several months, the *Hebrew Hour* continued to give voice to the emerging horrors while also striving to present a regular broadcast heavy on music. Increasingly, however, that sense of normalcy was difficult to maintain. On March 23, 1940, the evening of Purim, Allouche made clear the stakes of the present, which suddenly seemed not that distant from the ancient Persian past commemorated by the Jewish holiday:

> In every generation—bekhol dor ve dor—we are told in the Scripture, "in every generation," an adversary arises but justice always triumphs in the end.
>
> Today again [ . . . ] Do France, England not rightly fight against the Spirit of Evil to render justice to the weak, those whom the Malicious One has struck, beaten? Haman has been reborn as Hitler but like the Persian minister, the Fuhrer will also buckle under the weight of his own iniquity.[46]

He most likely concluded with the following pronouncement, although a series of cross-outs in red pencil on this part of the text may indicate that it was moved around, altered, or even discarded by the French censor.

> Dear listeners, I would like for you, during this Purim in the year 5700, this Purim 1940, to get everything you want—and that especially in the next year, with the defeat of the new Haman, the total Victory of the Allies.[47]

In this version of the transcript, Mizrahi followed Allouche. He chanted from the Book of Esther. Then, Babi Bismuth sang "Mi kamokha" (Who is like you, God?), another piyyut by Yehuda Halevi, this one traditionally sung by North African Jews on the Sabbath before Purim.[48]

On May 9, 1940, as France prepared for German attack, the *Hebrew Hour* was moved from Saturday to Monday evenings.[49] No explanation for the change was given but the exigencies of an unfolding war must have contributed to the decision to free up a coveted time slot. The following day, Germany began the invasion of the neutral Low Countries. France was next. It had been less than three months since Allouche had yearned for the "total Victory of the Allies" but his hopes had been quickly dashed. With the French-German armistice in June 1940, the *Hebrew Hour* was taken off the air.[50] Its removal occurred months before Vichy, the authoritarian and anti-Semitic regime led by Marshal Philippe Pétain that replaced the Third Republic, promulgated its notorious anti-Jewish statutes (*statuts des juifs*) in Tunisia.

## Germany in Paris, and Vichy on Both Sides of the Mediterranean

As the war of the airwaves raged across the southern Mediterranean, a number of Moroccan, Algerian, and Tunisian musicians made their way north to metropolitan France. In Paris, established and emerging acts flocked to the Latin Quarter, where cabarets catered to an expanding North African clientele. Among those sites was El Djazaïr, located at 27 rue de la Huchette, just south of the Seine, and owned by an Algerian Muslim who went by the name of Mohamed Seghir. By the mid-1930s, Tunisia's Louisa Tounsia served as in-house entertainment for the Paris venue, having relocated to the capital following a 1934 recording session with the French Perfectaphone label. In time, Tounsia became the face of El Djazaïr itself, with her visage adorning its promotional postcards.[51]

The Parisian press eventually caught wind of the transnational musical phenomenon in its midst. On May 21, 1939, *Paris-Soir* ran a photo essay capturing an evening at El Djazaïr.[52] Flanked, at turns, by her orchestra and North Africa's biggest names in boxing, Tounsia was at the center of the action. That same year, Halali's Pathé releases, made with Algerian Muslim musicians Mohamed El Kamal and Mohamed Iguerbouchène, put him on the map at home and abroad. By March 1940, French journalists had anointed

him the "Oriental Tino Rossi," a reference to the popular French recording artist and film actor with whom he now shared a city.[53]

On June 14, 1940, Paris fell to German forces. Less than ten days later, France signed an armistice with Germany that divided the country between the two entities. Nazi Germany now occupied northern France, including the capital. Marshal Philippe Pétain, hero of the First World War, led the accommodationist and authoritarian French State (*l'État français*) in southern France from the resort town of Vichy. The Vichy government, which maintained control over Morocco, Algeria, and Tunisia, was technically a neutral power but cooperated, sometimes enthusiastically, with the Nazi regime.

On June 14, 1940, as the Germans entered Paris, Halali was still there, as were El Kamal and Iguerbouchène. Bsiri remained too. Tounsia, it seems, had departed earlier. Back in Tunisia, however, she now found herself under Vichy rule. For those who did not or could not cross the Mediterranean but remained in the so-called Unoccupied Zone of France, the same was true.

## Radio Silence

Almost immediately following the surrender of France to Germany and the concomitant rise of Vichy, much of the music and many of the musicians once heard with regularity on radio, in theaters and cafés, and in public spaces in North Africa became ever more difficult to hear. In similar fashion, some of the musical inclusivity and permissibility that had helped produce the unique sound of the interwar period would come to a dramatic close beginning in summer 1940. Vichy's promulgation of the anti-Jewish statutes in Morocco, Algeria, and Tunisia, alongside their extension of the conservative ideological program known as the "national revolution" (*la révolution nationale*), provided the framework for an expunging of North African Jewish artists from public view.

The effort to silence Jewish musicians, in fact, had roots that immediately predated Vichy, at least in Algeria. In April 1940, as Malcolm Théoleyre and Jonathan Glasser have shown, Salah Arzour, head of "Muslim broadcasts" for Radio Alger, circulated a report among French officials in which he pronounced the then-current state of "urban music in Algiers" as one of "decadence."[54] The problem stemmed, Arzour argued, from musicians' lack of knowledge of classical Arabic, their tendency toward instruments of foreign origins (like the piano) but, above all, to a single (Jewish) source: Edmond Nathan Yafil, whose pathbreaking songbook the *Majmu ʿ* was "very poorly done and riddled with huge errors."[55] To remedy the situation, he called for the formation of a single Radio Alger orchestra, drawn from the best musicians from the capital's best orchestras. All of this was to be done, "with the exception of societies composed mostly of Jewish elements," for whom improvement would prove "practically unattainable."[56] El Moutribia, the celebrated orchestra led by Bachetarzi, a Muslim, whose members were Jewish almost to a one and which appeared regularly on the station, was the obvious target. So was its rival El Andaloussia, an entirely Jewish ensemble which had split from El Moutribia in 1929 but with which it now shared airtime on Radio Alger.

On October 3, 1940, the Vichy regime applied the first of its anti-Jewish statutes to the Unoccupied Zone, including Algeria. In addition to the promulgation of Jewish racial laws that hewed closely to those of Nazi Germany, Article 5 prohibited Jews from working in film, theater, and radio, mostly in a managerial capacity but also as directors, producers, and other creatives behind the scenes.[57] On October 13, 1940, the three state radio stations in North Africa—Radio Alger, Radio Maroc, and the newcomer Radio Tunis—were subsumed under Vichy and placed under the direct control of France's national broadcasting authority.[58] On October 31, 1940, the anti-Jewish statutes were extended to Morocco.[59] In Tunisia, the resident general applied nearly identical restrictions on November 30, 1940.[60]

With the promulgation of the anti-Jewish statutes in Algeria, El Moutribia and El Andaloussia would no longer be permitted to appear on Radio Alger. The same was true for national and municipal theaters and other public performance venues. Bachetarzi was thus faced with a difficult decision as to how to proceed. "Personally," he writes in his memoirs, "I preferred to dissolve El Moutribia rather than having to remove the Jewish members with whom I had worked for almost twenty years."[61] In other words, understanding the implications of the anti-Jewish statutes, Bachetarzi dismantled El Moutribia in its entirety rather than dismembering it along Jewish-Muslim lines. On December 10, 1940, an ominous announcement thus appeared in *L'Écho d'Alger*: members of El Moutribia were slated to gather the following day to discuss "the reorganization of the society."[62] From that date until early 1943 (just after the end of Vichy rule in Algeria), El Moutribia disappeared from the radio and so, too, from the pages of *L'Écho d'Alger*. El Andaloussia did as well.

It is possible that a handful of the lesser-known Jewish members of El Moutribia continued to perform on Radio Alger for a time. Bachetarzi, in fact, would claim that he supplied some Jewish artists with Muslim pseudonyms in order to facilitate their continued appearance on radio.[63] Such a maneuver would have required the cooperation of Radio Alger's Muslim broadcasters, like Salah Arzour, and French administrators, the same individuals who communicated regularly with Vichy officials and who were intimately familiar with the well-known Jewish regulars on the station like Labassi. Bachetarzi's plan, in fact, either never happened or was a failure. "My father," Labassi's son Robert Castel (né Moyal) would write in his memoir, "musician-singer-lyricist-composer of Andalusian music, was banned from Radio Alger to the great satisfaction of the director of the station who could not accept that Lili Labassi was superior to his Algerian Muslim protégés." For Castel, the treatment of his father under Vichy long maintained its sting, in large part because it remained unacknowledged. "Apparently, my father's records were not broadcast," Castel bemoaned, "he was the most important lyricist-composer of his age, but he was a JEW." For his father, those were the "dark years."[64]

In Morocco, in accordance with the first anti-Jewish statute of October 31, 1940, protectorate authorities dismissed Jews from managerial and administrative positions at Radio Maroc. It remains unclear, however, whether Moroccan Jewish musicians were able to continue to perform live on radio. What is more certain is that while the concert scene did not dry up under Vichy, Jewish artists from elsewhere across North Africa, like the Tunisian Louisa Tounsia, were no longer able to tour Moroccan cities as they had done in the interwar years. Indeed, the musical atmosphere had already changed in a number of ways. On November 21, 1940, for example, Resident General Charles Noguès issued order number 5.728/2.C., which prohibited restaurants, bars, cafés, and cinemas from playing records other than those containing "classical music or [music] of patriotic inspiration," which nonetheless still required submission to the censor.[65] One year later, an updated version of the order clarified that the target was that which was "trivial," including "all jazz and dance music."[66]

On August 5, 1941, two additional anti-Jewish statutes were enacted in Morocco by way of official decree. The first dahir "applied anti-Jewish discrimination with an even greater degree of severity, especially increasing the range and scope of professions from which Jews were excluded."[67] The second order created the mechanism to carry out an official census of Moroccan Jews and their property. Here, spoliation (Aryanization) was the goal. On the same day that the two anti-Jewish statutes were issued, a Mr. Tomasi, chief superintendent of Casablanca's police department, expedited an intelligence report to the director of Public Security in Rabat. He announced that the orchestra of Bouchaib Ben Ahmed and Abdesselem Talbi, which was composed of three "natives" (Muslims) and four Jews, had recently performed at the Municipal Theater of Casablanca. Even though the group was well known and proceeds from the concert were slated to be given to a "Muslim charity," very few spectators attended. Tomasi recounted that "a certain criticism was exercised against the orchestra due to the presence of the four Jewish musicians." He warned that should the Jewish-Muslim orchestra be given a chance to perform on Radio Maroc, "it would give rise to a certain dissatisfaction among a part of Casablanca's public."[68] Whether that slice of the Casablanca public was representative of urban centers, in general, or even the cultural capital, in particular, is difficult to say. But in light of new anti-Jewish actions taken by the government, Tomasi saw fit to alert his superiors of a possible shift in musical tastes.

Tunisia under Vichy forged a path midway between Morocco and Algeria. In accordance with the promulgation of the first anti-Jewish statute there on November 30, 1940, Tunisian Jews were removed as managers and administrators at Radio Tunis. Given that Radio Tunis was located at 1 Place de l'École Israélite, next to the AIU school in the heart of the Hafsia quarter, many of the discharged Jewish employees would have continued to pass the studio on a regular basis, making the sting of dismissal that much more difficult to bear. In addition, explicitly Jewish content, like the *Hebrew Hour*, was taken off the air in early summer 1940. And while individual Jewish artists performed live on Radio Tunis through 1940 and 1941, their continued presence elicited criticism from at least some in the Tunisian press.

With Vichy rule, the women's journal *Leïla* had shifted gears considerably. In December 1940, its editor Mahmoud Zarrouk transformed the monthly publication into a weekly newspaper. In its new guise, *Leïla* was now no longer concerned with either the emancipation of women or "the modern girl" but instead with delineating the boundaries of a rigidly constructed Tunisian national culture. Evocatively, Nadia Mamelouk has described this reorientation of the periodical as a "whirlwind," as both "tumultuous" and "confused."[69] In the course of *Leïla's* pivot, the newspaper's two anonymous radio and music critics—known respectively as "the enthusiast" (*l'amateur*) and "the listener" (*l'auditeur*)—launched an attack against celebrated Jewish recording artists and composers. Their broadsides, laden with Wagnerian overtones, invoked the decadence and decline of Tunisian music at the hands of a class of frauds, from which Muslim musicians were exempt.[70] That the articles of "the enthusiast" and "the listener" appeared alongside reproductions of the anti-Jewish statutes in plain language (for the benefit of their readership) and columns which lavished praise on Vichy chief of state Pétain (Zarrouk was a supporter) makes their uneven criticism all the more troubling.[71] On December 21, 1940, "the enthusiast" described a solo by violinist Albert Abitbol that he had heard on Radio Tunis as nothing short of "musical parody."[72] According to the pseudonymous author, Abitbol, a frequent collaborator of Bsiri and among the most important and technically adept instrumentalists of the era, "does not deserve the honors of the microphone."[73] In an echo of Arzour's Radio Alger report of April 1940, "the enthusiast" wrote incessantly of "the charlatans of art" and their "pseudo-talent," maintaining, alongside "the listener," a particular focus on Jewish composers like Bsiri.[74] On January 1, 1941, for example, an unattributed article, likely written by "the listener," castigated "the Attouns, the Bsiris, and other amateurs of all types who exploit the shallows of the city of Tunis or draw from their vaporous imagination."[75] But while Maurice Attoun, or Louisa Tounsia for that matter, another frequent target of *Leïla*'s ire, could respond to the war of words waged against them from Tunisia itself, Bsiri could not. Like other North African Jewish musicians, he was still marooned in Nazi-occupied Paris.

## Lives Suspended and Careers Continued

On October 7, 1940, mere days after the implementation of the first anti-Jewish statute in France, Pétain's government abrogated the Crémieux Decree in Algeria. In doing so, Vichy removed the French citizenship held by the overwhelming majority of Algerian Jews since 1870. The move returned musicians like Labassi and Halali to a state of legal indigeneity at the same time that their Jewishness was transformed into a racial category holding the weight of law. For Algerian Jews living in Paris like Halali, the reversal of Crémieux rendered them stateless at a moment when papers of state were determinate factors in survival. If in North Africa the careers of artists like Labassi were put on hold as a result of the October 1940 orders, then, in metropolitan France, the very lives of North African Jewish musicians were seriously compromised.

In German-occupied Paris, some North African Jews, including Halali and Bsiri, attempted to survive the war by passing as Muslims. In doing so, Bsiri managed to perform publicly for a time after the fall of the Third Republic in June 1940.[76] The same was likely true for Halali, as we will soon see. Such a feat would have meant considerable risk to themselves and required the clandestine collaboration of others. On September 27, 1940, for example, all Jews, French citizens and noncitizens alike, were required to register themselves with the French police. In addition, special identity cards had to be carried on their persons at all times.[77] Just a few months later, the Gestapo initiated a series of large-scale arrests and roundups. Foreign Jews, of which Halali was now one, were especially vulnerable. Given his celebrity—in March 1940, he had headlined a fundraiser at the famed Théâtre des Bouffes-Parisiens alongside actors from the Comédie-Française—all the more so.[78]

To be sure, Halali was known to French officials and functionaries in Vichy Algeria, who communicated regularly with their counterparts in the metropole. On December 22, 1941, a Mr. Delahaye of the Centre des hautes études d'administration musulmane (CHEAM) in Algiers distributed a confidential paper to his fellow administrators entitled "Propaganda in Muslim Countries: Arabic-Language Cinema and Records." It was riddled with anti-Semitism. Echoing Bachagha Smati's 1937 report on the relationship of the North African recording industry to nationalism, Delahaye lamented, for instance, the fact that "all of the labels that specialize in Arabic recording were in the hands of Jews [*israélites*]." Oscillating between the confessional *israélite*, the preferred verbiage of the Third Republic, and the ethnic designation *juif*, Delahaye added that "all of these Jews (*Juifs*) see nothing but the commercial side of the business. Pan-Islamic politics don't interest them." In other words, like Smati, Delahaye deemed Jews inadvertent auxiliaries of nationalism, a factor which he attributed to their supposed rapacious behavior. Toward the end of his eighteen-page report, he turned to the subject of Halali. Characterizing "Arja' l-biladak"—Halali's nationalist record—as "nothing other than the longing for one's country of birth" rather than "seditious," he nonetheless acknowledged its popularity and that of the voice behind it. "The young Jew Selim Helali," Delahaye wrote, again using the word *Juif*, "seemed to have become a popular star at the moment that the war broke out."[79] Appearing to have knowledge of the fact that Halali was still in Paris, he also understood that living in the Occupied Zone interrupted the career of "the young Jew," if not threatened his life.

By Halali's own early account, he was also on the radar of German officials in Paris. In an October 1946 interview given to *La France au Combat*, the bulletin of the French resistance, the journalist M. N. framed his conversation with Halali in the following way: "The Germans tried to use him to transmit their orders to his compatriots. He refused, was arrested, roughed up by the Gestapo, and went into hiding, spending the occupation years in a state of terror. His seventeen-year-old sister, already married, was shot. Her

brother-in-law's eyes were gouged out by the occupiers."[80] In spite of his re-
fusal to join Radio Paris-Mondial on behalf of the Germans, and even as the
Gestapo closed ranks around his family, "the late" Algerian Jewish musician
not only resisted but did somehow survive.

In the liner notes for a 1990 CD, Ahmed Hachlef first outlined a story in
which he identified Si Kaddour Benghabrit, the rector of the Grand Mosque
of Paris in the fifth arrondissement, as the individual responsible for hiding
and saving Halali during the war.[81] Hachlef, an Algerian, began serving as artistic director for Pathé's North African catalog at mid-twentieth century; he
was well placed to glean such information given that he oversaw many of the
recording sessions of Halali just after the war.[82] As Ethan Katz has shown,
"the first public account of the Grand Mosque as a refuge for Jews" during
the Holocaust dates to 1983.[83] In Albert Assouline's entry in the *Almanach du
Combattant*, the Algerian Jewish Holocaust survivor recounted that he was
hidden at the Grand Mosque not by Benghabrit per se but by the imam Si
Mohamed Benzouaou, who "took considerable risks in order to camouflage
Jews by furnishing them with certificates saying that they were Muslim."[84]
Assouline's account bears a strong resemblance to Hachlef's retelling of
Halali's experience, which is all the more remarkable given that the latter was
certainly unaware of the former's testimony. According to Hachlef:

> In 1940, he [Halali] was saved from the concentration camps thanks to the
> intervention of Si Kaddour Ben Ghabrit, rector of the Paris Mosque, who
> issued him a certificate of conversion to Islam under his father's name and
> in order to corroborate that, engraved that name on a tomb in the Muslim
> cemetery of Bobigny. In addition, he employed him at the café of the Paris
> mosque, where he performed regularly with equally important artists, like Ali
> Sriti and Ibrahim Salah.[85]

If we are to take Hachlef's account at face value, then the papers, the engrav-
ing, and the entire act would have had to pass considerable muster since
Halali was known to both the Germans and the French police as well as to
the North Africans frequenting the café. Here we are reminded of Bachetarzi's attempt to provide similar cover for Jewish musicians on Radio Alger.

Still, as Katz has illustrated, the Grand Mosque's reticence to open
its archives—as well as Benghabrit's own mixed record of resistance and

accommodation—has introduced some lingering questions about the actual mechanics of Halali's rescue.[86] In lieu of corroborating documents in official or institutional archives, Benghabrit's biography may offer additional support for Hachlef's narrative and a way out of the impasse. The fact that Benghabrit was not only a known music fan but an amateur musician himself may have made him more likely to shelter an artist of Halali's stature in the first place. Benghabrit, for example, was an invited guest at the Cairo Congress of Arab Music in 1932, one of the most important regional musical gatherings of the era.[87] While in Egypt, he was interviewed by an Alexandria-based newspaper and boasted that "I love the ʿud and would even say without vanity that I play it quite well."[88] Although a passion for Halali's music is not incontrovertible evidence of Benghabrit's intervention, it is also possible that it may very well have helped the Jewish artist survive.

At the same time that Halali lived a suspended, imperiled life under Nazi rule, some of his Algerian Muslim compatriots in the music business continued on with their careers, including in service to the Germans. On April 23, 1941, Vichy's Service for Algerian Affairs identified five North African venues in Paris "frequented by a large German clientele, which seems to have their sympathy."[89] Among them was Mohamed Seghir's El Djazaïr, the cabaret where Tounsia had headlined just before the war. Not only did Seghir cater to Germans but he was reported to have acted as an informant as well.[90] Meanwhile, Mohamed Iguerbouchène and Mohamed El Kamal went to work for Radio Paris-Mondial, which in 1940 had been transformed into a German propaganda outfit.[91] The Centre d'Information et d'Études (CIE), part of the intelligence apparatus in Algeria, concluded at the time that Iguerbouchène was being "bankrolled by the German occupiers."[92] In addition to his broadcasting activities, El Kamal continued to record for Pathé in Paris, at the height of the war. On June 8, 1942, he made a half-dozen Arabic-language jazz and dance records, a number of which were destined to become among his most iconic songs.[93] One month later, French police perpetrated the Vel' d'Hiv Roundup, interning thousands of Jews before ultimately sending most of them on to Auschwitz. Over the next year, the pace of arrest and deportation hastened. Among those caught in the expanding dragnet were Berthe "Beïa" Valaix (née Halali), Salim's sister, and her young child Claude.[94] On August 17, 1943, Berthe was arrested and interned at Drancy along with the

six-month-old Claude. On September 2, 1943, the two were sent to Auschwitz and murdered.[95]

## "Qulu ma ʿaya (Vive le Maréchal)" (Say it with me [Long live the marshal])

At the very moment that Jewish musicians like Halali faced grave danger in
metropolitan France, the show went on across North Africa. In Algeria, a
mix of established, emerging, and itinerant Muslim acts filled the void left by
Jews beginning in fall 1940. At Radio Alger, an orchestra drawn from various
Muslim associations replaced El Moutribia as the station's in-house Andalusian ensemble.[96] But while El Moutribia was sidelined, its president was not.
In fact, Bachetarzi toured at breakneck speed under Vichy. He did so armed
with a new repertoire and a new purpose: songs in praise of Vichy leadership,
which sometimes dipped into overt anti-Semitism.

At a distance from the center of European action and horror, Bachetarzi
provides a case study for how some artists in North Africa responded to the
events of World War II. We will recall that the high-profile tenor claimed to
have disbanded El Moutribia, his own orchestra, to avoid having to implement
Vichy's anti-Jewish race laws. At the same time, he maintained that he supplied Jewish musicians with Muslim pseudonyms to circumvent said legal regime at state institutions like Radio Alger. But by Bachetarzi's own admission
in his memoirs, we are confronted with his other wartime behavior: his enthusiastic and engaged support for Vichy.[97] On October 13, 1940, for instance, just
days after the publication of the first anti-Jewish statute and the abrogation
of the Crémieux Decree, Bachetarzi took the stage at the Majestic Cinema in
Algiers. One French intelligence report described the Majestic that evening as
"full to the breaking point." Some agents estimated at least three thousand in
attendance. Others suggested the theater had reached its capacity of five thousand. For the three-hour program, Bachetarzi, so accustomed to performing as
the sole Muslim among Jews, appeared for the first time in his career with an
all-Muslim troupe.[98] For much of the night, he sang in praise of Vichy leadership. So did actor and recording artist Rachid Ksentini, whose former comic
partner, the Jewish Marie Soussan, was no longer permitted on stage.[99] In her
absence, Ksentini lauded Pétain and his "national revolution." The thousands-
strong crowd applauded the performers and their words vigorously.[100]

By the end of 1940, Bachetarzi had already written several "patriotic songs" dedicated to Vichy.[101] He did so as conditions in Algeria worsened for considerable swaths of the population, especially for recently denaturalized Jews. Due to the *numerus clausus* stipulations under the anti-Jewish statutes, large numbers of Jewish men and women had been dismissed from their jobs.[102] Quotas likewise applied to the French schooling system, where most Jewish children were soon expelled.[103] Food insecurity became a rampant problem. As Vichy officials implemented a rationing system, enterprising Algerians forged the "marché noir," the black market.

In his memoir, the Algerian Jewish pianist Maurice El Médioni (b. 1928) recalled that "autumn 1940 and winter through to 1941 were 'rigorous' and extremely difficult" in his native Oran.[104] According to El Médioni, his widowed mother awoke daily at 3 a.m. in order to queue for basic provisions (stores did not open until many hours later).[105] Even before his expulsion from l'École Saint-André, the school's European director subjected El Médioni and other Jewish students to anti-Semitic violence. Capturing the sounds of the physical punishment, he writes:

> One of the humiliations which he practiced on us most often was during break-time. He would come up to us with a cane in his hand and, to the rhythm of a particular Arabic word specially chosen for us, like *hamar* (donkey) or *halouf* (pig), he would hit each one of us on our back or on our knees, his favourite targets for pain delivery.[106]

Worse yet for the family, however, was the moment when El Médioni's older, military-age brother Alexandre was "demilitarized" by the French army and sent to the Vichy concentration camp of Bedeau. Located just south of Oran, Bedeau was one of the many "places of confinement" that dotted the North African landscape from Morocco to Libya—but one of the few reserved for Jews.[107] With Alexandre's condition there unknown, El Médioni framed his and his mother's suffering in relative terms:

> Panic was growing all the time and we were getting more and more nervous about what might be in store for our brothers "concentrated" in Bedeau. We now thought a lot less about our empty stomachs, about the tiny daily ration of bread. I don't remember anymore exactly how many grams it was. But I

remember that the ration was enough for one meal [ . . . ] just [ . . . ] and the
bread was black, made from rotten rye.[108]

Of course, Bachetarzi's experience of the war years was decidedly different.

In January 1941, Bachetarzi embarked on a tour of Algeria supported and
coordinated by the CIE and the Press and Propaganda Services office of the
governor general of Algeria.[109] The multicity concert and theatrical series was
promoted widely on Radio Alger.[110] Proceeds were earmarked for the French
national relief fund and for Algerian Muslim prisoners of war held by Germany.[111] For the next year, Bachetarzi's intensive touring schedule brought
him and his troupe, including the actor Ksentini, to the far reaches of all three
Algerian departments. In this way, a pro-Vichy ideological program, which at
times veered into anti-Semitism, reached the largest halls in Algeria's larger
cities and smaller venues in the country's interior.

FIGURE 14. The audience at a performance of *El Mechehah*, October 27,
1940. Source: "Les Tournées Mahieddine: El-Mechehah," n.d., Archives
nationales d'outre-mer (ANOM). Reprinted with permission.

For much of 1941, performances began with a staging of *El Mechehah* (*al-Mashhah*), Bachetarzi's adaptation of Molière's *L'Avare* (The miser). He played the principal role of El Mechehah, the usurer Harpagon in the original, while Ksentini acted opposite him as Cléante, Harpagon's son, who was now renamed "Samuel."[112] In fact, as Joshua Cole has suggested, the choice of an explicitly Jewish name for Cléante was clearly intended to explicate the association between avarice, usury, and Jewishness embedded in *L'Avare* to a Muslim audience largely unfamiliar with the trope.[113] Following every staging of *L'Avare* was a concert. For audiences, its highlight was Bachetarzi's original composition, "Qulu ma'aya (Vive le maréchal)": "Say it with me (Long live the marshal)."

For Bachetarzi, "Qulu ma'aya," his panegyric to Marshal Pétain, was a stunning departure from just a few years earlier. Almost immediately after the 1936 election of Léon Blum, the first Jewish and socialist prime minister of France, for example, Bachetarzi sang his praises and that of his Popular Front government in songs like "Sawt al-Jaza'ir" (The voice of Algeria) and "Al-Ittihad" (Unity).[114] As Blum, together with his minister of state Maurice Viollette, pushed forward the Blum-Viollette plan, a reform proposal which aimed to increase rights for Algerian Muslims including providing some 21,000 to 25,000 with French citizenship, Bachetarzi, like others, found both hope and inspiration.[115] Remarkably for someone who already had a considerable voice, his "Sawt al-Jaza'ir" concluded with the line, "it is really thanks to Léon Blum that I have been able to speak."[116]

In "Qulu ma'aya," by contrast, Bachetarzi sang of an authoritarian leader to a martial rhythm. The chorus, a repetition of the titular line, resembled a political chant at a mass rally:

> Say it with me, "Long live the Marshal"
> Yes, say it with me, "Long live the Marshal."[117]

In the first verse, meanwhile, he addressed an imagined "son of Algeria" and sang of a new dawn in which "misery" was ending and a "glorious era" beginning. Léon Blum, for his part, was no longer the laudable figure invoked in "Sawt al-Jaza'ir" but the enemy of truth and God. While never mentioning Blum by name, Bachetarzi lauded his arrest and imprisonment by Vichy. Blum's replacement, on the other hand, was clearly identified.

We were under the reign of demagogy and illusion,
Now we are waking up from our lethargy,
God has confounded the liar.
Politicians have been expelled and the most
honorable of men is now here:
Pétain.[118]

More than just honorable, Bachetarzi exalts Pétain in the song's final verse as "God's chosen one," who sat at the head of a coalition of "Frenchman and Arabs," who were both "the children of France." Jews had not only been removed from his orchestra but from his vision of a future Algeria as well.

The audiences that purchased tickets for Bachetarzi's performances were large and diverse. Women of various social classes were well represented among the crowds.[119] As French intelligence reports reveal, a minority of Algerian Jews eager for Arabic-language music and theater attended as well. On February 12, 1941, Bachetarzi and his troupe performed before nine hundred spectators "of all classes" at the Alhambra cinema in Bougie (Béjaïa) in the Kabylie region on Algeria's Mediterranean coast. As usual, the evening began with *El Mechehah* and then moved on to "Qulu maʿaya" and other songs of Vichy. But at the end of the night, as Cole has demonstrated, Bachetarzi veered off what had already become a well-worn script. It seems doubtful that this was a one-time occurrence. According to the French police commissioner of Bougie, the former president of El Moutribia brought the evening to a close with a warning to be "on guard against the schemes of the Jews [ . . . ] who, while our masters, never stopped sinking their teeth into us and who, now downgraded, caress us as brothers."[120] After imploring the crowd to "put [its] faith in Marshal Pétain and his collaborators," the report noted that the audience erupted in applause. What it failed to mention was the reaction of the "thirty or so" Jews in attendance that night, who must have been considerably more muted.[121]

In Algeria, Bachetarzi was not alone in amplifying the Vichy regime through song, but he was likely its highest-profile bard. Many others elected to work closely with the CIE, including the celebrated musician Mahieddine Lakehal of El Djazaïria and recording artists El Hadj Mahfoud[122] and Abdelhamid Ababsa.[123] In Ababsa's case, he approached the CIE in what its chief commander Wender described as "a spirit of collaboration" and was "ready to further develop collaboration between the French and Muslims."[124] Alongside the famed and the well-known, Muslim scouting troupes and children's choirs shared the stage, performing "Maréchal, nous voilà" (Marshal, here we are) and other songs dedicated to Vichy well past the end of its rule in Algeria in November 1942.[125] In the weekly markets where itinerant performers made their stages, similar ballads could be found. By early 1941, these roaming storyteller-musicians, who attracted large, paying crowds not likely to frequent venues like the Alhambra or the Majestic, were brought to the attention of the CIE and soon onto the payroll of the Bureau of Muslim Affairs. In doing so, the reach of Vichy propaganda was substantially extended. At the end of March 1941, for example, Mabrouk Berchi and Tahar Ben Messaoud were recruited to spread the Vichy message some 380 miles south of Algiers in the hamlet of Touggourt in the Algerian Sahara.[126]

Of course, Berchi and Ben Messaoud were not Bachetarzi. And it is likely that neither had the historic and profound relationship with Jews that the famed tenor did. Nor did either possess the level of information about Vichy to which the well-connected star was privy. Cole has suggested a number of frames for coming to terms with Bachetarzi's actions in service to Vichy, among them "opportunism," disappointment with "the failure of colonial reform projects," backlash against the surveillance he was subjected to under the Third Republic, and the state of his finances at the time.[127] Rightly, Cole has also labeled Bachetarzi's engagement with anti-Semitism as a "betrayal" of his erstwhile Jewish colleagues. In light of such a reading, Bachetarzi's self-announced circumvention of anti-Jewish racial laws in the fall of 1940 suddenly reads definitively as an act of expediency rather than altruism. This is especially true when considering the wartime choices made by other North African Muslim actors, especially those that subverted Vichy rule.[128] For his part, Katz has urged scholars to consider "Muslims' war time behavior and sentiment in terms that go beyond simply assessing their level of anti-Semitism."[129] Indeed, Bachetarzi would rekindle and develop relationships with Algerian Jewish musicians after the war, including the pianist Maurice El Médioni and El Moutribia's interwar conductor Joseph "Cheb" Kespi.[130] Nonetheless, as Arlette Roth has alluded to, after the war many Algerian Muslims were unable to forgive Bachetarzi's behavior under Vichy, a fact that may have contributed to his temporary and self-imposed exile in Paris for much of the Algerian War (1954–62) and through the early Algerian independence period.[131]

By the end of 1941, Bachetarzi had concluded his first, year-long tour for the Vichy regime. After fifty-six performances, at the pace of more than one a week, he had raised tens of thousands of francs for the national relief fund and brought *El Mechehah* and "Qulu ma ʿaya" to tens of thousands around Algeria. Audiences had now committed the song to memory and were reported to sing it in chorus with him. Despite his success, there were setbacks. Some had grown tired of Bachetarzi's habit of auctioning off a portrait of Pétain to the highest bidder in the course of every show.[132] And yet the practice continued. On November 24, 1941, Bachetarzi penned a letter to the governor general of Algeria proposing another tour of the country.[133] It was soon approved.

## The Arrival of *al-Mirikan*

"Ayayayay! Nothing good is going to come of this. The
   Americans were here."
      —Hocine Slaoui, recorded as "A-Zin wa-l-ʿayn" (later
      released as "Al-Mirikan") for Pathé in 1949, Morocco[134]

"The bad times came when the Americans arrived,
They were like cockroaches, filling the streets."
      —Hamed Ben Ali Bel Abbes, sung on April 24, 1943,
         adjacent to the Jewish cemetery in Oran, Algeria[135]

"The Allies have come and removed the Germans from our
   midst."
      —Simon de Yacoub Cohen, "Khamus Jana," ca. 1943–
         44, published by Imprimerie Uzan, Tunisia[136]

On November 8, 1942, over 100,000 American and British troops stormed the shores of Morocco and Algeria in the largest amphibian landing in human history. Three days later, Operation Torch, which ultimately aimed to overrun Morocco through Tunisia in order to drive Axis forces out of Libya and Egypt while also setting the stage for an Anglo-American incursion into

Europe, came to an end with the surrender of the Vichy regime in North Africa. The operation, a stunning success thanks in large part to a notable group of Algerian Jews known as the Géo-Gras group, had devastating consequences.[137] The Allied victory prompted a German takeover of the southern half of France and direct occupation of Tunisia. Six months later, the war took another dramatic turn. In May 1943, the Allies pushed German and Italian forces out of Tunisia and from there initiated the Italian campaign from Sicily.

The hardships and deprivations of the war did not immediately abate in the aftermath of Operation Torch. Many Vichy officials, for instance, maintained their positions in the new French administration, providing a direct continuity between the war years and those that followed. Anti-Jewish legislation, for that matter, was repealed neither in Morocco nor Algeria until March 14, 1943. In Algeria, the reinstatement of the Crémieux Decree, hardly a fait accompli, would be delayed until October 1943.[138] In the meantime, food shortages persisted across North Africa. By 1943, the cost of staples, including oil, coffee, and sugar, had risen to ten times their prewar prices.[139] Cigarettes and candy, simple pleasures before the onset of Vichy rule, remained all but impossible to procure outside of the black market but with one notable exception: the Americans. The American forces, nearly everywhere and always a visible and physical presence after November 1942, were known to dole out such indulgences and much more.[140]

For many North African Jews, the Americans, who had vanquished Vichy and would eventually drive out the Germans from Tunisia, came to represent liberation from an existential threat. That sentiment was captured in the moment by both musicians and their music. On March 31, 1944, for example, the Moroccan Jewish recording artist Zohra El Fassia, who we will learn more about soon, sent a letter to the American Consul in Casablanca about the theft of her mail by her neighbor, coreligionist, and American protégé Rahamim Azoulay. "The actions of this gentleman," El Fassia reminded Azoulay's benefactors, "do not befit a nation to whom we owe our liberation."[141] The feeling of a debt owed to the United States was sincere and shared by many North African Jews at the time and since. Not mentioned in her letter was the fact that El Fassia had been displaced from Casablanca, the city she had called home since she had first begun recording there for the Polyphon label in 1938. Pushed "back" into the mellah of Fez due to Vichy's anti-Jewish race laws, El Fassia had been deprived of the large cross-confessional audiences which had gathered around her at the end of the interwar period. With the American presence and within months of writing the letter, she would be back on stage in Casablanca, appearing alongside Louisa Tounsia, who had begun touring again across North Africa. For her first post-Vichy tour, Tounsia appeared at the Vox Cinema for a series of "freedom" events to raise funds for the French Committee of National Liberation.[142]

In the songbook of some North African Muslims, however, the new American reality in their midst came to hold a very different meaning. One emerging negative, if satirical, attitude toward "the Americans" (*al-Mirikan*) was captured most iconically in the Moroccan popular artist Hocine Slaoui's "A-Zin wa-l-'ayn" (The handsome and [blue]-eyed), recorded for the Pathé label in 1949 but very likely composed and performed earlier.[143] Over five stanzas punctuated by the humorous refrain "the beautiful and blue-eyed brought all kinds of good things" (*A-zin wa-l-'ayn al-zarqa jana bi-kul khayr*), Slaoui's song gives voice to a scene of consumerism and gendered corruption plaguing Morocco in the aftermath of the American arrival. After years of shortages and scarcity, he sings, chewing gum and candy (!)—rather than basic needs—are now everywhere. So is rum. Young girls act brazenly and married women flock to American soldiers. Worse yet for Slaoui, Moroccan men cannot compete. Emblematic is the song's fourth verse, which ends as the others do, with a hook peppered with Moroccan approximations of American English:

> They gave candy today and gum tomorrow.
> The girls covered their faces with powder made
> from chickpeas,
> And they ate bonbons.
> And even the hags sat drinking rum with
> the Americans.
> And you heard: *Hokay* [Ok], *hokay* [Ok]!
> *Come on! Bye bye!*[144]

For many scholars, "the song stands as a rejoinder to accounts of the seamlessness of the entry of American soldiers."[145] For others, it is an allegory,

ripe with irony, which makes allusion to French colonialism and an emerging postwar Moroccan nationalism.[146] Whatever the case, the song was in-
credibly popular and reflected, for some, a jarring experience. In her memoir,
Fatima Mernissi, born in 1940, recalls her aunt explaining the song's meaning
to her in the early 1950s in its plainest form:

> Casablanca men were really quite upset. Not only did the Americans chase
> women whenever they spotted one from the docks, but they also gave them
> all kinds of poisonous gifts, such as chewing gum, handbags, scarves, ciga-
> rettes, and red lipstick.[147]

To be sure, others took a much grimmer view than Slaoui. Such was
the case with a certain Hamed Ben Ali Bel Abbès, an itinerant Algerian
musician, who was arrested in Oran on April 24, 1943. Just before sundown
that Saturday evening, Bel Abbès was apprehended outside of the city's Jewish cemetery for singing a song which, according to the intelligence agent
Mustapha Hanaoui, "ridiculed our American allies and extolled the power
of Hitler's Germany." For his "defeatist" chant, he had gathered a crowd of
some 150, including a number of Muslim soldiers, and compared Americans
to "cockroaches."[148]

According to the police report, Bel Abbès had been performing the unnamed song for months. Hanaoui and other agents found it difficult to determine whether this was an original composition. Bel Abbès named a number
of sources for the song during interrogations but it was unclear whether any
of them were valid. If written by someone else, it meant the problematic lyrics were being diffused well beyond the hundreds of curious onlookers who
had been gathering since at least February 1943. Either way, the twenty-two-
year-old had raged against what he called "this year of scarcity" for quite a
while. In addition to castigating the Americans for the disease and death that
plagued Algerians postwar, he concluded his song with a wish that the police
found particularly troublesome. "We pray to God," Bel Abbès sang, "that He
sends us Hitler so that we will be happy."[149] He invoked those lines as Hitler's
troops were still occupying neighboring Tunisia.

Meanwhile, North African Jews also sang of "Al-Mirikan." In their
songs, however, which were printed in songbook form beginning in 1943, the
Americans were rendered saviors, whose intervention was nothing short of

divine.[150] Some utilized traditional Jewish liturgical forms, as with Prosper Hassine's "Megillat Hitler" (The Hitler Megillah) and Nissim Ben Shimon's "Haggada di Hitler" (The Hitler Haggadah), both produced in Casablanca and which resembled, respectively, the central texts of Purim and Passover.[151] Others took the form of the qasida, the strophic song-texts associated with the Andalusian repertoire, like the Moroccan Matatya Ben Simhon's "Qasida di Hitler" (The qasida of Hitler).[152] In Tunisia, the *qina* (pl. *qinot*), a type of ballad, was used for laments like "Qinat Hitler" (The dirge of Hitler) penned by the Tunisian poet "Y. B."[153] Popular genres like the Tunisian ughniyya prevailed too.[154] Such was the case with Allouche Trabelsy's "Ughniyyat al-madhlumin" (The song of the oppressed), written by a very young disciple of Acher Mizrahi.[155] While many of these songs faded from memory in the decades after the war, not all did. Among those that are still sung is "Khamus jana" (The Allies have come to us).

Simon de Yacoub Cohen published "Khamus jana" in Tunis sometime in 1943 or 1944. With great irony and subversiveness, he based the melody on another song of the era: the popular and pro-Axis "Tayar jana" (The pilot has come to us).[156] Cohen's "Khamus jana" begins with the arrival of the Germans in Tunisia, as in "Tayar jana," but here the two diverge. Among the first transgressions against the Jewish community the song calls attention to is a sonic one, namely, "the requisition of our radios" (*khdha lana al-radiola*). Cohen then proceeds to enumerate the other offences. "They rounded us up" (*b'ath lana al-rafl*) and erected a Jewish "council" (*al-kumita*). "O Lord" (*ya rabbi*), Cohen laments, "how they called me a Yid" (*kif qaluli juif*).[157] But the refrain serves as a constant reminder of their salvation: "the Allies have come to us and removed the Germans from our midst" (*khamus jana kharraj l-alman min bahdhana*).[158]

In "Khamus jana," the Americans enter not to defile, as in other songs from the period, but "like a bride" (*kif l'arusa*).[159] And what is carried along with them does indeed resemble a dowry:

They brought flour
Delicious chocolates
They distributed to us
And gave us candy

The Allies came to us
Money was exchanged
A hallowed time
And the banks were full

Soap and sugar
Chewing gum and cigarettes
Sweet milk
Our Americans.[160]

Finally, the song ends with praise of the Allied leaders:

Roosevelt light of our eyes
De Gaulle and Stalin
And Churchill the compassionate
Protect them, our Lord.[161]

Like "A-Zin wa-l-ʿayn," in Morocco, "Khamus jana" circulated widely in postwar Tunisia. In his memoirs, the Tunisian Jewish recording artist Raoul Journo recalled performing "the American song 'khamous jènè'" following liberation.[162] Whenever he sang it, he remembered, the audience "rained dollars" upon him.

One final song by an Algerian Jewish recording artist deserves mention: Lili Boniche's "Marché noir" (Black market), recorded for the Pacific label in 1947. Unlike "Khamus jana," Boniche's "Marché noir" was intended for a much wider North African audience and in this way captures a shared Jewish-Muslim feeling toward the Americans and toward the war years that preceded their entry. Boniche, like his contemporary Halali, was on the path to stardom before the war broke out. By 1938, for example, he had been heralded as El Moutribia's "new star" in the orchestra's own promotional materials.[163] "Marché noir" was part of his comeback.

The song begins with piano and droning violin before Boniche arrives at his prolonged lament in Arabic:

Oh, the good old days, I wonder if they will return
Their lightness became darkness
Time lost its meaning.[164]

The young Algerian Jew, sidelined under Vichy and only twenty-five years old at the time of the recording, was invoking the prewar moment. More than three minutes into the song and toward the very end of the first side of the record, Boniche reaches the mostly French-language refrain. As with Slaoui, Boniche too begins with the dirge, "ayayay."

> Ayayay
> Ayayay
> Ayayay
> It's the black market.
>
> Ayayay
> Ayayay
> And our customers
> will pay this evening.[165]

While never identified by name, the Americans *are* there in the decidedly modern, up-tempo "Marché noir," but not as a root cause of misery. If Boniche's compatriots are paying for goods and services in dollars, as he sings, the implication is that the inflated prices are the result of the Vichy years and not the American presence that followed. Rather than focusing on American consumerism or on the corruption of women that accompanied it, Boniche sings of quotidian difficulties, wherein "everyone's heart is broken" (*kul wahid qalb majruh*). Like Slaoui, Boniche also inserts English into his verses, but its use among Algerians signals postwar destitution and desperation, as opposed to immorality:

> Rebecca, Rachel, and Mouni only say,
> "Give me money,"
> If they do not buy a wallet,
> they will spend it all [lit., billions].[166]

If Moroccan men of a certain disposition are the principal victims in Slaoui's "A-Zin wa-l-ʿayn," Boniche's "Marché noir" is far more egalitarian. Significantly for the postwar period, Jews, like "Rebecca, Rachel, and Mouni," are identified by Boniche not only as having suffered, much like Muslims, but as belonging to the Algerian people as well. Again, Boniche ends on a note of hope since the arrival of the Americans:

> Now that goods are available,
> The situation is settled, thank God.
> We can tell our sons and daughters
> this story of the Black Market.[167]

Listening to Slaoui alongside Boniche, or to Hamed Ben Ali Bel Abbès against "Khamus jana" for that matter, makes clear that American liberation was accompanied by and produced many different sounds. At the same time, as discussed earlier, experiences were often shaped along Muslim-Jewish confessional lines. Perhaps it is telling then that one of the first records that the rising Moroccan star Samy Elmaghribi, the subject of the next chapter, would release in 1948 was a cover of the Algerian "Marché noir" rather than a song closer to home, "A-Zin wa-l-'ayn."[168]

## Survivors and Victims

Following Operation Torch in November 1942 and the liberation of Tunisia in May 1943, prominent Jewish musicians returned to the North African stage and appeared once again on radio, but overall their numbers were much diminished. Under Vichy rule, Muslims had come to dominate a soundscape once largely the domain of Jews. El Moutribia, for example, was replaced by an all-Muslim orchestra on Radio Alger in 1940 and just barely survived the war as an institution. After three decades of making music, it would tour Algeria one final time in 1943.[169] To be sure, tastes had changed. But the legal silencing of the mostly Jewish orchestra had not helped much either.

In fall 1943, Mahieddine Bachetarzi wrote to the head of the CIE on El Moutribia letterhead.[170] In light of the fact that the curfew had been lifted in Algiers, he was requesting permission to resume evening shows. Within a year, he moved Chez Mahieddine to an outdoor location just behind the Majestic Cinema. No one yet knew the fate of Salim Halali, but his absence in Algeria led some to presume that he had not survived.

While Halali did survive, other musicians did not. With each of their deaths a world of music passed down from master to disciple disappeared.

FIGURE 15. An early postwar recording by Salim Halali with
Gaston Bsiri credited as lyricist. Personal collection of author.

Sometime in early 1942, for example, Gaston Bsiri, the Tunisian Jewish composer and musician attacked in the pages of *Leïla* in 1941, was arrested by the
Gestapo.[171] On April 8, 1942, he met his end in Auschwitz.[172] The reverberations of his death were felt well beyond the confines of continental Europe.

At war's end, Halali's former collaborators El Kamal and Iguerbouchène
were interrogated by Free French forces but did not ultimately serve prison
time.[173] For his part, Halali worked little with either again (if at all). Beyond
the betrayal, he no longer needed their services. After World War II, he rode
a wave of immense popularity. In part, it was derived from the staggering
number of records he released beginning again in 1945. Almost all of that

initial output had one thing in common: Gaston Bsiri was credited as either the composer, the lyricist, or both.[174] Did Halali and Bsiri know one other in Paris? If so, how and when did Bsiri transmit his compositions to Halali? Whether the postwar writing credits constituted mere coincidence or an act of homage on Halali's part is unclear. Regardless, Halali had managed to amplify the voice of a fellow North African Jewish musician silenced by World War II and the Holocaust.

# CHAPTER 5

# SINGING INDEPENDENCE

On August 17, 1956, five months after Morocco gained independence from France, the Moroccan national icon Samy Elmaghribi wrote his brother Simon Amzallag in Marseilles. Simon, watching the shifting Moroccan political climate from afar, had grown concerned about how his brother was faring as the country's best-known recording artist and its most prominent Jewish cultural figure. The brothers were usually punctual about their correspondence. After all, the two had a transnational business to run. The affairs of Samyphone, Elmaghribi's independent Moroccan record label, required near daily back and forth between its Casablanca headquarters and France, where Simon and his family, like so many other Moroccan Jews, had dwelled since 1949. But Elmaghribi had grown quiet of late.

In his August 1956 letter to Simon, Elmaghribi apologized for the delay but admitted there was little he could do given the situation. "On three occasions over the last three weeks, His Highness has needed me and my orchestra to perform at soirées at which Salim Halali and his orchestra were also working," he explained, making reference to the Algerian Jewish artist now settled in Morocco.[1] It seemed that Sultan Mohammed ben Youssef, the Moroccan sovereign since 1927, could hardly get enough of Elmaghribi. Nor could Crown Prince Hassan or his brothers. "My song 'Allah ouatani oua soultani' [God, my country, and my sultan]," Elmaghribi wrote of his wildly successful record, "was happily danced to by the princes and their guests" at those recent royal events.[2] There was no need to worry, he assured his brother. He and his brand of patriotic music, which celebrated the Moroccan nation in expansive terms, were in constant demand from the *makhzan* (the central Moroccan government). "The Guard and Royal Army are learning to play it as well," he added of the song, "in order to perform my march [ . . . ] at every possible occasion." In some ways, the military was behind the times. Ordinary Moroccans, Algerians over the border, and North Africans in France had already committed "Allah, watani, wa-sultani," to memory. As Simon wrote Elmaghribi some ten days later, the record was "causing a furor here and in the Arab world." Audiences from Marseilles to Algiers were finding inspiration in Elmaghribi and the sounds of his liberatory music.[3]

To date, Samy Elmaghribi has eluded the historiography of postwar Moroccan nationalism.[4] In fact, most musicians and most music have. Instead, the literature treating the anticolonial moment culminating in national liberation has mostly followed political parties, especially the largest of them, the *Hizb al-Istiqlal* (Independence Party), its counterpart in the Spanish zone, the *Hizb al-Islah al-Watani* (Party of National Reform, PNR), smaller competitors like the *Hizb al-Shura w-al-Istiqlal* (Party of Democracy and Independence, PDI), and, more recently, the Moroccan Communist Party (PCM).[5] In doing so, as Susan Gibson Miller has demonstrated with regard to the Istiqlal, the accounting of a pivotal episode in Moroccan national history remains bound up in self-interested actors' own teleological reading of the march to independence.[6] That narrative, as Fadma Ait Mous writes convincingly, has rested upon the notion of a "diffusionist model," whereby an Arabo-Islamic-oriented nationalism centered on particular male figures (like Allal al-Fasi, for example) is understood to have spread from an "original core," in this case, the interwar Comité d'action marocaine (CAM; the predecessor to the Istiqlal discussed in chap. 3), to a single, undifferentiated periphery. This has meant that "the historiography of Moroccan nationalism has long privileged the macro-scale, thus masking the socio-political processes and networks of actors at work at the micro-level." The result is a "stereotyped history of Moroccan nationalism" that is both "linear and monolithic," and in which the earlier sounds of Messika, Labassi, and Halali have been drowned out by a selective focus on the latif protests and the men who would point back to them toward the end of World War II.[7]

Much as David Stenner has uncovered how Moroccan nationalists, far from going it alone or operating in a "linear" fashion, engaged a web of transnational actors—ranging from Eleanor Roosevelt to executives at Coca-Cola—to advocate for their cause postwar, this chapter amplifies still other in-country voices whose commitment to Moroccan independence at mid-twentieth century proved crucial to its ultimate success. Few were more prominent than Samy Elmaghribi, a superstar without affiliation to any one political party, who performed a widely disseminated and capacious form of patriotism in concert, on the radio, and by way of disc to great effect throughout the 1950s.[8] His nationalism, centered on both Sultan Mohammed ben Youssef and the valorization of a single Moroccan people across the French and Spanish protectorates, played a critical role in what Miller has described as an intense atmosphere of "monarchy fever" that pervaded Morocco just before the end of French and Spanish colonial rule.[9] In fact, Daniel Zisenwine has argued that at various points French officials feared "sultanian nationalism" even more than the Istiqlal.[10] By the late 1940s, the sultan had not only become a potent symbol of Moroccan anticolonial nationalism—nearly unanimously across the political spectrum—but a strategic nationalist himself.[11] His invocation by Elmaghribi in a range of songs, including "Allah, watani, wa-sultani," was no accident, nor was it the continuation of some sort of traditional reverence for the Moroccan sovereign.[12] It was nationalism. It was political. And it was in the service of a movement for independence. As we follow Elmaghribi in concert and the journey of his records, we will learn that his message resonated not only in Morocco but in Algeria during its war for liberation as well.

Elmaghribi's rise to national prominence, along with the high-profile careers of other Moroccan, Algerian, and Tunisian Jewish musicians at the same time, provides for additional rethinking of the Jewish trajectory in postwar North Africa. In this way, this chapter builds on a rich historiographical terrain of recent years, in which scholars have pointed to active Jewish participation in mid-twentieth-century nationalist movements across the Middle East and North Africa despite the absence of such a discussion in the foundational literature.[13] In most of these studies, however, emphasis has been placed on leftists and communists but rarely on the vast middle. By contrast,

Elmaghribi, especially given his wide appeal among both Jews and Muslims, offers a case study in Jewish engagement with a broad-based, popular nationalism which existed alongside and outside of party politics.

In related fashion, Elmaghribi's very career, launched in the year of Israel's establishment in 1948 and reaching its apex in the year of Moroccan independence in 1956, corresponds to a period which has been framed in terms of Jewish exodus and exile from Morocco to Israel, France, and Canada.[14] This is not without justification given that a range of factors, including the conflation of Zionism with Judaism in the Moroccan press and on the street, episodes of anti-Jewish violence in cities like Oujda and Djerada, Morocco's orientation to the Arab League, general economic uncertainty, and even, as Aomar Boum has demonstrated, Jewish messianism rooted in the rebirth of the Jewish state, reduced the Moroccan Jewish community from a postwar peak of approximately 250,000 souls to 160,000 by 1960.[15] But as a result of the scholarly emphasis on outmigration to France, Israel, and the Americas, the question of how Jews lived in Morocco during those years has been largely neglected in favor of detailing how Jews left.[16] In turn, voices like those of Elmaghribi and the two-thirds of Moroccan Jewry that remained in the country through Moroccan independence have largely been silenced. As treatment of the celebrity musician will make clear, not only did Jews have a place in Morocco at the dawn of a new political era—in what Alma Heckman has referred to as the "politics of belonging"—but so too did this highly visible minority actively shape its national sounds from center stage.

Finally, while this chapter casts a spotlight on Elmaghribi, it also tracks a number of other North African musical figures who likewise provided postwar nationalism in the region with some of its sounds. Among them, as mentioned in Elmaghribi's correspondence with his brother Simon, was the Algerian Salim Halali. So too will we hear from the Tunisian recording artist Raoul Journo, whom we first met briefly as he sang a song celebrating his country's liberation from Nazi occupation.

## The Postwar Moroccan Musical Landscape

At the end of World War II and in the years immediately afterward, the musical marketplace and concert scene in Morocco grew especially crowded.

To begin with, there were the emerging local acts, including young Muslim innovators like Mohammed Fouiteh, Ahmed Jabrane, and Abdelwahab Agoumi, as well as veteran Jewish performers, like Zohra El Fassia (born Zohra Hamou in Sefrou in 1905).[17] The postwar period had actually afforded El Fassia a remarkable revival after the Vichy anti-Jewish statutes had pushed her out of her adopted Casablanca, back to the mellah of Fez, and off the stage. In addition, visiting acts of considerable repute from Tunisia and Algeria toured Morocco's major cities, including again those quieted in one way or another under Vichy. Among them were figures we have come to know: the Tunisian star of popular song Louisa Tounsia, and the Algerians Lili Labassi, Lili Boniche of the song "Marché noir," and Salim Halali.[18] Halali, in fact, after touring Tunisia and Morocco for the first time at the end of 1945, soon became a regular in cities like Casablanca, Marrakesh, and Rabat, where he would cross paths with Egyptian musicians of regional renown like Farid El Atrache.[19]

Almost all of these musicians would grace venues like Rabat's Cinéma Royal, owned by a Moroccan Jew by the name of Mr. Zafrani and one of a number of concert halls and theaters where the nationalist politics of the era were duly performed alongside the era's hits. In fact, it was in the Moroccan capital, not far from the Cinéma Royal, that the Istiqlal was founded in December 1943. Some months later, in 1944, the party issued a manifesto calling for Moroccan independence from France, "within the framework of a constitutional-democratic monarchy" at whose head would sit Sultan Mohammed ben Youssef.[20] Two years later, Allal al-Fasi returned home from exile—donning the "halo of a national martyr"—and helped to grow the Istiqlal into a formidable party of some thousands.[21] Other parties with similar goals but somewhat divergent ideologies, like the PDI, emerged as well.

On August 30, 1946, the ʿudist and vocalist Abdelwahab Agoumi began his concert at the Cinéma Royal by "glorifying HM [His Majesty] the Sultan," as P. Feraud, head of regional security for Rabat, noted in a confidential report. Among the five hundred that attended the Agoumi concert, Feraud's agents identified them as "for the most part, nationalists."[22] But if Agoumi's praise for the sultan could be forgiven by Feraud—His Majesty did, after all, theoretically govern alongside the French resident general—the musician's short speech in praise of Istiqlal leader Allal al-Fasi which followed would have crossed a line. But for a growing percentage of the Moroccan public, the sultan and the Istiqlal were in many ways beginning to converge. Thus, Agoumi, after invoking al-Fasi, concluded the evening by asking the audience to rise as he performed what he called "the Sultan's hymn" (*L'Hymne sultanien*), an anthem of his own, recent creation. As he left the stage, Agoumi prepared for a trip to Egypt. "The cost of this sojourn in Egypt," Feraud indicated, "will be paid for by the Istiqlal party." The Istiqlal's goals for Agoumi in Egypt rested at the nexus of politics and music. From Cairo, he would spread the party's "propaganda in the Middle East." At the same time, he would work toward "the modernization of Andalusian music in Morocco" through a close study of the Egyptian classical repertoire.

The convergence of the sultan and the Istiqlal resonated most loudly on April 10, 1947. On that day, Mohammed ben Youssef approached a microphone before a Moroccan and French audience at the Roosevelt Club in Tangier and gave a defiant speech in which he called on his country to "regain its rights and to endeavor toward progress that will place [ . . . ] Morocco as a whole among the league of countries and most civilized and refined nations."[23] In pronouncing an urgent desire for independence from France, he "rose up like a lion to meet his historical destiny," as Miller has written. Like al-Fasi and others in the Istiqlal, he also spoke passionately of the country's "'Arabo-Islamic' destiny" while at the same time praising the Arab League.[24]

Where Moroccan Jews (or Berbers, for that matter) fit into the "Arabo-Islamic" configuration was not always clear.[25] This was especially true for the Istiqlal and the PDI, even as some among its leadership courted Jews and as a minority joined these parties.[26] In an independent Morocco, the groups argued, Jewish citizenship would be contingent on a rejection of Zionism.[27] The distinction between Judaism and Zionism, however, was often muddled. By the end of 1947, the Istiqlal began a countrywide anti-Zionist campaign which culminated in a boycott of Jewish businesses.[28] At the same time, the PDI's newspaper *al-Ra'y al-'Am* encouraged Moroccans "to avoid any Zionist commercial enterprise" while simultaneously conflating Jews with Zionists.[29]

The reverberations of Israel's establishment on May 14, 1948, and the concomitant Palestinian *nakba* (catastrophe) were felt among Jews and Muslims in Morocco as elsewhere across the region.[30] On June 7–8, 1948, Muslim attacks against Jews spread from Oujda, close to the Algerian border, to the mining town of Djerada, resulting in some forty-two dead, dozens injured, and hundreds of millions of francs in damage to Jewish-owned businesses.[31] Rightly, Jonathan Wyrtzen has described it as "the most intense episode of anti-Jewish violence in Morocco during the protectorate period."[32] By the end of 1949, more than 2,700 Moroccan Jews had departed for Israel, in addition to those who had left for France.[33] In the years that followed, many more thousands would migrate, with numbers subject to a certain ebb and flow depending on local conditions and external wars.[34]

Music was hardly immune from the new atmosphere produced in the wake of 1948. In a testament to the imprecision of the "neat, binary categories" on which both colonial domination and nationalist revolt could rely, however, the results were sometimes strange.[35] In early 1951, for instance, according to French regional security officers in Rabat, the Istiqlal launched an anti-Zionist campaign against Farid El Atrache, Egyptian superstar of Syrian Druze origin, as he arrived in Morocco alongside dancer Samia Gamal and an ensemble of fifteen Egyptian actors and musicians.[36] Intelligence reports identified two driving forces behind the effort targeting El Atrache, both of which revolved around questions of Jewishness, not Zionism. First, Istiqlal chatter-cum-protest came to focus on El Atrache's Egyptian Jewish tour manager David Salama, who had accompanied the high-profile artist to Morocco. According to an initial statement written on February 1, 1951, the manager's mere presence led to the Istiqlal "reproaching actors for having worked with the Jewish impresario SALAMA." Second, and in similarly curious fashion, a follow-up report sent on February 8, 1951, noted that "there is a widespread rumor in Casablanca that the Egyptian actor Farid El Atrache is of Jewish origin."[37] Nonetheless, the Istiqlal's attempted boycott of El Atrache fell flat. Each of his concerts overflowed with enthusiastic fans. Moroccan Jews, whose national loyalty was constantly being questioned, behaved exactly like their Muslim compatriots. On February 5, 1951, some three hundred of them packed Casablanca's Cinéma Vox to see the Syro-Egyptian star, who had lately added a song exalting Marrakesh to his repertoire. During that performance, as with his others, El Atrache also took to the microphone in praise of the sultan, for which he earned a thunderous applause from the Jewish audience.[38]

## Becoming Samy Elmaghribi

Into this political maelstrom stepped a young Moroccan Jew by the name of Salomon "Samy" Amzallag. Amzallag was born to a Jewish family of modest means in the coastal city of Safi on March 7, 1922. Four years later, his father Amram moved the family to Rabat.[39] In the Moroccan capital, the young Amzallag began to sing. He quickly showed musical promise. By the age of ten, his voice was already in demand at his local synagogue, the Slat Aflalo.[40] According to his own reckoning, his talent was first recognized there when a visiting delegation of the makhzan happened upon him chanting and took note. Samy, as family and friends called him, marked that encounter as the launch of his career in music.[41]

Amzallag's passion for music was fueled by artists close to home, across the border, and around the globe. He was first and foremost a pupil of his father Amram, himself a devotee of piyyut. As he recalled on a number of occasions, the elder Amzallag filled the family home with music every Sabbath and on all of the Jewish festival holidays.[42] The young Amzallag was further exposed to such music while at the local Talmud Torah (Jewish religious primary school). At the Alliance israélite universelle (AIU) school in Rabat, which he attended in parallel to the Talmud Torah, he was introduced to French songs and *Shirei Eretz Yisrael* (Songs of the land of Israel). His enthusiasm for music led him to skip school on occasion in order to catch a gathering of musicians playing at the local, Jewish-owned haunt Chez Cohen.[43] Passing by any of the myriad cafés of Rabat with their street-facing radios and phonographs, Amzallag was also exposed to Moroccan, Algerian, Tunisian, and Egyptian voices, along with jazz, rumba, and other forms of popular music. He would later cite the Egyptians Mohamed Abdel Wahab and Um Kulthum, along with the Algerian Labassi, as inspiration.[44]

Amzallag came of age during the difficult years of World War II. Upon war's end in Morocco, he found work as an accountant at a commercial firm.[45] He also enrolled at the Conservatory of Moroccan Music, where he drew closer to the thought of a career as a musician. In 1947, he made the necessary leap. In January of that year, he entered a star-search competition run by the Camérafrique company in Casablanca.[46] It was actually two competitions in one. The stakes for the "European candidates" of the contest were considerable. First place, selected by a jury of cinematographers and celebrities, carried with it a contract to star in a European film. For the "North African candidates," which included Amzallag alongside other Jews and Muslims, top placement landed the winner a role in an Arab film. As a finalist, his photo was circulated widely in the press. That photo identified his profession as that of an "artist" but did not identify him by his future stage name of "Samy Elmaghribi." For now, as the caption read, he was still "Salomon Amzallag, 21 years old."

The year 1947, which also marked the United Nations' decision to partition Palestine, the start in Morocco of boycotts against Jewish-owned businesses, and a nationalist orientation to the country's "Arabo-Islamic destiny," could have been considered an inauspicious time to begin a career as a Jewish musician in Morocco or anywhere else in North Africa for that matter. Nor was it necessarily a moment when already established Jewish acts could have been expected to flourish. But the timeline plotted by artists like Amzallag proved otherwise.

In April 1948, as conflict in Palestine intensified and mere weeks before Israel declared independence, a twenty-six-year-old Amzallag was tapped by L. A. Vadrot, the local head of Pathé, to make a series of recordings for the label in Paris. Vadrot, though, did not just intend for the young Moroccan Jewish musician to be but one artist among many. Rather, he believed him to be the future of Pathé in North Africa. Vadrot made that clear in his April 30, 1948, letter to the civil controller of Casablanca requesting permission for Amzallag to travel abroad to record. He described "Mr. Salomon Amzallag" as "indispensable" to the effort of "revitalizing our Arab catalog."[47] In 1948, then, just as some nationalists were circumscribing Moroccan and Arab identity in ways that could exclude Jews, Pathé saw little issue with a Moroccan Jew serving as anchor to its Arab catalog. And just as 1948 has often been regarded as the beginning of the end of Moroccan Jews in situ, given that thousands would soon depart, a Moroccan Jew was beginning his meteoric ascent to the national spotlight. He did so alongside a number of his coreligionists.

When Amzallag finally exited Pathé's Paris studios on September 13 and 14, 1948, he did so under the stage name of "Samy Elmaghribi" (Samy the Moroccan).[48] By choosing such an appellation, he made explicit his identification with the Moroccan nation. The sixteen sides that Elmaghribi recorded in late 1948 already hinted at his brand of nationalism. Like other Moroccan musicians at the time, some of his first records included interpretations of modern Egyptian music, in which he exalted iconic figures like the Egyptian king and "the fellah."[49] On still other records, Elmaghribi, in collaboration with the Moroccan Muslim pianist and composer Ahmed Ben Hadj Bouchaib Boudroi, also drew on Egyptian modes but now blended them with up-tempo Andalusian rhythms and Latin genres like tango and paso doble to produce an emerging brand of modern Moroccan music that was popular and often patriotic. It was also quickly regarded as a national form.[50] Typical was Elmaghribi's "Shubban al-riyada" (Youth of sport), in which he sang the praises of the athletic prowess of young Moroccans alongside music that was at once in the 6/8 rhythm known as *birwali* and, at the same time, a march.[51] Moroccans responded positively. The same was true for his records "Hubb al-banat" (Love of girls) and "Khitana" (Gypsy woman), which were overnight sensations. Pathé's Vadrot had not been wrong in trusting the label's future to Amzallag.[52]

In 1949, as Amzallag became Samy Elmaghribi, his siblings Simon and Denise settled in Marseilles. If Jewish departure from Morocco tends to be framed in the aggregate and as unidirectional and discrete, the Amzallag family journey sheds light on the personal and multidirectional nature of exile-as-process in the middle of the twentieth century.[53] In other words, it was not the case that all of the Amzallags left Morocco in 1949, and yet it was certainly true that the absence of his brother and sister weighed heavily on Elmaghribi. Denise would return to Morocco in 1953 to live with Elmaghribi, but only temporarily. And it was far from clear that Simon's departure was permanent—at least initially. Writing to Elmaghribi from Marseilles on December 23, 1949, Simon expressed great joy at his younger brother's burgeoning career in Morocco while also informing him that he had "completely abandoned the project to return there to live."[54]

As Simon and Denise adjusted to life in France, their brother was beginning to make a name for himself on both sides of the Mediterranean. On September 11, 1949, Elmaghribi appeared on the evening radio program *La Gazette de Paris* on Radiodiffusion et Télévision Françaises (RTF).[55] By October 1949, a year since debuting with Pathé, Elmaghribi had given three concerts on Radio Maroc.[56] Later that month, he made another series of

FIGURE 16. Pathé promotional photo for Samy Elmaghribi, ca. 1951.
Source: Samy Elmaghribi archive. Reprinted with permission.

records for Pathé in Paris.[57] By November 1949, Elmaghribi premiered on the Arabic-language broadcast of RTF.[58] At year's end, he could claim growing audiences in France and Morocco. He even bridged the gap. In December 1949, Elmaghribi served as in-house entertainment on the vessel *Koutoubia* as it sailed between Marseilles and Casablanca and returned him home.[59]

Although Elmaghribi's sojourn abroad was for little more than business, hundreds of Moroccan Jews who had emigrated in the late 1940s and early 1950s returned to Morocco as well. Between 1949 and 1953, 2,466 Moroccan Jews officially reestablished themselves in Morocco after having tried their hands at life in Israel.[60] Others did the same but returned from France. In addition, many Algerian Jews made their way to Morocco during the same period. Salim Halali, who had survived the horrors of the Holocaust while hiding in Paris, was among them. Why Halali chose to set down roots in the cultural capital of Casablanca is unclear, although the war and its devastation likely played a role in his decision to leave France. Whatever the reason, he could be certain that he already had fans there. Just a few years prior, in the midst of the Second World War, Halali could be heard across Morocco despite his own silencing in the Nazi-occupied French capital. "Arja' l-biladak," we may recall, his nationalist record addressed to Algerian workers in France, was banned from sale and play in Morocco beginning in July 1942.[61] Six years later, in August 1948, the French residency demanded that Radio Tanger International, founded in the international zone of Tangier by an intrepid American by the name of Herbert Southworth, cease its play of the still-banned song. According to a confidential report filed by the political section of the Ministry of Interior, Halali's record was being "broadcast three or four times a day," having been repeatedly "requested by certain listeners in our zone" and adopted by Moroccan nationalists.[62] The issue was raised with U.S. diplomats and then with Southworth himself. Under pressure, he agreed that "that incriminated disc would no longer be played on his station." In 1949, months after the record was again taken off the air, Halali arrived in Casablanca. There he established Le Coq d'Or, a cabaret at 19 rue du Consulat d'Angleterre in the heart of Casablanca's Jewish quarter. How or why the protectorate authorities allowed such a move is unclear.

Le Coq d'Or's own promotional material depicted the venue as "the most beautiful oriental cabaret in Morocco" and by all accounts it was.[63] The

# SALIM HALALI'S COQ D'OR

FINEST BELLY DANCING IN THE ENTIRE MIDDLE EAST.
UNDER THE PERSONAL DIRECTION OF
FAMED SINGER OF ORIENTAL SONGS

## SALIM HALALI

Authentic

decorations

Wonderful clean

tasty Moroccan food.

Genuine Oriental

Music.

Large bar

Serving complete

assortment of

drinks.

Largest assemblage of Dancing and Singing Girls in the Middle East.

and

The greatest singer of them all...in person...

## SALIM HALALI

19. Rue du Consulat d'Angleterre, Casablanca, Phone: 260-49

FIGURE 17. Advertisement for Salim Halali's Casablanca cabaret Le Coq
d'Or. Source: *The English Language Guide to Morocco*, ed. Art Rosett, 1961.

cabaret, a cavernous space packed with tables, adorned with photos of Halali, and located in a decidedly working-class neighborhood, gathered Moroccans of many social classes eager to catch a performance of "the famous international artist with his large orchestra and traditional Arab show." It also served to incubate new talent like a young Muslim ʿaita and popular singer by the name of Hajja Hamdaouia.[64] Elmaghribi too would pass through Le Coq d'Or's doors, but he soon outgrew the venue.

## Revolutionary Music

By the early 1950s, Moroccans had begun to imagine independence.[65] For many, it may have sounded like Elmaghribi. In tandem with a national struggle waged by the Istiqlal in global forums like the United Nations, Elmaghribi was sating Moroccans back home with what he called his "sensational revolution in Oriental music."[66] And it could be heard nearly everywhere: from the concert hall to the radio and from the royal palace to the marketplace. His revolutionary music celebrated urban and rural, north and south, locations in the French protectorate and the Spanish one, while making no distinction between Arab or Berber nor Muslim or Jew. All were Moroccan. But if his nationalism was more capacious than that of the political parties it was no less nationalist. On the country's largest stages and on its most symbolic ones, Elmaghribi donned the national colors, toured alongside Muslims, and sang of and for the nation. In each setting where his music was performed, Elmaghribi's audiences learned to perform his inclusive brand of Moroccan nationalism as well.

"The echoes of your brilliant success," Simon wrote to his brother from Marseilles on February 17, 1950, "have reached me all the way up here."[67] By early 1950, Elmaghribi's success was so compelling that Simon encouraged him to remain in Morocco instead of joining him on a permanent basis in Marseilles. In late summer 1950, Elmaghribi, whose music was already broadcast with regularity on Radio Maroc, embarked on his first concert tour of Morocco. "Les Samy's Boys," his six-piece orchestra, accompanied him on stops that included Rabat, Fez, and Mazagan.[68]

In the promotional materials for his 1950 tour, Elmaghribi demonstrated the independent style, sartorial confidence, and musical modernism that helped set him apart. The poster for his September 9, 1950, concert in

Mazagan, for instance, which adorned kiosks throughout the city, first carried his slogan of a "revolution in Oriental music."[69] It also included a large photo of a dapper, perfectly coiffed Elmaghribi, bespoke in white suit at the microphone, surrounded by Les Samy's Boys. With all eyes fixed on their bandleader, his orchestra practically swooned in admiration. "For the first time in Morocco," the poster announced in French, "Samy Elmaghribi and his dynamic ensemble, 'Les Samy Boys' (before their departure for Paris)," were to appear. Catch him for a hometown show, the marketing suggested, before the rest of the world grabbed hold of him. And with reasonably priced tickets, Moroccan audiences could afford his revolution. That rebellion of "modern music and song" was true to form and included such styles as "Franco-Arab, flamenco, Egyptian, Algerian, Tunisian, [and] Moroccan."

As his advertisements promised, Elmaghribi's early set lists included music that ranged across North Africa and the Middle East, across styles, and across languages. Emblematic were his breakout record "Luna lunera," a bolero written by the Cuban composer Tony Fergo, which Elmaghribi translated into Arabic while maintaining whole verses in Spanish.[70] But it was one disc in particular that ingratiated Elmaghribi to a wide swath of the Moroccan public: "Lukan al-milayin" (If I had millions).[71] Perhaps it was its aspirational quality that endeared the singer and the song so.

In "Lukan al-milayin," Elmaghribi dared dream the impossible so long as French rule persisted in Morocco. In the song, which employed a 6/8 birwali rhythm, Elmaghribi articulated the lengths he would go to pursue the love of his life.

> Ay ay ay, if only I had millions
> I know what I would do with them at that time.
>
> On boats—in planes
> I would cross oceans and traverse the skies
> To search for my love in every place.[72]

But if Moroccan audiences gravitated toward "Lukan al-milayin," they would have also relished its folly. Traveling by boat and plane in order to reach "the East and Lebanon, India and Yemen" (*fil-sharq wa-lubnan, fil-hind wa-l-yaman*), as Elmaghribi crooned, would have been recognized as pure fantasy when considering that the majority of Moroccans needed permission to travel abroad. And yet, the realm of possibility that was part and parcel of the appeal of a song like "Lukan al-milayin" would also have suddenly seemed within grasp as the national struggle gained ground. Elmaghribi's music was providing Moroccans with a taste of their possible future.

By 1951, Elmaghribi was increasingly in demand within an ever-widening circle of Moroccan fans, among them the political establishment, the well-heeled, and the working class. While his earliest concerts had already attracted a multiconfessional Moroccan audience, he actively cultivated Jewish-Muslim diversity in the years to come. Initially, he did so in a number of ways, including through the promotion of his shows with Arabic-language concert posters and by featuring highly regarded Muslim artists on the bill like Lahbib Kadmiri and Bouchaïb El Bidaoui. Thanks to a combination of factors—his look, his voice, his choice of song, his charisma, and the shows that he assembled—Elmaghribi could report the following to Simon:

> My success in Morocco is certainly immense and I am recognized and surrounded very quickly no matter which city I'm in, in Casa, [cities] small and big, everyone points out Samy with their finger, with a smile [ . . . ] the great success of the day remains the Song of the Millions (my creation) in Arabic of which you have the record and which is hummed by Arabs and Jews, young and old, men and women, in all the cities of Morocco.[73]

He could hardly move in Morocco without drawing attention or being swarmed by fans. The veneration of Elmaghribi by Moroccans even caused some Jews who had left the country to second-guess their decision, at least momentarily. "Moroccan Jews arriving in France are speaking about your success with pride and admiration," Simon informed his brother on August 14, 1951. "I would have paid dearly to find myself in Morocco these days," he continued, "to be intoxicated by your rise to success; I miss this Morocco."[74]

In 1952, Elmaghribi started explicitly flying the colors of Moroccan nationalism—or at least wearing them. "I have ordered from a fine tailor six splendid outfits for the six best performers in Morocco, who will accompany me on my tour," he wrote to his brother on February 22, 1952. "These wool outfits are in the Moroccan colors: red vests with satin-lined lapels and green pants," he added with pride. In the midst of composing, recording, performing, and preparing for yet another concert tour in April and May 1952, Elmaghribi had been contacted by the sultan. "These [outfits] were designed," he noted, "for our presentation to His Majesty the Sultan and then the Glaoui [Thami El Glaoui, the pasha of Marrakesh], which is going to give me a good helping hand in my climb to success."[75] The red-and-green outfits seem to have done just the trick.

Over the next year, the relationship between Elmaghribi and the sultan, the central symbol of Moroccan anticolonialism and its attendant liberation movement, strengthened considerably. By the end of summer 1952, Elmaghribi had given his first of many private concerts for the royal family. He provided his brother Simon with sumptuous play-by-play. "Last Sunday, Prince Moulay Hassan, son of the Sultan, sent for me and I sang until the break of dawn," he wrote on August 22, 1952. This was no audition. Crown Prince Hassan was more than familiar with Elmaghribi and his music. "My hits were requested by His Highness himself," he noted.[76] After having brought him to his Casablanca villa, the crown prince promised the artist an invitation to the most iconic venue of all.

On November 17, 1952, just before midnight, Elmaghribi took the microphone at Dar al-Makhzan, the royal palace and official residency of the sultan in Rabat. For the occasion of Throne Day ('id al-'arsh), a holiday invented by nationalists in 1933, the sultan himself had requested the presence of the Jewish artist.[77] In the early hours of November 18, 1952, Elmaghribi sang two patriotic compositions of his own creation as well as other songs "before some 2,000 Muslims and before Moulay el Hassan, who presided over the soirée where the best musical and theatrical troops of Morocco had passed through." If his relationship to the monarchy could once be considered private, his association with the royal family was now public. Again he communicated his triumph to his brother in Marseilles. "My success has exceeded the limits of my wildest dreams," Elmaghribi proclaimed. "The ovation given to me by the public was nothing like the simple applause received by other artists," he boasted. "Then came the congratulations of all the Muslim personalities, which touched me," he added.[78] Elmaghribi's "sensational revolution in Oriental music" was now firmly aligned with the royal family. That alignment came as the sultan grew increasingly independent of his French handlers and as "the tempo of protest rose" in Morocco, especially in the aftermath of the

French assassination of Tunisian nationalist Ferhat Hached, secretary general of the General Tunisian Workers Union.[79]

## A National Brand and International Celebrity

In 1952, the same year that Elmaghribi first wore the Moroccan colors on stage and began performing his fidelity to the sultan in front of the royal entourage, the artist himself became a national brand. As the purchase of radios spread across Morocco and as the signals of stations from Radio Tanger International to Radio Maroc strengthened, Elmaghribi became not just ubiquitous but largely inseparable from the era's sound.[80] To be sure, his live performances on radio and the constant playing of his records on air helped cement his status as the nation's voice during a formative political moment. But that omnipresence also owed to his foray into the world of commercial advertising.

In February 1952, Elmaghribi became an official spokesperson for Coca-Cola in Morocco. His spoken dialogues and musical hooks for the soft drink company were played in heavy rotation on Radio Tanger International and Radio Maroc over the next several years.[81] The association was more than just business. As both Wyrtzen and Stenner have shown, the soft drink company maintained deep connections to the royal palace and the Istiqlal.[82] During this period, Elmaghribi became the sound of brands like Gillette, Palmolive, Canada Dry, and Shell Oil as well. So too did his family. In one such ad for Angel Chewing Gum, the artist, his wife Messody, and their children sang the virtues of the company's many flavors while backed by a small orchestra performing modern Moroccan music. By the end of the year, every Moroccan within earshot of a radio could hear Elmaghribi singing "How sweet is Angel Chewing Gum" (*Ma ahla shuwin-gum anjil*) on Radio Maroc with the near universal resonance of the midcentury radio jingle. With his radio ads, in addition to his concerts and records, Elmaghribi was providing many Moroccans with the soundtrack to their lives in the 1950s. But as with boundaries of genre, physical borders could barely contain the musician or his growing international appeal.

On July 24, 1952, Elmaghribi made his first of many live broadcasts for Radio Alger.[83] The demand for the artist was no longer just a Moroccan one. In fact, although much of the music-related literature on North Africa has tended to adhere to national lines, Elmaghribi's relationship with Algeria and Algerians reminds us that musical histories follow transnational flows, even during periods of intense nationalist fervor. By mid-1952, Algerian fans were clamoring for Elmaghribi, and Algerian musicians had even started performing his repertoire. On June 23, 1952, Simon informed his brother that the Algerian Jewish comic singer Blond Blond, the disciple of Lili Labassi who would go on to release a cover of "Où vous étiez mademoiselle," had recorded Elmaghribi's "Lukan al-milayin" for Radio Paris's Arab broadcast.[84] "A large number of Arab listeners," he reported from Marseilles, "were requesting the song daily."

Meanwhile, Elmaghribi's stature as a national figure back home was bolstered by the electric coverage he received in the Moroccan press. Outlets like *Le Petit Marocain*, *La Vigie marocaine*, *Maroc-Presse*, and the bilingual *Radio-Maroc* magazine covered his radio appearances, provided his recording and travel schedules, reviewed his concerts, and even announced the birth of his triplets. In short, the media captured his nearly every move. This was especially the case for his live performances. "As for the singer himself, he alone is a whole show," gushed *Maroc-Presse* in the review of his April 26, 1953, concert in the city of Mazagan. Although especially rich in description, the write-up was on no account atypical. "First there is the composer, the romantic," the unnamed journalist wrote, "with his Algerian tangos, his flamenco-like pasos, and his Tunisian songs; then, there is the dreamer, with his cheerful choruses, like 'the Song of the Millions,' which causes the crowd, already warmed up, to explode." The temperature in the concert hall rose throughout the evening. "It was a lot for an already excited room," the paper mused. "From the very first notes of his songs, which most already knew," *Maroc-Presse* concluded, "Samy Elmaghribi had 'his' public."[85]

For the moment, however, the Moroccan press seemed to tread lightly on at least one facet of Elmaghribi's life: his relationship to the sultan. Nonetheless, the association between the musician and Sultan Mohammed ben Youssef only deepened as the French residency moved in to immobilize the Moroccan nationalist movement. In May 1953, Elmaghribi traveled from Casablanca to the newly constructed royal palace in Rabat known as Dar al-Salam, where he was once again received by the sultan. This invitation came at a particularly tense time. It was a moment when the Moroccan sovereign was recovering from an injury, and while Thami El Glaoui, the pasha of Marrakesh and French ally, was setting the wheels in motion to dethrone ben Youssef. Given his physical state and the psychological pressure he was facing, the sultan, according to Elmaghribi, had ordered a temporary halt on visitors to the palace, with the musician seeming to prove the exception. Writing to Simon on May 20, 1953, Elmaghribi informed his brother that when accepting the invitation, he had announced to the crown prince that he was "a slave to His Majesty."[86] The following day, El Glaoui, with French support, circulated a petition calling for the sultan's ouster.[87] On May 30, 1953, the petition, signed by hundreds of Moroccan tribal and religious leaders, was sent to Paris.[88] Morocco was on the brink of crisis.

Elmaghribi's devotion to the sultan was understood well by the police. That a popular Moroccan musician and the voice of the people had aligned himself with such a potent figure and symbol was cause for concern. In April 1953, French police first trailed the musician. Immediately following his April 11, 1953, concert at the Municipal Theater in Mazagan, a confidential intelligence report on the "Tour of the SAMY ELMAGHRIBI troupe" was stamped by the police commissioner and then rushed to Rabat, where it was delivered to the Ministry of Interior. But the police officer behind the report was unsure of what to make of the evening. Although the "hall was packed with an audience composed exclusively of Moroccans, Muslims and Jews, who were pleased with the event," he also "noted the absence that evening of local nationalist elements."[89] Looking past the content of Elmaghribi's music and, remarkably, past his orchestra's red and green outfits, the officer had been looking for nationalism only via membership in the Istiqlal, PDI, or other political parties. Perhaps a superior officer recognized this, for the surveillance of Elmaghribi continued. Sometime later, an anonymously authored handwritten list of Moroccan musical acts was slipped into an expanding police file on "Arab and Jewish theater." Elmaghribi's name was on it.[90]

The surveillance apparatus that ensnarled Elmaghribi was indicative of the French residency's growing impatience with Moroccan nationalism and Sultan Mohammed ben Youssef. On August 20, 1953, in a final, dramatic attempt to decapitate the figurehead of the independence movement, the French residency removed the sultan from the throne. Two days later Elmaghribi wrote cryptically to his brother of his hope for a return to calm.[91]

But with the sultan deposed and exiled to Madagascar, Morocco was far from at ease. Nor would Elmaghribi's life assume the tranquility he sought. Nonetheless, it was at this politically tumultuous time that the musician, already working at a frenetic pace, expanded the bounds of his stardom. For some, this was predictable. "Samy El Maghribi, a brilliant Moroccan star," a *Maroc-Presse* journalist wrote on March 15, 1954, "could one day become a star of the entire Arab world."[92]

That same month, the Tunisian star Raoul Journo responded to a request from Elmaghribi to tour together in Morocco. "I can't thank you enough dear Samy for your proposal," Journo wrote, "but I'm doing very well in Tunis."[93] Journo was doing so well that he could afford to politely decline Elmaghribi's invitation. Journo, born in 1911 in a working-class neighborhood in Tunis, had a similar profile to Elmaghribi, even if a decade and a half older.[94] Journo also began singing at an early age. Like Elmaghribi, he learned to do so at home, in the neighborhood synagogue, where some of the standout musicians and recording artists of his era gathered to chant, and from the phonograph. He too attended both a traditional Jewish school and the AIU (where his music teacher and private tutor was Gaston Bsiri).[95]

At the age of fifteen, Journo assembled a small ensemble and began performing at private gatherings and celebrations. Shortly thereafter, he started acting alongside (or in the shadows of) Habiba Messika and Dalila Taliana.[96] In the early 1930s, the pianist Messaoud Habib, Pathé's artistic director in-country, arranged for him to make his first records. As Elmaghribi performed for the sultan, so Journo performed regularly for Lamine Bey, the Tunisian monarch who was growing closer to an emboldened Neo-Dustur party. He also toured across North Africa, including in Morocco alongside Elmaghribi at venues like Le Boléro, close to Salim Halali's Le Coq d'Or.[97]

"I have work every night," Journo informed Elmaghribi on March 31, 1954, "and I am supposed to leave for Paris to record with Decca." Making oblique reference to the gains of the Neo-Dustur, the increase in public protests, and the subsequent French suppression of both, Journo reported that "the situation has calmed down and we have started working again like normal." He was not only "working again" but was overworked. "I'm flush with Jewish and Arab events and weddings," he informed Elmaghribi. That situation persisted even after French Prime Minister Pierre Mendès France announced to Lamine Bey on July 31, 1954, that Tunisia was to be given internal autonomy, a process which ushered in the end of the protectorate there less than two years later.

As Journo headed to Paris, Elmaghribi crossed the border into Algeria, where his celebrity soared. What started in April 1954 as a recording session with Radio Alger ended in December of the same year with an acclaimed, multicity concert tour of the country, which was then in the initial throes of the Algerian War. "I have been very well received here in the Arab artistic milieu," Elmaghribi wrote to Simon from Algiers on April 13, 1954. He also gave one concert while there that spring, "where I sang the Millions and where I was showered with applause and ululation from an audience that was entirely Muslim."[98] Just as he had "his public" in Morocco, he was finding another one in Algeria.

During his April 1954 sojourn in Algeria, Elmaghribi added a song to his repertoire that he had not previously performed in Morocco. That abstention, given his public profile and the climate back home, was understandable. While in studio at Radio Alger, he recorded what he referred to in his letters as a *taqtouqa djeblia* (*taqtuqa jabaliyya*), a light, popular form from Morocco's northern Rif region. The song in question was "Habibi diyali" (My love). Its titular lyric, "Ayli ayli, my love, where is he?" (*Ayli ayli habibi diyali fin huwa*), repeated throughout and punctuated by the anguish of the singer who longs for his lost but "not forgotten" love, was suddenly everywhere in late 1953 and through 1954. Elmaghribi was not the only musician to start singing "Habibi diyali" at the time, despite the fact that the song had long been in circulation. Nor was he even the only Moroccan Jewish artist to record it. In the period immediately after the sultan's exile, "Habibi diyali" was recorded by an array of Jewish musicians, including the veteran El Fassia and newcomer Albert Suissa.[99] Others performed it regularly, and Salim Halali would later record its best-known version.[100] The song's popularity, as Elmaghribi surely knew, was largely derived from the refrain, which, in the current context, was understood by audiences as alluding to the exiled sultan. That point was certainly clear to El Fassia, who was also close to the sultan. Halali, another frequent guest of the palace, no doubt recognized its potency as well.

Through songs like "Habibi diyali," Moroccan Jewish musicians, including Elmaghribi, performed their patriotism outside of the limits of political parties. Their sonic contribution to the cause célèbre that was the sultan was understood as nationalist at the time. Already in January 1954, the *qa'id* (tribal governor) of Settat, about fifty-five miles south of Casablanca, informed the civil controller of the region that "Habibi diyali," which was played constantly on Radio Maroc, "makes allusion to the exile of the ex-sultan."[101] A short while later an unsigned letter from a division within the resident general's Office of Political Affairs stated with alarm that "the record 'Ayli Ayli, Hbibi dyali' has been recorded by three different singers in three different manners." The note, passed on to the Ministry of Interior, continued, "that of Albert Suissa (Olympia, 1.005–1.006) contains political allusions."[102] Quick action was necessary. The Olympia label, owned by the Moroccan Jewish Azoulay-Elmaleh firm, had just pressed and then received shipment of another 935 copies of the Suissa record containing "political allusions" to the deposed sultan. Once again, Jewish purveyors of records, alongside musicians, were complicit in facilitating and fomenting a form of nationalism.

Elmaghribi embarked on his first official concert tour of Algeria just as a robust Algerian anticolonial liberation movement emerged and then eventually coalesced into the Front de libération nationale (FLN, *jabhat al-tahrir al-watani*, National Liberation Front). On November 1, 1954, the FLN, which had drawn strength and inspiration from nationalist successes in Morocco and Tunisia, carried out dozens of attacks across Algeria through its armed wing, the Armée de libération nationale (ALN, *jaysh tahrir al-watani*, National Liberation Army). That same day the FLN announced its commitment to "national independence by (1) the restoration of the sovereign, democratic and social Algerian State within the framework of Islamic principles, [and] (2) the respect of all basic freedoms without distinction of race or religion." The Algerian War had begun. In almost eight years' time, Algeria would gain independence, bringing an end to 132 years of French rule. It came at an incalculable human cost, with somewhere on the order of 250,000–300,000 Algerians killed.[103]

At the end of December 1954, Elmaghribi arrived first in Algiers and then in Oran with "Habibi diyali" and other hits in tow. He found a ready Jewish and Muslim audience and a sympathetic press. On December 23, 1954, the *Alger républicain* featured photos of the Moroccan Jewish musician posing alongside Algerian musical figures Mohamed Tahar Fergani (known as the

"Nightingale of Constantine") and Ahmed Wahby, a popular artist and FLN supporter who would eventually join the party's artistic troupe.[104] On December 28, 1954, H. Abdel Kader, writing in *La Dépêche quotidienne*, declared Elmaghribi's recent concert at the Algiers Opera, where he debuted alongside Mahieddine Bachetarzi, a "triumph."[105] The journalist delighted in the idea that the mostly Muslim audience had also included "many Jews who had come to applaud their idol." With "Habibi diyali" and "Lukan al-milayin," Abdel Kader announced that the well-dressed Elmaghribi had "conquered the Algerois public." Elmaghribi did the same at the Oran Opera the following evening. As in Algiers and with distance from the residency in Rabat, Elmaghribi had ended his concerts in Oran with "Habibi diyali," which the *Oran républicain* noted was "very much appreciated by the Oranais public," who likely also found a nationalist message in it that may have resonated with their own.[106]

In interviews with the press in the midst of his Algerian tour, Elmaghribi basked in his national-turned-international celebrity. "I have never received a welcome like the one I received in Algiers and Oran," Elmaghribi told *Echo soir* journalist El Bouchra.[107] While not making direct reference to "Habibi diyali," he revealed that, as much as he delighted in performing in classical Arabic, he was passionate about "composing melodies and words understood by all." Elmaghribi informed El Bouchra that "music need not be an abstract language, on the contrary, it should serve as a message of friendship and mutual understanding." In his interview, Elmaghribi reflected on "Lukan al-milayin." "Some time ago, I wrote a song that I called, 'Ah, if I had millions.' It was very well received by the vendors in the markets of Casablanca, who called out to their clients with the chorus." That adoption and adaptation of a popular song of malleable meaning was once the highlight of his career, he divulged. It had been replaced, he said, by his reception from Algerians, who were now putting "Habibi diyali" and other songs to their own use.

## Waltzing to Independence

In the fall of 1955, Elmaghribi found himself outside of Morocco during a critical political time. In November 1955, Sultan Mohammed ben Youssef and members of the royal family were removed from exile in Madagascar and installed in Paris. The continued absence of the rightful sultan was no longer politically tenable for the French. Neither was the protectorate. On November 6, 1955, the sultan was reinstated to the throne while in the French capital. Ten days later, he touched down in Morocco. The country was on the verge of independence. Since July 1955, Elmaghribi had been a temporary resident in Paris as well. There he headlined nightly at Soleil d'Algérie, among the Latin Quarter's many North African cabarets. As the sultan prepared for his return, Elmaghribi was forced to question the expediency of his own. For many Moroccan Jews, theirs was the opposite choice: whether to remain in Morocco or start over elsewhere.

Although Elmaghribi's contract at Soleil d'Algérie ran until February 1956, he had always planned to return to Morocco. He was in Paris for work but little more. Over the course of the previous year, he had established Samyphone, one of the first postwar independent record labels in North Africa. In addition to serving as a vehicle for his own recordings, Samyphone took the form of a brick-and-mortar store in Casablanca. In Morocco, he had a career, a national brand, and financial assets to consider. Yet, in Morocco, he would also remain separated from his brother and sister, who had concluded, as had thousands of other Moroccan Jews, that life there was no longer tenable.

In late fall 1955, the bond between the sultan and the Istiqlal had frayed and the beginnings of a power struggle were evident. To Morocco's east, the Algerian War was more than a year in the making, with little sign of letting up. For the father of a growing family, who also happened to be a leading musician, Elmaghribi could have been forgiven for choosing the political stability of a life outside of Morocco.

But at that decisive hour, Elmaghribi tied his destiny to that of his country. On November 4, 1955, from his room at the Hotel Derby in Paris, Elmaghribi recorded the first in a series of explicitly nationalist songs released on his own Samyphone label. Among those recordings was "Fi ʿid ʿarshik ya sultan" (On your throne day, O sultan), a "Moroccan anthem" (*nashid maghribi*) of his own composition, which drew on birwali as much as it leaned on waltz.[108] It also featured a young, up-and-coming Algerian Jewish musician named Lucien "Luc" Cherki.[109] Elmaghribi's song expressed an unequivocal pride in the sultan, which seemed to mirror that of many Moroccans, whether Muslim or Jewish.[110] That pride was especially palpable in the chorus.

On your Throne Day, O Sultan
The people extend their congratulations
Today every Moroccan is happy
My heart rejoices and I sing my song.[111]

Like the music of that anthem, Elmaghribi's lyrics were inclusive of the constitutive parts of a broadly conceived Moroccan nation. In the verses that followed, Elmaghribi invoked "the brave of the Rif and Atlas" (*shuj'an al-rif wa-l-atlas*), citizens "from Agadir to Fez" (*min agadir hatta l-fas*), and those who "come from the cities and the ports to delight in your Throne Day, my Sultan" (*jayin min al-mudun wa-l-maras, yafrahu fi 'id 'arshik ya sultani*). Two days after recording "Fi 'id 'arshik ya sultan," as well as the equally zealous "Alf haniyya wa haniyya" (1,001 congratulations), Elmaghribi performed the two nationalist compositions before Sultan Mohammed ben Youssef and Crown Prince Hassan in Saint-Germain-en-Laye, just outside of Paris.[112] If in the past Elmaghribi's devotion to the sultan was performed away from the camera, his fidelity to the royal family—and by extension, to the Moroccan nation—was now captured both on disc and in black and white. On November 6, 1955, an official photo was snapped of Samy Elmaghribi grasping the sultan's hand and bending at the knee. The image, widely circulated, tellingly displayed Samy Elmaghribi's name above that of the sultan.[113] The former was still the real Moroccan star, and his compatriots were anxiously awaiting his return as well.

Elmaghribi understood that the nationalist songs he had just recorded would make waves in Morocco. Within days of their recording, Radio Maroc had already played them on prime time alongside an interview with the artist. "In spite of all this," Elmaghribi wrote to Simon on November 14, 1955, "I will think about a return to Morocco only when I will be assured of absolute calm there."[114] He was concerned, "especially for the safety of my little ones." But that assurance was rather quick in coming. By December 12, 1955, Elmaghribi had ordered that a thousand of his nationalist records be pressed for his Samyphone label. "I intend to go to Morocco to sell them myself and on the best terms," he informed Simon.[115] For weeks Simon attempted to dissuade his younger brother from returning to Morocco. On January 7,

سامـــي المغـربـي عنــد ساحب الجلالـة سيـدي محمد الخامس
بـان جـرمـان أن لي

*Samy Elmaghribi*
reçu par SA MAJESTE SIDI MOHAMMED V
à St-Germain-en-Laye le 6 novembre 1955

FIGURE 18. Samy Elmaghribi being received by Sultan Mohammed ben Youssef just outside of Paris on November 16, 1955. Source: Samy Elmaghribi archive. Reprinted with permission.

1956, Simon gave it one last try, but to no avail. Then, for over two weeks, the letters stopped. Elmaghribi had returned to Morocco. It was an interminable silence, given their twice-weekly correspondence and coming as the sultan and the Istiqlal were beginning to jostle for control of the country.

When Elmaghribi resumed writing to Simon on January 23, 1956, he did so at a moment of exasperation, which itself stemmed from the demands on his schedule. "Since my arrival in Casa," Elmaghribi wrote, "my days have been consumed with getting the records out of customs, frequent trips to the palace in Rabat, and sales at the store."[116] His initial return to Morocco had been busy. Among other activities, he headlined the inaugural gala of al-Wifaq (the Entente), a Jewish-Muslim nationalist association presided over by Crown Prince Hassan, performed alongside Salim Halali in support of the Jewish Anti-Tubercular Society, and met frequently with the sultan and crown prince, who "promised me I had a future here in Morocco."[117] His return was heralded in the press. He had been out of the country for less than six months but there was concern that the Moroccan national figure was contemplating exile. "Is your return to Morocco permanent?" one journalist asked desperately. Elmaghribi responded positively. "I have returned to my country to see His Majesty again," Elmaghribi said, "and after a few days here, I need to go back to the French capital, pick up my family, and then return to Morocco for good."[118]

On March 22, 1956, Morocco gained formal independence from France. That same day, Elmaghribi wrote to Simon from Paris. The tickets were booked. He had decided to return to "his public" on the very day that Moroccans had regained their sovereignty. It was the ultimate performance of patriotism. For that act, both the palace and the public would reward him. Within days of his arrival, Elmaghribi was called upon to sing for the crown prince. In April 1956, during the first two nights of Ramadan, the Jewish artist gave a private concert for the sultan.[119] Just a few weeks after the Spanish protectorate came to an end and the two Moroccos were rejoined into one, he wrote to his brother that "the situation here is not as alarming as you think."[120]

In May 1956, as the Moroccan kingdom navigated a future independent of France and now Spain, Elmaghribi was doing better than he could have imagined. He had moved his Samyphone store to a tony and very visible location on Boulevard de Bordeaux in Casablanca. In the meantime, his

nationalist music had become more explicit and that much more in demand
by the palace, the Moroccan public, and the newly constituted Moroccan
Royal Armed Forces. On May 15, 1956, he wrote to Simon.

> Saturday, I recorded verses in classical Arabic (written and composed by me)
> for Radio Maroc, a military song extolling the glory of His Majesty, His Im-
> perial Highness, Moroccan freedom, and the Royal Armed Forces, whose pa-
> rade took place yesterday. [ . . . ] This was the only Moroccan song presented
> to radio listeners on the occasion of the first parade of the Moroccan army.[121]

Elmaghribi added that he had been flooded by both compliments and record
orders since the song's broadcast. On May 25, 1956, he entered a Casablanca
studio to cut a record of the anthem that was already causing a frenzy among
Moroccans: "Allah, watani, wa-sultani" (God, my country, my sultan).[122] In
this post-independence patriotic effort, he was joined by other Jewish artists. Albert Suissa, for example, released a record entitled "Ughniyya sayyid
Muhammad al-Khamis" (The song of Liege Mohammed V), and Zohra El
Fassia recorded "Al-Malik ben Youssef" (King Ben Youssef) in support of
the sultan and the Moroccan nation.[123] This did not happen only in Morocco.
In Tunisia, Journo composed four songs on the theme of Tunisian independen-
ce, at least two of which were performed live on Radio Tunis.[124] In 1958,
Journo also performed for the Algerian FLN from their base in Tunis.[125]
That same year, Journo's younger colleague El Kahlaoui Tounsi (né Elie
Touitou), a regular on Radio Tunis and an in-demand composer and percussionist for a great number of Tunisian musicians, recorded the nationalist
record "Jaza'ir" (Algeria), which by January 1959 had been banned for sale in
Algeria itself.[126] As for the tone of much of that music, "Allah, watani, wa-
sultani"—practically a military march—provides a good indication with its
booming endorsement of the sultan, the cause of independence, and Moroccan soldier-citizens.

Chorus:
God, my Country, and my Sultan
This goal of every Moroccan soldier
O goal of every Moroccan soldier
God, my Country, and my Sultan

First verse:

Under your command, O Merciful Lord

And thanks to our liege the Sultan

And with the generosity of our national leaders

Our Morocco is independent and tranquil.[127]

Immediately after "Allah, watani, wa-sultani" was performed during Morocco's first military parade, Elmaghribi informed his brother that the Moroccan Royal Armed Forces band was now in the process of learning the song as well.[128]

———

In independent Morocco and with the militaristic "Allah, watani, wa-sultani," Samy Elmaghribi had reached the height of fame. The Jewish artist arrived at that moment, in part, by providing Moroccans, and sometimes Algerians, with an inclusive soundtrack to national liberation. His Muslim and Jewish audiences responded enthusiastically. Neither Israel's establishment in 1948 nor Moroccan independence in 1956 were an end for the Jewish musician in Morocco, who not only remained in the country during that period but whose astonishing climb to national and transnational fame in North Africa was measured by those very years. And, while a singular figure, Elmaghribi was not the only North African Jewish musician to express a form of sonic nationalism that sometimes crossed borders. Alongside and in communication with him were the Algerian Salim Halali, who had relocated postwar to Casablanca, and the Tunisian Raoul Journo, who sang of Tunisian independence and, on at least one occasion, of Algerian independence as well. Finally, that careers first launched in the colonial period continued to flourish after 1956, the year of independence for both Morocco and Tunisia, reminds us that decolonization should be studied as a process, not as rupture.

When Elmaghribi did leave Morocco three years after independence, he did so for a set of complicated reasons born of gossip. On March 1, 1959, he wrote to his brother of pernicious "rumors that some jealous and envious people are spreading, even going as far as to speak of my final departure [from Morocco] following an expulsion order."[129] In the same breath, Elmaghribi announced that he intended to repaint and redecorate his apartment and then hold a press conference there in order to dispel the false charge. The next day, he wrote again to Simon. "It has become clear that the noise bubbling up around me," he explained, "was due to an erroneous interpretation of the truth: my name was simply confused with that of Salim Halali." According to Elmaghribi, Halali had been arrested after a police raid on his cabaret.[130] Elmaghribi then asked his brother to keep all of this to himself. Halali did not take kindly to people talking about him. Whatever calm had washed over Elmaghribi in that letter to his brother dissipated shortly thereafter. Our final chapter picks up with that moment of uncertainty.

# CHAPTER 6

# CURTAIN CALL

On September 8, 1959, Samy Elmaghribi wrote to his brother-in-law Émile Cohen from Marseilles.[1] His travel to France, of course, was nothing new. He had been recording and performing there for a decade. And in the months since the unfounded rumor about his possible expulsion from Morocco had circulated, he had gone back and forth across the Mediterranean regularly. But the tone of this letter was different. He instructed Cohen, for example, to give his apartment in Casablanca a fresh coat of interior paint and to fix whatever needed repair. He was planning to sell it. For anyone and everyone "who asked the big question," he provided Cohen with a ready-made response: tell them he "was on vacation." For those who then (naturally) wondered about the sale of the apartment, his brother-in-law was instructed to inform questioners that Elmaghribi was in the process of moving to a larger place in the city or even to a villa on the beach. The superstar musician had in fact left Morocco to settle in France, but he wanted no one back home to know.

Until very recently, the migration of North African Jewry in the midst of decolonization in the 1950s and 1960s has been framed as unidirectional and final. That scholarship, deeply informed by French historiography and its more recent turn to the colonial context, has focused mostly on France and the reception and integration of Jewish migrants there. What this has meant, however, is that the frame of action has often been shifted away from

North Africa itself. As a result, the very real connections North African Jews retained with their homelands, not only from France but from Israel as well, have been artificially severed. Music, as this chapter demonstrates, serves as a corrective to that singular northward gaze. While Elmaghribi departed Morocco toward the end of 1959, for instance, he remained intimately tied to his country for years afterward. From France, he managed to run his Casablanca-based Samyphone label. He also wrote and recorded music aimed at his compatriots back home. Like so many others, he also continued to read the Moroccan press and requested goods not available (or of inferior quality) in France to be sent to him from Morocco.

If Jewish departure from North Africa in the 1950s and 1960s has been presented as rupture alone, the ties binding new centers with old centers have been for the most part overlooked. Those connections include Israel, where an independent record label run by a Moroccan migrant named Raphaël Azoulay rereleased music originally recorded in North Africa for local consumption. At the same time, North African records made in Israel and released on his R. Zaky (and later Zakiphon) imprint soon made their way clandestinely to Morocco, Tunisia, and even Algeria in the 1960s, where such products were legally forbidden.[2]

None of this happened in a vacuum. Many professional Jewish musicians—often the most recognizable figures in their communities—remained in Morocco through the early 1960s. The same was true in Tunisia. So it was that these performers became a bellwether for the future of Jewish life in North Africa in the second half of the twentieth century. Nowhere was this more apparent than in Algeria. There, the assassination of the venerated Cheikh Raymond Leyris near the end of the seven-and-a-half-year Algerian War (1954–62) signaled to many Jews that their future was elsewhere. And yet, other Algerian Jewish musicians followed different paths. Some went on to celebrate Algerian independence from exile. Some returned to Algeria after independence in July 1962. Others never left. Still, for the majority of Jewish musicians who did eventually leave, their final appearances in situ coincided with the very moment that the shellac record, the fragile musical medium that had carried their voices for half a century, was phased out and replaced with the vinyl record. In the shuffle, many sounds faded from the scene.

But given the gradual quality of Jewish displacement, one which did not immediately portend their silence, the result could be confusion for Muslims in North Africa. In the days after his departure, many already asked after Elmaghribi. After all, his store was still there and open for business even in his absence. Whispers turned to rumors. Misunderstanding and misjudgment sometimes carried with them lethal consequences, as was the case with Leyris in Algeria. Nonetheless, "the inaccuracies in these stories," as Luise White has written in another context, "make them exceptionally reliable historical sources as well: they offer historians a way to see the world the way the storytellers did, as a world of vulnerability and unreasonable relationships."[3] In treating the whispers that circulated and the rumors that swirled as the Jewish present was becoming the Jewish past in the 1960s, this chapter builds on Aomar Boum's pioneering generational approach to the shifting Muslim memories of Jews over time.[4] In doing so, the aim is to raise new questions about the living memory of Jews in North Africa at the moment of their curtain call.

## Running Samyphone from Afar and Rumors Closer to Home

When Elmaghribi and his family departed Casablanca for Marseilles in late summer 1959, he left Samyphone, the brick-and-mortar record store he had founded in 1955, in the hands of Jacob Benzaquen, a longtime employee, and Émile Cohen, his wife Messody's young brother who, while a music enthusiast, had no experience in the music business.[5] Benzaquen served as a supervisor and Cohen as the day-to-day manager. Because of the family ties, most of the communication involved Elmaghribi and Cohen. That there was much to do meant that multiple letters carrying instructions flowed from Marseilles to Casablanca on a weekly basis. At the same time, Cohen faced two sets of questions that required immediate answers. The first was how to handle the rumors which had begun to surface. The other was how best to run a business that involved transnational shipping and an ever-complicated customs regime, especially as newly independent Morocco distanced itself from its former colonial master.

Given his public persona, Elmaghribi's departure was almost immediately noticed. Already on September 10, 1959, just a few weeks after he had left the country, Cohen reported that people were approaching him asking about his brother-in-law's whereabouts.[6] On September 15, 1959, Elmaghribi wrote back to Cohen: "Not a word to anyone about our sojourn in Marseilles—not even Benzaquen."[7] Even the supervisor at Samyphone was being kept in the dark. But if Cohen had been instructed to respond "to the big question" with the message that Elmaghribi "was on vacation," it satisfied little. "Arabs and Jews," Cohen wrote to his brother-in-law two weeks later, were constantly dropping by the centrally located Samyphone store on boulevard de Bordeaux, some to seek employment but others out of mere "curiosity."[8] "You can also tell everyone that I am in Paris to make recordings for Samyphone, which will take me a few months," Elmaghribi strongly suggested to Cohen on November 12, 1959, "after which I intend to return home to Morocco."[9] But before that letter reached him, Cohen had written another. "I also want to tell you that the rumors are starting up again as before," Cohen updated him on November 13, 1959, "and everyone has his own theory, I receive nonstop visits throughout the day. You know that I can't prevent people from talking."[10] Even if some believed "the sojourn" was temporary, the explanation could not always satisfy. By the end of the year, a certain Mireille Toledano had hoped to hire Elmaghribi to perform at her son's bar mitzvah.[11] She was not the only one who sought out his services. But clearly she would have to make other arrangements.

That Elmaghribi was so intent on keeping his departure a secret was not unusual for Moroccan Jewish migrants at the time. Those who remained silent about their movements during this period, however, tended to be those bound for Israel.[12] Much as in 1947–48, political parties like the Istiqlal continued to be animated by an opposition to Zionism (with which Judaism was still often conflated). Elmaghribi, by contrast, had additional concerns that justified his keeping quiet on his whereabouts. He was seeking to maintain his business in Morocco and, in many ways, his presence there, even as he settled in France. Given that he never took French citizenship, he may have also wanted to leave a window of opportunity for returning to North Africa in the future. To that end, he made one final tour of Algeria in June 1960, doing so at a moment of relative calm in the Algerian War.[13]

There was also a logic to Elmaghribi's installation in France in order to run a business in Morocco—and Algeria, where his records were also distributed. In 1959, the North African recording industry was by definition transnational, just as it had been for over half a century. Elmaghribi's back catalog, for example, including his earliest records on Pathé and his more recent ones on Samyphone, was pressed in France (the latter by the Philips company), as was true of most Moroccan records at the time. Indeed, throughout the 1950s, a number of other independent labels, now with Muslims at the helm, emerged as the industry shifted from making 78 rpm records on shellac to 45 rpm and 33 rpm records on vinyl. Among them were Boudroiphone, established by Ahmed Ben Hadj Bouchaib Boudroi, the pianist and composer who had earlier recorded with Elmaghribi, as well as Boussiphone and Orikaphone. Their records too were initially recorded locally, pressed in France, and then shipped back to Morocco, but without the infrastructure afforded by a trusted employee operating on the other side of the Mediterranean. For Boussiphone especially, this would change in the coming years, as its founder Mohammed Boussif's children established themselves in Brussels and Paris.[14]

Coordinating orders and shipments in the hundreds from France to North Africa was thus facilitated greatly by Elmaghribi's installation, first in Marseilles and, shortly thereafter, in Paris. In addition, independent recording outfits in both of those cities had emerged in recent years to capture the voices of newly arrived North African migrants. Among the records Cohen requested from Elmaghribi for the Casablanca store, for instance, were those on Disques Tam Tam, a Marseilles-based label run by Jacques Derderian, himself an Armenian migrant.[15] But movement went in both directions. While the Samyphone records Elmaghribi sold in France were obtained from a pressing plant in the capital, their sleeves were still printed in and then airmailed from Casablanca.[16]

The management of Samyphone in Casablanca, from paying salaries and vendors to supplying his store and other stores across Morocco and in Algeria with his records, largely fell to Elmaghribi in France. For his efforts from afar, the musician drew an income from his Morocco-based business. Among other things, this required Cohen to wire him money monthly, something Elmaghribi's young brother-in-law had never done before stepping into the position of manager. Elmaghribi would therefore have had to direct him from a distance, a process facilitated only by typed or handwritten letter. The success of Samyphone in Morocco and Algeria and Samy Elmaghribi in France therefore required transnational business matters to run smoothly,

even flawlessly, as the global recording industry transitioned to the new format of vinyl. That did not always happen. Already on September 18, 1959,
Émile reported to Elmaghribi that a large order of Samyphone sleeves for
their 45 rpm records had been "poorly done" and would now need to be reprinted.[17] This hitch would delay record distribution in North Africa and in
France as well.

Likewise, the coordination of payments through bank checks and money
orders, already a cumbersome and time-consuming process, was slowed as
Elmaghribi's signature was initially required before Cohen was eventually
vested with the authority to sign. And soon, after years of sputtering, the
Moroccan economy stalled completely. Since independence in 1956, the majority of Moroccans had been confronted with a series of problems inherited
from the protectorate regime, namely "high unemployment, scarce housing,
inadequate schooling, understaffed health services, and a stagnant economy
depleted by the flight of foreign capital."[18] On October 16, 1959, therefore,
Cohen reminded Elmaghribi "about the situation in Morocco. . . . As I already told you in my last letter with regard to business, things are very quiet,
especially with us."[19] That "quiet" meant cash flow was tight. As a result,
Elmaghribi's records sent from France sat in Moroccan customs longer. On
a number of occasions, lack of prompt payment to the customs office meant
parcels destined for Samyphone were returned to France.

Beyond Samyphone, Elmaghribi and his family remained intimately tied
to Morocco in other ways. At their request, Cohen regularly sent goods like
olive oil, tea, flour, wormwood, and almonds to his sister Messody and his
brother-in-law in France.[20] In addition, Elmaghribi continued to subscribe
to the paper *La Vigie marocaine*. As he explained to Cohen, "we are very
thirsty for news from our dear country, which we are sincerely pining for."[21]
Reading the daily Moroccan press also allowed him to keep up with many
of the new developments back home. It was Elmaghribi, for example, who
informed Cohen of a new dahir which had increased salaries in Morocco by
5 percent, including his.[22] In addition and whenever possible, the musician
also provided financial support to various family members and friends in
Casablanca, Rabat, and Salé.

As best he could and at a distance, Elmaghribi sought to satisfy the musical needs of his compatriots. After Cohen informed Elmaghribi that the

Andalusian standard "Shams al-ʿashiyya" (The evening sun) was "very in demand" among Moroccans, the musician quickly recorded it for his Samyphone label.[23] The 45 rpm record was in many ways a departure for the artist
as it was the first to feature and foreground his children. In fact, the disc
itself was credited to his son Dédé Elmaghribi (Amram Amzallag) and "his
sisters." Their famous patriarch provided accompaniment on the ʿud. Eager
to learn about its reception in Morocco, Elmaghribi dashed off a letter to
Cohen. "Provide me with the details of the sale of Chems el âchi through today and if you think this record is a hit, especially among Muslims."[24] Cohen
responded on January 19, 1960. "You asked if it was a hit, without a doubt, for
that matter, you will see the [accounting] statements and understand that it
is a hit among all Muslims and Jews."[25]

## "Qissat Agadir"

Late on February 29, 1960, the Moroccan port city of Agadir was struck
by a powerful earthquake. More than fifteen thousand were killed. Among
those victims were an estimated 1,500 Jews, representing not only 10 percent
of all fatalities but some two-thirds of the total Jewish community there as
well.[26] Thousands more were injured. Refugees sought shelter in the area but
also much farther north.[27] Hundreds of the remaining Jewish survivors fled
to Casablanca in order to benefit from the communal infrastructure in the
cultural capital still very much in place.

On March 3, 1960, Cohen attempted to convey the enormity of the situation to Elmaghribi. "This tragedy," he wrote, "has touched all of Morocco and
business has ground to a standstill."[28] But Elmaghribi already knew full well
many of the devastating details. Not only did he receive *La Vigie marocaine*
but, unlike Cohen, he also had access to French television. "All we talk about
is this catastrophe," Elmaghribi informed Cohen, "which is causing us great
sorrow."[29] In fact, by the time he had received Cohen's letter, he had already
channeled that grief into a song. He had also recorded it, sent it to the pressing plant in Paris, and designed its cover art, which featured a "a beautiful
view of Agadir before the catastrophe."[30] On March 5, 1960, Casablanca record dealers, including Samyphone, had already ordered a thousand copies of
"Qissat Agadir" (The story of Agadir) for their stores.[31] The record was now
bound for Radio Maroc in Rabat and Radio Africa in Tangier as well.

"Qissat Agadir" was not the only song composed or recorded by Moroccan Jews to commemorate the tragic events of February 1960. Against the backdrop of what Cohen described as a scene of fasting, fundraising, and "the cries of women and children" in Casablanca, Rabbi David Bouzaglo, the great paytan and pillar of Moroccan Jewry, had also written something to mark the tragedy and soothe Jewish mourners.[32] That version may very well have been performed by Bouzaglo on Radio Maroc, as the rabbi remained a regular performer on the Jewish program *La Voix des Communautés* until his departure for Israel in 1965.[33] In Israel, a number of *qasaʾid* (s., *qasida*; sung poems) on the Moroccan tragedy appeared as well.[34] There, a second "Qissat Agadir," written by a certain Jacob Dahan and recorded by Sliman Elmaghribi (no relation, né Ben Hamo) was released on the Jaffa-based R. Zaky label.[35] But few could compete with Elmaghribi and his reach among both Jews and Muslims.

In the weeks after the earthquake, Elmaghribi's slow-moving lament became something of an anthem for Moroccans not just in the diaspora but in Morocco as well. His record, on which he intoned "in the middle of the night one Tuesday, O listeners, the ground thundered and Agadir collapsed" (*laylat talata fi wast a-layl, ya sada, traʿadat l-ard w-bilad Agadir nakhlat*), was broadcast regularly on Radio Maroc. Meanwhile, other musicians began to perform Elmaghribi's "Qissat Agadir" on Moroccan radio as well.[36] As a consequence, the Samyphone record sold quite well. For a time it buoyed the label. "May God bless you and may the Lord protect you and guide you" (*Tabarkallah ʿalayk al-rabbi huwa yanzik wa-yahdik*), Émile wrote, switching from French to Moroccan Arabic.

Despite his physical absence from the country for more than six months, Elmaghribi's voice was now once again a powerful presence in Morocco. He was present in other ways as well. His face, for example, graced the popular "Qissat Agadir" record, which of course was sold both on his own label and from his very visible Samyphone store in the heart of Casablanca. For Elmaghribi, the record was more than just a commercial venture. He proposed, for instance, that one-third of the profits be designated for aid relief in Agadir itself.[37] On May 10, 1960, he tasked Cohen with contacting their local representative in Casablanca to inquire about where the money might be best directed. "Send him my greetings," Elmaghribi wrote, "inform him of my desire to do my duty like any citizen of this country."[38] Whether the proceeds ever reached their destination is unclear. As best he could, Cohen cautioned his brother-in-law against the idea, given what he perceived to be rampant corruption in the distribution of charitable funds, in particular, and in other sectors, more generally.[39]

No matter how intimately he remained connected to Morocco, El-maghribi was necessarily far from the action. Thus, he not only had to evaluate all manner of rumor from afar but was also forced to compete with musicians still on the ground as well as the growing number of local labels with exclusive access to them. In addition, the political situation had shifted. In the midst of discussions related to the "Qissat Agadir" record, Elmaghribi inquired about his contemporaries operating in Casablanca. He had heard, for example, that the Muslim artist Ahmed Jabrane had been jailed.[40] (He had). He inquired after Halali and whether his venue Le Coq d'Or had really been shut down. (It had been temporarily.) At the time of the Agadir earthquake, Morocco was in the midst of seismic changes marked by a move toward political repression. By 1959, King Mohammed V, who had exchanged his old title of sultan for his new one two years earlier, had successfully "outmaneuvered" the main rival to his authority, the Istiqlal, forcing it to splinter into a number of factions. In May 1960, the king expanded his powers considerably as he sacked his prime minister, Abdallah Ibrahim, dissolved the government, and installed himself in Ibrahim's place.[41] For his part, Crown Prince Hassan was not only observing his father in action but perfecting a slide into authoritarianism as he grabbed hold of the national security reins.

Among those Elmaghribi asked about in his letters to Cohen was Zohra El Fassia, the Jewish grande dame of Moroccan performers, as she returned to the stage after Vichy and sang for the sultan postwar. Although El Fassia was nearly two decades older than Elmaghribi, she was still very much in her prime in the late 1950s. And while the younger star had left in fall 1959, El Fassia stayed in place, at least for the moment. In doing so, she assumed his mantle, becoming the highest-profile Moroccan Jewish artist in the country. To that end, she remained highly visible and audible. She was a fixture of Radio Maroc, a headliner at vaunted venues in Casablanca like Dancing Vox (part of the two-thousand-seat Cinéma Vox) and Le Bristol, and a regular at the royal palace. She also continued to record extensively for the

FIGURE 19. The celebrated artist Zohra El Fassia at mid-twentieth century. Source: Zohra El Fassia archive. Reprinted with permission.

Pathé and Philips labels, including songs deeply invested in the same brand of Moroccan nationalism that had helped Elmaghribi cement his status as national icon.

In the weeks following the release of "Qissat Agadir," El Fassia recorded a version of it for Radio Maroc. By May 1960, *her* interpretation of the Elmaghribi record was played every Saturday morning on the national station.[42] It was sometime that month that El Fassia walked through the doors of Samyphone and approached Cohen. She was interested in recording the song for the Samyphone label. Cohen was excited by the proposal. It would "sell like hotcakes" (technically, "rolls," or *les petits pains*), he announced to Elmaghribi on May 28, 1960.[43] But the record deal never came to pass. El Fassia had requested an exorbitant sum of money: an advance of 25–50,000 Moroccan francs and a total contract worth four times that amount. Operating two Samyphone establishments between France and Morocco on exceptionally thin margins and unsure of whether the interest in the song would persist, Elmaghribi passed on the opportunity.[44] It would be a year before another one like it presented itself. Meanwhile, upstarts like Boudroiphone, Boussiphone, and Orikaphone were actively recruiting and recording a new generation of artists in-country. The growth of their catalogs was aided by the ease and availability of reel-to-reel tape recording, which since 1948 had largely replaced the more cumbersome process of creating wax masters.[45] In other words, anyone with a tape recorder and a bit of will could now make a record.

## Memories of Presence

On June 3, 1960, Cohen wrote to Elmaghribi with concern. In the previous days, the police had visited Samyphone twice, each time questioning him about the nature of his brother in-law's departure.[46] On the last visit, the officers had read through their extensive correspondence. For some time thereafter, Elmaghribi would exercise caution in what he disclosed to Cohen by letter. But Cohen would prove less inhibited. His communications also reveal that the police were not the only ones to wonder about Elmaghribi, although their inquiries were certainly the most menacing. The letters sent by Cohen to Elmaghribi between mid-1960 and the end of 1961 shine a light on emerging Muslim concerns with the absence of a high-profile Moroccan Jew. What surfaces as well is the confusion of at least some segments of

the Muslim population vis-à-vis Jewish migration. This stemmed from the
fact that other prominent Jewish voices, like El Fassia and Halali, were still
considerable presences in the country, as was Elmaghribi—although he was
nowhere physically to be found.

In his work on memory, Boum has painted a remarkably sensitive portrait
of how four generations of Moroccan Muslims came to remember a Jewish
community that numbered some 250,000 at its height at mid-twentieth century. To amplify the memories of a generation he refers to as "parents"—those
who came of age in early independent Morocco—he has paid careful attention to the press. With regard to Moroccan Jews after 1956, he has described
them persuasively as "shadow citizens": visible in some ways, invisible in others; talked about but not dialogued with, protected but disenfranchised.[47]
Moving beyond the public sphere, then, the realm of hearsay and rumor al-
lows for an even deeper engagement with the real-time perceptions and concerns of a generation.

Less than five days after first alerting Elmaghribi to the unwanted police
visits to Samyphone, Cohen wrote to him again about yet another house call.
This time, officers asked Cohen as to whether he had a passport and for the
address of Samyphone in Paris.[48] If intimidating, Cohen's main concern continued to be growing the business in Morocco.[49] For Elmaghribi, the concern
was much the same but it was made difficult by his absence and the specula-
tion surrounding it. His response to Cohen was directed at putting an end to
the inquiry, at least as far as the police were concerned. "I would love for you
to come here as soon as possible," he wrote to Cohen on July 1, 1960, from
Paris, "so that you can take my place as the manager here." He continued,
"that will allow me to return to Morocco and attend to my artistic and commercial activities [ . . . ] it is more important than here and what is more I
miss my country, its atmosphere, and my friends."[50] To be sure, the longing
was deeply felt. But was Elmaghribi actually contemplating swapping places
with his brother-in-law and returning to Morocco? Almost certainly not.
Still, in committing those words to paper, he may have also been trying to
convince himself of the idea's merit.

While the police speculated and interrogated, others deliberately spread
misinformation. Some of it emanated from his competition in the music
business. On August 18, 1960, for example, Cohen reported that "there is a

rumor being spread that Samyphone records are banned [in Morocco], it is the Casablanca dealers who are trying to sabotage the Samyphone label in Casa."[51] Rather than seek outside intervention, Elmaghribi promised to personally bring them before "Moroccan justice" should the misinformation campaign persist.[52]

During the early months of 1961, the gossip subsided, at least temporarily. The frequent closures of businesses in Casablanca and across the country during that time, including Samyphone, contributed to the quiet. So did the tense atmosphere. Between January 3 and 7, 1961, Morocco hosted the Casablanca Conference, which brought United Arab Republic President Gamal Abdel Nasser to the country, along with other members of the Arab League as well as African leaders. As Alma Heckman has written, the presence of Nasser, who represented the very embodiment of pan-Arabism and confrontation with Israel, culminated in violence against the Jews of Casablanca, producing considerable anxiety for the entire Jewish community.[53] According to Cohen, it was the visit of the Egyptian head of government that prompted what amounted to a nearly weeklong public holiday.[54] Curiously, he made no mention of the anti-Jewish attacks and arrests but instead expressed apprehension over the financial impact of the prolonged shuttering on Samyphone. Less than two months later, on February 26, 1961, the death of King Mohammed ben Youssef ground Morocco to a halt once again. By mid-March, as King Hassan II amalgamated power, Cohen relayed to Elmaghribi that much in the country was still closed.[55] In the meantime, the pace of Moroccan Jewish emigration, which had slowed in the years immediately after independence, quickened precipitously. Beginning in November 1961 and lasting through spring 1964, Operation Yakhin, "a complex plan involving the Mossad, the Jewish Agency, the United HIAS [Hebrew Immigrant Aid Society] Service, and King Hasan II," brought some 92,000 Moroccan Jews to Israel.[56]

As Morocco reopened in the months after Nasser's visit and King Mohammed V's death, the police returned to Samyphone for regular questioning. "I'm bringing to your attention," Cohen wrote to Elmaghribi on May 25, 1961, "that the police came to tell me that your file is still open and that they are waiting for you to come [to the station] in order to close it."[57] As Cohen rightly concluded, however, the dossier in question likely did not exist.

Meanwhile, others visited as well. In June, a Muslim friend informed Cohen that Elmaghribi was an ongoing subject of conversation at the palace. According to the same individual, the story circulating among the royal circle was that Elmaghribi had fled, rather than left of his own accord, due to an unidentified indiscretion.[58] Just a couple of weeks later, a Moroccan Jew by the name of Salomon Boulhbal, a percussionist (*drabki*) from Rabat, provided a different story. Boulhbal swore "on all of his ancestors" that he had heard King Hassan II himself ask about Elmaghribi in front of "all the musicians" but with none of the insinuation associated with Cohen's Muslim informant.[59]

By the fall of 1961, Cohen informed Elmaghribi that the rumors had turned into something else: a collective plea for his homecoming. "I have learned that everyone wants you to return to Morocco," Cohen wrote on September 6, 1961. This included "the employees of the second arrondissement," an allusion not just to local powerbrokers in Elmaghribi's old neighborhood but to the very police officers with whom Cohen was now quite familiar.[60] Then, on October 10, 1961, Cohen brought something "very serious" to Elmaghribi's attention. On two separate occasions, he had recently been visited by another Muslim friend of his who was close to a nephew of the late king. According to Cohen's contact, King Hassan II was prepared to personally facilitate Elmaghribi's reentry into Morocco and had committed to financially supporting the Jewish celebrity during the relaunch of his career on Moroccan soil. But something did not sit right with Cohen. He was skeptical. "Everyone is trying to get you to come by whatever means," Cohen alerted his brother-in-law, "be very careful, do not trust anyone."[61] He described the effort as "a trap" and warned him that his "life was at stake": "Do not leave Paris." Just a few days later, Elmaghribi responded. "Thank you for your information and advice," he wrote, "I have neither the desire nor the means to move away from here. My occupation also does not allow me to do so."[62] That Elmaghribi mentioned his lack of "means" was telling. At the very least, it indicated that he had some desire to relocate to Morocco, even if it was fleeting. And that his occupation—a musician and musical impresario oriented toward North Africans—permitted him to support his family in France, even more so than in Morocco, speaks once again, as André Levy has shown, to the ways in which new centers for Moroccan Jewry were deeply enmeshed with old Moroccan centers that for the moment could not sustain them.[63]

## Samyphone in Israel, Zakiphon and Jo Amar in Morocco

In August 1960, Elmaghribi signed a contract with Raphaël Azoulay, providing the latter with exclusive concession for the distribution of Samyphone records in Israel.[64] Azoulay had scored a major coup. While the Moroccan Jewish artist's music had been heard in Israel for years—the ethnomusicologist Deben Bhattacharya had captured recently arrived Moroccan Jews singing Elmaghribi's "Qaftanak mahlul" (Your caftan is open) on a set of 1957 field recordings he released on the American Westminster label—this was the first time his records would find official channels of distribution in the Jewish state.[65]

Raphaël and Messaouda Azoulay had arrived in Israel from Morocco in September 1948 with four boys in tow. After first landing in Haifa, the family established itself in Givat Aliyah in southern Jaffa. Both parents worked outside of the home: Messaouda operated a small falafel business while Raphaël resold items purchased at auction, including phonographs. Along with his eldest son Zaki (Isaac), the father soon learned to repair the machines. Shortly thereafter, the two began to purchase Egyptian records from Palestinian distributors in Jaffa's Ajami neighborhood, reselling them to Jewish migrants from North Africa and the Middle East.[66] Seizing on an opportunity, father and son then turned their sights to the many accomplished and emerging Jewish musicians from the Islamic world for whom the major Israeli labels, like Hed Artzi and Makolit, showed little interest.[67] By the mid-1950s, the Azoulays had established a record label known alternately as R. Zaky, Sacchiphon, and Zakiphon, which served as the first and, for a long while, only port of call in Israel for arabophone Jewish artists.[68] As with North African records since the beginning of the twentieth century (and cylinders just before then), Zakiphon records began with a spoken announcement identifying the label and the name of the artist in Arabic.

For the tens of thousands of Jews from North Africa and the Middle East who arrived in Israel in the years immediately after 1948, neglect and outright discrimination manifested outside of the music business as well.[69] Unlike most Ashkenazi immigrants, the diverse communities who came to be labeled collectively as *Mizrahim* (Easterners) were forced to settle in transit camps (*maabarot*) with little to no infrastructure and in so-called development towns, far from urban centers, on Israel's borders. With scant access to either power or resources, Mizrahim suffered high unemployment rates and debilitating poverty. "When it came to Moroccan Jews, however," as Emily Benichou Gottreich has written, "their 'absorption' into Israel was additionally marked by strong anti-Arab cultural biases and Eurocentric ideas of 'modernization,' not unlike what had already been undergone by these same communities in Morocco with regard to programs of French acculturation in the schools of the AIU."[70] As Bryan K. Roby has shown, Moroccan Arabic was even criminalized on occasion, as was the case when three residents of a transit camp in Binyamina were arrested for distributing flyers in their native language.[71] On July 9, 1959, the discontentment of Mizrahim, especially North Africans, manifested in the Wadi Salib riots, an event in which hundreds of residents of Haifa came out to protest the police shooting of a Moroccan Jewish immigrant by the name of Ya'akov Akiva (Elkarif).[72] In the following months, demonstrations spread to other cities, part and parcel of a growing movement for Mizrahi rights and recognition which would take shape over the next decade.

Inspired and incensed by the Wadi Salib riots, the Zakiphon artist Jo Amar wrote and recorded a searing critique of Israel's treatment of Moroccans entitled "Lishkat avodah" (Employment office).[73] By the time of its release around 1960, Amar, born in Settat, Morocco, in 1930, was already a veteran of two different but connected recording industries. In Morocco, he had recorded in Arabic for the Philips label under the name of Joamar Elmaghribi (Jo Amar the Moroccan). After his arrival in Israel in 1956, he would initially do the same for Zakiphon.[74] As Amar, together with his label, sought a wider Israeli audience, he dropped the Arabic place identifier from his stage name and gravitated increasingly, although not exclusively, toward Hebrew song. "Shir haShikor" (The drunkard's song), "Shalom leben dodi" (I greet my cousin), and "Barcelona"—all originally recorded in Hebrew for Azoulay and his sons—catapulted Amar into wider Israeli stardom and eventually onto the global stage.[75] In 1965, Amar became the first Moroccan and North African to perform at Carnegie Hall in New York.[76] But alongside his hits like "Shir haShikor," Amar continued to record for a specifically Moroccan audience. Such was the case with "Lishkat avodah," his six-minute song about anti-Moroccan discrimination in Israel, narrated in a mix of Moroccan Arabic and Hebrew.

I went to the employment office
He said where are you from
I said from Morocco
He said get out.

I went to the employment office
He said where are you from
I said from Poland
He said please come in.[77]

In fall 1961, Cohen reported to Elmaghribi that Zakiphon records were beginning to appear in Morocco. His customers were increasingly clamoring for Amar in particular.

As Israeli-produced Moroccan records arrived in Morocco, Samyphone struggled. In September 1961, Cohen informed Elmaghribi that the country had raised customs fees on foreign goods by 25 percent.[78] To compensate, Samyphone records, made in France, either had to raise their prices or face a considerable decrease in their profits. For a time, Elmaghribi entertained the thought of moving all of the production of Samyphone records to Casablanca. To remedy the situation, Cohen encouraged him to record new material, something he had not done since his release of "Qissat Agadir" in March 1960. He would have to wait until August 1962 for such records to arrive.[79] In the interim, Elmaghribi faced increased competition from the dizzying array of on-the-ground labels whose diverse catalogs at competitive prices featured a rising class of Muslim stars, alongside a minority of Jewish artists like Haim Botbol, Felix El Maghribi (né Weizman), Karoutchi Elmaghribi (né Hananiah Karoutchi), and "Petit Robert" Gabai (who sometimes went by the stage name of "Little Salim" due to his predilection for the music of Salim Halali).

In 1963, Elmaghribi decided to make a record that strayed considerably from the previous output on which he had built his career. In March of that year and timed to arrive in Morocco just before the start of the Passover holiday, Elmaghribi released "La Hagada de Pessah" (The Passover Haggadah), a full-length LP (long-playing vinyl record) on Samyphone.[80] The foray into explicitly Jewish content owed, no doubt, to the competition from Zakiphon, which, given its captive market in Israel, could afford to release both sacred Hebrew and profane Arabic music, sometimes even on the same record. On "La Hagada de Pessah," Dédé, his eldest child and only son, pronounced instructions drawn from the central Passover text in French while Elmaghribi, accompanying himself on ʿud, chanted the blessings and songs associated with the ritual meal known as the seder. The whole family joined in chorus to sing "amen." On March 29, 1963, the first batch of "La Hagada de Pessah" albums arrived at Samyphone in Casablanca. It was a momentous occasion for Jews in Morocco, who could now bring the religious repertoire of one of their secular idols into their living rooms in advance of that most important of Jewish holidays. But Elmaghribi was not the only one with the idea to record the Passover seder on LP. In short order, Cohen informed his brother-in-law that "he had competition from Jo Amar's Haggadah."[81] Unbeknownst to Elmaghribi, Israel's Amar had recorded his "Haggadah De Pessach" on the Disques Tam Tam label, based in Marseilles. That LP was now flooding the market. Making matters worse, the second shipment of Elmaghribi's much-anticipated record only arrived in Morocco on April 7, 1963, the day before the start of the holiday. According to Cohen, the copies in question were "defective."[82] Elmaghribi would have to try again the following year.

In the midst of the Passover holiday, Cohen confided in his brother-in-law that he was "overwhelmed and exasperated."[83] Elmaghribi, running low on stock and requiring an influx of capital to press more records, found himself in a difficult position.[84] By fall 1963, a distressed Moroccan economy was sent into free fall by the War of the Sands, a border conflict between Morocco and Algeria, which, as Cohen reported, hit businesses hard.[85] On November 12, 1963, Elmaghribi learned that Egyptian records, a considerable portion of the inventory at Samyphone and most other Moroccan record stores, were temporarily banned from sale in the country on account of Egypt's support for Algeria in the midst of this iteration of the Arab Cold War.[86] Frustrated, the musician decided to shift his focus away from Morocco and to France, where a Samyphone store was set to open in Paris's historic Jewish quarter, Le Marais.

In the early to mid-1960s, others in Morocco made similar moves to re-orient themselves, including emigration from the country. Those decisions

were almost always influenced by a desire to reunite with family. Sometime
at the end of 1962, for example, Zohra El Fassia left Morocco for Israel, where
two of her children resided. The choice, while not made lightly, must have
been a last-minute one. In early 1963, as a hand-scrawled note in a datebook
indicates, she was scheduled to perform at the "Assouline anniversary party"
and the "Luski marriage" in Rabat.[87] She never made either. In 1963, Salim
Azra, among Morocco's most accomplished masters of the *qanun* (the trap-
ezoidal zither) and a mainstay of the royal palace, left too—first for France
and then for Montreal, Canada, where he settled with his family in 1965.[88] In
November 1963, Cohen reached out to his sister Messody (Elmaghribi's wife)
for help.[89] More than just an older sibling, Messody was the matriarch of the
Cohen family as well as a trusted advisor and partner to her husband.[90] One
month later, in December 1963, Elmaghribi concluded it was time to start
thinking about selling the Casablanca store.[91]

In January 1964, Cohen requested more releases from Israel, "even if they
are in Hebrew, because here we love Jo Amar records as well as the Zakiphon
label and all that is recorded on it."[92] And in March 1964, Elmaghribi shipped
the improved "La Hagada de Pessah" to Cohen. After praying to "all of the
saints" for support, Cohen was finally able to provide Elmaghribi with some
good news: "now that I write this letter the [sale of the] Haggada does not
stop, from morning to night."[93] Still, running the transnational operation
proved difficult, if not impossible. It was too little, too late. By June 1964,
Elmaghribi had begun to make plans to shutter both stores and move from
France to Montreal. "You will come with us," he told Cohen, "God is great."[94]

In 1965, Elmaghribi sold his store and its stock to a young Muslim en-
trepreneur by the name of Jalal. Istwanat Jalal (Disques Jalal, Jalal Records)
would operate out of that same Samyphone location for more than four decades. In the same year that Samyphone changed hands, a fire tore through
Salim Halali's cabaret Le Coq d'Or. That it was unoccupied at the time of
the blaze gave rise to a number of rumors. So did the fact that Halali left for
France shortly thereafter.

## Rumors of a Different Sort

In the fall of 1960, some months after Elmaghribi's last tour in Algiers, Algeria found itself in a different place politically than Morocco and Tunisia, even

as independence appeared to be increasingly likely. Some four years after Moroccans and Tunisians had begun to chart a path without France, Algeria was still French-controlled. For that matter, most of Algeria's Jewish community of approximately 140,000 remained in 1960, despite the fact that the last six years of the Algerian War had rattled them considerably. Since late 1955 and early 1956, the Algerian war of independence had intensified with the FLN's "deliberate ramping up of revolutionary violence and the consequent punitive actions of the French 'forces of order.'" By July 1956, nearly 400,000 French soldiers had been deployed to Algeria in an extraordinary show of force.[95]

In August 1956, the leadership of the FLN met in Algeria's Soummam Valley to lay out a program of national unity and a platform for their state-in-the-making. The Soummam platform, as Ethan Katz has written, "treated Jews as compatriots in waiting." "The Algerians of Jewish origin," the FLN platform read, "have not yet overcome their trouble of conscience, nor chosen [a side]. Let us hope that they will follow in large numbers the path of those who have responded to the call of the generous fatherland, given their friendship to the Revolution and already demanded proudly their Algerian nationalism."[96] As Pierre-Jean Le Foll-Luciani has shown, quite a few answered the nationalist call, even as "Algerians of Jewish origin" continued to suffer from FLN attacks.[97]

As Katz has pointed out astutely, Algerian attitudes toward and experiences of an ever-shifting war were "remarkably multidirectional and uncertain," especially when considered in real time.[98] Even as violence surged around them and as many within the FLN and other parties would come to define the bounds of national belonging in exclusively Arab and Muslim terms, Algerian Jewish musicians continued to occupy center stage on radio, in concert, and on the new medium of television. Labassi, for instance, who had been sidelined under Vichy, was a regular on Radio Alger throughout the war and one of the first arabophone musicians, Jewish or Muslim, to appear on Algerian television when it debuted at the end of 1956.[99] He also continued to compose and record new material that became anthemic shortly after its release, as was the case with "Wahran al-bahiyya" (Oran the radiant), released on both shellac and vinyl for RCA.[100] Given that a war was being waged over the future status of cities like Oran, its Arabic-language exaltation by Labassi might be read as staking a certain claim. Muslim audiences at the time seemed to react that way. During an end-of-decade Ramadan concert in Oran, the crowd roared when the master of ceremonies announced that Labassi, described as "the famed and well-known popular (*sha'bi*) artist," would perform "Wahran al-bahiyya."[101]

Beginning in late 1960, the Algerian War entered its final phase. In November of that year, French president Charles de Gaulle referred for the first time to "an Algerian republic, which will exist one day."[102] On January 8, 1961, nearly five years after Moroccan and Tunisian independence, France went to the polls to vote in a referendum on Algerian independence. More than six years after the start of the Algerian War, the overwhelming majority of French citizens, which had included Algeria's Muslims since 1947, cast their ballots in favor of the idea. Among the Algerian Jews who supported the initiative was Raymond Leyris, the master interpreter of the Andalusian tradition of the Algerian-Tunisian border, who hailed from the repertoire's spiritual center of Constantine.[103]

That spring, Leyris, a fixture of Algerian radio and television, traveled briefly to France for a visit.[104] Like Elmaghribi, he had any number of reasons

FIGURE 20. Cheikh Raymond records (vinyl on left, shellac on right) on his own Hes-El-Moknine label. Personal collection of author.

for ongoing travel to the metropole, especially professional ones. The shellac and increasingly vinyl records on his label Hes-El-Moknine (*has al-muqnin*), established in 1948, were pressed in Paris by Pathé. Shipment from France to the other side of the Mediterranean and then distribution to sellers across Algeria required his personal attention. In addition to owning and operating independent North African record labels, Leyris and Elmaghribi shared other commonalities. Both, for instance, were fathers of large families consisting of several girls and one boy. Both were deeply connected to the synagogue, as to the stage. Both were partisans of a certain type of postwar nationalism. And both were subject to rumors that carried with them consequences.

Leyris was born in Constantine in 1912 to a Jewish father named Jacob Lévi and a Catholic mother named Céline Leyris. After his father was killed in World War I, his widowed mother arranged for his adoption. Leyris was subsequently raised by Maïma Halimi, the young Jewish nurse who had in fact delivered him. As a teenager, he developed a talent for the ʿud, which was quickly recognized by Constantine's most celebrated Muslim masters of the Andalusian repertoire: Omar Chakleb, Abdelkrim Bestandji, and Si Tahar Benkartoussa.[105] We can begin to glean some of his early political sensibilities from a couple of sources. The first, as Joshua Cole has unearthed, came in the immediate aftermath of the Constantine Riots of 1934, the startling interwar episode of Muslim-Jewish violence in which twenty-five Jews and three Muslims were killed.[106] In the weeks after the violence of August 1934, many Jews and Muslims in Constantine had kept their distance from one another—but not Leyris. According to a police report, on the evening of September 17, 1934, the Jewish musician had not only shared a drink with a Muslim musician by the name of Mohamed ben Abdelmoumène Amri but also sought to warn him about potential impending state violence to be carried out against Muslims.[107] When Leyris made his first recordings three years later as "Cheikh Raymond," he did so not for one of the major labels but for Taieb ben Amor's Constantine-based Diamophone, a recording outfit which quickly came under suspicion from Algeria's Bureau of Native Affairs for its nationalist activity.[108]

Beginning in the late 1940s, Leyris became connected to the Algerian Communist Party (PCA) although, as with Diamophone, the depth of that

association is difficult to ascertain. In 1947, he and his Jewish-Muslim orchestra gave a rare interview to Chérif Attouche, a journalist with the PCA's
weekly *Liberté*.[109] In the course of a conversation which took place in the
evocative setting of a garden overlooking the Rhumel River, the violinist Syl-
vain Ghrenassia, father of Gaston Ghrenassia (the future Enrico Macias),
suggested to Attouche there was "no better bond than music" and offered as
evidence the fact that Leyris's orchestra consisted of both Jews and Muslims.
For his part, Leyris spoke of the Andalusian repertoire as a shared Jewish-
Muslim tradition, "one of the cornerstones of 'originality' in our country,"
while criticizing "the authorities" for not doing enough to safeguard it.[110]
Their comments aligned closely with the type of capacious "Algerianness"
(*algériennité*) regularly promoted by the PCA's *Liberté*, which on at least
one occasion invoked Leyris himself as its symbol. In the same year that
Attouche's article appeared and in those that followed in the 1950s, Leyris
and his orchestra performed regularly at the PCA's annual gatherings.[111]

But by 1961, as Leyris momentarily left Algeria, much had changed and
the nuance of his political program was overshadowed by other events. On
December 11, 1960, the Grand Synagogue of Algiers, just outside the lower
Casbah, was attacked by supporters of the FLN. In February 1961, following
the referendum on Algerian independence, the French paramilitary Organ-
isation de l'armée secrète (OAS) was formed in order to maintain French
Algeria by whatever means necessary, including terrorism.[112] With Leyris
temporarily absent, at least two rumors emerged. The first was the outland-
ish claim that he had joined the newly formed OAS.[113] The second story to
surface was that Leyris had left not for France but for Israel, a path taken by
a decided minority of Algerian Jews.[114]

While in France, Leyris was informed by his family in Constantine that
a direct threat had been made on his life by the FLN. To assuage concern, he
returned home at once. In an echo of Tawfiq al-Madani's interwar tripartite
nationalist slogan, "Islam is my religion, Arabic is my language, Algeria is
my country," Leyris declared that "Algeria is his country, his music is Arab,
his identity is not European."[115] To himself and his family, he justified his
return in stark terms: "I would rather die in Algeria than live in France."[116]
By March 1961, Leyris was performing in public once again, appearing at

the Cinéma Vox in Constantine. "In the hall, the public squeezed together," Raphaël Drai recalled of one particular Saturday evening, "Jews and Muslims side by side."[117]

## A Letter and Signal from Constantine

In May 1961, *Droit et Liberté*, the journal of the French antiracism organization Le Mouvement contre le racisme et pour l'amitié entre les peuples (MRAP), published "A Letter from Constantine," written by "a group of Algerian Jewish patriots."[118] In their missive, the group demanded Algerian independence, called for Jewish solidarity with their Muslim compatriots, and condemned colonialism alongside Zionism. So too did the "vanguard," as the Algerian Jewish patriots likewise referred to themselves, issue a "solemn appeal to their Jewish brothers" to reflect upon their outsized role in shaping Algerian culture. "Look at how many of you who have enriched Algerian cultural heritage are held in high esteem!" the authors exclaimed.[119] "Is the Constantine singer and musician Raymond not dear to the hearts of Muslims?" the vanguard asked. "They love him," they reminded readers, "because he has helped to preserve and enrich the very Algerian folklore that the colonialists wanted to suppress."

On June 22, 1961, a month after the appearance of "A Letter from Constantine," a bullet struck Leyris in the neck as he strolled with his daughter Viviane through the market at Place Négrier close to the entrance to Constantine's old Jewish quarter. The city's best-known musician, Jewish or otherwise, had been assassinated, in all likelihood by members of the FLN, although the assailants were never and have never been named.[120] In the immediate aftermath of his murder, the daily *La Dépêche de Constantine et de l'est algérien* found Constantine's Muslim population to be "deeply aggrieved."[121] In July 1961, *Information Juive*, the monthly journal of the Comité juif algérien d'études sociales (CJAES), similarly reported that "the attack aroused considerable emotion in the Jewish community." In commenting on Leyris's esteem among Jews and Muslims, the journal made reference to the now tragic letter written by the group of Algerian Jewish patriots of the previous month.[122] The 1962 American Jewish Year Book (AJYB), the annual publication of the American Jewish Committee, observed that "strong feeling was aroused by the assassination on June 22 [1961], in the Jewish quarter of

Constantine, of Raymond Leyris, one of the masters of oriental music, a man universally admired by both the Jewish and Moslem communities."[123] It ranked the weight of the murder alongside that of the December 1960 attack on the Grand Synagogue of Algiers, which had similarly shaken the Jewish community to its core.

The following year, the French Jewish writer Arnold Mandel, reporting on Algeria for the AJYB, provided additional details as to how that "strong feeling" manifested itself. "In Constantine," he wrote, "panic and precipitate rush to ship and plane had already begun after the murder in June 1961 of Raymond Leyris, an oriental singer popular among Jews and Moslems."[124] Later memoirists, including scholars, would validate Mandel's real-time assessment of the impact of Leyris's death. "That was the turning point," Benjamin Stora, born in Constantine in 1950, writes in *Les clés retrouvées*, "the moment when what remained of the Jewish community of Constantine in 1961, chose to leave for France. The question was no longer whether to leave or not but: 'What would become of us there?'"[125]

In his 1963 Algeria country report for the AJYB, Mandel again spoke of Leyris, a testament to his stature and impact, but this time described him rather curiously as "an Arab Christian converted to Judaism."[126] Perhaps he had confused the fact that the musician was born to a Jewish father and Catholic mother or that he had been adopted as a child. Or maybe in summer 1962, when the report was completed, in the early days of Algerian independence and with roughly half of Algeria's Jews—some 70,000 souls—departed for France and another 60,000 to soon follow, an arabophone Algerian Jewish shaykh was already understood by him to be an impossible figure of improbable origin. He suggested something else about Leyris, albeit with little evidence to substantiate his claim. "He was also a thoroughly loyal partisan of [the] FLN," Mandel wrote, "who had signed a manifesto disavowing any Jewish need or desire for guarantees in an independent Algeria." He continued:

> Many Constantine Jews had counted on Leyris and the few other FLN-aligned Jews to protect them. Yet Leyris was murdered by Moslems, not by OAS. It was the signal for the Jews to flee.[127]

If for many the Leyris assassination at the near end of the colonial period has come to embody an obvious end of the line for Algeria's Jews in-country,

Mandel's observations lay bare another possibility. For the Jews of Constantine and potentially elsewhere, Leyris did not only represent a reified past but became a symbol of their possible future in postcolonial Algeria.

———

That the murder of Raymond Leyris, an Arabic-speaking Jew, an Algerian national icon, a possible partisan of the FLN, *and* a musician "was the signal for the Jews to flee" has certainly given scholars pause, but it offered little else by way of conclusion as to the centrality of music in history. While Leyris's murder was singular, the continued exaltation of Jewish artists in the midst of decolonization was not. The gossip surrounding Elmaghribi and his departure, for example, whether emanating from Moroccan Muslim passersby, the police, or the palace, demonstrates that the potential absence of a Jewish celebrity could be of profound concern to them. For those spreading rumors or merely passing along information determined by them to be true, this disquiet was not a political calculation but one of national, sometimes existential, import. Musicians and their music mattered, especially to everyday people.

Leyris and Elmaghribi belong to a much longer lineage of Jews who shaped the very sounds of North Africa from the turn of the twentieth century through at least the beginning of the postcolonial period. Even if diminished by waves of departures at midcentury, fixing an end date to that dialectical relationship can still prove elusive. At the end of 1962, the revered Algerian Jewish pianist Sariza Cohen (née Saïac) returned from temporary residence in France to her native Oran. There she resumed her position at the Oran Conservatory, where she taught the Andalusian repertoire to a new generation of mostly Muslim students. She also served, alongside the Tlemcen-born Muslim Cheikh Abderrahmane Sekkal, as the copresident of a new music association evocatively named "Ennahda" (*al-Nahda*, the Renaissance).[128] Others never left. The singer and 'ud player Alice Fitoussi, for instance, who had begun her recording career around 1930, not only stayed in Algeria after independence but remained a central member of Radio Alger's Andalusian orchestra for years afterward. Of course, the music lingered as well. In 1964, three years after Leyris's assassination, his Hes-El-Moknine records were still being pressed in Paris and distributed in Algeria.[129] His tragic end did not diminish the power of his voice. The same was true for countless other Jewish musicians whose records continued to circulate in North Africa and whose music was covered by others in the absence of their physical presence. The same early recording by Elmaghribi that the ethnomusicologist Bhattacharya had heard being sung by Moroccan Jews in Israel in the late 1950s, for example, was recorded again a decade later by an Algerian Muslim musician named Abdelkader Brahmi for Disques El Manar, one of the many Algerian labels which had appeared after 1962.[130] On the flip side was a cover of Salim Halali's "Sidi H'bibi" (an updated version of Ayli ayli habibi diyali). Wherever Abdelkader had first encountered the music—in concert, on a record, or elsewhere—it was clearly still around and resonated.

In May 1967, Elmaghribi returned to Morocco from France after a nearly eight-year absence. He was there to give a series of much anticipated concerts. When he touched down in Casablanca, reporters welcomed the national icon on the airport tarmac in the same style as other figures of historical significance. "Who are you, Samy Elmaghribi?" a certain M. P. from *Le Petit Marocain* asked provocatively of the Jewish artist. Without missing a beat, he responded: "First of all, a Moroccan."[131]

# CONCLUSION

In 1962, as Algeria gained independence, Lili Labassi (né Elie Moyal) settled with his family in Paris. In France, he joined 130,000 other Algerian Jews whose move to the metropole was facilitated by their French citizenship. Nonetheless, the year of his departure was a difficult one. Within twelve months of his arrival, his wife Léonie passed away. As the Moyals' son Robert Castel, the successful actor known for his perfection of the patois and humor of the European settler population, later wrote in the vexed language of the so-called *pieds-noirs*, "one year after the repatriation, my mother left us. She was traumatized by this forced exile."[1] Labassi's own mother Hachiba was likewise "repatriated" to a country that she had spent little time in. She died the following year. As for "the famed and well-known sha'bi artist," as Labassi had been heralded at a Ramadan celebration just a few years earlier, he was starting life over in his mid-sixties in a strange city. By 1963, apart from his son, he was in many ways alone.

In the course of roughly half a century, Labassi had become synonymous with modern Algerian music itself. In concerts, on radio, and lately on television, he performed his popular compositions with great gusto before adoring Jewish and Muslim audiences and interpreted the Andalusian repertoire with a certain flair and fidelity that satisfied even the most demanding of aficionados. Over four decades, his voice was carried on hundreds of individual releases for major labels including Gramophone, Columbia, Polyphon,

Parlophone, and RCA. Many of those shellac records, which ranged from the scandalous "Mamak" to the unintentionally subversive "Lillah ya-l-ghadi li-l-sahra" to the anthemic "Wahran al-bahiyya," became standards in their time, not only in his native Algeria but across North Africa. They also made him a star.

In Paris, however, Labassi was no longer in the spotlight, even though he found himself surrounded by increasing numbers of Jews and Muslims from Algeria—and from Morocco and Tunisia as well. And while a North African recording industry was beginning to take shape there, it was not what he was used to. Meanwhile, tragic circumstances had intervened. In 1964, he would have just emerged from the traditional Jewish mourning period for his mother, whose death had come just after that of his wife, whose passing followed their traumatic passage to a new country. But sometime shortly thereafter, as Castel recalled, Labassi "suddenly decided to record six 45 rpm records, as if an immanent emergency dictated this decision to him imperatively."[2] At a recording studio in the nightlife district of Pigalle, Disques Lili Labassi (Lili Labassi Records) was born. The first record issued on the eponymous label was a striking, original composition entitled "Ma ninsashi biladi" (I will not forget my country).[3]

> I will never forget my country.
> I miss it, and my soul is tormented.[4]

He referred, of course, to Algeria.

Accompanied by his son Castel, the pied-noir celebrity who was very well versed in his father's music, the in-demand Algerian pianist Maurice El Medioni, and an unknown percussionist, Labassi sang with pathos of his separation (*fraq*) and loneliness (*wahhash*). Together the two ideas constituted among the most important leavening ingredients of the genre of North African songs of exile (*ghurba*) then emerging, one more commonly associated with Muslim musicians of the period.[5] The slight echo on the roughly twelve-minute recording, the result of a tape problem, produces a haunting effect. That Labassi, among the million or so "repatriates" to France at the time, sang of Algeria in Arabic, a tongue common not to the European settler population but to Muslims and Jews, made a powerful statement. We might consider such songs to be among the first memoirs crafted by this generation of North African Jewish migrants to France, produced and performed in real time and in a language long thought abandoned by them.

Such music, of course, brought many North African Jews and Muslims together in exile. In France, Jewish and Muslim musicians reconstituted ensembles, formed new partnerships, and gave voice to a very real longing. Raoul Journo, who had written to Samy Elmaghribi of how well he was doing in Tunisia on the eve of independence there, would later describe his resettlement in Paris in February 1967 as one of "exile and heartbreak."[6] The "fateful decision" to depart was finally made because he and his wife Émilie could no longer bear to be away from their children, who had moved to France some years earlier. But even after making that difficult choice to leave, Journo was hardly contented. As he writes in his memoir:

> This thought did not make me happy and I kept procrastinating. Leaving my native Tunisia, abandoning my cherished audience was unbearable for me. Dark thoughts jostled in my head. I was consumed with worry and grief.[7]

His iconic "Al-Wahhash wa-l-ghurba" (Loneliness and exile), first recorded on shellac for Polyphon in 1938, took on new meaning. As he recounted, it now left him "shaken" every time he sang it.[8] The same was likely true for his audiences.

As Journo rebuilt his life and career in Paris and as Labassi recorded "Ma ninsashi biladi," the Algerian Muslim popular artist Dahmane El Harrachi, who had been settled in France since 1949, expressed strikingly similar sentiments in songs like "(Kifash ninsa) Bilad al-khayr" (How could I forget the land of abundance) and "Ya Rayah" (O you who leaves), the latter first recorded for the Algerian label Edition Atlas.[9]

> You who leave, where are you going, growing weary, going onward?
> How much did they regret, the unwary ones who went before you and me?
> How many crowded cities have I seen, and emptied countrysides?
> You who are absent, in the land of others, how you'll grow weary . . .[10]

In the 1990s, "Ya Rayah" would be reprised to great effect by the Algeria-born French rock legend Rachid Taha.[11]

In navigating a different recording industry, new types of sounds, and new settings, the challenges faced by some musicians proved particularly daunting and, at times, insurmountable. Such was the case with Zohra El Fassia when she arrived in Ashkelon, Israel, from Casablanca. Reduced to public housing, her most natural audience scattered to the country's periphery, a younger generation increasingly preferring Hebrew over Arabic, El Fassia did as best she could. In the years after her arrival, she recorded for the Azoulays' Zakiphon label, performed at concerts that were more intimate than she was accustomed to, and entertained at weddings with much smaller music budgets. Still musical tastes were changing among Moroccan Jews in Israel, and a more general Israeli audience proved elusive. In January 1965, an exhibit on North African Jews, their culture, and "their contribution to Israel's development" was organized by Le Comité de Coordination des Unions d'Originaires d'Afrique du Nord en Israel at the International Cultural Center for Youth in Jerusalem's German Colony neighborhood. Presided over by Israel's president Zalman Shazar, the well-publicized event attracted considerable foot traffic. On the first floor of the exhibit, guests would have encountered El Fassia in person, sitting on a low sofa placed atop a number of carpets and surrounded by silver platters and samovars in "a reproduction of the salon of a well-to-do Moroccan family."[12] All of the exhibited possessions, in fact, belonged to her. Tragically, while still in her prime Zohra El Fassia was being reduced to a museum piece and the life she once lived to spectacle.

Other musicians managed to reprise their careers (at least temporarily), reinvent themselves, or both. After departing Morocco in 1965, Salim Halali returned to France, established himself in Cannes, and set up shop as an antiques dealer. At the same time, he stepped back into the spotlight with a series of legendary concerts. This included a 1969 performance at the Pleyel Hall in Paris, a theater with seating for 2,400, and a 1975 concert at the Place des Arts in Montreal for an audience of roughly 1,800.[13] After returning to Morocco to tour in 1967, Samy Elmaghribi was recruited to serve as the cantor at Montreal's historic Spanish and Portuguese Synagogue. Now associated with his birth name albeit with an added title, Cantor Salomon Amzallag served the growing congregation of Moroccan Jews at Canada's oldest synagogue for seventeen years. While an older generation recognized his celebrity, a younger generation would have had to learn about it secondhand from their parents.

Although Labassi, Journo, El Fassia, Halali, and Elmaghribi were no longer physically present in North Africa, their shellac discs could still be found there. But their records faced increasingly stiff competition. The LP, but especially the 45 rpm record, became the preferred format of a generation, as music like raï, a genre born in Oran, tackled themes of a changing society along the lines of the popular songs of the interwar years; the new music now proliferated on new labels across the Mediterranean. While some of the original recordings of the earlier artists were indeed rereleased as LPs and 45s, including on the state-run En'nagham label in Tunisia and on the independent Zed El Youm label in Algeria, the overwhelming majority never made the technological jump to the new medium. In the transition, the major and minor labels lost a great deal of master recordings, discovered many broken, and discarded others still. And so the only extant copies of certain discs remained on bookshelves and in basements or lingered on the platters of aging phonographs in foyers and flea markets.

But by the 1970s, Les Artistes Arabes Associés (AAA), a label run in Paris by the Algerian impresario Ahmed Hachlef, the former artistic director for Pathé in North Africa, began rereleasing the original Pathé recordings of artists like Salim Halali and Samy Elmaghribi on LP, 45, and cassette. For Elmaghribi's part, he personally signed off on the six albums and many more singles distributed on AAA in France, North Africa, and elsewhere around the world. But much was missing, including all of the nationalist and a great deal of their popular repertoire. In addition, the Arabic-language spoken introductions, which had graced the start of all of his original recordings, as had been the tradition in North Africa since the industry's start, were now excised. Notwithstanding his producer's best intentions, Elmaghribi's output had been condensed to a fraction of what it once was and in many ways lacked its provenance and context. Given the continued and dramatic expansion of the North African recording industry, the diffusion of cassette tapes, and the surging popularity of raï and its young artists, the market share and exposure of Jewish musicians necessarily diminished. Like history, the music business forgets, too.

In the age of the CD, the vinyl and cassette offerings made by AAA and others were transformed once again. In the 1980s, a CD series entitled "Trésors de la chanson judéo-arabe" (Treasures of Judeo-Arabic song) appeared on Mélodie Distribution in France. Each CD focused on one of a handful of Algerian and Tunisian Jewish artists and tended to feature four to six recordings originally made for the Paris-based Dounia label, operated by Tunisian Jewish musician El Kahlaoui Tounsi since the 1960s. Similarly, in the early 1990s, AAA, which was now also known as Le Club du Disque Arabe, released two volumes of what it called "Musique judeo-arabe." In the 2000s and 2010s, Buda Musique purchased the rights for "Trésors de la chanson judéo-arabe," redesigned the cover art, and added a few more musicians to the roster, including Elmaghribi and Halali. In this way, individual artists, whose releases spanned decades and genres, were reduced to their "Judeo-Arabic song," a category that never existed, whose contents stretched to no more than forty minutes.[14]

By the time I walked through the doors of an aging record store in Casablanca in 2009, I was too late. Or so I thought. But in Morocco, the varied guardians of physical music soon schooled me. There was a deeper past: buried in actual grooves rather than refracted through jewel cases. And it was still out there. This book is a product of that lesson learned. Soon, music-purveyors brought me behind counters to hold and behold older records not for sale. One tape seller, waxing poetic about musicians who were no longer, propped up a rickety ladder that led me to an attic where a box of old discs sat well preserved. A waiter at a café moved a sliding door over a midcentury hi-fi system to reveal a small stack of fragile discs from decades earlier. To demonstrate that these were the real deal and not plastic (vinyl), he flicked a lighter and brought the flame to the shellac. Like the Biblical burning bush, the record was not consumed.

In the late 1890s, Edmond Nathan Yafil was gripped by a fear that his music, shared among Jews and Muslims, was at risk of forever disappearing. Well aware that the endangered records of voices past, in this case, manuscripts, were still around but privately owned, he began to "knock on many doors and show an obstinate perseverance" in order to collect them.[15] More than a century later, I understood Yafil acutely. This time, the music of the first half of the twentieth century was at a precipice: the records dispersed around the globe and most of the musicians themselves gone.

One of the many doors I eventually knocked on was but half a mile from where I now live in Montreal. On the second floor of a three-story apartment building, I found an archivist the likes of whom I have never encountered: Yolande Amzallag, the youngest daughter of Samy Elmaghribi. For years, alongside a demanding translation business, she has preserved a lifetime of materials that her father and mother first packed hurriedly but carefully in Morocco in 1959, then sent by ship to France, and then across the Atlantic in 1968. Records, handwritten lyrics, concert ephemera, film, photos, a copy of Yafil's magnum opus (!)—everything was there—including the letters *he* had sent from Casablanca to Marseilles in the 1950s and from Paris to Casablanca in the 1960s, all of which he eventually retrieved. Contained therein was the story of twentieth-century North Africa: of Jews and Muslims; of nation building and nationalism; of crossing borders and thresholds; of dislocation and diaspora; of separation and loneliness; and of sounds extraordinary and everywhere. Like the music driving that history, its telling demanded collaboration, improvisation, and, more often than not, being in the right place at the right time.

As this book has endeavored to make clear, every record tells a story. In tracing the trajectories of but a sampling of musical figures and their sounds, I have recorded a different history of North Africa and the Jewish-Muslim past there through a history of music itself. This approach has allowed us to situate the early twentieth-century Algerian impresario Edmond Nathan Yafil not solely in relation to his French citizenship and not only as a bridge to an earlier moment but as a sonic nation-builder who established an industry dedicated to Arab music's future by grounding it in a working-class Jewish base. It has also permitted us to tease out the popular sounds of North African modernity in the interwar period and the women who gave voice to them. In coming to a focus on Habiba Messika, the very embodiment of the era, we have also been able to identify her as a nationalist, whose coveted records, subject to censorship due to their politics and popularity, would prove consequential for what could be heard in the region for years to come. In similar fashion, a methodology focused on musicians and their output has granted us a rare opportunity to listen into World War II and for its impact on Jews, Muslims, and the musical culture of a critical period. At the same time, it has enabled us to reanimate the postwar life of figures like Samy Elmaghribi, whose voice brought Moroccan Jews and Muslims together in the push for his country's independence and inspired Algerians in the quest for theirs, well after Jews and Muslims were supposed to have gone their separate ways. Finally, in cupping our ears to the early postcolonial period, we have been afforded the opportunity to get a better sense of the living memory of Jewish recording artists and their music in North Africa before what we might consider their curtain call. There are other takeaways here as well. With sound, music, and records, class surfaces time and again, cities and regions thought previously unconnected are connected, women quite literally take center stage, forms of nationalism outside of political party manifest themselves, and social dynamics are better understood.

The question that remains now is whether all of this should somehow be treated as exceptional. To do so, I believe, is to silence. It is to silence the musicians, each a world unto themselves and only a fraction of whom were mentioned in the previous pages and chapters. It is to silence their vast audiences, the large numbers of historical actors for whom we are so invested in better comprehending. It is to silence their music and the meaning of that music, nationalist and otherwise but always of consequence, which set hearts aflame and continues to do so in profane and sacred spaces alike. Music, after all, is "what makes a society [ . . . ] move, tick, create, cohere."[16]

To be sure, this book is a history not of political culture but culture as politics, a history that sounds different from its devocalized analogues, but one that resonates deep into the present and may very well change how we think about the past.

# NOTES

## Introduction

1. Castel, *Je pose soixante-quinze*, 311.

2. Much of the literature on Andalusian music in early to mid-twentieth century North Africa focuses on specific national contexts. On Morocco, see, e.g., Davila, *Andalusian Music of Morocco*; Schuyler, "Moroccan Andalusian Music," 33–43; and Chottin, *Tableau de la musique Marocaine*. On Algeria, see, e.g., Glasser, *Lost Paradise*; Serri, *Chants andalous*; Saidani, *La musique du constantinois*; Merdaçi, *Dictionnaire des musiques et des musiciens de Constantine*; and Bouzar-Kasbadji, *L'émergence artistique algérienne au XXe siècle*. On Tunisia, see, e.g., Davis, *Ma'lūf: Reflections*; El-Mahdi and Marzuqi, *Al-Ma'had al-rashidi li-l-musiqa al-tunisiyya*; Rizqi, *Al-Aghani al-tunisiyya*; and D'Erlanger, *La musique arabe*. On Libya, see Ciantar, *Ma'lūf in Contemporary Libya*. For North Africa–wide approaches, see Shannon, *Performing al-Andalus*; Langlois, "Music and Politics in North Africa," 207–27; Reynolds, "Musical 'Membrances of Medieval Muslim Spain," 229–62; Poché, *La musique arabo-andalouse*; *Le chant arabo-andalou*, ed. Marouf; and Guettat, *La musique classique du Maghreb*.

3. On raï, see, e.g., Swedenburg, "On the Origins of Pop Rai," 7–34; Daoudi and Miliani, *L'Aventure du raï*; Schade-Poulsen, *Men and Popular Music in Algeria*; and Virolle, *La chanson raï*.

4. "Contrat," February 27, 1952, Samy Elmaghribi archive (hereafter SEA).

5. Raphael Levy, "El Maghribi à la place des arts," *La Voix sepharade–Montréal*, June–July 1978, 11, SEA.

6. Hachlef and Hachlef, *Anthologie de la musique arabe*, 215.

7. Bachetarzi, *Mémoires, 1919–1939*, 356.

8. See reference for "El hay ram gadol ashira" (track 13), *Sacred Music of the Moroccan Jews. From the Paul Bowles Collection*, Rounder Select 82161-5087-2, edited with notes by Edwin Seroussi (2000), n.p.

9. Castel, *Je pose soixante-quinze*, 310.

10. Yafil, *Majmuʿ*.

11. Yafil, *Majmuʿ*.

12. Shannon, *Performing al-Andalus*, 35; Davila, *Andalusian Music of Morocco*, 295. On the myth-making around Ziryab, see also Reynolds, "Al-Maqqarī's Ziryab," 155–68.

13. Shiloah, "Al-Manṣūr al-Yahūdī," 679.

14. Shiloah, "Al-Manṣūr al-Yahūdī."

15. Shannon, *Performing al-Andalus*, 38.

16. Glasser, *Lost Paradise*, 85.

17. See, e.g., Davila, "Andalusi Turn," 159.

18. On stambeli, see Jankowsky, *Stambeli*.

19. On the *diwan* and the Bilaliyya, see Turner, "The 'Right' Kind of Ḥāl," 113–30.

20. Davila, "Andalusi Turn," 154.

21. On the limits of the Crémieux Decree, see Stein, *Saharan Jews*.

22. Memmi, *Colonizer and the Colonized*, 13.

23. Memmi, *Colonizer and the Colonized*, 15.

24. On Yafil, see Glasser, "Edmond Yafil and Andalusi Musical Revival," 671–92.

25. For a central text on the "modern girl," see *The Modern Girl around the World*, ed. Weinbaum et al.

26. Audisio, "Enregistrements algériens," 57.

27. Scales, "Subversive Sound," 384–417.

28. Bachetarzi, *Mémoires*, 1:155.

29. On the impact of World War II on North African Jewish political subjectivities, see Heckman, *The Sultan's Communists*.

30. Gottreich and Schroeter, introduction, *Jewish Culture and Society in North Africa*, ed. Gottreich and Schroeter, 16.

31. Seroussi, "Music: Muslim-Jewish Sonic Encounters," 429–48.

32. Thanks is due to Sami Everett and Rebekah Vince for first coming up with a similar formulation and then imploring me to speak on the matter during a 2019 workshop at the Camargo Foundation in Cassis, France.

33. On the recording industry in MENA, see Racy, "Record Industry and Egyptian Traditional Music," 23–48; Moussali, "Les premiers enregistrements"; and Hachlef and Hachlef, *Anthologie de la musique arabe*. To date, the global history of the recording industry has yet to be written.

34. For a parallel example, see Jones, *Yellow Music*.

35. See, e.g., Starr, *Togo Mizrahi and the Making of Egyptian Cinema*; Gitre, *Acting Egyptian*; Reynolds, *A City Consumed*; Fahmy, *Ordinary Egyptians*; and Armbrust, *Mass Culture and Modernism in Egypt*.

36. On popular music in early twentieth-century MENA, see, e.g., Fahmy, *Street Sounds*; Davis, "Jews, Women and the Power to Be Heard, 187–206; Armbrust, "Formation of National Culture in Egypt," 155–80; Danielson, *Voice of Egypt*; Dougherty, "Badia Masabni, Artiste and Modernist," 243–68; Sakli, "La chanson tunisienne"; and Lagrange, "Musiciens et poètes en Égypte."

37. See, e.g., Heckman, *The Sultan's Communists*; Sternfeld, *Between Iran and Zion*; Marglin, *Across Legal Lines*; Katz, *Burdens of Brotherhood*; Le Foll-Luciani, *Les juifs algériens*; Boum, *Memories of Absence*; Bashkin, *New Babylonians*; and Beinin, *Dispersion of Egyptian Jewry*.

38. Seroussi, "Music: The 'Jew' of Jewish Studies," 3.

39. The question here is of the integration of music into MENA historical scholarship. It needs to be mentioned, however, that studies specifically dedicated to sound and radio in the region in the early to mid-twentieth century have grown in recent years. See, e.g., Abbani, "Beirut's Musical Scene," 54–77; Mestyan, "Upgrade? Power and Sound," 262–79; Stanton, "*This Is Jerusalem Calling*"; Jackson, *Mixing Musics*.

40. Rath, "Hearing American History," 417.

41. Seroussi, "Music: The 'Jew' of Jewish Studies," 3.

42. See gharamophone.com.

43. See comment on "Elie Touboul dit Pinhas El Saidi—Istikhbar Zidane + Ya Saki Ou S̜ki Habibi (Columbia, c. 1928)," Gharamophone, https://soundcloud.com/gharamophone/elie-touboul-dit-pinhas-el-saidi-istikhbar-zidane-ya-saki-ou-ski-habibi-columbia-c-1928.

44. Schafer, *Soundscape*, 132.

45. James, *Beyond a Boundary*, 72, 71, 70.

46. Ross, *The Rest Is Noise*, 61, xv.

## Chapter 1: The Birth of the Recording Industry in North Africa

1. On the activities of Dillnutt and other sound engineers, see Kelly, Gramophone Company Matrix Series 1898–1932.

2. Unfortunately, Driss's full name still remains unknown despite the pivotal role he played in the early twentieth century Algerian recording industry and the music scene more generally. For biographical information on him, see Bachetarzi, *Mémoires, 1919–1939*, 91–94; and Wail Labassi, "Driss 'le flûtiste' (1878–1953)," *Le Groupe YAFIL Association*, http://yafil.free.fr/document_driss_flutiste.htm.

3. "Qum yassir lana al-qata'an" is performed today as an *insiraf* in the Andalusian suites (nuba, pl. nubat) of *mazmum* and *rasd ad-dhil* or as an *inqilab*, a repertoire distinct from but often attached to the *nuba*, in the mode of *sika*.

4. The lyrics are gleaned from Mahieddine Bachetarzi, "Ah ya m'allim (Yafil)," Gramophone K 2655, 1924. Personal collection of author.

Ah ya m'allim ya m'allim
Ah ya m'allim ya m'allim
Ah ya m'allim ya m'allim

Ya la la la
Ya la la la
Ya la la la
Ya la la lan.

5. On Andalusian music and the twin tropes of loss and revival, see esp. Glasser, *Lost Paradise*, and Shannon, *Performing al-Andalus*.

6. Letter from Alfred Clark to T. B. Birnbaum, September 9, 1908, EMI-UK, un-catalogued country reports, France 1906.

7. See Glasser, *Lost Paradise*; Théoleyre, "Musique arabe, folklore de France?"; Miliani, "Crosscurrents," 177–87; and Bouzar-Kasbadji, *L'émergence artistique algérienne*.

8. See Yafil, *Majmu'*.

9. For the printed texts in question, see Yafil, *Répertoire de musique arabe et maure*, and Yafil, *Majmu'*.

10. On criticism of Yafil's *Majmu'*, see Glasser, *Lost Paradise*, esp. chap. 5.

11. Yafil was appointed to the position in 1922. See Bouzar-Kasbadji, *L'émergence artistique algérienne*, 51.

12. Glasser, "Edmond Yafil and Andalusi Music," 673–74.

13. On the problem of sources and Yafil, see Glasser, "Edmond Yafil and Andalusi Music," 673–74; Théoleyre, "Musique arabe, folklore de France?," 116; and Bouzar-Kasbadji, *L'émergence artistique algérienne*, 12.

14. Bouzar-Kasbadji, *L'émergence artistique algérienne*, 44.

15. See Glasser, *Lost Paradise*, 139; Miliani, "Le cheikh et le phonographe," 44–45; Bouzar-Kasbadji, *L'émergence artistique algérienne*, 53.

16. The few works that treat the recording industry in North Africa include Ouijjani, "Le fonds de disques"; Miliani, "Le cheikh et le phonographe," 43–67; Hachlef and Hachlef, *Anthologie de la musique arabe*; and Moussali, "Les premiers enregistrements."

17. Glasser, *Lost Paradise*, 135. Chez Maklouf was well regarded and received considerable coverage in the press. For an evocative description of the restaurant, see J. Ter-zualli, "Types Algériens: Chez Maklouf," *Les clochettes algériennes et tunisiennes: journal littéraire, humoristique et commercial, paraissant le dimanche*, June 7, 1903, 5–6, https://gallica.bnf.fr/ark:/12148/bpt6k51423267?rk=42918;4.

18. Glasser, *Lost Paradise*, 135.

19. See Mahieddine Bachetarzi, "Texte de la causerie de Mr: Mahieddine Bachetarzi à l'occasion du Séminaire National sur la Musique Souvenirs sur les vieux Musiciens d'Alger," ca. 1974, 5, http://data.over-blog-kiwi.com/1/21/68/62/20170206/ob_236e8b_causerie-mahieddine-bachetarzi-1964.PDF.

20. Bachetarzi, "Texte de la causerie," 5.

21. See, e.g., McDougall, *History of Algeria*; *Histoire de l'Algérie à la période coloniale*, ed. Bouchène et al.; Brower, *Desert Named Peace*; and Julien, *Histoire de l'Algérie contemporaine*.

22. Brower, *Desert Named Peace*, 15.

23. For an excellent synthesis on Emir Abdelkader, see McDougall, *History of Algeria*, 58–72.

24. McDougall, *History of Algeria*, 89–100, 77–85, 77–85.

25. Brower, *Desert Named Peace*, 4.

26. Schreier, *Arabs of the Jewish Faith*, 51.

27. Schreier, *Arabs of the Jewish Faith*, 51. On the consistory system, see Hyman, *Jews of Modern France*, 53–76.

28. Hyman, *Jews of Modern France*, 82. On the consistorial connections between France and Algeria, see as well Leff, *Sacred Bonds of Solidarity*.

29. Schreier, *Arabs of the Jewish Faith*, 176. It needs to be recalled that the Crémieux Decree was legislated rather than a voluntary measure. On Jewish resistance to the legal injunction, see Friedman, *Colonialism and After*, esp. 10, and Schreier, *Arabs of the Jewish Faith*, esp. 143–76.

30. McDougall, *History of Algeria*, 118–28.

31. Schreier, *Arabs of the Jewish Faith*, 8.

32. On European settler anti-Semitism in Algeria, see Roberts, *Citizenship and Antisemitism*, and esp. 80–110.

33. Roberts, *Citizenship and Antisemitism*, 95.

34. "Lettres d'Algérie," *Le Temps*, February 5, 1898, n.p., https://gallica.bnf.fr/ark:/12148/bpt6k235511r?rk=21459;2.

35. "Naissance de Martial Maklouf Yafil," May 31, 1898, Archives nationales d'outre mer (hereafter ANOM), État civil, Alger, Algérie, http://anom.archivesnationales.culture.gouv.fr/caomec2/osd.php?territoire=ALGERIE&acte=938443.

36. Sfindja and Seror began performing together no later than the early 1890s and probably earlier. See "Échos Algériens," *Patriote Algérien*, April 19, 1891, n.p., https://gallica.bnf.fr/ark:/12148/bpt6k6231567q.item.

37. Glasser, *Lost Paradise*, 136.

38. Bachetarzi, "Texte de la causerie," 6.

39. See Yafil, "La musique arabe," *La Dépêche algérienne*, October 1, 1927, 3.

40. See "Rouanet, Jules (1858–1944)," Notice de personne, Bibliothèque Nationale de France (hereafter BNF) General Catalogue, https://catalogue.bnf.fr/ark:/12148/cb103294998.

41. On the Petit Athénée school, see Théoleyre, "Musique arabe, folklore de France?," 111–13.

42. Yafil, "La musique arabe," 3.

43. Yafil, *Répertoire de musique arabe et maure*. At least twenty-seven installments of the *Répertoire* were published. Numbers 26 and 27 were authored by Yafil alone. See Glasser, *Lost Paradise*, 137–39.

44. Yafil, *Répertoire de musique arabe et maure*, made repeated reference to saving Andalusian music from "oblivion." See Glasser, *Lost Paradise*, 137–39.

45. Roberts, *Citizenship and Antisemitism*.

46. Yafil, *Répertoire de musique arabe et maure*. As Todd Shepard has reminded us, Algerian Jews, despite their French citizenship, remained a distinct category in colonial censuses until 1931. See Shepard, *Invention of Decolonization*, 35.

47. Yafil, *Répertoire de musique arabe et maure*.

48. Yafil, *Majmu'*, 1904.

49. Yafil, *Diwan al-aghani min kalam al-andalus*. Here I employ the English translation offered by Glasser.

50. Yafil, *Majmu'*.

51. Glasser, "Edmond Yafil and Andalusi Music," 675.

52. See Glasser, *Lost Paradise*, 161.

53. Glasser, *Lost Paradise*, 159. For the original French, see Desparmet, *La poésie arabe actuelle*, 440.

54. Desparmet, *La poésie arabe actuelle*, 27.

55. On Yafil's studies at the Lycée d'Alger, see Bachetarzi, "Texte de la causerie," 6.

56. See, e.g., Yafil's *Diwan*, held in the Kiev Judaica Collection at Gelman Library Special Collections, The George Washington University.

57. "Diwan Yafil," *Portail du Patrimoine Culturel Algérien*, http://patrimoineculturel algerien.com/ecole.html?ecole=1&id=undefined.

58. On Bouali and Maqshish, see Glasser, *Lost Paradise*, esp. 132–35.

59. "Cylindres enregistrés pour phonographes et graphophones: catalogue general," Compagnie Française du Gramophone, January 1, 1901, https://perso.crans.org/ ~woessner/catalogue.html.

60. On Emile Berliner's invention of the disc, see Read and Welch, *From Tin Foil to Stereo*, 119–36.

61. On the competition between Thomas Edison's cylinder and Emile Berliner's disc, see Read and Welch, *From Tin Foil to Stereo*, 151–76.

62. Document #68861, November 25, 1902, EMI-UK, uncatalogued country reports, France 1902.

63. This type of division had its precedent in the race to patent phonograph technology in the United States and then around the world at the very end of the nineteenth century. See Read and Welch, *From Tin Foil to Stereo*, 139.

64. Document #55960, September 19, 1902, EMI-UK, uncatalogued country reports, France 1902.

65. Document #36475, October 29, 1906, EMI-UK, uncatalogued country reports, France 1906.

66. Document #25836, April 24, 1906, EMI-UK, uncatalogued country reports, France 1906.

67. Document #34936, October 1, 1906, EMI-UK, uncatalogued country reports, France 1906.

68. Document #34936, October 1, 1906, EMI-UK, uncatalogued country reports, France 1906.

69. Document #36475, October 29, 1906, EMI-UK, uncatalogued country reports, France 1906.

70. Letter from Clark to Birnbaum, September 9, 1908.

71. See *Le Radical*, November 16, 1905, n.p., https://gallica.bnf.fr/ark:/12148/bpt6k5095786z/. The cylinders were sold from Yafil's home office at 24 rue Bab-El-Oued, which also served as a recording studio. Interestingly, a Spaniard by the name of J. Chelpi, who was also engaged in recording activities at that time, is attached to the advertisement and the address. Finally, it should be noted that among Yafil's first cylinder recordings were selections of Hebrew paraliturgy performed by Elie Narboni of the Grand Synagogue of Algiers.

72. Clark to Birnbaum, September 9, 1908.

73. For the Moroccan case, see Marglin, *Across Legal Lines*; Schroeter, *Merchants of Essaouira*.

74. Clark to Birnbaum, September 9, 1908.

75. Jules Rouanet, "La musique arabe," *Bulletin de la Société de géographie d'Alger et de l'Afrique du nord*, 9e année, 2e trimestre (1905): 327.

76. Of course, early records, intended to safeguard specific music or voices, did not necessarily lend themselves to long-term preservation given their fragility and limited production runs. Many of the earliest recordings, for example, whether in North Africa or elsewhere, went missing not long after their initial release. Archival materials, after all, need to be stewarded. On the notion of preservation in early American recording, see Sterne, *Audible Past*, 287–334.

77. Eden and Anker also began recording in Tunisia at this time.

78. In the scholarship on Yafil, there has been a claim that Rouanet also served as an artistic director for Gramophone in Algeria, although I have seen no evidence that he served in this capacity. I believe this may stem from an error in Hachlef and Hachlef, in which "orchestration Rouanet et Yafil" is misidentified as "orchestre Rouanet et Yafil." See Hachlef and Hachlef, *Anthologie de la musique arabe*, 288.

79. Clark to Birnbaum, September 9, 1908.

80. On Disque Yafil records, the Odeon moniker was relegated to a smaller font just below Yafil's name. It is also of interest to note that the original design for Disque Yafil records featured a six-pointed rather than five-pointed star. See Chamoux, "Dépôts de marques phonographiques françaises," http://www.archeophone.org/rtf_pdf/Marques _phonographiques_inpi.pdf.

81. Gronow, "Record Industry," 263.

82. This practice dated to the very beginning of the recording era. Since cylinders, unlike discs, did not carry a printed label with company and artist information, an announcement was made instead. See Read and Welch, *From Tin Foil to Stereo*, 179.

83. I again borrow the translation of Glasser. For treatment of the text in question, see Glasser, *Lost Paradise*, 151–52.

84. Théoleyre, "Musique arabe, folklore de France?," 730–31, 121.

85. See "Pathéphone: Répertoire algerien des disques Pathé," 1912, BNF, Département de l'Audiovisuel, Service des documents sonores.

86. See the Hebrew language recordings (listed in Hebrew script) included in "Chant Arabe enregistrés à Alger et à Oran, 1910," Disques Gramophone, 1910, BNF, Département de l'Audiovisuel, Service des documents sonores.

87. For more on how acoustic recording works, see, e.g., Wurtzler, *Electric Sounds*; Morton, *Sound Recording*; Sterne, *Audible Past*; and Read and Welch, *From Tinfoil to Stereo*.

88. For a number of exemplary figures from China, see Jones, *Yellow Music*.

89. In rare cases, recordings were carried out over several double-sided discs to capture the entirety of a piece. Consider, e.g., Cheikh Zouzou's interpretation of the famed "Gheniët Ben Soussan," recorded in eight parts over four records for Polyphon in 1937.

90. See file 333135, "Nathan Yafil dit Edmond," *Société des auteurs, compositeurs et éditeurs de musique* (hereafter SACEM), April 11, 1914, also https://musee.sacem.fr/index .php/Detail/objects/59121.

91. See file 333135, "Nathan Yafil dit Edmond," SACEM, June 22, 1914.

92. See *Archives commerciales de la France: Journal hebdomadaire*, June 10, 1908, 755, https://gallica.bnf.fr/ark:/12148/bpt6k57955206.item.

93. See Englund and Lotz, "Online Discography," http://www.lotz-verlag.de/ lindstroem-mx-masterfile.htm.

94. Kelly, Gramophone Company Matrix Series 1898–1932.

95. Roger Hazan, son of Raoul Hazan, conversation with the author, June 25, 2018.

96. See "La Maison Bembaron et Hazan," *L'Afrique du nord illustrée: Journal hebdomadaire d'actualités nord-africaines: Algérie, Tunisie, Maroc*, May 19, 1928, 59, https:// gallica.bnf.fr/ark:/12148/bpt6k5851977778/f205.

97. "La Maison Bembaron et Hazan," *L'Afrique du nord illustrée*.

98. During the late 1920s, the French branch of the German Polyphon label began recording in Tunisia (as it did already in Algeria and Morocco) and Bembaron again came to hold exclusive concession—across North Africa.

99. Polyphon record sleeves made for Bembaron. Personal collection of author.

100. Polyphon record sleeves made for Bembaron. Personal collection of author.

101. Polyphon record sleeves made for Bembaron. Personal collection of author.

102. I thank Kasper Janse at the Pianola Museum in Amsterdam (Netherlands) for bringing the number and titles of the music rolls to my attention.

103. See "Répertoire TUNISIEN des disques Pathé, J. & A. Bembaron, 5. Rue Es-Sadikia—TUNIS, Concessionaires pour la Tunisie," Pathé, 1926, BNF, Département de l'Audiovisuel, Service des documents sonores.

104. Bachetarzi, *Mémoires*, 1:125.

105. See the series of letters between Yves Sicot, director of Political Affairs in Rabat, Morocco, and Théodore Khayat of the Baidaphon label: Centre des Archives Diplomatiques de Nantes (hereafter CADN) MA/200/193.

106. See letter from Khayat to Sicot, May 5, 1937, CADN/MA/200/193. Khayat states that in Paris, for example, Baidaphon records "distracted" Moroccans from more pressing matters.

107. See, e.g., "Politique Indigène," December 3, 1930, CADN/MA/200/193.

108. See "Enregistrements Algériens," Parlophone, 1930, ANOM/9x/24.

109. Electrical recording, which utilized the microphone instead of the phonograph horn, permitted far better musical fidelity and range. Intriguingly, Michael Denning has argued that the incredible amount of music recorded immediately after the advent of the electrical method, especially in port cities under colonial rule, made possible no less than the "decolonization of the ear" in capturing new, sometimes subversive sounds, and then connecting them with listeners laboring far from home in metropolitan capitals. See Denning, *Noise Uprising*.

110. For a French intelligence perspective on Rsaissi, see "A/S de la famille rsaissi," November 11, 1940, ANOM/15h/32.

111. See Miliani, "Le cheikh et le phonographe," 51; and Chamoux, "Dépôts de marques phonographiques françaises."

112. "A/S. enregistrement de disques arabes par la Société 'Electra' de Casablanca," October 22, 1935, CADN/MA/200/193.

113. Letter from deputy director of French Gramophone to headquarters, August 30, 1928, EMI-UK, uncatalogued country reports, France 1928.

114. Gronow, "Record Industry," 282, 283.

115. Bachetarzi, *Mémoires*, 1:110.

116. Document #4570, May 15, 1928, EMI-UK, uncatalogued country reports, France 1928.

117. See, e.g., Jean Coupet-Sarrailh, "A propos de la pièce de si Kaddour Ben Ghabrit, Comment la musique arabe fut suavée de l'oubli: L'oeuvre de M. Yafil, musicien, chanteur et éditeur algérois," *Le Petit Journal*, July 16, 1926, 1, 3, https://gallica.bnf .fr/ark:/12148/bpt6k629614w.

118. On the Rouanet-Yafil fallout, see, e.g., Miliani, "Déplorations, polémiques et strategies patrimoniales," 27–41; and Glasser, *Lost Paradise*, esp. 140–41.

119. Jules Rouanet, "La musique musulmane," *La Dépêche algérienne*," September 25, 1927, 3.

120. Cited in Glasser, *Lost Paradise*, 140.

121. Glasser, *Lost Paradise*, 140.

122. Edmond Nathan Yafil, "La musique arabe," *La Dépêche algérienne*, October 1, 1927, 3.

123. Cited in Glasser, *Lost Paradise*, 141.

124. As Glasser has shown, the editors at the publication *Notre Rive: Revue nord-africaine illustrée* turned the phrase on its head and accused Yafil of being little more than "a human phonograph" (see *Lost Paradise*, 141). It should be noted that Rouanet's accusation fits a paradigm. In Germany, playwright Bertolt Brecht made similar (baseless) accusations again composer Kurt Weill. See Ross, *The Rest Is Noise*, 206.

125. Jules Rouanet, "La musique arabe," *La Dépêche algérienne*, October 1, 1927, 3.

126. Bachetarzi, *Mémoires*, 1:107.

127. "Les obsèques de M. Ed. Yafil," *L'Écho d'Alger*, October 9, 1928, n.p., https:// gallica.bnf.fr/ark:/12148/bpt6k75812299/f1.image.

128. "Mr. Ed. Yafil," *l'Afrique du Nord illustrée*, October 13, 1928, 9, https://gallica.bnf .fr/ark:/12148/bpt6k5583775g/f19.image.r.

129. "Les obsèques de M. Ed. Yafil."

## Chapter 2: The Arab Foxtrot and the Charleston

1. *Wa-ʾalash ma tihinnitsh la taqulik l-mama.* See Cheikha Aicha La Hebrea, "Ma taqulash l-mamak," Pathé 58618, ca. 1930, BNF, Département de l'Audiovisuel, Service des documents sonores, https://gallica.bnf.fr/ark:/12148/bpt6k1310289m/f2.media.

2. See Simon Ohayon and Hazar Cohen, "Ma taqulash l-mamak," Pathé 58717, ca. 1931, BNF, Département de l'Audiovisuel, Service des documents sonores, https:// gallica.bnf.fr/ark:/12148/bpt6k1310212z.

3. Among them were Joseph Morjean, "Mamak," Parlophone 46.523, 1930; Madame Ghazala, "Mamak," Columbia GF 200, 1930; Madame Louisa "Al-Israʾiliyya," "Mamak Mamak," Gramophone K 4421, ca. 1930; Méââllem Et-Ouati el-ouahʾrani, "Mamak Mamak," Gramophone K 4213, ca. 1930, and Jojo (Fils de Saoud), "Ma taqulash l-mamak," Polydor 550067, ca. 1931.

4. See Lili Labassi, "Mamak," Columbia GF 262, 1930.

5. On Cheikha Aicha La Hebrea's career in Spain, see David A. Wacks, "A Moroccan Jewish Nightclub Artist Sings Sáetas to the Virgin in León: Aicha la Hebrea," posted May 4, 2020, *David A. Wacks: Research and Teaching on Medieval Iberian and Sephardic Culture*, https://davidwacks.uoregon.edu/2020/05/04/a-moroccan-jewish-nightclub-artist-sings-saetas-to-the-virgin-in-leon-aicha-la-hebrea/.

6. On colonial modernity, see esp. *Formations of Colonial Modernity*, ed. Barlow; Shin and Robinson, *Colonial Modernity in Korea*; and Jacob, *Working Out Egypt*.

7. The term "garçonne" originates in Victor Margueritte's novel *La garçonne* (Paris: Ernest Flammarion, Éditeur, 1922).

8. On the concept of the New Woman, a good starting place is *A New Woman Reader: Fiction, Articles, and Drama of the 1890s*, ed. Carolyn Christensen Nelson (Peterborough, ON: Broadview Press, 2001). On early twentieth-century feminism in Egypt, including the appearance of the New Woman, see, e.g., Baron, *Egypt As a Woman*; Russell, *Creating the New Egyptian Woman*; Badran, *Feminists, Islam, and Nation*; Booth, *May Her Likes Be Multiplied*; and Baron, *Women's Awakening in Egypt*. On feminism in early twentieth-century Tunisia, where much of this chapter focuses, see Clancy-Smith, "From Household to Schoolroom Women," 200–231; Mamelouk, "Anxiety in the Border Zone; Bakalti, *La femme tunisienne*; *Mémoire de femmes*, ed. Kazdaghli; Marzouki, *Le mouvement des femmes en Tunisie*; and Raccagni, "Origins of Feminism in Egypt and Tunisia."

9. Glenn, *Female Spectacle*, 4.

10. Glenn, *Female Spectacle*, 5.

11. Gontran Dessagnes, "La musique populaire musulmane en Afrique du Nord," *Liberté*, April 25, May 2, and May 9, 1946. Cited in Théoleyre, "Musique arabe, folklore de France?," 573.

12. Dessagnes, "La musique populaire musulmane en Afrique du Nord."

13. Barbès, "La musique musulmane en Algérie"; also cited in Théoleyre, "Musique arabe, folklore de France?," 540.

14. Barbès, "La musique musulmane en Algérie."

15. Some important exceptions include Silver, "Nationalist Records"; Miliani and Everett, "Marie Soussan"; and Davis, "Retelling the Jewish Past in Tunisia," 61–120; Davis, "Jews, Women and the Power to Be Heard," 187–206; and Sakli, "La chanson tunisienne."

16. Two works that do treat the role played by women in early twentieth-century Tunisian music deserve recognition: Alyson E. Jones, "Playing Out"; and L. Jafran Jones, "A Sociohistorical Perspective on Tunisian Women," 69–83.

17. See Glasser, *Lost Paradise*, 5.

18. On the conservatory in Rabat, see Pasler, "Teaching Andalousian Music." On El Djazaïria, see Glasser, *Lost Paradise*, and Bouzar-Kasbadji, *L'emergence artistique algérienne*. On La Rachidia, see Davis, *Ma'lūf*.

19. See Glasser, *Lost Paradise*, esp. 195–99 and 217–30; and Davis, *Ma'lūf*, esp. 71–90.

20. See, e.g., El-Mahdi and Marzuqi, A*l-Ma'had al-rashidi li-l-musiqa al-tunisiyya.*

21. See Guettat, *La musique arabo-andalouse*, 238; cited in Davis, *Ma'lūf*, 194.

22. Guettat, La musique arabo-andalouse, 238.

23. See "Pathéphone: Répertoire algerien des disques Pathé," 1912, BNF, Département de l'Audiovisuel, Service des documents sonores.

24. "Statuts de 1912 de l'association El-Moutribia," Archives de la Wilaya d'Alger, July 4, 1912, 1Z6/420; also cited in Théoleyre, "Musique arabe, folklore de France?," 117.

25. "'El Moutribïa,' Association amicable des anciens élèves de l'École gratuite de Musique Arabe d'Alger," Journal Officiel de la République Française, July 31, 1912; also cited in Théoleyre, "Musique arabe, folklore de France?," 115.

26. "Statuts de 1912 de l'association El-Moutribia."

27. "Statuts de 1912 de l'association El-Moutribia." On headwear and its symbolism in early twentieth-century Algeria, see McDougall, *History of Algeria*, 148–52; and Rahnama, "Hijabs and Hats," 429–46. On the fez in Egypt, see Jacob, *Working Out Egypt*, esp. chap. 7.

28. "El Moutribia," *L'Écho d'Alger*, October 20, 1912, n.p., https://gallica.bnf.fr/ark:/12148/bpt6k75744962.item; also cited in Théoleyre, "Musique arabe, folklore de France?," 114.

29. "Au Square de la Republique," *L'Écho d'Alger*, September 12, 1912, n.p., https://gallica.bnf.fr/ark:/12148/bpt6k7574466x.item.

30. Carlier, "Medina and Modernity," 63.

31. Carlier, "Medina and Modernity," 62.

32. Glasser, *Lost Paradise*, 181, 183.

33. See mention of the dancer Baya, "Nouveau théâtre," *L'Afrique du nord illustrée*, November 8, 1919, 14, https://gallica.bnf.fr/ark:/12148/bpt6k5585778b/f19.item#.

34. On Egyptian theater, see Cormack, *Midnight in Cairo*; Gitre, *Acting Egyptian*; and Mestyan, "Arabic Theatre," 117–37.

35. On the violence of the French conquest of Tunisia and some of the resistance it engendered, see, e.g., Ayadi, "Insurrection et religion en Tunisie," 166–75; Mahjoubi and Karoui, *Quand le soleil s'est levé à l'ouest*; and Dellagi, "Une campagne sur l'insécurité des colons de Tunisie en 1898," 99–106.

36. Lewis, *Divided Rule*, 1.

37. Perkins, *History of Modern Tunisia*, 45.

38. On the French educational initiatives in the early protectorate period, see, e.g., Clancy-Smith, "L'École Rue du Pacha, Tunis," 33–55; Sraieb, "L'idéologie de l'école en Tunisie coloniale (1881–1945)," 239–54; Arnoulet, "Les problèmes de l'enseignement," 31–62; and Bakalti, "L'enseignement féminin," 249–74.

39. On the Young Tunisians and early Tunisian nationalism, see Ayadi, *Mouvement réformiste et mouvements populaires à Tunis (1906–1912)*; Mahjoubi, *Les origines du mou-*

*vement national en Tunisie (1904–1934)*; Tlili, "Socialistes et Jeunes-Tunisiens," 49–134; Julien, "Colons français et Jeunes Tunisiens (1892–1912)," 87–150.

40. Ben Halima, *Un demi-siècle de théâtre arabe.* On theater across North Africa, see also Amin and Carlson, *Theatres of Morocco, Algeria, and Tunisia.*

41. Perkins, *History of Modern Tunisia,* 90. El Adab's full name in Arabic is *Al-Adab al-ʿarabiyya.*

42. In Arabic, *Al-Shahama al-ʿarabiyya.* Much of that same theater was performed and originated in the Levant and Egypt. See, e.g., Khuri-Makdisi, *Eastern Mediterranean,* esp. chap. 3.

43. Ben Halima, *Un demi-siècle de théâtre arabe,* 86. Al-Tarraqi's full name in Arabic is *Jawq al-tarraqi al-israʾili.*

44. See Kelly, Gramophone Company Matrix Series 1898–1932.

45. See "Pathéphone: Répertoire tunisien des disques Pathé," 1910, BNF, Département de l'Audiovisuel, Service des documents sonores.

46. See "117–16: Documents Divers, Annotations, Brouillons," Archives Ennejma Ezzahra, https://ennejma.tn/archives/fr/2015/07/11/117-16-documents-divers-annotations-brouillons/.

47. For foundational studies of the AIU, see, e.g., Rodrigue, *French Jews, Turkish Jews*; Laskier, *Alliance Israélite Universelle*; and Chouraqui, *L'Alliance israélite universelle.*

48. On the Damascus Affair, see Frankel, *The Damascus Affair.*

49. Heckman, *The Sultan's Communists,* 10.

50. See Sebag, *Histoire des Juifs de Tunisie,* 190.

51. As Sebag has shown, in 1931, e.g., only 22 percent of Jewish children attended AIU schools in Tunis. While he assumes that the remainder went to French public schools, no data are offered to substantiate that claim. He also mentions that the Talmud Torah continued to function. See Sebag, *Histoire des Juifs de Tunisie.* On the question of modernity and the AIU, see Marglin, "Modernizing Moroccan Jews," 574–603.

52. "Bulletin trimestriel des Écoles de Tunis," Alliance israélite universelle (AIU), no. 5 (Finzi: October–November–December, 1922), https://www.bibliotheque-numerique-aiu.org/viewer/alto/17552.

53. On the Bsiri family's origins, see Davis, "Time, Place, and Memory," 73. For Bsiri's acumen as a Hebrew teacher, see "Bulletin trimestriel des Écoles de Tunis," Alliance israélite universelle (AIU), no. 6 (Finzi: January–February–March 1923), https://www.bibliotheque-numerique-aiu.org/viewer/alto/17553. On his role as music teacher, see Journo, *Ma vie,* 72.

54. Bsiri, "*Al-qism al-awwal.*"

55. See, e.g., Bsiri, "Les Dernières Créations et 25 autres chansons égyptiennes" (Tunis: Imprimerie de l'Orient, n.d.), NLI, Rare Collection.

56. Bsiri, "Les Dernières Créations."

57. In Arabic transliteration:

Lillah sawt habiba idh annahu
fi-l-qalb awqaʻ min siham ʻuyuniha
la khayr fi ʻud bi-ghayr akuffiha
Allah yaksiruhu ka-kasr jufuniha

See "Istawanat Baidaphon, karwana tunis al-anisa Habiba Messika," Katalawg haziran 1928, held at Le Centre des musiques arabes et méditerranéennes (hereafter CMAM).

58. On the state of musical ecstasy known as tarab, see, e.g., Racy, *Making Music in the Arab World*; Danielson, *Voice of Egypt*; Shiloah, *Music in the World of Islam*; and Rouget, *Musique et transe chez les arabes*.

59. For the name of Messika's mother, see Jeanne Faivre d'Arcier, *Habiba Messika: La brûlure du péché* (Paris: Belfond, 1997). Faivre d'Arcier's historical fiction is based on interviews with figures like Messika's nephew and adopted son Serge Arrouas, her musical contemporaries like Raoul Journo, and scholars in France and Tunisia.

60. Khailou Esseghir recorded for labels like Pathé, Columbia, and Odeon. Sfez made an incredible number of recordings including for Anker, Eden, Pathé, and Odeon.

61. Jankowsky, *Ambient Sufism*, 141.

62. Messika's sister's name and year of birth are provided by Faivre d'Arcier, *Habiba Messika*.

63. One *Awlad Messika* record is held at CMAM and another is held at the Staatliche Museen zu Berlin.

64. Faivre d'Arcier, *Habiba Messika*, 11.

65. Machado, "Habiba Messika," 28.

66. Faivre d'Arcier, *Habiba Messika*, 25.

67. Ben Halima, *Un demi-siècle de théâtre arabe*, 161.

68. Faivre d'Arcier, *Habiba Messika*, 49, 56. Raoul Journo discusses listening to records at cafés and at the homes of neighbors in *Ma vie*, 71–74.

69. "Pathé, Supplément au Répertoire Tunisien," 1925, held at the Bibliothèque nationale de France (BNF), Département de l'Audiovisuel, Service des documents sonores.

70. Ben Halima, *Un demi-siècle de théâtre arabe*, 71–72.

71. See, e.g., Perkins, *History of Modern Tunisia*, 90–93; and Ben Halima, *Un demi-siècle de théâtre arabe*, 72.

72. Perkins, *History of Modern Tunisia*, 93.

73. Document no. 354, April 2, 1921, Archives nationales de Tunisie (hereafter ANT). Cited in Machado, "Habiba Messika," 142.

74. Document no. 2542, May 18, 1921, ANT. Cited in Machado, "Habiba Messika," 142.

75. For a good starting place on French reactions to Tunisian-Egyptian connections, see Perkins, *History of Modern Tunisia*, esp. chap. 3.

76. Document reproduced from ANT in H. Zramdini, *"Habiba M'sika, la Marilyne tunisienne," Le Temps*, May 12, 2012.

77. Ben Halima, *Un demi-siècle de théâtre arabe*, 72.

78. Cormack, *Midnight in Cairo*, 31.

79. For mention of one of Messika's concerts in Algiers, see "3e Gala du Ramadan, Devant le triomphe remporté hier par la grande et véritable vedette Mlle Habiba Messika," *L'Écho d'Alger*, March 13, 1927, n.p., https://gallica.bnf.fr/ark:/12148/bpt6k75837072 .item.

80. Criticism of Messika usually revolved around her playing male roles. See, e.g., Ben Halima, *Un demi-siècle de théâtre arabe*, 80. For an early reference to Messika's "soldiers of the night," see Abdelaziz Laroui, "Les soldats de la nuit (Une évocation de Habiba Messika)," *Le Petit Matin*, October 9, 1937; cited in Turki, *Abdelaziz Laroui*, 242.

81. Bourguiba, *Ma vie, mes idées*, 168–69.

82. Bachetarzi, *Mémoires*, 1:50.

83. See Arrouas, *Livre d'or*, 132.

84. The *rebaybiyya* recording in question is Habiba Messika, "'Ala bab darik," Pathé 18.507, 1926. On the song's provenance, see Jankowsky, *Ambient Sufism*, 141–42.

85. Habiba Messika, "Habibi al-awwal," Pathé 18.517, 1926.

86. In Arabic transliteration:

Ya layl, ya 'ayuni
Habibi al-awwal wa-Allah la ninsa
Habibi al-awwal 'umri la ninsa
Habibi al-awwal mahabbatu fi qalbi
La tatahawwal wa-Allah 'umri ma ninsa

Lyrics are gleaned from Habiba Messika's second recording of "Habibi al-awwal," Baidaphon B 86362, 1928, held by CMAM.

87. Wartani was inspired by Huda Sha'rawi, the founder of the Egyptian Feminist Union who first appeared unveiled in 1923. On Wartani, see Clancy-Smith, "From Household to Schoolroom Women," 216; and Raccagni, "Origins of Feminism in Egypt and Tunisia," 186.

88. For the "superstar" designation, see "Pathé, Supplément au Répertoire Tunisien," 1925. For the reference to Messika as "the star of the theatres" and the salary she commanded, see Ben Halima, *Un demi-siècle de théâtre arabe*, 80.

89. "Hafla faniyya kubra," Tunis, May 7, 1928. The handbill in question once appeared online but, like so much with Messika, has now disappeared.

90. For an incisive treatment of Um Kulthum, see Danielson, *Voice of Egypt*. On Mounira al-Mahdiyya, see Cormack, *Midnight in Cairo*, esp. chaps. 2, 3.

91. Raccagni, "Origins of Feminism in Egypt and Tunisia," 194; Clancy-Smith, Tunisian Revolutions, 23. For Haddad's publication, see *Imra'tuna fi al-shari'a wa-l-*

*mujtama* (Tunis: Dar al-ma'rif li-l-tiba'a wa-l-nashr, 1997). On Haddad, see as well Weideman, "Tahar Haddad after Bourguiba and Bin Ali," 47–65; and Zayzafoon, *Production of the Muslim Woman*, esp. chap. 4.

92. "Le Théâtre Arabe," *Le Petit Matin*, March 20, 1924, 2; cited in Machado, "Habiba Messika," 96.

93. The literature on Bernhardt is extensive. For recent works, see Glenn, *Female Spectacle*, esp. chap. 1; Roberts, *Disruptive Acts*; *Sarah Bernhardt*, ed. Ockman and Silver; Duckett, *Seeing Sarah Bernhardt*; Marcus, *Drama of Celebrity*.

94. Darmon, *La Goulette et les Goulettois*, 41. On Tunisian Jewish female body types, see Salamon and Juhasz, "'Goddesses of Flesh and Metal,'" 1–38.

95. For the Messika image in question, see Hamrouni, *Habiba Msika*, 8. For the corresponding photograph of Sarah Bernhardt, see Gaspard-Felix Tournachon, "Sarah Bernhardt, French actress, c. 1865," www.gettyimages.com, Hulton Archive, editorial #464427941, 1865, https://www.gettyimages.ca/detail/news-photo/sarah-bernhardt -french-actress-c1865-sarah-bernhardt-was-news-photo/464427941?.

96. Hamrouni, *Habiba Msika*, 8.

97. Arrouas, *Livre d'or*, 132.

98. "Pathé, Supplément au Répertoire Tunisien," 1925.

99. "Quelques-uns des artistes du répertoire tunisien de disques," Pathé, n.d., CMAM. For an example of a "Habiba Messica" sticker, see "Ana achakt (III), Messika, Habiba," Phonobase.org, http://www.phonobase.org/simple_search.php?Tout=Habiba %20&langue=fr&Ordre=&ligne=0&limite=1.

100. Tamzali, *Images retrouvées*, 72–74. Tamzali was the daughter of Albert Samama Chikly, Tunisia's first filmmaker. She was also Messika's neighbor.

101. "Habiba Messika 'Chikhat' réputée victime d'une vengeance, meurt après avoir été afreusement brûlée," *L'Écho d'Alger*, February 22, 1930, 6, https://gallica.bnf.fr/ark:/ 12148/bpt6k75852128.item.

102. Henry Bordeaux, "La terre africaine," *Revue des deux mondes*, May 1, 1930, 71, https://gallica.bnf.fr/ark:/12148/bpt6k4319480?rk=21459;2.

103. Bordeaux, "La terre africaine," 71.

104. "La grande vedette tunisienne Habiba Messika a été assassinée," *L'Afrique du nord illustrée*, March 8, 1930, 7, https://gallica.bnf.fr/ark:/12148/bpt6k5791286p?rk=214593;2.

105. "Habiba Messika 'Chikhat' réputée victime d'une vengeance," 6.

106. Eliaou Mimouni died on March 15, 1930.

107. For her obituary in the Egyptian press, see "Masra' mummithila tunisiyya," *Ad-Dunya al-Musawarra*, March 27, 1930, https://digitale-sammlungen.ulb.uni-bonn .de/ulbbnioa/periodical/pageview/7285738.

108. Dotan (Maklouf Nadjar), "Qinat al-artist Habiba" (Tunis, n.d., 5), NLI, Rare Collection.

109. Tobi and Tobi, *Judeo-Arabic Literature in Tunisia, 1850–1950*, 132, 133.

110. Tobi and Tobi, *Judeo-Arabic Literature in Tunisia, 1850–1950*, 146–47. I have provided the transliteration from the Judeo-Arabic below:

min yisabar nasha al-hazana
fi al-ladhi matat bi-ghayr ajil
min yisabar al-'ud wa-l-jarana
fi-l-artist al-ladhi tizatil
min yisabir ashab al-hana
fil-mughniyya al-ladhi tihabil
u-min yisabirni hata ana ghayrik
ya rabb al-basar

111. Asal, "Bayn Evar le-arev," 11, 36.

112. See the reference to Asher "Ashriko" Mizrahi in Yehoshua, *Yaldut bi-Yerushalayim*, 212.

113. Acher Mizrahi, "Qissat Habiba Messika," Parlophone B 81009, ca. 1930, held by CMAM; Ratiba Chamia, "Qissat Habiba," Baidaphon B 93749, ca. early 1930s; Flifla Chamia, "Mawt Habiba Messika," Gramophone K 4355, ca. 1931. On Flifla Chamia and her recording, see Christopher Silver, "Flifla Chamia—Moute Habiba Messika—Gramophone, c. 1930," Gharamophone, https://gharamophone.com/2018/02/22/flifla-chamia-moute-habiba-messika-gramophone-c-1930/.

114. Flifla Chamia, "Mawt Habiba Messika," Gramophone K 4355, "Fiche de Stocks—Arabes," Les Archives d'EMI-France.

115. Madeleine Cohen-First, conversation with the author, February 22, 2018.

116. Bachir Fahmy, "Habiba Matit," Baidaphon B 93580, ca. 1931.

117. Bichi Slama, "Surat Habiba Messika," Pathé X 65068, ca. 1931, held by CMAM.

118. Redouane Ould Chikh Elarbi, "Habiba Messika," Gramophone K 4412, ca. 1931. Half a dozen Moroccan laments to Messika are held at the NLI.

119. L. V., "Le théâtre arabe à Tunis," 537, 542.

120. L. V., "Le théâtre arabe à Tunis," 543.

121. L. V., "Le théâtre arabe à Tunis," 544.

122. Lagrange, "Women in the Singing Business," 227.

123. Lagrange, "Women in the Singing Business," 227.

124 L. V., "Le théâtre arabe à Tunis," 544.

125. "Columbia en Tunisie," 1931, held in the Collection phonographique du CNRS—Musée de l'homme, Le centre de recherche en ethnomusicologie (CREM), Paris, France.

126. See "Demandez à ecouter les disques 'Polyphon' enregistrés par la première super-vedette tunisienne LOUISA TOUNSSIA chez Bembaron & Cie, Agents exclusifs" (sic), *L'Écho d'Alger*, March 25, 1931, http://gallica.bnf.fr/ark:/12148/bpt6k7581666z/f8.item.r.

127. "Un grand gala artistique arabe à l'Alhambra," *L'Écho d'Alger*, February 12, 1931, http://gallica.bnf.fr/ark:/12148/bpt6k75816251/f5.item.r.

128. Abbonizio, "Musica e colonialismo nell'Italia Fascista (1922–1943)," 110.

129. "Columbia en Tunisie." On the debate on the haik in the Algerian press, see Rahnama, "Hijabs and Hats."

130. Perkins, *History of Modern Tunisia*, 104.

131. Raccagni, "Origins of Feminism in Egypt and Tunisia," 235. On *Leïla*, see esp. Mamelouk, "Anxiety in the Border Zone."

132. Mamelouk, "Anxiety in the Border Zone," 215.

133. Issues of *Leïla* are held by L'institut des belles lettres arabes de Tunis. I sincerely thank Morgan Corriou for helping me to acquire scans of the magazine.

134. Cited in Mamelouk, "Anxiety in the Border Zone," 215.

135. Louisa Tounsia, "Hukm al-niswan," Pathé X 55269, ca. 1931. See Christopher Silver, "Louisa Tounsia—Heukm Ennessouane—Pathé, ca. 1930–1931," Gharamophone, https://gharamophone.com/2018/03/29/louisa-tounsia-heukm-ennessouane-pathe-c -1930-1931/.

136. In Arabic transliteration:

Fi dunya ma ʿad aman
fi bali ma nwitu shi
Hadha takhir al-zaman
shufu kif ndimtu shi.
A-tiflat qassu shaʿrhum
hata nisa illi bi-rijalhum
Kul haja ila fi shawarhum
u-ma nakhfa ʿalaykum shi
Ma yʿadiyu kan kalamhum
wa rijalhum ma tahki shi

137. Lili Labassi, "Hadha takhir al-zaman," Gramophone K 3991, ca. 1928. Personal collection of author.

138. Joseph "Sosso" Cherki, "Al-Sharlistun," Columbia 17006, ca. late 1920s. Personal collection of author. The same version of the song was recorded by the artist Mohamed Abdel Aziz (who was possibly Tunisian) on Baidaphon and by the Egyptian duo Mary and Nina on Odeon.

139. Louisa Tounsia, "Ma fish flus," Polyphon V 45673, ca. 1935.

140. In Arabic transliteration:

Ma fish flus
ma fish kalam

ruh ya habibi
ah fi salam

kinik mabsut ya nur ʿayniyya
hubbik al-nas al-kulha
w-al-bint hatta tikun ghniyya
qulik taʿa ya salam

kan ʿandik min mal sirra
taadi dima al-ʿaisha hurra
hatta maratik taqbil dhurra
bilash arka, bilash khisam

141. My thanks to Cormac O'Donoghue for bringing this to my attention.

142. In the original:

Chérie, combien je t'aime
Nitakalimlik bikalam
ʿUmri, combien je t'aime
Kif tukhrij mil-hammam
. . . . . . . . . . . . . .
Viens chez moi un moment
Wahdi fi dar
Tu verras comment
Naṭfiyu hadhik al-nar
J'oublierai mes tourments
Ana bi ʿayunik al-kbar

Louisa Tounsia, "Viens chez moi" ("Taʿala ʿandi"), Polyphon 46147, 1937. Personal collection of author.

143. Ben Halima, for example, identifies her not as Jewish but as Italian (see Ben Halima, *Un demi siècle de théâtre arabe*, 86). For the memory of Taliana as Jewish, see Davis, "Jews, Women and the Power to Be Heard," 188.

144. Ben Halima, Un demi siècle de théâtre arabe, 86.

145. Darius Milhaud, "Chronique des Disques," *Art et décoration: Revue mensuelle d'art moderne*, October 1930, 8, http://gallica.bnf.fr/ark:/12148/bpt6k6106726z/f55.

146. "Exposition Coloniale Internationale," Disques Pathé, 1931. Personal collection of Claude Fihman in Paris, France.

147. In the original:

Où vous étiez mademoiselle
Kul yawm asal ʿalayki
Je vous aime, oh ma belle

Je deviens fou ma bayn yadiki
Ma parole d'un homme mademoiselle

. . . . . . . . . . . . . . . . . . .

Où vous etiez, mish sa ʾila fiyya
Mish ʿarifti illi habbitik
Kul yum, astana shwiyya
On dirait fou janib baytik
Ma parole d'un homme, mademoiselle

. . . . . . . . . . . . . . . . . . .

Nous allons prendre un rendez-vous
Shufi fusha très gentil
Allah maʿaki l'amour est doux
Vous êtes la seule dans ma vie
Ma parole d'un homme, mademoiselle

Lyrics gleaned from Dalila Taliana, "Où vous étiez mademoiselle," Gramophone K 4680, ca. 1931. Personal collection of author.

148. Dalila Taliana, "Où vous étiez mademoiselle," Gramophone K 4680, "Fiche de Stocks—Arabes," EMI-France.

149. See "Fiche de Stocks—Arabes," EMI-France.

150. See, e.g., Louisa Tounsia, "Mademoiselle," Polyphon 45634, ca. 1935, personal collection of author; Ratiba Chamia (Tounsia), "Où étiez-vous mademoiselle," Oum-El-Hassen 55.052, ca. early 1930s; and Fadhila Khetmi, "Mademoiselle," Baidaphon B 93016, ca. early 1930s.

151. "Gala oriental d'ʾEl-Moutribiaʾ à l'Opera d'Alger," *L'Écho d'Alger*, January 3, 1934, 7, https://gallica.bnf.fr/ark:/12148/bpt6k7583565t.item.

152. Favre, *Tout l'inconnu de la Casbah d'Alger*, 209, 210, 213.

153. Lucienne Jean-Darrouy, "Grande soirée orientale," *L'Écho d'Alger*, January 14, 1934, 4, https://gallica.bnf.fr/ark:/12148/bpt6k7583576m.item.

154. Jean-Darrouy, "Grande soirée orientale," 4.

155. Mac Orlan, *Le Bataillon de la mauvaise chance*, 43.

156. Mac Orlan, *Le Bataillon de la mauvaise chance*, 43–44. The Zouave battalions were light infantry units of the French army in North Africa and included many Jewish and Muslim members. The baharias (in Ar., *bahariyya*) were sailors. The working-class character of Ragabouche first appeared in Arthur Pellegrin's *Les Aventures de Ragabouche* (Tunis: Editions de la Kahena, 1932). Like the Cagayous figure popularized by Musette (Auguste Robinet) in Algeria, Ragabouche speaks the *patois* of working-class Europeans and inhabits many of the same spaces as his Jewish and Muslim counterparts.

157. The "virtuoso pianist" in question was Messaoud Habib.

158. Mac Orlan, *Le Bataillon de la mauvaise chance*, 45.

159 Mac Orlan,. *Le Bataillon de la mauvaise chance*, 45.

160. On the corporate mergers of record labels during the interwar years, see Read and Welch, *From Tin Foil to Stereo*, esp. chap. 27.

161. Bachetarzi, *Mémoires*, 2:165.

162. Bachetarzi, *Mémoires*, 2:165.

163. See Blond Blond, "Où vous étiez mademoiselle," Dounia 1267, ca. 1960s.

164. Mahdi and Marzuqi, *Al-Maʿhad al-rashidi li-l-musiqa al-tunisiyya*, 25.

165. As quoted in Davis, "Time, Place, and Memory," 50.

## Chapter 3: Nationalist Records

This chapter draws on material previously published as: "Nationalist Records: Jews, Muslims, and Music in Interwar North Africa." In *Jewish-Muslim Interactions: Performing Cultures between North Africa and France*, ed. Samuel Sami Everett and Rebekah Vince, Liverpool: Liverpool University Press, 2020, 61–80. Copyright © 2020 Liverpool University Press and the Society for Francophone Postcolonial Studies. Reproduced with permission of The Licensor through PLSclear.

1. "Note pour M-le Dr de la Sûreté," February 23, 1930, as cited in "Entre histoire culturelle et histoire politique: La Tunisie des années vingt," *Wathaʾiq*, nos. 24–25, Institut supérieur d'histoire du mouvement national (Tunis: Université de Tunis, 1998–99), 126.

2. Habiba Messika, "Al-Nashid al-watani al-misri," Baidaphon, B 086520, 1928.

3. Habiba Messika, "Inti suriya biladi," Baidaphon, B 086596, 1928. See Christopher Silver, "The Life and Death of North Africa's First Superstar," *History Today*, April 24, 2018, https://www.historytoday.com/miscellanies/life-and-death-north-africas-first-superstar.

4. Habiba Messika, "Nashid jalalat al-Malik Faysal," Baidaphon B 086530, 1928.

5. Habiba Messika, "Salam sidna bay tunis habib al-shʿab," Baidaphon B 086622, 1928, held by CMAM.

6. "Note pour M-le Dr de la Sûreté," 126.

7. "A/S des obsèques de Habiba Messika," February 24, 1930, as cited in "Entre histoire culturelle et histoire politique: La Tunisie des années vingt," 1998–99. *Wathaʾiq*, nos. 24–25, 122–23.

8. Hamrouni, *Habiba Msika*, 21.

9. "A/S des obsèques de Habiba Messika," 122.

10. The Europeans in attendance could have been "curious" French men and women, like those who attended the Louisa Tounsia concert described in chap. 2, or members of the Maltese or Sicilo-Italian communities. On these latter communities, see Clancy-Smith, *Mediterraneans*.

11. My sincere thanks to Reem Abdulmajid for bringing Messika's reference to "enemies" to my attention.

12. See, e.g., Wyrtzen, *Making Morocco*; Miller, *History of Modern Morocco*; Brown, "The Impact of the *Dahir Berbère* in Salé," 201–21; Halstead, *Rebirth of a Nation*.

13. Halstead, *Rebirth of a Nation*, 181.

14. For discussion of North African Jewish engagement with communist politics during the interwar years, see Heckman, *The Sultan's Communists*; and Le Foll-Luciani, *Les juifs algériens*. On Moroccan nationalist attitudes *toward* Jews between the two world wars, see Wyrtzen, *Making Morocco*, chap. 6; Kenbib, *Juifs et Musulmans au Maroc, 1859–1948*, pt. 2, chap. 4.

15. On approaching North Africa through the framework of a "horizontal axis," see Clancy-Smith, *Mediterraneans*.

16. The party's full name was al-Hizb al-Dusturi al-Hurr al-Tunisi (Parti libéral constitutionnel Tunisien).

17. See Erez Manela, *Wilsonian Moment*.

18. For a sonic and musical approach to the 1919 Revolution, see Fahmy, *Ordinary Egyptians*.

19. Perkins, *History of Modern Tunisia*, 85, 91.

20. "A/S des obsèques de Habiba Messika," 122–23.

21. "A/S des obsèques de Habiba Messika," 122–23.

22. "Propaganda étrangère par les phonographs," May 30, 1930, Centre des archives diplomatiques de Nantes (hereafter CADN)/MA200/193.

23. On Baidaphon's activities in Germany, see Rainer Lotz, "The German 78rpm Record Label Book," http://www.recordingpioneers.com/docs/BAIDA-TheGerman78 rpmRecordLabelBook.pdf.

24. On electrical recording, see Read and Welch, *From Tin Foil to Stereo*.

25. "Istawanat Baidaphon, karwana tunis al-anisa Habiba Messika." Similar letters were included in Egyptian Baidaphon catalogs. See Racy, "Record Industry and Egyptian Traditional Music," 39.

26. In Morocco, Algeria, and Tunisia, the French authorities regularly complained about the nationalist quality of Egyptian film and music. See, e.g., "Contrôle des disques de gramophone de langue étrangère," December 4, 1937, ANOM/GGA/15h/32.

27. Habiba Messika, "Baladi ya baladi," Baidaphon B 086405, 1928, held by BNF.

28. Habiba Messika, "Marsh jalalat al-Malik Fuad," Baidaphon, B 086473, 1928.

29. In Arabic transliteration:

al-mawtu yaladhdhu lana ma damat . . . sama'u l-haqqi ta'akhina
hubbu l-awtani min al-imani . . . wa-ruh Allah tunadina
al-haqqu lana wa-yadu l-mawla . . . tajri min fawqi ayadina
in lam yajma'na l-istiqlalu . . . fa-fi al-firdaws talaqina

fal-yanzil ghadabu sh-sha'bi 'ala . . . man yatasadda li-watanina
wa-l-tahya misr al-istiqlal . . . wa-l-tahya fiha al-wataniyya
wa-l-yahya al-sha'b ya'zizaha . . . shubban wa-filahu al-qirya
wa-l-yahya Sa'du wa-man ma'hu . . . wa-l-yahya dahaya l-hurriyya

30. "Activité des jeunes marocaines," May 16, 1930, CADN MA/200/193.

31. "Activité des jeunes marocaines."

32. "A.S. hymne chanté par des élèves du Collège Musulman de Rabat," May 30, 1930, CADN MA/200/193.

33. Halstead, *Rebirth of a Nation*, 71, 72.

34. Miller, *A History of Modern Morocco*, 123–24.

35. On "repurposing" the latif, see Wyrtzen, *Making Morocco*, 138–39. The translation of the latif is taken from Halstead, *Rebirth of a Nation*, 181.

36. Wyrtzen, *Making Morocco*, 144.

37. Halstead, *Rebirth of a Nation*, 170, 167.

38. "Activité des jeunes marocaines."

39. "Propagande anglaise," May 5, 1930, CADN/MA/200/193.

40. Foreign in this case meant non-French. "Propaganda étrangère par les phonographs," May 30, 1930, CADN MA/200/193.

41. Letter from civil controller of Rabat to director general of Native Affairs and Military Cabinet, February 18, 1931, CADN MA/200/193.

42. "Contrôle des enregistrements sonores," May 27, 1931, CADN MA/200/193.

43. "A/S de disques arabes," February 27, 1931, CADN MA/200/193.

44. "A/S introduction et vente au Maroc, de disques phonographiques," May 1, 1930, CADN MA/200/193.

45. "Introduction et vente au Maroc de disques phonographiques, May 6, 1930, CADN MA/200/193.

46. "Disques phonographiques," December 6, 1930, CADN/MA/200/193.

47. "Note pour Monsieur le Directeur des Affairs Indigènes au G.G.," January 26, 1931, ANOM/GGA/15h/32.

48. Halstead, *Rebirth of a Nation*, 181.

49. Miller, *History of Modern Morocco*, 129–30, 131. On Throne Day, see also Wyrtzen, *Making Morocco*, 161–62.

50. Miller, *History of Modern Morocco*, 135, 136.

51. Halstead, *Rebirth of a Nation*, 250.

52. "A/S Propagande par disques phonographiques: Disques subversif relatif à ALLAL EL FASSI," October 27, 1938, CADN MA/200/193.

53. "Propagande par disques phonographiques," November 2, 1938, CADN MA/200/193.

54. In Arabic transliteration:

Ya l-ghadi li-bilad al-ghazal
Idha laqit li ghazali
Qulu qulu mazal mazal
Ghayr ma yahla li
Lillah ya l-ghadi li l-sahra shuf li ghazal

Lili Labassi, "Lillah ya-l-ghadi li-l-sahra," Polyphon V 46.117, 1937. Personal collection of author.

55. Henriette Azen, "La Chanson de Bensoussan: Complainte Judéo-arabe à propos d'un crime passionnel survenu à Oran en 1889" (No publisher, 1996), 11–12. My thanks to Jonathan Glasser for providing me with a copy of this text.

56. "Columbia en Algérie," 1931, uncatalogued, CREM.

57. On al-Fasi and anti-Semitism, see Heckman, *The Sultan's Communists*, 42. On Labassi and al-Fasi, see also Silver, "Listening to the Past," 243–55.

58. "Propagande par disques phonographiques," November 2, 1938, CADN MA/200/193.

59. "Note de renseignements," November 7, 1938, CADN MA/200/193.

60. On hawzi and its relationship to the Andalusian repertoire, see Glasser, *Lost Paradise*, 102.

61. "Propagande par disques phonographiques," November 4, 1938, CADN MA/200/193.

62. "Disque subversif relatif à ALLAL EL FASSI," November 19, 1938, CADN MA/200/193.

63. "Propagande par disques phonographiques: Disque subversif relatif à ALLAL EL FASSI," November 18, 1938, CADN/MA/200/193.

64. "Propagande par disques phonographiques." November 18, 1938, CADN/MA/200/193.

65. "Propagande par disques phonographiques." November 18, 1938, CADN/MA/200/193.

66. "Propagande par disques phonographiques." November 18, 1938, CADN/MA/200/193.

67. "Disque subversif relatif à allal el fassi, November 12, 1938, CADN MA/200/193.

68. "Letter from civil controller of Casablanca to director of Political Affairs," December 9, 1938, CADN MA/200/193.

69. "Propagande par disques phonographiques: Disque subversif relatif à ALLAL EL FASSI," November 28, 1938, CADN MA/200/193.

70. "Propagande par disques phonographiques: Disque subversif relatif à ALLAL EL FASSI," November 18, 1938, CADN/MA/200/193.

71. "Propagande par disques phonographiques : Disque subversif relatif à ALLAL EL FASSI," November 18, 1938, CADN/MA/200/193.

72. Scales, "Subversive Sound," 399. On Bachagha Smati, see as well Miliani, "Crosscurrents."

73. Bachagha Smati, "Causerie faite par M. Bachagha Smati au cours de perfectionnement des affaires indigènes. Le disque en langue arabe," February 1937, ANOM/GGA/15H/32.

74. Scales, "Subversive Sound," 400.

75. The song, written by famed Iraqi Jewish composer Ezra Aharon (Azuri Harun), had become even more popular in the wake of King Faysal's death in 1933.

76. Smati, "Causerie." Miliani provides a slightly different translation.

77. Smati, "Causerie."

78. "Disque subversif relatif à ALLAL EL FASSI," May 21, 1940, CADN/MA/200/193.

79. "Ordre," May 30, 1940, CADN MA/200/193.

80. "Emission de Berlin de 17 h 30," July 9, 1939, CADN/2MI/791,.

81. In Arabic transliteration:

Arja' ya bin adam l-biladak
'alash baqi gharib?

Salim Halali, "Arja' l-biladak," Pathé PR 230, 1939. Personal collection of author.

82. Madeleine Louis-Guerin, "Arrivé sans chasseurs à Paris: Salim Halali, 10 ans plus tard, repart avec la voiture d'un sultan," *Le monde vu de Paris*, October 3, 1947, n.p.

83. See Laloum, "Des juifs d'afrique du nord," 47–83.

84. Laloum, "Des juifs d'afrique du nord," 56. For more on Au Petit Marseillais, see Katz, *Burdens of Brotherhood*, 69–71.

85. Bachetarzi, *Mémoires*, 1:358. In another rendering, Halali was discovered in a Moroccan restaurant in the Montparnasse neighborhood by a Mr. Finckel, head of the "Oriental" section of Pathé. See Louis-Guerin, "Arrivé sans chasseurs à Paris."

86. On El Kamal, see Hachlef and Hachlef, *Anthologie de la musique arabe*, 271–72.

87. On Iguerbouchène, see Miliani, "Diasporas musiciennes et migrations maghrébines," 155–69; and Ounnoughene, *Mohamed Iguerbouchène*.

88. On the Grand Mosque of Paris and on the surveilling of Muslims in interwar Paris, see Davidson, *Only Muslim*; and Rosenberg, *Policing Paris*.

89. Les Archives d'EMI-France, uncatalogued, "Fiche de Stocks—Arabes."

90. Scales, "Subversive Sound," 414.

91. For a later interpretation of the Halali lyric in question, see Aidi, *Rebel Music*, 321.

92. "A/S-d'un disque phonographique," May 26, 1939, ANOM/GGA/15h/32.

93. "Ordre," July 1, 1942, CADN/MA/200/193.

## Chapter 4: Listening for World War II

1. "Le cabaret oriental chez mahieddine sera transfere à partir de demain aux bains Nelson," *L'Écho d'Alger: Journal républicain du matin*, August 24, 1944, n.p., https://gallica.bnf.fr/ark:/12148/bpt6k7600693k?rk=4399163;2.

2. Abdelhamid Ababsa (1918–98) was a prolific Algerian recording artist who is known best for his patriotic songs. For a short biography of Ababsa, see Hachlef and Hachlef, *Anthologie de la musique arabe*, 233–35. Little by way of biography can be found on the Tunisian jazz pianist Aziz, who is not to be confused with the Algerian musician Abderrahmane Aziz and who also performed on August 25, 1944. It is possible that Aziz was a Tunisian Jew by the name of Edmond Rubins although this is difficult to verify. See Bachetarzi, *Mémoires*, 1:357. The dancer and singer Djamila hailed from Tripoli, Libya.

3. "Ce soir, à 21 h. 30, gala d'ouverture du cabaret oriental chez mahieddine, transfere pour le ramadhan aux bains Nelson," *L'Écho d'Alger*, August 25, 1944, n.p., https://gallica.bnf.fr/ark:/12148/bpt6k76006940/f2.item. While profiles now escape for acts like Aouaoueche, newspapers at the time needed do little more than supply her first name and diminutive in order for her to be recognized by the public.

4. It is likely that Bachetarzi supplied information about his concert to the press. This would mean that he was the one—and not a journalist with *l'Écho d'Alger*—who believed Halali had died.

5. Miller, *Years of Glory*; Heckman, *The Sultan's Communists*, esp. chap. 2; Simon, *Jews of the Middle East and North Africa*; *The Holocaust and North Africa*, ed. Boum and Stein; *Les Juifs d'Afrique du nord*, ed. Michman and Saadoun; Schroeter, "Vichy in Morocco," 215–50; Miller, "Filling a Historical Parenthesis," 461–74; Baida, "American Landing,"518–23; Kenbib, "Moroccan Jews and the Vichy Regime, 1940–42," 540–53; Boum, "Partners against Anti-Semitism," 554–70; Driss Maghraoui, "The *Goumiers* in the Second World War," 571–86; Slyomovics, *How to Accept German Reparations*, esp. chap. 6; Saraf, *The Hitler Scroll*; and Abitbol, *Les Juifs d'Afrique du nord sous Vichy*.

6. Corriou, "Radio and Society in Tunisia," 371.

7. Scales, "Subversive Sound," 388–389.

8. Corriou, "Radio and Society in Tunisia," 370.

9. Scales, "Subversive Sound," 388–389.

10. See Fanon, *Dying Colonialism*, 71; and Corriou, "Radio and Society in Tunisia," 371.

11. There is a relatively robust literature on Radio Bari's efforts in the Mediterranean. See, e.g., Asseraf, *Electric News in Colonial Algeria*, chap. 4; Marzano, *Onde fasciste*; Scales, "Subversive Sound"; Corriou, "Radio and Society in Tunisia"; Williams, *Mussolini's Propaganda Abroad*; Bessis, *La Méditerranée fasciste*; MacDonald, "Radio Bari," 195–207; and Grange, *La propagande arabe de Radio Bari*.

12. "Note sur la radiodiffusion et les populations indigenes d'Algerie," February 25, 1938, ANOM/15h/32.

13. Numerous reports made this suggestion including through the Vichy period. For an example, see "Organes d'information indigènes (Radio, cinéma, etc.)," February 22, 1938, ANOM/15h/32. On jamming, see Scales, "Subversive Sound," 405.

14. Scales, "Subversive Sound," 385.

15. Grange, *La propagande arabe de Radio Bari*, 171.

16. Ageron, "Les populations du Maghreb face à la propaganda Allemande," 14. See as well Baïda, "Maroc et la propagande du IIIème Reich," 91–106.

17. See Corriou, "Radio and Society in Tunisia," 386–387.

18. For an important evaluation of Axis radio in the context of Palestine, see René Wildangel, "More than the Mufti: Other Arab-Palestinian Voices on Nazi Germany," 101–25. Wildangel has noted, for instance, that for the minority of Palestinians who tuned into German radio, they did so only to listen to their "popular musical programs" (116).

19. See, e.g., *Radio araba di Bari: Pubblicazione mensile della stazione radio di Bari*, January 1938, AN/F/60/710.

20. Sarfatti, *Jews in Mussolini's Italy*, 156.

21. "Emission de Berlin de 17 h 30," July 9, 1939, CADN/2MI/791.

22. Corriou, "Radio and Society in Tunisia," 391.

23. Surprisingly little has been written on Allouche. See Silver, "Radio Tunis' Hebrew Hour"; and Hamli, "Allouche, Félix," 181.

24. "Projet d'organistion d'une heure hebraique a Tunis-ptt," late 1938 or early 1939, Central Zionist Archive (hereafter CZA)/A397.

25. As the linguist Keith Walters has written, drawing upon historian of Tunisian Jewry Paul Sebag, Arabic rather than French remained the dominant language for Tunisian Jews outside of the capital and its surrounds through Tunisian independence in 1956. In fact, as Walters shows, Sebag dates the beginning of the displacement of Arabic among Jews in Tunis to the end of World War II, far later than is often presumed. See Walters, "Education for Jewish Girls," 258, 269–70; and Sebag, *Histoire des Juifs de Tunisie*, esp. 253, 264.

26. "Projet d'organistion d'une heure hebraique a Tunis-ptt"; emphasis in original.

27. "Projet d'organistion d'une heure hebraique a Tunis-ptt."

28. *Catalogue général des disques arabes*, Gramophone, ca. 1931, ANOM/9x/24.

29. "Programme de la première émission," April 1, 1939, CZA/A397.

30. Among other activities, Joseph "Babi" Bismuth made a number of Hebrew language recordings for Pathé in Tunisia in the mid-1920s, including the Zionist anthem Ha-Tikvah. See "Répertoire tunisien des disques Pathé, J. & A. Bembaron, 5. Rue Es-Sadikia—Tunis, Concessionaires pour la Tunisie," Pathé, 1926, BNF, Département de l'Audiovisuel, Service des documents sonores. Throughout the 1930s, Bismuth and Fragi

Senouf served as paytanim at the Rabbi Messaoud El Fassi synagogue in Tunis. See Journo, *Ma vie*, 45.

31. Letter from Jacques Tebeka to director of Tunis P.T.T., April 21, 1939, CZA/A397.

32. "A Monsieur le Directeur de Radio P.T.T.-Tunis," April 28, 1939, CZA/A397.

33 "A Monsieur le Directeur du Poste, Radio P.T.T.-Tunis," May 16, 1939, CZA/A397.

34. Famille Fellous to director, Radio Tunis P.T.T., May 17, 1939, CZA/A397.

35. V. K. to director, Radio P.T.T.-Tunis, May 15, 1939, CZA/A397.

36. "Muslim Tunisian listener" to director, Radio P.T.T.-Tunis, May 15, 1939, CZA/A397.

37. *Ta'lil* literally means "entertainment" in Arabic. Mrs. Fargeon to director, May 26, 1939, CZA/A397.

38. Joseph Bijaoui to Mr. Secretary, June 7, 1939, CZA/A397.

39. "Heure Hébraique," June 17, 1939, CZA/A397.

40. Razlogova, *The Listener's Voice*, 9.

41. The interpretive translation of the title is taken from *Selected Poems of Yehuda Halevi*, trans. Halkin, 22.

42. My thanks to Edwin Seroussi for providing me with background on Riahi in Israel.

43. "Heure Hébraique," June 24, 1939, CZA/A397. The records referenced are Hermann Fleishmann, "Kaddisch," Parlophon 57041, 1928, and Darius Milhaud, "La Séparation, Chanson populaire hébraique," 4–32844, Gramophone, 1928.

44. "Heure Hébraïque du samedi 23 septembre 1939," n.d., CZA/A397/20.

45. "Heure Hébraïque du samedi 7 octobre 1939," n.d., CZA/A397.

46. "Heure Hébraïque de Radio-Tunis, samedi 23 mars 1940," n.d., CZA/A397. This transcript, like some others in the archive, may have been a draft of a final product. Nonetheless, crossed-out sections often made it to broadcast, albeit in a different order than the one initially proposed.

47. "Heure Hébraïque de Radio-Tunis, samedi 23 mars 1940," n.d., CZA/A397.

48. Other Sephardi communities recite "Mi kamokha," based on the Book of Esther, on the afternoon of Shabbat Zakhor, the Sabbath before Purim. Shabbat Zakhor is also sometimes known as Shabbat Mi kamokha due to the recitation of the piyyut on that day. Thanks again to Seroussi.

49. Administrative secretary of broadcasts, Radio-Tunis to Félix Allouche, May 9, 1940, CZA/A397.

50. "Rapport pour M. Charles Haddad, Président de la communauté Israelite de Tunis, et de la Fédération des communautés Israelites de Tunis sur 'La voix d'Israel,' Emission juive de Radio-Tunis," February 3, 1954, CZA/A397. Indeed, the last transcripts in the CZA before the postwar period date to May 1940.

51. Postcard in personal collection of author.

52. "Une 'diffa' en plein Paris," *Paris-Soir*, May 21, 1939, 6a, https://gallica.bnf.fr/ark: /12148/bpt6k7644450g.item.

53. See, e.g., the theater listings in *Excelsior*, March 14, 1940, https://gallica.bnf.fr/ ark:/12148/bpt6k4611295o.item.

54. See Théoleyre, "Musique arabe, folklore de France?," 446–48; and Glasser, *Lost Paradise*, 215. For the original report, see "Rapport sur les emissions musulmanes à Radio-P.T.T. Alger," April 1940, ANOM/15H/32.

55. Théoleyre, "Musique arabe, folklore de France?," 446–48; Glasser, *Lost Paradise*, 215; "Rapport sur les emissions musulmanes à Radio-P.T.T. Alger," April 1940, ANOM/15H/32.

56. Glasser, *Lost Paradise*, 215.

57. "Loi portent status des juifs," *Journal officiel de la Republique Française*, October 18, 1940, 5323. Also discussed in Théoleyre, "Musique arabe, folklore de France?," 452. On the anti-Jewish statutes in Algeria, see Simon, *Jews of the Middle East and North Africa*, esp. chap. 12; Roberts, *Citizenship and Antisemitism*, esp. chap. 6; Allouche-Benayoun, "Intermittently French," 219–30; Cantier, *L'Algérie sous le régime de Vichy*, esp. pt. 2, chap. 7; Abitbol, *Les Juifs d'Afrique du nord sous Vichy*; and Marrus and Paxton, *Vichy France and the Jews*, esp. chap. 5.

58. Corriou, "Radio and Society in Tunisia," 372.

59. Schroeter, "Vichy in Morocco," 219.

60. "Decret du 30 novembre 1940 portant statut des Juifs en Tunisie," November 30, 1940, AMAE/Vichy/P–Tunisie/8GMII/18.

61. Bachetarzi, *Mémoires*, 2:29.

62. "Communications diverses," *L'Écho d'Alger*, December 10, 1940, n.p., https:// gallica.bnf.fr/ark:/12148/bpt6k7586894h.item.

63. Bachetarzi, *Mémoires*, 2:29.

64. Castel, *Je pose soixante-quinze*, 17.

65. "Ordre," April 10, 1941, CADN/MA/200/193.

66. "Ordre," August 26, 1941, CADN/MA/200/193.

67. Schroeter, "Vichy in Morocco," 221.

68. "Note de Renseignements," August 5, 1941, CADN/MA/200/193.

69. Mamelouk, "Anxiety in the Border Zone," 25, 22, 257.

70. Much has been written on Richard Wagner, anti-Semitism, and his infamous essay(s), "Judaism in Music" ("Das Judenthum in der Musik"). For a succinct overview, see Ross, *Wagnerism*, esp. chap. 6. See as well HaCohen, *Music Libel against the Jews*, esp. chap. 5; Loeffler, "Richard Wagner's 'Jewish Music,'" 2–36; and Katz, *Darker Side of Genius*.

71. See, e.g., "L'oeuvre du Maréchal Pétain," *Leïla: Hebdomadaire Tunisien Independent*, année 5, no. 2, December 7, 1940, 7; and "L'organe des Juifs de Tunisie," *Leïla: Hebdomadaire Tunisien Independent*, année 5, no. 4, December 21, 1940, 2.

72. "La Radio," *Leïla: Hebdomadaire Tunisien Independent*, année 5, no. 4, December 21, 1940, 4.

73. On Albert Abitbol, see Christopher Silver, "Albert Abitbol and Gaston Bsiri—al-Bashraf al-Kabir [Sides 1–2]–Disques Oum-El-Hassen, c. 1930s," Gharamophone, https://gharamophone.com/2019/10/21/albert-abitbol-and-gaston-bsiri-al-bashraf-al -kabir-sides-1-2-disques-oum-el-hassen-c-1930s.

74. See, e.g., "Les airs synthetiques de l'Egypto-Tunisien," *Leïla: Hebdomadaire Tunisien Independent*, année 6, no. 6, January 8, 1941, 4.

75. "Musique et lieux communs," *Leïla: Hebdomadaire Tunisien Independent*, année 5, no. 5, January 1, 1941, 3.

76. Valensi, "Une conversation entre Raoul Journo, Jacques Taïeb et Lucette Valensi (juin 1999)," 215.

77. Mitchell, *Nazi Paris*, 38.

78. See, e.g., "Confidence d'une Turque," March 9, 1940, *Paris-Soir*, 4, https://gallica .bnf.fr/ark:/12148/bpt6k7644065j.item.

79. M. Delahaye, "La Propagande en pays musulman: Le cinéma et le disque de langue arabe," Exposé no. 47, December 22, 1941, AN/CHEAM/20000002/18.

80. M. N., "L'Ange du rythme: Débute de l'écran," *La France Au Combat*, October 17, 1946, BNF, département Arts du spectacle, 8-RK-18493, https://gallica.bnf.fr/ark: /12148/btv1b52505499b.

81. See, "Salim Halali en Algérie," Les Artistes Arabes Associés (AAA) 023, liner notes by Ahmed Hachlef, 1990; also reproduced in Hachlef and Hachlef, *Anthologie de la musique arabe*, 215. For a cinematic depiction of Halali's rescue, see *Les hommes libres* (dir. Ismaël Ferroukhi, 2008). The film, a work of historical fiction in which Algerian historian Benjamin Stora served as consultant, has been criticized by some historians and by members of the Halali family. For the former case, see Pierre Haski, "Benjamin Stora répond aux critiques des 'Hommes libres,'" *l'OBs avec Rue89*, October 4, 2011, https://www.nouvelobs.com/rue89/rue89-rue89-culture/20111004.RUE4731/benjamin -stora-repond-aux-critiques-des-hommes-libres.html, and for the latter, see Laloum, "Cinéma et histoire," 116–28. For scholarly works that have drawn on the Hachlef narrative, see, e.g., Katz, *Burdens of Brotherhood*; and Aidi, *Rebel Music*.

82. Hachlef and Hachlef, *Anthologie de la musique arabe*, 14.

83. Albert Assouline, "Une vocation ignorée de la mosquée de Paris," *Almanach du Combattant* (1983): 123–24, as cited in Katz, *Burdens of Brotherhood*, 272.

84. Assouline, "Une vocation ignorée de la mosquée de Paris."

85. Hachlef, "Salim Halali en Algérie." Curiously Hachlef's text has been reproduced many times but rarely (if ever) cited.

86. Katz, "Did the Paris Mosque Save Jews?," 259.

87. "A/S participation de l'Algérie au congrès de la musique arabe du Caire," January 22, 1932, ANOM/14h/41. On the Cairo Congress, see, e.g., Katz, *Henry George*

*Farmer*, *Congrès de Musique Arabe du Caire 1932, Édition intégrale des Enregistrements*, Jean Lambert and Pascal Cordereix, liner notes by Bernard Moussali (Paris Bibliothèque Nationale de France and the Abu Dhabi Tourism and Culture Authority, 2015); Racy, "Historical Worldviews of Early Ethnomusicologists," 68–94.

88. Interview d'Essi Kaddour Ben Ghabrit, ministre plenipotentiaire du Maroc à Paris, "Nadinnil" d'Alexandrie, April 5, 1932, ANOM/14h/41.

89. "Etablissements Nord Africains à Paris," April 23, 1941, Archives Départementales des Bouches-du-Rhône (hereafter ADBdR)/76 W 205. I thank Ethan Katz for sharing the ADBdR files with me.

90. See "Renseignment," May 10, 1941, ADBdR/76 W 205; and "Renseignment," May 20, 1941, ADBdR/76 W 205.

91. Hachlef and Hachlef, *Anthologie de la musique arabe*, 235.

92. "A/S d'une suggestions du Président de la Région Economique d'Algérie et Chef de la Mission Economique du Gouvernement Général dans la Métropole, tendant à la création d'un Service des Affaires Indigènes, à Paris," October 1942, ANOM/ALG/GGA/1h/40.

93. On June 8, 1942, El Kamal recorded six titles in Paris for Pathé corresponding to issue numbers CPT 5434 to 5439.

94. Laloum, "Cinéma et histoire," 124.

95. Laloum, "Cinéma et histoire," 124.

96. Théoleyre, "Musique arabe, folklore de France?," 463–64.

97. Bachetarzi, *Mémoires, vol. 2*, esp. 28–49.

98. "Soiree de la troupe Mahieddine, au Majestic, le dimanche 13 octobre," October 18, 1940, ANOM/ALG/GGA/9h/37.

99. On Soussan, see Miliani and Everett, "Marie Soussan."

100. "Représentation théatrale organisée au Majestic par la troupe Mahiéddine," October 14, 1940, ANOM/ALG/GGA/9h/37.

101. "A/S Chanson de Mahieddine," December 26, 1940, ANOM/ALG/GGA/9h/37.

102. For precise figures, see Cantier, *L'Algérie sous le régime de Vichy*, 132–34.

103. Cantier, *L'Algérie sous le régime de Vichy*, 132–34.

104. El Médioni, *Maurice El Médioni*, 69. El Médioni was the nephew of famed recording artist Saoud l'Oranais (né Medioni). In January 1943, Saoud l'Oranais and his thirteen-year-old son Joseph were arrested in Marseilles. Along with hundreds of others the two were sent to the Drancy internment camp. On March 23, 1943, the iconic musician, together with his child, were murdered at Sobibor. See Allouche and Laloum, *Les Juifs d'algérie*, 278.

105. El Médioni, *Maurice El Médioni*, 69.

106. El Médioni, *Maurice El Médioni*, 78.

107. El Médioni, *Maurice El Médioni*, 88. On the Bedeau Camp, see Slyomovics, "'Other Places of Confinement,'" 95–112.

108. El Médioni, *Maurice El Médioni*, 89.

109. "Mahieddine Bachtarzi à Monsieur le Sous-Prefet de Bougie," January 31, 1941, ANOM/ALG/GGA/9h/37. On Bachetarzi and Vichy, see Joshua Cole, "À chacun son public: Politique et culture dans l'Algérie des années 1930," *Sociétés & Représentations*, 2014/2 no. 38, 21–51; and Roth, *Le théâtre algérien*, 29–30.

110. "Mahieddine Bachtarzi à Monsieur le Sous-Prefet de Bougie," January 31, 1941, ANOM/ALG/GGA/9h/37.

111. "La Tournée Mahieddine, au profit des prisonniers de guerre musulmans," n.d., ANOM/ALG/GGA/9h/37.

112. "Les Tournées Mahieddine: El-Mechehah," n.d., ANOM/ALG/GGA/9h/37. Elsewhere in his memoirs, Bachetarzi uses "Samuel" as a stand-in Jewish name. See Bachetarzi, *Mémoires*, 1:134.

113. Cole, "À chacun son public," 46.

114. "Recueil des chansons Mahieddine, 1937," n.d., ANOM ALG/GGA/9h/37.

115. On the Blum-Viollette plan and its reception among Algerian Muslims and Jews, see, e.g., Katz, *Burdens of Brotherhood*, 105–9.

116. Katz, *Burdens of Brotherhood*, 104.

117. Unfortunately, only the French translation of the original lyrics has survived. "Dites avec moi: 'Vive le maréchal,' oui, dites avec moi: 'Vive le maréchal,'" n.d., ANOM/ALG/GGA/9h/37.

118. In French:

Nous étions sous le règne de la démagogie et de l'illusion
Nous sommes maintenant sortis de notre léthargie,
Dieu a confondu le menteur.
Les politiciens sont expulsée c'est le plus
valeureux des hommes qui est là maintenant:
Pétain

119. "Les Tournées Mahieddine: El-Mechehah," n.d., ANOM/ALG/GGA/9h/37.

120. "Rapport Special," ANOM/ALG/GGA/9h/37, February 13, 1941; and Cole, "À chacun son public," 46.

121. "Rapport Special," ANOM/ALG/GGA/9h/37, February 13, 1941.

122. "Pour Monsieur le Directeur du Cabinet," April 8, 1941, ANOM/ALG/GGA/9h/37.

123. See memo from Captain Wender dated November 4, 1940, ANOM/ALG/GGA/9h/50.

124. Memo from Captain Wender.

125. "Division d'Alger: Censure Théatrale," December 27, 1941, ANOM/ALG/GGA/9h/37.

126. "Propagande par conteurs," April 22, 1941, ANOM/ALG/GGA/9h/50.

127. Cole, "À chacun son public," 47.

128. Corriou, "Radio and Society in Tunisia," 376. Not all in his position followed the same path. As Corriou has shown, Radio Tunis announcer Abdelaziz Laroui "skilfully used the texts given to him by the [Vichy] propaganda department to spread his own messages" during his daily broadcasts.

129. Katz, *Burdens of Brotherhood*, 114.

130. See letter from Maurice El Médioni to Samy Elmaghribi, March 31, 1954, SEA.

131. Roth, *Le théâtre algérien*, 71–72.

132. "Soirée Mahieddine," February 7, 1942, ANOM/ALG/GGA/9h/37.

133. "Les Tournées Mahieddine," November 24, 1941, ANOM/ALG/GGA/9h/37.

134. In Arabic transliteration:

Ai yai yai yai yai yai yai yai
ʿala had zman washnu sar
dakhilat al-mirikan

Hocine Slaoui, "A-Zin wa-l-ʿayn," Pathé PV 97 (CPT 7120), 1949. The translation here is taken from Bowles, *Points in Time*, 68.

135. "Rapport: Propos défaitistes," April 27, 1943, ANOM/ALG/GGA/9h/37.

136. De Yacoub Cohen, "Khamus jana," NLI, Rare Collection.

137. On Operation Torch and Algeria, see, e.g., Katz, "Who Were the Jewish Underground of Algiers?"; Roberts, "Jews, Vichy, and the Algiers Insurrection of 1942," 63–88; Amipaz-Silber, *Role of the Jewish Underground*; Funk, *Politics of Torch*.

138. Schroeter, "Vichy in Morocco," 231, 232.

139. Simon, *Jews of the Middle East and North Africa*, 170.

140. On the distribution of candy by American forces, see Walters, *Silent Missions*, 52.

141. "À Monsieur le Consoul [*sic*] Général des États-Unis d'Amérique," March 31, 1944, Zohra El Fassia archive (hereafter ZEF).

142. See, e.g., "Grande kermesse de liberté," May 26, 1944, *Le Petit Marocain*, n.p., https://gallica.bnf.fr/ark:/12148/bpt6k4692178n/f1.image.

143. When Pathé rereleased Slaoui's "A-Zin w-al-ʿayn" as a 45 rpm record ca. 1960, the song started carrying the parenthetical title "Al-Mirikan" (The Americans). For the most in-depth treatment of Hocine Slaoui, see Bargach, "Liberatory, Nationalising and Moralising by Ellipsis," 61–88.

144. In Arabic transliteration:

farqu al-fanid fliyu zadu shwin-gum

u katru al-ghabra

wa-l-hamir

zadu al-bun-bun

hata min al-gayzat al-yawm sharbu rum

al-mirikan

tsma᾽ ghayr hokay hokay kaman bai bai

Bowles, *Points in Time*, 68–69.

145. Edwards, *Morocco Bound*, 59.

146. Bargach, "Liberatory, Nationalising and Moralising by Ellipsis," 73.

147. Mernissi, *Dreams of Trespass*, 183.

148. "Rapport: Propos défaitistes," April 27, 1943, ANOM/ALG/GGA/9h/37.

149. "Rapport: Propos défaitistes," April 27, 1943, ANOM/ALG/GGA/9h/37.

150. On the Judeo-Arabic songbooks in question, see, e.g., Guedj, "Post-Second World War Praise Poetry," 455–71; Tobi and Tobi, *Judeo-Arabic Literature in Tunisia, 1850–1950*; and Saraf, *The Hitler Scroll*. North African Jews also released songbooks and sheet music in French on themes like American liberation. See, e.g., the Algerian Jewish musician's Jean Bécache's "La première libération," ca. 1943, Collection Jean Bécache, held by Institut Européen des Musique Juives, http://media1.cfmj.fr/partition/extrait/P _S048/P_4846_EX.jpg; and the Tunisian Jewish recording artist and composer Youssef Hagège's "Consolation," 1944, Collection Youssef Hagège, held by Odysseo, http:// odysseo.generiques.org/medias/customer_28/pdf/FRGNQ_PM001_036/FRGNQ _PM001_036.pdf.

151. Hassine, "Megillat Hitler" (Casablanca, ca. 1942), NLI, Rare Collection; and Ben Shimon, "Haggada di Hitler" (Rabat, ca. 1945), NLI, Rare Collection.

152. Ben Simhon, "Qasida di Hitler" (Casablanca, ca. 1944), NLI, Rare Collection.

153. Y. B., "Qinat Hitler" (Tunis, ca. 1943), NLI, Rare Collection.

154. For the most complete treatment of the Judeo-Arabic songs of World War II and the Holocaust, again see Saraf, *The Hitler Scroll*.

155. Trabelsy was apparently twelve years old when he authored the song. See Allouche Trabelsy, "Ughniyyat al-madhlumin," (Tunis, n.d.), NLI, Rare Collection.

156. For one version of the song, see "Tayar jana ughniyya zamaniyya min akuda," April 14, 2018, https://www.youtube.com/watch?v=yWJ4vH47Xq8.

157. Cohen, "Khamus jana," 3.

158. The name "Khamus" derives from *khamsa*, the popular five-fingered amulet.

159. Cohen, "Khamus jana," 5.

160. In the original:

jab al-farina . . . shawkawlat bnina

fraq ᾽alina . . . Kanfit ᾽atina

jana khamus . . . Badal al-flus

waqt al-qadus . . . wa-bankat miliyana

sabun wa-sukar . . . shwin-gum wa-sigar

wa-halib maʿatar Amirikana

Cohen, "Khamus jana," 6.

161. In the original:

rusavilt dhawʾ al-ʿayn . . . digal wa-staline

wa-shurshil al-hanin . . . ansurhum ya mulana

Cohen, "Khamus jana," 7.

162. Journo, *Ma vie*, 171.

163. "Grande fête de fin du Ramadan," November 23, 1938, ANOM/2i/41.

164. In the original:

Ya hasra ʿala duk ay-yam, ya tarahum yaʿudu

Dhawʾuhum rjʿa dhilam

Wa-zaman dar maqsudu

Lili Boniche, "Marché noir," Pacific CO 7010, ca. 1947. Personal collection of author. The label indicates that the lyrics were written by Bachetarzi, although it should be mentioned that the attachment of his name to a project is not a guarantee of his authorship.

165. In the original:

Ai yai yai

Ai yai yai

Ai yai yai

C'est le marché noir.

Ai yai yai

Ai yai yai

Et nos clients

me paieront ce soir

166. In the original:

Ribika, rashil, wa-muni yaqulu ghayr

'Give me money,'

Wila ma shrash porte monnaie

yarjaʿ yasraf bil-milliyar

167. In the original:

Durk ki silaʿ rahi jat

Grace à Dieu a-dʿawa frat

Nahki l-awlad wa-l-banat

Cette histoire de marché noir

168. Samy Elmaghribi, "Al-Marché noir," Pathé CPT 6863, 1948.

169. The Jewish orchestra El Andaloussia would reemerge again only on April 14, 1944. "Société musicale 'El Andaloussia,'" *Alger républicain*, April 14, 1944, ANOM/ALG/GGA/9h/37.

170. "Mon colonel," November 9, 1943, ANOM/ALG/GGA/9h/37.

171. Valensi, "Une conversation entre Raoul Journo, Jacques Taïeb et Lucette Valensi (juin 1999)," 215.

172. Klarsfeld, *Memorial to the Jews Deported from France*, 10.

173. Hachlef and Hachlef, *Anthologie de la musique arabe*, 235.

174. See, e.g., Christopher Silver, "Salim Halali—Je t'appartiens (tango)—Pathé, c. 1945," October 23, 2017, Gharamophone, https://gharamophone.com/2017/10/23/salim-halali-je-tappartiens-tango-pathe-c-1945/.

## Chapter 5: Singing Independence

This chapter draws on material previously published as Christopher Silver, "The Sounds of Nationalism: Music, Moroccanism, and the Making of Samy Elmaghribi," *International Journal of Middle East Studies* 52, no. 1 (2020): 23–47. Reproduced with permission.

1. Correspondence, August 17, 1956, SEA.

2. Samy Elmaghribi, "Allah, watani, wa-sultani," Samyphone no. 8, 1956.

3. Correspondence, August 28, 1956, SEA.

4. For an exception, see Silver, "Sounds of Nationalism," 23–47. For other works that treat Elmaghribi, see Roda and Schwartz, "Home beyond Borders," 609; Seroussi, "Elmaghribi, Samy (Amzallag)," 165–66; and El Haddaoui, "Symbiose judeo-arabe au Maroc."

5. There is no shortage of first-rate scholarship on the Istiqlal and, to a lesser extent, the PNR and PDI. See, e.g., Stenner, *Globalizing Morocco*; Wyrtzen, *Making Morocco*; Miller, *History of Modern Morocco*; Zisenwine, *Emergence of Nationalist Politics in Morocco*; Zaki, *Le Mouvement de libération marocain*; Ghallab, *Tarikh al-haraka al-wataniyya bi-l-Maghrib*; Benjelloun, *Le nord du Maroc*; Joffé, "The Moroccan Nationalist Movement," 289–307; Ayache, *Le mouvement syndical au Maroc*; Laroui, *L'Histoire du Maghreb*; Waterbury, *Commander of the Faithful*; Halstead, *Rebirth of a Nation*; Rézette, *Les partis politiques marocains*; El Fassi, *Independence Movements in Arab North Africa*; and Julien, *L'Afrique du nord en marche*. For a recent study of the PCM and Moroccan Jews, see Heckman, *The Sultan's Communists*.

6. Miller, "Filling a Historical Parenthesis," 461–74.

7. Ait Mous, "Moroccan Nationalist Movement," 738.

8. Stenner, *Globalizing Morocco*.

9. Miller, *History of Modern Morocco*, 148.

10. Zisenwine, *Emergence of Nationalist Politics in Morocco*, 122.

11. Miller, *History of Modern Morocco*, 148.

12. Halstead goes as far as to say that "a 'Moroccan Jewish nationalist' was almost a contradiction in terms, and there were exceedingly few of them." See Halstead, *Rebirth of a Nation*, 100.

13. See, e.g., Heckman, *The Sultan's Communists*; Sternfeld, *Between Iran and Zion*; Wyrtzen, *Making Morocco*, esp. chap. 6; Le Foll-Luciani, *Les juifs algériens*; Boum, *Memories of Absence*, esp. chap. 5; Bashkin, *New Babylonians*; and Beinin, *Dispersion of Egyptian Jewry*, esp. chaps. 2, 3.

14. Consider Kenbib's magisterial *Juifs et musulmans au Maroc, 1859–1948*, which tellingly concludes with the year 1948. His more recent *Juifs et musulmans au Maroc: Des origines à nos jours* (Paris: Tallandier, 2016), now brings that history to the present.

15. On the emigration of Moroccan Jews in the years after 1948, see Baïda, "Emigration of Moroccan Jews, 1948–1956,"; Bin-Nun, "Contribution of World Jewish Organizations," 251–74; Hatimi, "Al-Jamaʿat al-yahudiya al-maghribiya"; Laskier, *North African Jewry*.

16. Heckman's *The Sultan's Communists* is a welcome exception. On the historiographical shift of late toward situating MENA Jews in their Middle Eastern and North African milieu, see Bashkin, "Middle Eastern Shift," 577–80; and Stein, "The Field of In-Between," 581–83.

17. Fouiteh, Jabrane, and Agoumi were among a number of artists who married Egyptian music to Moroccan music and established a national form that has been referred to as "modern Moroccan music" (in Arabic, ʿasri; in French, *la musique marocaine moderne*); see Cherki, *La musique marocaine*. On Zohra El Fassia, see Silver, "Sonic Geniza."

18. See, e.g., "Soirée de Gala a la Brasserie Vox avec le concours de la grande vedette nord-africaine Louisa Tounsia et de notre chanteuse Marocaine Zohra el Fassia. Accompagnées par un orchestre de choix," *Le Petit Marocain*, June 3, 1944, n.p., https://gallica.bnf.fr/ark:/12148/bpt6k4692185s.item; "Lili Boniche [ . . . ] chanteur franco-musulman se produira pour la prèmeire fois a Casablanca avec son orchestre oriental au Rialto dans le gala des vedettes," *Le Petit Marocain*, April 21, 1945, n.p., https://gallica.bnf.fr/ark:/12148/bpt6k469143lz/f2.item; "Lili Labassi à Casablanca? Bien sur! Mais ou va-t-il débuter?," *Le Petit Marocain*, January 22, 1946, n.p., https://gallica.bnf.fr/ark:/12148/bpt6k4691643v/f1.image; "L'unique représentation de la piéce arabe déjà célèbre d'Edmond Khayat chanson d'amour avec le concours du grand chanteur et musicien Salim Halali et son orchestra," *Le Petit Marocain*, April 13, 1946, n.p., https://gallica.bnf.fr/ark:/12148/bpt6k469III9g/f1.image.

19. Farid El Atrache was born in Syria in 1917. He was a nephew of Sultan al-Atrash, the Druze leader who led the 1925 Great Syrian Revolt against the French. As a result of the French occupation, El Atrache and his family departed for Egypt, where he would spend the duration of his career. He died in Beirut, Lebanon, in 1974 and is buried in Cairo, Egypt. A musician, composer, and film star, El Atrache was one of the most highly regarded Middle Eastern artists of the twentieth century.

20. Stenner, *Globalizing Morocco*, 4, 21.

21. Miller, *History of Modern* Morocco, 147–48.

22. "Concert de musique orientale," August 31, 1946, CADN/MA/200/193.

23. Stenner, *Globalizing Morocco*, 25.

24. Miller, *History of Modern Morocco*, 148.

25. On Moroccan Jewish positionality vis-à-vis the Arabo-Islamic formulation, see Wyrtzen, *Making Morocco*, esp. 180–218. On the Istiqlal and Moroccan Jews, see Kenbib, *Juifs et musulmans au Maroc*, 661–87.

26. Heckman, *The Sultan's Communists*, 104.

27. Kenbib, *Juifs et musulmans au Maroc*, 664.

28. Wyrtzen, *Making Morocco*, 213.

29. Heckman, *The Sultan's Communists*, 118. On discussion of Jews in the newspapers of the Istiqlal and PDI, see also Wyrtzen, *Making Morocco*, chap. 6; and Boum, *Memories of Absence*, chap. 5.

30. On Palestine, Israel, and their impact on Jewish-Muslim relations in North Africa and France, see, e.g., Katz, *Burdens of Brotherhood*; and Mandel, *Muslims and Jews in France*.

31. On the attacks in Oujda and Djerada, see, e.g., Heckman, *The Sultan's Communists*, 120–22; Wyrtzen, *Making Morocco*, 214–15; Laskier, *North African Jewry*, 94–101; and Kenbib, *Juifs et musulmans*, 679–87.

32. Wyrtzen, *Making Morocco*, 214.

33. Laskier, *North African Jewry*, 126.

34. See chart in Laskier, *North African Jewry*, 126.

35. Reynolds, *A City Consumed*, 4.

36. "Casablanca," February 1, 1951, CADN/MA/200/193.

37. "Casablanca," February 8, 1951, CADN/MA/200/193. Farid El Atrache was Druze, not Jewish. His origins, unfamiliar to many Moroccans, may have confused. Confusion may have also stemmed from an association of popular entertainment with Jewishness. In Sherifa Zuhur's book on El Atrache's sister Asmahan, who was herself a major star of the interwar period and the subject of numerous rumors, the author argues that Egyptians of the era believed that musicians and film actors were for the most part Jewish and Christian. See Zuhur, *Asmahan's Secrets*, 16.

38. "Note de Renseignements," February 8, 1951, CADN/MA/200/193.

39. Untitled short biography, SEA.

40. Charles Lugassy, "Samy El-Maghribi à la Place des Arts," *La Voix Sepharade-Montréal*, August-September 1977, 4, SEA.

41. Lugassy, "Samy El-Maghribi à la Place des Arts."

42. Lugassy, "Samy El-Maghribi à la Place des Arts."

43. Raphael Levy, "El Maghribi à la Place des Arts," *La Voix Sepharade-Montréal*, June–July 1978, 11, SEA.

44. Levy, "El Maghribi à la Place des Arts."

45. Yolande Amzallag, conversation with the author, May 9, 2016.

46. "Grand Concours Camerafrique," January 6, 1947, SEA.

47. L. A. Vadrot to Monsieur le Chef de Bataillon Perrony, contrôleur du secteur Ancienne Médina, April 30, 1948, SEA.

48. The original French spelling was in fact "Elmoghribi" but would soon change to the more familiar "Elmaghribi."

49. See Samy Elmaghribi, "Nahdat al-fallah" (The peasant's awakening), Pathé CPT 6859, 1948; and "Nashid al-malik" (The king's anthem), Pathé CPT 6869, 1948.

50. See Cherki, *La musique marocaine*.

51. Samy Elmaghribi, "Shubban al-riyada," Pathé CPT 6873, 1948. Personal collection of author. The 6/8 birwali rhythm is typical of many North African musical practices. It signals the popular and is often tied to dancing, clapping, and ululating.

52. Samy Elmaghribi, "Hubb al-banat," Pathé CPT 6865, 1948; and "Khitana," Pathé CPT 6867, 1948. Both are in the personal collection of author.

53. For the traditional view of the departure of Moroccans Jews, see Laskier, *North African Jewry*. For a fresh perspective, see Moreno, "Beyond the Nation-State," 1–21.

54. Correspondence, December 23, 1949, SEA.

55. "A Monsieur Samy El Moghrabi," September 11, 1949, SEA.

56. Note from Radio Maroc, October 19, 1949, SEA.

57. Note from L. A. Vadrot, October 20, 1949, SEA.

58. "Emissions Arabes," November 29, 1949, SEA.

59. "Koutoubia," December 4, 1949, SEA.

60. The figure of 2,466 represents the return to Morocco of some 15 percent of all émigrés at the time. Laskier, *North African Jewry*, 126.

61. "Ordre," July 1, 1942, CADN/MA/200/193.

62. "Disques interdits," September 18, 1948, CADN/MA/200/193.

63. Business card for "Coq d'Or." Personal collection of author.

64. Mohamed Ameskane, "Hajja Hamdaouia: La ayta pop en deuil!," *VH Magazine*, April 10, 2021, https://www.vh.ma/actualite-news-express-maroc/hajja-hamdaouia-la-ayta-pop-en-deuil/. There is growing scholarly interest in ʿaita. For two excellent studies, see Ciucci, "'The Text Must Remain the Same," 476–504; and Kapchan, *Gender on the Market*.

65. Miller, *History of Modern Morocco*, 149.

66. This phrase adorned Elmaghribi's early concert posters.

67. Correspondence, February 17, 1950, SEA.

68. Sometimes "Les Samy Boys."

69. "Sensationnel revolution dans la Musique Orientale!" September 9, 1950, SEA.

70. Samy Elmaghribi, "Luna lunera," Pathé CPT 8842, 1952. Personal collection of author.

71. Samy Elmaghribi, "Lukan al-milayin," Pathé CPT 8051, 1951. Personal collection of author.

72. In the original:

Ay ay ay lukan kanu 'andi al-milayin
n'arif ma n'amil bihum fi dal zman.

. . . . . . . . . . . . . . . . . . .

fil baburat—fil-tayarat
naqt'a bahur wa-nalali fi smawat
naftash 'ala gharami fi kul makan

Lyrics can also be found in "Accouplement," n.d., SEA.

73. Correspondence, August 24, 1951, SEA.

74. Correspondence, August 14, 1951, SEA.

75. Correspondence, February 22, 1952, SEA.

76. Correspondence, August 22, 1952, SEA.

77. On Throne Day, see Wyrtzen, *Making Morocco*, 161, and Miller, *History of Modern Morocco*, 131.

78. Correspondence, November 24, 1952, SEA.

79. Miller, *History of Modern Morocco*, 127.

80. According to Elmaghribi, Radio Maroc received a new transmitter in winter 1952. See Correspondence, January 15, 1952, SEA.

81. "Attestation," February 28, 1952, SEA.

82. Stenner, "Networking for Independence," 216. Wyrtzen has written that the residency believed that Coca-Cola supported the Moroccan nationalist cause (*Making Morocco*, 260–61). Coca-Cola also sponsored Elmaghribi's concerts.

83. Correspondence, July 28, 1952, SEA.

84. Correspondence, June 23, 1952, SEA.

85. "Une salle comble pour écouter Samy Elmaghribi," *Maroc-Presse*, April 30, 1953, SEA.

86. Correspondence, May 20, 1953, SEA.

87. Zisenwine, *Emergence of Nationalist Politics in Morocco*, 211.

88. Sater, *Morocco: Challenges to Tradition and Modernity*, 28.

89. "Tournée de la troupe Samy Elmaghribi," April 12, 1953, CADN/MA/200/193.

90. "Troupes théâtres," CADN/MA/200/193.

91. Correspondence, August 22, 1953, SEA.

92. S. O., "Les émissions arabes de la télévision marocaine: Samy El Maghribi a son enthousiasmé son public," *Maroc-Presse*, March 15, 1954, SEA.

93. Correspondence, March 31, 1954. SEA.

94. On Journo, see Christopher Silver, "Raoul Journo—Habbit ana habbit [Sides 1–2]—Philips (Polyphon), 1937," Gharamophone, https://gharamophone.com/2020/11/20/raoul-journo-habbit-ana-habbit-sides-1-2-philips-polyphon-1937/.

95. Silver, "Raoul Journo."

96. Silver, "Raoul Journo."

97. Journo, *Ma vie*, 125, 172, 187.

98. Correspondence, April 13, 1954, SEA.

99. Zohra El Fassia, "Ayli ayli habibi diyali," Philips 78.120 H, ca. 1954–55; and Albert Suissa, "Ayli ayli", Olympia 1005, ca. 1954. Both in personal collection of author.

100. The song is usually associated with Halali, who later recorded it for the Polydor label under the title "Sidi H'bibi" (*Sidi habibi*), Polydor 2215015, ca. 1960s.

101. "Émissions arabes de Radio-Maroc," January 14, 1954, CADN/MA/200/193.

102. "Disques arabes," February 15, 1955, CADN/MA/200/193.

103. See McDougall, *History of Algeria*, 198, 232–33.

104. "Les volleyeuses du CAF et les footballeurs de ASPTT ont fêté leurs succès en compagnie des artistes Ahmed Wahbi, Samy El Maghribi, et Mohamed Tahar Fergani," *Alger républicain*, December 23, 1954, SEA.

105. H. Abdel Kader, "Un triomphal succès a été réservé à Samy el Maghribi, grande vedette de la chanson," *La Dépêche quotidienne*, December 28, 1954, SEA.

106. "Magnifique succès de Sami el Moghribi et de Abdelwahab Agoumi," *Oran républicain*, December 29, 1954, SEA.

107. El Bouchra, "Au Théâtre Municipal: Samy el Moghrebi et Omar el Tantawy (que les Oranais ne connaissaient pas) et Abd el Wahab Agoumi (que les Oranais connaissaient bien) ont été éblouissants," *Écho Soir*, December 27, 1954, SEA.

108. Samy Elmaghribi, "Fi 'id 'arshik ya sultan," Samyphone no. 7, 1955. *Nashid* can refer to a song, hymn, or anthem. It is also a genre of devotional Islamic song that is mostly performed a cappella. The anthemic quality of Elmaghribi's nationalist music resonates with what Fahmy describes as "the rhythmic martial music beat" of the post–World War I nationalist songs of Egypt's Sayyid Darwish. See Fahmy, *Ordinary Egyptians*, 166.

109. Cherki, *Itinéraire d'un chanteur juif pied-noir déraciné*, 66. My thanks to Ted Swedenburg and Hisham Aidi for sharing Cherki's memoir with me.

110. Kably, *Histoire du Maroc*, 632.

111. In the original:

Fi ʿid ʿarshik ya sultan
al-shʿab yujadid al-tuhani
kul maghribi al-yawm farhan
yafrah qalbi wa-nanashid alhani

"Accouplement," n.d., SEA.

112. Samy Elmaghribi, "Alf haniya wa haniya," Samyphone no. 7, 1955. Personal collection of author. Correspondence, November 14, 1955, SEA.

113. "Samy Elmaghribi reçu par Sa Majesté Sidi Mohammed V à St-Germain-en-Laye le 6 novembre 1955," November 6, 1955, SEA. Yes.

114. Correspondence, November 14, 1955, SEA.

115. Correspondence, December 12, 1955, SEA.

116. Correspondence, January 23, 1956, SEA.

117. Correspondence, January 23, 1956, SEA. On al-Wifaq, see also Heckman, "Dream of Al-Wifaq," 305–22; and Boum, *Memories of Absence*, esp. chap. 5.

118. Untitled newspaper clipping, January 1956, SEA.

119. By embracing Elmaghribi post-independence, along with other Jewish artists, the sultan asserted his musical preferences while positioning himself as the leader of all Moroccans, regardless of ethnoreligious or social divisions. This move also may have served to undercut the Istiqlal.

120. Correspondence, May 11, 1956, SEA.

121. Correspondence, May 15, 1956, SEA.

122. The song "Allah, al-watan, wa-l-malik" (God, country, king) appeared on the other side of the disc (Samyphone no. 8). That triptych was enshrined as the national motto in Morocco's first constitution in 1962.

123. See Albert Suissa, "Ughniyya Sayyid Muhammad al-Khamis," Editions N. Sabbah no. 45, ca. 1956; and Zohra El Fassia, "Al-Malik Ben Youssef," Pathé CPT 12169, 1957.

124. Journo, *Ma vie*, 172.

125. See letter from FLN to Journo, reproduced in Mahfoufi, *Chants kabyles de la guerre d'indépendence. Algérie 1954–1962*, annex 1.

126. Délégation générale du gouvernement en Algérie, *Recueil des actes administratifs de la Délégation générale du gouvernement en Algérie: Lois, décrets arrêtes, décisions, circulaires, avis, communications, informations et annonces*, 322, February 10, 1959, https://gallica.bnf.fr/ark:/12148/bpt6k9776390r/.

127. In the original :

Allah watani wa-sultani
da maqsud kul ʿaskri maghribi
wa-maqsud kul ʿaskri maghribi

Allah watani wa-sultani

. . . . . . . . . . . . .

Bi-amrik ya rabna al-rahman

wa-b-fadhlik ya sidna al-sultan

wa-bijud zu'ama al-watan

maghribna mustaqil wa-hani

Yigal Nizri and Yassine Touati first shared with me their translation of "Allah, watani wa-sultani" in 2014. Based on lyrics found in the SEA, the translation has been amended slightly. All errors are mine alone.

128. Correspondence, May 15, 1956, SEA.

129. Correspondence, March 1, 1959, SEA.

130. Correspondence, March 2, 1959, SEA.

## Chapter 6: Curtain Call

1. Correspondence, September 8, 1959, SEA.

2. Morocco, e.g., joined the Arab postal union in 1959, which theoretically resulted in "the immediate cessation of all communications with Israel." See Heckman, *The Sultan's Communists*, 159.

3. White, *Speaking with Vampires*, 5.

4. Aomar Boum, *Memories of Absence*. For other important works on questions of memory and Moroccan Jews, see Levy, *Return to Casablanca*; Yolande Cohen, "The Migrations of Moroccan Jews to Montreal: Memory, (Oral) History, and Historical Narrative," *Journal of Modern Jewish Studies* 10, no. 2 (2011): 245–62; Trevisan Semi and Sekkat Hatimi, *Mémoire et représentations des Juifs au Maroc*; and Rosen, *Culture of Islam*, esp. chap. 6. On Algeria, see esp. Bahloul, *Architecture of Memory*.

5. No known relation to Léon Benzaquen, the Moroccan Jewish doctor who served as Morocco's first Minister of P.T.T. (postal, telegraph, and telephone services).

6. Correspondence, September 10, 1959, SEA.

7. Correspondence, September 15, 1959, SEA.

8. Correspondence, October 3, 1959, SEA.

9. Correspondence, November 12, 1959, SEA.

10. Correspondence, November 13, 1959, SEA.

11. Correspondence, December 24, 1959, SEA.

12. Trevisan Semi, "Double Trauma and Manifold Narratives," 118.

13. "L'Aïd-Kebir fêté par les E.L.A.K. à la R.T.F," *La Dépêche quotidienne d'Algérie*, June 8, 1960, SEA.

14. See "Interview de Abderrahim BOUSSIF," June 5, 2018, https://www.boussifreres.com/post/interview-de-abderrahim-boussif.

15. Correspondence, late 1959, SEA.

16. Correspondence, October 7, 1959, SEA.

17. Correspondence, September 18, 1959, SEA.

18. Miller, *History of Modern Morocco*, 158–59.

19. Correspondence, October 16, 1959, SEA.

20. Elmaghribi and Cohen both used the Arabic for wormwood (*shiba*) and almonds (*al-luz*). Correspondence, December 3, 1959, SEA.

21. Correspondence, October 20, 1959, SEA.

22. Correspondence, November 4, 1959, SEA.

23. Dédé Elmaghribi et ses soeurs, "Shams al-ʿashiyya," Samyphone no. 25, 1959. Personal collection of author. Correspondence, October 16, 1959, SEA.

24. Correspondence, January 19, 1960, SEA.

25. Correspondence, January 19, 1960, SEA.

26. "1,500 Jews Reported Killed in Agadir Earthquake: J. D. C. Rushes Aid," *Jewish Telegraphic Agency* (JTA), March 4, 1960, https://www.jta.org/1960/03/04/archive/1500-jews-reported-killed-in-agadir-earthquake-j-d-c-rushes-aid.

27. On the Agadir earthquake of 1960 and the displaced, see Segalla, "Natural Disaster, Globalization, and Decolonization," 101–28.

28. Correspondence, March 3, 1960, SEA.

29. Correspondence, March 7, 1960, SEA.

30. Correspondence, April 1, 1960, SEA. The rapid production and distribution of the record was aided by the fact that Elmaghribi formally established a branch of Samyphone in Paris by early 1960. See Correspondence, January 8, 1960, SEA.

31. Samy Elmaghribi, "Qissat Agadir," Samyphone no. 26, 1960. Personal collection of author. Correspondence, March 5, 1960, SEA.

32. Correspondence, March 8, 1960, SEA.

33. *La Voix des Communautés* was launched on Radio Maroc in 1950 and remained on air in Morocco until 1965. On Bouzaglo and his recording activities, see Seroussi, "Sanctity and Celebrity.".

34. In ZEF, for example, there exists an anonymously authored "Qasida di Agadir," typewritten in Moroccan Judeo-Arabic and printed in Israel.

35. Sliman Mougrabi, "Qissat Agadir," R. Zaky 7060, 1960. Personal collection of author.

36. *Ya rabbi ʿafu ʿalina.* Correspondence, March 24, 1960, SEA.

37. Correspondence, April 1, 1960, SEA.

38. Correspondence, May 10, 1960, SEA.

39. Correspondence, May 12, 1960, SEA.

40. Correspondence, May 23, 1960, SEA.

41. Miller, *A History of Modern Morocco*, 155, 159.

42. Correspondence, May 23, 1960, SEA.

43. Correspondence, May 28, 1960, SEA.

44. Correspondence, May 30, 1960, SEA.

45. Read and Welch, *From Tin Foil to Stereo*, 350.

46. Correspondence, June 3, 1960, SEA.

47. Boum, *Memories of Absence*, chap. 5.

48. Correspondence, June 8, 1960, SEA.

49. Correspondence, June 14, 1960, SEA.

50. Correspondence, July 1, 1960, SEA.

51. Correspondence, August 18, 1960, SEA.

52. Correspondence, September 6, 1960, SEA.

53. Heckman, *The Sultan's Communists*, 154–58. On Nasser's visit and the Jewish community, see as well Gottreich, *Jewish Morocco*, 155–56.

54. Correspondence, January 6, 1961, SEA.

55. Correspondence, March 10, 1961, SEA.

56. The Mossad is Israel's national intelligence agency; the Jewish Agency is a parastate organization which oversees immigration to Israel. HIAS, founded in New York in 1881, is a Jewish aid society engaged in refugee resettlement. Laskier, *North African Jewry*, 238. On Operation Yakhin, see Laskier, *North African Jewry*, chap. 7.

57. Correspondence, May 25, 1961, SEA.

58. Correspondence, June 14, 1961, SEA.

59. Correspondence, August 1, 1961, SEA.

60. Correspondence, September 6, 1961, SEA.

61. Correspondence, October 10, 1961, SEA.

62. Correspondence, October 16, 1961, SEA.

63. See Levy, "A Community That Is Both a Center and a Diaspora."

64. Contract, August 17, 1960, SEA.

65. Samy Elmaghribi, "Qaftanak mahlul," Samyphone no. 4, 1955. The song is labeled "Shikka (Arabic Romance)" on *In Israel Today, vol. 2: Music of the Jews from Morocco*, ed. Bhattacharya, Westminster 12027, 1957.

66. Wertheim, "Ha-khanut ba-kikar ha-sha 'on," 82, 83.

67. On Hed Artzi and Hataklit, which operated Makolit, see Regev and Seroussi, *Popular Music and National Culture in Israel*.

68. The label also recorded artists who sang in Turkish, Persian, and all manner of Bollywood styles.

69. There is a considerable scholarly literature on the experiences of North African and Middle Eastern Jews in Israel. For a few examples in English among many, see Bashkin, *Impossible Exodus*; Roby, *Mizrahi Era of Rebellion*; Chetrit, *Intra-Jewish Conflict in Israel*; Behar, "Palestine, Arabized Jews, and the Elusive Consequences," 581–611; Massad, "Zionism's Internal Others," 53–68; and Shohat, "Sephardim in Israel," 1–35.

70. Gottreich, *Jewish Morocco*, 174.

71. Roby, *Mizrahi Era of Rebellion*, 52.

72. On the Wadi Salib riots, see Roby, *Mizrahi Era of Rebellion*, esp. chap. 5; Weiss, *Confiscated Memory*; and Chetrit, *Intra-Jewish Conflict in Israel*, esp. chap. 2.

73. Ben Shalev, "The Hardest-hitting Protest Song Ever Written in Israel," June 6, 2018, Haaretz.com, https://www.haaretz.com/israel-news/.premium.MAGAZINE-the-hardest-hitting-protest-song-ever-written-in-israel-1.6152410.

74. (Joamar) Elmaghribi was sometimes rendered as Moghrabi on R. Zaky releases.

75. All were released on Pairaphon (a sublabel of R. Zaky and Zakiphon) in the mid-late 1950s. The issue numbers, respectively, are Pairaphon 10012, 10094, and 10040.

76. Robert Shelton, "Concert for Israel Offers New Singer," *New York Times*, May 20, 1965, 54, https://timesmachine.nytimes.com/timesmachine/1965/05/20/118062868.html.

77. Jo Amar, "Lishkat Avodah," Zakiphon EP-020, c. 1960. Transliteration is my own. *Mshit* is the Moroccan Arabic word for "I went." The rest of the quoted lyrics are in Hebrew. An English translation of the lyrics can be found in Shalev, "The Hardest-hitting Protest Song."

Mshit lishkat avodah
Amar li me-ayfoh atah
Amarti lo mi-maroko
Amar li titzey mi-po

Mshit lishkat avodah
Amar li me-ayfoh atah
Amarti lo mi-polonia
Amar li tikanes bevakasha

78. Correspondence, September 13, 1961, SEA.

79. Correspondence, August 2, 1962, SEA.

80. Samy Elmaghribi et ses enfants, "La Hagada de Pessah," Samyphone no. 42, 1963. Personal collection of author.

81. In Émile Cohen's letter, the artist's name is spelled Jeo Amar. Correspondence, March 29, 1963, SEA.

82. Correspondence, April 7, 1963, SEA.

83. Correspondence, April 11, 1963, SEA.

84. Correspondence, May 27, 1963, SEA.

85. Correspondence, October 23, 1963, SEA.

86. Correspondence, November 12, 1963, SEA. On the Arab Cold War, see, e.g., Kerr, *Arab Cold War*.

87. Silver, "Sonic Geniza."

88. Correspondence, May 10, 1963, SEA.

89. Correspondence, November 1963, SEA.

90. Yolande Amzallag, in conversation with the author, June 18, 2021.

91. Correspondence, December 1, 1963, SEA.

92. Correspondence, January 1964, SEA.

93. Correspondence, March 25, 1964, SEA.

94. Correspondence, June 2, 1964, SEA.

95. McDougall, *History of Algeria*, 200, 206.

96. Katz, *Burdens of Brotherhood*, 173.

97. Le Foll-Luciani, *Les juifs algériens*.

98. Katz, *Burdens of Brotherhood*, 157.

99. For the television appearance in question, see "Lili Labbassi_Concert inaugural de la télévision algérienne_Mçedder sika_Ya nass ma tâdirouni 1956," El Hassar Salim, https://www.youtube.com/watch?v=t73xbu5BZNc, posted November 20, 2020.

100. Lili Labassi, "Wahran al-bahiyya," RCA F 88.012, c. 1956. Personal collection of author.

101. "Concert Orchestre Blaoui & Guests—Oran (Aïd 1958)," Raï & Folk, https://soundcloud.com/raiandfolk/concert-orchestre-blaoui-fadila-dziria-hajira-bali-etc-oran-aid-1958.

102. Katz, *Burdens of Brotherhood*, 201.

103. Dicale, *Cheikh Raymond*, 252.

104. Dicale, *Cheikh Raymond*, 252.

105. Dicale, *Cheikh Raymond*, 53, 55, 101–3.

106. On the Constantine Riots, see, e.g., Cole, *Lethal Provocation*; Roberts, *Citizenship and Antisemitism*, esp. chap. 4; Katz, Burdens of Brotherhood, esp. chap. 2; Attal, *Les émeutes de Constantine*; and Ageron, "Une émeute anti-juive," 23–40.

107. Cole, *Lethal Provocation*, 179.

108. Scales, "Subversive Sound," 402.

109. Attouche's article is reprinted in Merdeçi, *Dictionnaire des musiques citadines de Constantine*, 41.

110. For a different perspective on Leyris's political allegiances, see Swedenburg, "Against Hybridity," 238–39.

111. Le Foll-Luciani, *Les juifs Algériens*, 121–22, 131–32.

112. On the OAS, see Shepard, *Invention of Decolonization*.

113. See Marolle, "Enrico Macias."

114. Macias, *Mon Algérie*, 161–62.

115. Dicale, *Cheikh Raymond*, 254, 256.

116. Macias, *Mon Algérie*, 164.

117. Drai, "L'aigle et le luth," 65.

118. "Lettre de Constantine," *Droits et Liberté*, May 1961, no. 200, 5, http://archives.mrap.fr/images/6/69/Dl61_2000pt.pdf; cited in Katz, *Burdens of Brotherhood*, 203–4.

119. "Lettre de Constantine," 5.

120. Le Foll-Luciani has pointed out that the attack on Leyris fits into a pattern of the FLN targeting high-profile Algerian Jews. See Le Foll-Luciani, *Les juifs algériens*, 166. On the nonclaim of responsibility by the FLN or any other group, see Dicale, *Cheikh Raymond*, 278–80.

121. Merdaçi, "Cheikh Raymond, the 'Hseïni' (1912–1961)," 982.

122. "Les Attentats," *Information Juive*, July 16, 1961, 3, accessed via Historical Jewish Press, http://www.jpress.nli.org.il/Olive/APA/NLI/SharedView.Article.aspx ?href=INF%2F1961%2F07%2F16&id=Ar00301&sk=8B794C1D.

123. "Algeria," *American Jewish Year Book*, vol. 63 (1962): 452–53, held by American Jewish Committee Archives, http://www.ajcarchives.org/AJC_DATA/Files/1962_14 _NSAfrica.pdf.

124. Mandel, "Algeria," *American Jewish Year Book*, vol. 64 (1963): 406, http://www .ajcarchives.org/AJC_DATA/Files/1963_13_NSAfrica.pdf.

125. Stora, *Les clés retrouvées*. In fact, Stora invokes the memory of Leyris in much of his writing. See, e.g., Stora, "Une enfance à Constantine," 243; and Stora, *Les trois exils juifs d'Algérie*, 159.

126. Mandel, "Algeria," 1963, 406.

127. Mandel, "Algeria," 406.

128. Fargues, *Mémoires de Pieds-Noirs*, 219.

129. "Enregistrements 78 T. arabes—(Responsable: M. Hachlef)," February 28, 1964, Catalogues Arabia, 1948–72, EMI-France.

130. Brahmi Abdelkader, "Qaftanak mahlul," Disques El Manar JVBS 1051, ca. 1960s. Personal collection of author.

131. M. P., "Entre Paris et New York: Samy El Maghribi donnera deux récitals au Maroc," *Le Petit Marocain*, May 5, 1967, SEA.

## Conclusion

1. Castel, *Je pose soixante-quinze*, 311.

2. Castel, *Je pose soixante-quinze*, 313.

3. Lili Labassi, "Ma ninsashi a-biladi," Disques Lili Labassi LL01, ca. 1965. Personal collection of author. The title is printed only in Latin characters.

4. In the original:

Ma ninsashi biladi abadan
Wa-yihiju l-mihan

5. On North African songs of exile in France, see, e.g., *Générations*, ed. Yahi et al.; and Daoudi and Miliani, *Beurs' melodies*.

6. Journo, *Ma vie*, 203.

7. Journo, *Ma vie*, 203.

8. Journo, Ma vie, 205.

9. Dahmane El Harrachi, "Bilad al-khayr," Pathé 45EA716, ca. 1960s; and Dahmane El Harrachi, "Ya rayih," Edition Atlas K 480, ca. 1973.

10. McDougall, *History of Algeria*, 137.

11. Rachid Taha, "Diwân," Barclay 539953–2, 1998.

12. "Exposition sur la culture des Juifs d'Afrique du nord et leur contribution au developpement d'Israel," ZEF.

13. Hachlef and Hachlef, *Anthologie de la musique arabe*, 216.

14. On the emergence of Judeo-Arabic as a discursive category, see Shohat, "Invention of Judeo-Arabic," 153–200.

15. Yafil, *Majmu'*.

16. Kafadar, "Between Past and Present, Part 2."

# DISCOGRAPHY AND BIBLIOGRAPHY

## Archives

ALGERIA

Archives de la Wilaya d'Alger, Algiers

Archives nationales d'Algérie, Algiers

TUNISIA

Archives nationales de Tunisie, Tunis (TNA)

Centre des musiques arabes et méditerranéennes, Ennejma Ezzahra, Sidi Bou Said (CMAM)

L'Institut des belles lettres arabes de Tunis, Tunis

FRANCE

Archives de l'Alliance israélite universelle, Paris (AIU)

Archives de la Société des auteurs, compositeurs et éditeurs de musique, Neuilly-sur-Seine (SACEM)

Archives départementales des Bouches-du-Rhône, Marseilles (ADBdR)

Archives du Ministère des affaires étrangères, La Courneuve (AMAE)

Archives nationales, Paris (AN)

Archives nationales d'outre mer, Aix-en-Provence (ANOM)

Bibliothèque nationale de France, Paris (BNF)

Centre des Archives diplomatiques de Nantes, Nantes (CADN)

Collection phonographique du CNRS, Musée de l'homme, Le Centre de recherche en ethnomusicologie, Paris (CREM)

Warner Music Archives, Saint-Ouen-l'Aumône (EMI-France)

ISRAEL

Central Zionist Archives, Jerusalem (CZA)

National Library of Israel, Jerusalem (NLI)

UNITED KINGDOM

EMI Archive Trust, Hayes (EMI-UK)

CANADA

Samy Elmaghribi archive, Montreal (SEA)

UNITED STATES

Zohra El Fassia archive, Los Angeles (ZEF)

## Magazines and Newspapers

*Ad-Dunya al-Musawarra* (Cairo)

*Alger républicain* (Algiers)

*Art et décoration: Revue mensuelle d'art modern* (Paris)

*Écho soir* (Oran)

*Excelsior* (Paris)

*Haaretz* (Tel Aviv)

*Ici-Alger: Revue mensuelle des émissions en langues arabe et kabyle de Radio-Algérie* (Algiers)

*Information juive* (Algiers)

*Jewish Telegraphic Agency* (JTA)

*Journal officiel de la République Française* (Paris)

*La Dépêche algérienne* (Algiers)

*La Dépêche quotidienne d'Algérie* (Algiers)

*La France au combat* (Paris)

*L'Afrique du nord illustrée: Journal hebdomadaire d'actualités nord-africaines: Algérie, Tunisie, Maroc* (Algiers)

*La Voix des communautés* (Rabat)

*La Voix sépharade* (Montreal)

*L'Écho d'Alger* (Algiers)

*Leïla: Revue de la femme* and *Leïla: Hebdomadaire tunisien independent* (Tunis)

*Le Monde vu de Paris* (Paris)

*Le Petit Journal* (Paris)

*Le Petit Marocain* (Casablanca)

*Le Radical* (Algiers)

*Le Temps* (Paris)

*Les Clochettes algériennes et tunisiennes: Journal littéraire, humoristique et commercial, paraissant le dimanche* (Algiers)

*Liberté* (Algiers)

*Maroc-Presse* (Casablanca)

*New York Times* (New York)

*Notre Rive: Revue nord-africaine* (Algiers)

*Oran républicain* (Oran)

*Paris-soir* (Paris)

*Patriote algérien* (Algiers)

*Revue des deux mondes* (Paris)

## Discography

Alphabetized by how the performer's name appears on the recording.

Acher Mizrahi. "Qissat Habiba Messika," Parlophone B 81009, ca. 1930.

Albert Abitbol and Gaston Bsiri. "Al-Bashraf al-kabir," Disques Oum-El-Hassen 55.120, ca. 1930s.

Albert Suissa. "Ayli ayli," Olympia 1005, ca. 1954.

———. "Ughniyya Sayyid Muhammad al-Khamis," Editions N. Sabbah no. 45, ca. 1956.

Bachir Fahmy. "Habiba matit," Baidaphon B 93580, ca. 1931.

Bichi Slama. "Surat Habiba Messika," Pathé X 65068, ca. 1931.

Blond Blond. "Où vous étiez mademoiselle," Dounia 1267, ca. 1960s.

Brahmi Abdelkader. "Qaftanak mahlul," Disques El Manar JVBS 1051, ca. 1960s.

Cheikha Aicha La Hebrea. "Ma taqulash l-mamak," Pathé 58618, ca. 1930.

*Congrès de Musique Arabe du Caire 1932, Édition intégrale des Enregistrements.* Jean Lambert and Pascal Cordereix, liner notes by Bernard Moussali. Paris Bibliothèque Nationale de France and the Abu Dhabi Tourism and Culture Authority, 2015.

Dahmane El Harrachi. "Bilad al-khayr," Pathé 45EA716, ca. 1960s.

———. "Ya rayih," Edition Atlas K 480, ca. 1973.

Dalila Taliana. "Où vous étiez mademoiselle," Gramophone K 4680, ca. 1931.

Darius Milhaud. "La Séparation, Chanson populaire hébraique," 4–32844, Gramophone, 1928.

Dédé Elmaghribi et Ses Sœurs. "Shams al-ʿashiyya," Samyphone no. 25, 1959.

Fadhila Khetmi. "Mademoiselle," Baidaphon B 93016, ca. early 1930s.

Flifla Chamia. "Mawt Habiba Messika," Gramophone K 4355, ca. 1931.

Hermann Fleishmann. "Kaddisch," Parlophon 57041, 1928.

Hocine Slaoui. "A-Zin wa-l-ʿayn," Pathé PV 97 (CPT 7120), 1949.

Jo Amar. "Lishkat avodah," Zakiphon EP-020, ca. 1960.

———. "Shir hashikor," Pairaphon 10012, ca. late 1950s.

———. "Shalom leben dodi," Pairaphon 10094, ca. late 1950s.

———. "Barcelona," Pairaphon 10040, ca. late 1950s.

Jojo (Fils de Saoud). "Ma taqulash l-mamak," Polydor 550067, ca. 1931.

Joseph "Sosso" Cherki. "Al-Sharlistun," Columbia 17006, ca. late 1920s.

Joseph Morjean. "Mamak," Parlophone 46.523, 1930.

Habiba Messika. "'Ala bab darik," Pathé 18.507, 1926.

———. "Habibi al-awwal," Baidaphon B 86362, 1928.

———. "Baladi ya baladi," Baidaphon B 086405, 1928.

———. "Marsh jalalat al-Malik Fuad," Baidaphon, B 086473, 1928.

———. "Al-Nashid al-watani al-misri," Baidaphon, B 086520, 1928.

———. "Nashid jalalat al-Malik Faysal," Baidaphon B 086530, 1928.

———. "Inti suriya biladi," Baidaphon, B 086596, 1928.

———. "Salam sidna bay tunis habib al-sh'ab," Baidaphon B 086622, 1928.

*In Israel Today. Volume 2: Music of the Jews from Morocco.* Westminster 12027, edited
    and with notes by Deben Bhattacharya, 1957.

Lili Boniche. "Marché noir," Pacific CO 7010, ca. 1947.

Lili Labassi. "Hadha takhir al-zaman," Gramophone K 3991, ca. 1928.

———. "Mamak," Columbia GF 262, 1930.

———. "Lillah ya-l-ghadi li-l-sahra," Polyphon V 46.117, 1937.

———. "Wahran al-bahiyya," RCA F 88.012, ca. 1959.

———. "Ma ninsashi a-biladi," Disques Lili Labassi LL01, ca. 1965.

Louisa Tounsia. "Hukm al-niswan," Pathé X 55269, ca. 1931.

———. "Ma fish flus," Polyphon V 45673, ca. 1935.

———. "Mademoiselle," Polyphon 45634, ca. 1935.

———. "Viens chez moi" ("Ta'ala 'andi"), Polyphon V 46147, 1937.

Madame Ghazala. "Mamak," Columbia GF 200, 1930.

Madame Louisa "Al-Isra'iliyya." "Mamak Mamak," Gramophone K 4421, ca. 1930.

Mahieddine Bachetarzi. "Ah ya m'allim (Yafil)," Gramophone K 2655, 1924.

Méââllem Et-Ouati el-ouah'rani. "Mamak Mamak," Gramophone K 4213, ca. 1930.

Rachid Taha. "Diwân," Barclay 539953–2, 1998.

Ratiba Chamia. "Qissat Habiba," Baidaphon B 93749, ca. early 1930s.

———. "Où étiez-vous mademoiselle," Oum-El-Hassen 55.052, ca. early 1930s.

Raoul Journo. "Habbit ana habbit," Philips (Polyphon), 1937.

Redouane Ould Chikh Elarbi. "Habiba Messika," Gramophone K 4412, ca. 1931.

Salim Halali. "Arja' l-biladak," Pathé PR 230, 1939.

———. "Je t'appartiens (tango)," Pathé CPT 5975, ca. 1945.

———. "Sidi H'bibi," Polydor 2215015, ca. 1960s.

Salim Halali en Algérie. Les Artistes Arabes Associés (AAA) 023, liner notes by Ahmed Hachlef, 1990.

Samy Elmaghribi. "Nahdat al-fallah," Pathé CPT 6859, 1948.

———. "Hubb al-banat," Pathé CPT 6865, 1948.

———. "Nashid al-malik," Pathé CPT 6869, 1948.

———. "Shubban al-riyada," Pathé CPT 6873, 1948.

———. "Al-Marché noir," Pathé CPT 6863, 1948.

———. "Khitana," Pathé CPT 6867, 1948.

———. "Lukan al-milayin," Pathé CPT 8051, 1951.

———. "Luna lunera," Pathé CPT 8842, 1952.

———. "Qaftanak mahlul," Samyphone no. 4, 1955.

———. "Fi ʿid ʿarshik ya sultan," Samyphone no. 7, 1955.

———. "Alf haniya wa haniya," Samyphone no. 7, 1955.

———. "Allah, al-watan, wa-l-malik," Samyphone no. 8, 1955.

———. "Allah, watani, wa-sultani," Samyphone no. 8, 1956.

———. "Qissat Agadir," Samyphone no. 26, 1960.

Samy Elmaghribi et Ses Enfants. "La Hagada de Pessah," Samyphone no. 42, 1963.

Simon Ohayon and Hazar Cohen. "Ma taqulash l-mamak," Pathé 58717, ca. 1931.

Sliman Elmaghribi. "Qissat Agadir," R. Zaky 7060, 1960.

Zohra El Fassia. "Ayli ayli habibi diyali," Philips 78.120 H, ca. 1954–1955.

———. "Al-Malik Ben Youssef," Pathé CPT 12169, 1957.

## Books and Articles

Abbani, Diana. "Beirut's Musical Scene: A Narrative of Modernisation and Identity Struggles under the French Mandate." In *Middle Eastern and North African Societies in the Interwar Period*, ed. Ebru Boyar and Kate Fleet, 54–77. Leiden: Brill, 2018.

Abbonizio, Isabella. "Musica e colonialismo nell'Italia fascista (1922–1943)." PhD diss., Università degli Studi di Roma, 2008–9.

Abitbol, Michel. *Les Juifs d'Afrique du nord sous Vichy*. Paris: G. P. Maisonneuve et Larose, 1983.

Ageron, Charles-Robert. "Une émeute anti-juive à Constantine (août 1934)." *Revue des mondes musulmans et de la Méditerranée* 13, no. 1 (1973): 23–40.

———. "Les populations du Maghreb face à la propaganda Allemande," *Revue d'histoire de la Deuxième Guerre Mondiale* 29, no. 114 (April 1, 1979): 1–39.

Aidi, Hisham. *Rebel Music: Race, Empire, and the New Muslim Youth Culture*. New York: Pantheon, 2014.

Ait Mous, Fadma. "The Moroccan Nationalist Movement: From Local to National Networks." *Journal of North African Studies* 18, no. 5 (2013): 737–52.

"Algeria." *American Jewish Year Book* 63 (1962): 444–54.

Allouche, Jean-Luc, and Jean Laloum. *Les Juifs d'Algérie: Images & Textes*. Paris: Editions du Scribe, 1987.

Allouche-Benayoun, Joëlle. "Intermittently French: Jews from Algeria during World War II," *Contemporary Jewry* 37, no. 2 (2017): 219–30.

Amin, Khalid, and Marvin Carlson. *The Theatres of Morocco, Algeria, and Tunisia: Performance Traditions of the Maghreb*. Houndmills, UK: Palgrave Macmillan, 2011.

Amipaz-Silber, Gitta. *The Role of the Jewish Underground in the American Landing in Algiers, 1940–1942*. Jerusalem: Gefen, 1992.

Armbrust, Walter. "The Formation of National Culture in Egypt in the Interwar Period: Cultural Trajectories." *History Compass* 8, no. 1 (2009), 155–80.

———. *Mass Culture and Modernism in Egypt*. Cambridge: Cambridge University Press, 1996.

Arnoulet, François. "Les problèmes de l'enseignement au début du protectorat français en Tunisie (1881–1900)." *Revue de l'Institut des Belles Lettres Arabes* 167 (1991): 31–62.

Arrouas, Albert. *Livre d'or: Figures d'hier et d'aujour'hui*. Tunis: Imprimerie Sapl, 1932.

Asal, Yaacov. "Bayn Evar le-arev: Hayav ve yatzirato shel Asher Mizrahi." MA thesis, Hebrew University, 2014.

Asseraf, Arthur. *Electric News in Colonial Algeria*. Oxford: Oxford University Press, 2019.

Attal, Robert. *Les émeutes de Constantine: 5 août 1934*. Paris: Éditions Romillat, 2002.

Audisio, Gabriel. "Enregistrements algériens." *La Revue musicale* 11, no. 106 (July 1930): 153–58.

Ayache, Albert. *Le mouvement syndical au Maroc*. 3 vols. Paris: L'Harmattan, 1982.

Ayadi, Taoufik. "Insurrection et religion en Tunisie: L'exemple de Thala-Kasserine (1906) et du Jellaz (1911)." In *Direction des Archives de France, révolte et société*, 166–75. Association "Histoire au présent." Paris: Publications de la Sorbonne, 1989.

———. *Mouvement réformiste et mouvements populaires à Tunis (1906–1912)*. Tunis: Publications de l'Université de Tunis, 1986.

Azen, Henriette. "La Chanson de Bensoussan: Complainte judéo-arabe à propos d'un crime passionnel survenu à Oran en 1889." Self-published, 1996.

Bachetarzi, Mahieddine. *Mémoires, 1919–1939; Suivis d'étude sur le théâtre dans les pays islamiques*. Algiers: Éditions nationales algériennes, 1968.

———. *Mémoires. Vol. 2: Première partie de 1939 à 1946, deuxième partie de 1947 à 1951*. Algiers: Entreprise Nationale du Livre, 1984.

Badran, Margot. *Feminists, Islam, and Nation: Gender and the Making of Modern Egypt*. Princeton, NJ: Princeton University Press, 2001.

Bahloul, Joelle. *The Architecture of Memory: A Jewish-Muslim Household in Colonial Algeria, 1937–1962*. Cambridge: Cambridge University Press, 1996.

Baida, Jamaâ. "The American Landing in November 1942: A Turning Point in Morocco's Contemporary History." *Journal of North African Studies* 19, no. 4 (2014): 518–23.

———. "The Emigration of Moroccan Jews, 1948–1956." In *Jewish Culture and Society in North Africa*, ed. Emily Benichou Gottreich and Daniel J. Schroeter. Bloomington: Indiana University Press, 2010.

———. "Maroc et la propagande du IIIème Reich." *Hespéris Tamuda* 28, no. 1 (1990): 91–106.

Bakalti, Souad. *La femme tunisienne au temps de la colonisation, 1881–1956*. Paris: L'Harmattan, 1996.

———. "L'enseignement féminin dans le primaire au temps de la Tunisie coloniale." *Revue de l'Institut des Belles Lettres Arabes* 166 (1990): 249–74.

Barbès, Léo-Louis. "La musique musulmane en Algérie," *Documents algériens*, no. 15, April 10, 1947. Algiers: Centre d'Information et Etudes.

Bargach, Jamila. "Liberatory, Nationalising and Moralising by Ellipsis: Reading and Listening to Lhussein Slaoui's Song 'Lmirikan,'" *Journal of North African Studies* 4, no. 4 (1999): 61–88.

Barlow, Tani E. *Formations of Colonial Modernity in East Asia*. Durham, NC: Duke University Press, 1997.

Baron, Beth. *Egypt As a Woman: Nationalism, Gender, and Politics*. Berkeley: University of California Press, 2005.

———. *The Women's Awakening in Egypt: Culture, Society, and the Press*. New Haven, CT: Yale University Press, 1994.

Bashkin, Orit. *Impossible Exodus: Iraqi Jews in Israel*. Stanford, CA: Stanford University Press, 2017.

———. "The Middle Eastern Shift and Provincializing Zionism." *International Journal of Middle East Studies* 46, no. 3 (2014): 577–80.

———. *New Babylonians: A History of Jews in Modern Iraq*. Stanford, CA: Stanford University Press, 2012.

Behar, Moshe. "Palestine, Arabized Jews, and the Elusive Consequences of Jewish and Arab National Formations." *Nationalism and Ethnic Politics* 13 (2007): 581–611.

Beinin, Joel. *The Dispersion of Egyptian Jewry: Culture, Politics, and the Formation of a Modern Diaspora*. Berkeley: University of California Press, 1998.

Ben Halima, Hamadi. *Un demi-siècle de théâtre arabe en Tunisie (1907–1957)*. Tunis: Publications de l'université de Tunis, 1974.

Benjelloun, Abdelmajid. *Le nord du Maroc. L'indépendance avant l'indépendance: Jean Rous et le Maroc, 1953–1956.* Paris: L'Harmattan, 1996.

Ben Shimon, Nissim. "Haggada di Hitler." Rabat, ca. 1945.

Ben Simhon, Matatya. "Qasida di Hitler." Casablanca, ca. 1944.

Bessis, Juliette. *La Méditerranée fasciste. L'Italie mussolinienne et la Tunisie.* Paris: Karthala, Publications de la Sorbonne, 1981.

Bin-Nun, Yigal. "The Contribution of World Jewish Organizations to the Establishment of Rights for Jews in Morocco (1956–1961)." *Journal of Modern Jewish Studies* 9, no. 2 (2010): 251–74.

Booth, Marilyn. *May Her Likes Be Multiplied: Biography and Gender Politics in Egypt.* Berkeley: University of California Press, 2001.

Bouchène, Abderrahmane, Jean-Pierre Peyroulou, Ouanassa Siari Tengour, and Sylvie Thénault, eds. *Histoire de l'Algérie à la période coloniale.* Paris: La Découverte and Barzakh, 2014.

Boum, Aomar. *Memories of Absence: How Muslims Remember Jews in Morocco.* Stanford, CA: Stanford University Press, 2013.

———. "Partners against Anti-Semitism: Muslims and Jews respond to Nazism in French North African Colonies, 1936–1940." *Journal of North African Studies* 19, no. 4 (2014), 554–70.

Boum, Aomar, and Sarah Abrevaya Stein, eds. *The Holocaust and North Africa.* Stanford, CA: Stanford University Press, 2018.

Bourguiba, Habib. *Ma vie, mes idées, mon combat.* Tunis: Publications du Secrétariat d'État à l'Information, 1977.

Bouzar-Kasbadji, Nadya. *L'émergence artistique algérienne au XXe siècle: Contribution de la musique et du théâtre algérois à la renaissance culturelle et à la prise de conscience nationaliste.* Algiers: Office des publications universitaires, 1988.

Bowles, Paul. *Points in Time.* New York: Ecco Press, 1982.

Brower, Benjamin. *A Desert Named Peace: The Violence of France's Empire in the Algerian Sahara, 1844–1902.* New York: Columbia University Press, 2009.

Brown, Kenneth. "The Impact of the *Dahir Berbère* in Salé." In *Arabs and Berbers: From Tribe to Nation in North Africa,* ed. Ernest Gellner and Charles Micaud, 201–21. London: Duckworth, 1973.

Bsiri, Gaston. "*Al-Qism al-awwal min shiray siyyon, piyyutim bi-tafsirihim.*" Tunis: Castro, n.p., n.d.

———. "Les Dernières Créations et 25 autres chansons égyptiennes." Tunis: Imprimerie de l'Orient, n.d.

Cantier, Jacques. *L'Algérie sous le régime de Vichy.* Paris: Odile Jacob, 2002.

Carlier, Omar. "Medina and Modernity: The Emergence of Muslim Civil Society in Algiers between the Two World Wars." In *Walls of Algiers: Narratives of the*

*City through Text and Image*, ed. Zeynep Çelik, Julia Clancy-Smith, and Frances Terpak, 62–84. Los Angeles: Getty Research Institute, 2009.

Castel, Robert. *Je pose soixante-quinze, mais je retiens tout: Soixante-quinze ans de souvenirs*. Paris: Ramsay, 2008.

Chamoux, Henri. "Dépôts de marques phonographiques françaises de 1893 à 1940: Documents tirés des bulletins de l'INPI," n.p., 2015; http://www.archeophone .org/rtf_pdf/Marques_phonographiques_inpi.pdf.

Cherki, Luc. *Itinéraire d'un chanteur juif pied-noir déraciné*. Self-published, 2012.

Cherki, Salah. *La musique marocaine*. N.p., 1982.

Chetrit, Sami Shalom. *Intra-Jewish Conflict in Israel: White Jews, Black Jews*. London: Routledge, 2010.

Chottin, Alexis. *Tableau de la musique Marocaine*. Paris: P. Geuthner, 1938.

Chouraqui, André. *L'Alliance israélite universelle et la renaissance juive contemporaine, 1860–1960*. Paris: Presses universitaires de France, 1965.

Ciantar, Philip. *The Maʾlūf in Contemporary Libya: An Arab Andalusian Musical Tradition*. Farnham, UK: Ashgate, 2012.

Ciucci, Alessandra. "'The Text Must Remain the Same': History, Collective Memory, and Sung Poetry in Morocco." *Ethnomusicology* 56, no. 3 (Fall 2012): 476–504.

Clancy-Smith, Julia. "From Household to Schoolroom Women, Transnational Networks, and Education in North Africa and Beyond." In *French Mediterraneans: Transnational and Imperial Histories*, ed. Patricia M. E. Lorcin and Todd Shepard, 200–231. Lincoln: University of Nebraska Press, 2016.

———. "L'École Rue du Pacha, Tunis: L'education de la femme arabe et 'La Plus Grande France' (1900–1914)." *Clio: Histoire, femmes, et société* 12 (2000): 33–55.

———. *Mediterraneans: North Africa and Europe in an Age of Migration, c. 1800–1900*. Berkeley: University of California Press, 2011.

———. *Tunisian Revolutions: Reflections on Seas, Coasts, and Interiors*. Washington, DC: Georgetown University Press, 2014.

Cohen, Yolande. "The Migrations of Moroccan Jews to Montreal: Memory, (Oral) History, and Historical Narrative." *Journal of Modern Jewish Studies* 10, no. 2 (2011): 245–62.

Cole, Joshua. "À chacun son public: Politique et culture dans l'Algérie des années 1930." *Sociétés & Représentations* 2, no. 38 (2014): 21–51.

———. *Lethal Provocation: The Constantine Murders and the Politics of French Algeria*. Ithaca, NY: Cornell University Press, 2019.

"Concert Orchestre Blaoui & Guests—Oran (Aïd 1958)." *Raï & Folk*; https:// soundcloud.com/raiandfolk/concert-orchestre-blaoui-fadila-dziria-hajira-bali -etc-oran-aid-1958.

Cormack, Raphael. *Midnight in Cairo: The Divas of Egypt's Roaring '20s.* New York: W. W. Norton, 2021.

Corriou, Morgan. "Radio and Society in Tunisia during World War II." In *The World in World Wars: Experiences, Perceptions and Perspectives from Africa and Asia*, ed. Heike Liebau, 369–97. Leiden: Brill, 2010.

Danielson, Virginia. *The Voice of Egypt: Umm Kulthūm, Arabic Song, and Egyptian Society in the Twentieth Century.* Chicago: University of Chicago Press, 1997.

Daoudi, Bouziane, and Hadj Miliani. *Beurs' melodies: Cent ans de chansons immigrées du blues berbère au rap beur.* Paris: Séguir, 2002.

———. *L'Aventure du raï. Musique et société.* Paris: Point Virgule-Le Seuil, 2006.

Darmon, Raoul. *La Goulette et les Goulettois: Notules.* Tunis: Société tunisienne de diffusion, 1969.

Davidson, Naomi. *Only Muslim: Embodying Islam in Twentieth-Century France.* Ithaca, NY: Cornell University Press, 2012.

Davila, Carl. *The Andalusian Music of Morocco: Al-Āla: History, Society and Text.* Wiesbaden: Reichert Verlag, 2013.

———. "The Andalusi Turn: The Nūba in Mediterranean History." Special Issue: The Mediterranean Voyage, *Mediterranean Studies* 23, no. 2 (2015): 159.

Davis, Ruth F. "Jews, Women and the Power to Be Heard: Charting the Early Tunisian *Ughniyya* to the Present Day." In *Music and the Play of Power in the Middle East, North Africa and Central Asia*, ed. Laudan Nooshin, 187–206. Farnham, UK: Ashgate, 2009).

———. *Ma'lūf: Reflections on the Arab Andalusian Music of Tunisia.* Lanham, MD: Scarecrow Press, 2004.

———. "Retelling the Jewish Past in Tunisia through Narratives of Popular Song." In *Jewish-Muslim Interactions: Performing Cultures between North Africa and France*, ed. Samuel Sami Everett and Rebekah Vince, 101–20. Liverpool: Liverpool University Press, 2020.

———. "Time, Place, and Memory: Songs for a North African Jewish Pilgrimage." In *Music and Displacement: Diasporas, Mobilities, and Dislocations in Europe and Beyond*, ed. Erik Levi and Florian Scheding, 71–88. Lanham, MD: Scarecrow Press, 2010.

Dellagi, Moncef. "Une campagne sur l'insécurité des colons de Tunisie en 1898." *Revue d'Histoire Maghrébine* 7–8 (1977): 99–106.

Denning, Michael. *Noise Uprising: The Audiopolitics of a World Musical Revolution.* London: Verso, 2015.

D'Erlanger, Rodolphe. *La musique arabe.* 6 vols. Paris: P. Geuthner, 1930–59.

Desparmet, Joseph. *La poésie arabe actuelle à Blida et sa métrique.* Paris: Ernest Leroux, 1907.

de Yacoub Cohen, Simon. "Khamus jana." Tunis: Imprimerie Uzan, ca. 1943–44.

Dicale, Bertrand. *Cheikh Raymond: Une histoire algérienne.* Paris: First, 2011.

Dotan (Maklouf Nadjar). "Qinat al-artist Habiba." Tunis: n.p., n.d.

Dougherty, Roberta L. "Badia Masabni, Artiste and Modernist: The Egyptian Print Media's Carnival of National Identity." In *Mass Mediations: New Approaches to Popular Culture in the Middle East and Beyond,* ed. Walter Armbrust, 243–68. Cambridge: Cambridge University Press, 1996.

Drai, Raphaël. "L'aigle et le luth." *Sillages: Revue littéraire et politique* (Winter 1983): 61–73.

Duckett, Victoria. *Seeing Sarah Bernhardt: Performance and Silent Film.* Urbana: University of Illinois Press, 2015.

Edwards, Brian T. *Morocco Bound: Disorienting America's Maghreb, from Casablanca to the Marrakech Express.* Durham, NC: Duke University Press, 2005.

El Fassi, Allal. *The Independence Movements in Arab North Africa.* Translated by Hazem Zaki Nuseibeh. Washington, DC: American Council of Learned Societies, 1954.

El Haddaoui, Mohammed. "Symbiose judeo-arabe au Maroc: La contribution des juifs marocains à la culture de leur pays; Samy El-Maghribi (Salomon Amzallag), sa production poétique et musicale." PhD diss., Université de Paris VIII–Vincennes à Saint-Denis, 1987.

El-Mahdi, Salah, and Mohamed Marzuqi. A*l-Maʿhad al-rashidi li-l-musiqa al-tunisiyya.* Tunis: Ministry of Culture, 1981.

El Médioni, Maurice. *Maurice El Médioni: A Memoir (From Oran to Marseilles, 1935–1990).* Edited by Max Reinhardt, translated by Jonathan Walton. London: Repeater Books, 2017.

Englund, Björn, and Rainer E. Lotz. "Online Discography: Matrix Blocks Used by the Carl Lindström AG"; http://www.lotz-verlag.de/lindstroem-mx-masterfile.htm.

Fahmy, Ziad. *Ordinary Egyptians: Creating the Modern Nation through Popular* Culture. Stanford, CA: Stanford University Press, 2011.

———. *Street Sounds: Listening to Everyday Life in Modern Egypt.* Stanford, CA: Stanford University Press, 2020.

Faivre d'Arcier, Jeanne. *Habiba Messika: La brûlure du péché.* Paris: Belfond, 1997.

Fanon, Frantz. *A Dying Colonialism.* New York: Grove Press, 1965.

Fargues, Dominique. *Mémoires de Pieds-Noirs.* Paris: Flammarion, 2008.

Favre, Lucienne. *Tout l'inconnu de la Casbah d'Alger.* Algiers: Baconnier Frères, 1933.

Frankel, Jonathan. *The Damascus Affair: "Ritual Murder," Politics, and the Jews in 1840.* Cambridge: Cambridge University Press, 1997.

Friedman, Elizabeth. *Colonialism and After: An Algerian Jewish Community.* South Hadley, MA: Bergin and Garvey, 1988.

Funk, Arthur Layton. *The Politics of Torch: The Allied Landings and the Algiers Putsch, 1942.* Lawrence: University Press of Kansas, 1974.

Ghallab, Abd al-Karim. *Tarikh al-haraka al-wataniyya bi-l-Maghrib.* Vol. 1. Casablanca: Matba'at al-najah al-jadida, 2000.

Gitre, Carmen. *Acting Egyptian: Theatre, Identity, and Popular Culture in Cairo, 1869–1930.* Austin: University of Texas Press, 2019.

Glasser, Jonathan. "Edmond Yafil and Andalusi Music Revival in Early 20th-Century Algeria," *International Journal of Middle East Studies* 44 (2012): 671–92.

———. *The Lost Paradise: Andalusi Music in Urban North Africa.* Chicago: University of Chicago Press, 2016.

Glenn, Susan A. *Female Spectacle: The Theatrical Roots of Modern Feminism.* Cambridge, MA: Harvard University Press, 2000.

Gottreich, Emily Benichou. *Jewish Morocco: A History from Pre-Islamic to Postcolonial Times.* London: I. B. Tauris, 2020.

Gottreich, Emily Benichou, and Daniel J. Schroeter, eds. *Jewish Culture and Society in North Africa.* Bloomington: Indiana University Press, 2010.

Grange, Daniel-Jacques. *La propagande arabe de Radio Bari* (1937–1939). Paris: Relations internationales, 1976.

Gronow, Pekka. "The Record Industry Comes to the Orient." *Ethnomusicology* 25, no. 2 (May 1, 1981): 251–84.

Guedj, David. "Post-Second World War Praise Poetry, Lament and a Utopian Treatise in Morocco: Historical Literature on the Theme of the Second World War," *Journal of Modern Jewish Studies* 17, no. 4 (2018): 455–71.

Guettat, Mahmoud. *La musique arabo-andalouse. L'Empreinte du Maghreb.* Paris: Editions El-Ouns, 2000.

———. *La musique classique du Maghreb.* Paris: Sindbad, 1980.

Hachlef, Ahmed, and Mohamed Elhabib Hachlef. *Anthologie de la musique arabe, 1906–1960.* Paris: Centre Culturel Algérien, Publisud, 1993.

HaCohen, Ruth. *The Music Libel against the Jews.* New Haven, CT: Yale University Press, 2011.

Halkin, Hillel, trans. *The Selected Poems of Yehuda Halevi.* New York: Nextbook, 2011.

Halstead, John P. *Rebirth of a Nation: The Origins and Rise of Moroccan Nationalism, 1912–1944.* Cambridge, MA: Harvard Middle Eastern Monographs, Harvard University Press, 1967.

Hamli, Mohsen. "Allouche, Félix." In *Encyclopedia of Jews in the Islamic World.* Vol. 1: A–C, ed. Norman Stillman, 181. Leiden: Brill, 2010.

Hamrouni, Ahmed. *Habiba Msika: Artiste Accomplie.* Tunis: L'Univers du livre, 2007.

Hassine, Prosper. "Megillat Hitler." Casablanca, ca. 1942.

Hatimi, Mohammed. "Al-Jamaʿat al-yahudiya al-maghribiya wa-l-khiyar al-saʿb bayna nidaʾ al-sahyuniya wa-rihan al-maghrib al-mustaqil, 1947–1961." PhD diss., Faculty of Letters, Université Mohammed V-Agdal, Sais-Fès, 2007.

Heckman, Alma Rachel. "The Dream of Al-Wifaq: Moroccan Muslim-Jewish Unity at the Moment of Independence." In *Moroccan Contemporary History: Past and Present Time. Historical Essays in Honor of Mohammed Kenbib*, vol. 1, ed. Khalid Ben-Srhir, 305–22. Rabat: Publications of the Faculty of Letters and Human Sciences, Mohammed V University in Rabat, 2021.

———. *The Sultan's Communists: Moroccan Jews and the Politics of Belonging*. Stanford, CA: Stanford University Press, 2020.

Hyman, Paula E. *The Jews of Modern France*. Berkeley: University of California Press, 1998.

Jackson, Maureen. *Mixing Musics: Turkish Jewry and the Urban Landscape of a Sacred Song*. Stanford, CA: Stanford University Press, 2013.

Jacob, Wilson Chako. *Working Out Egypt: Effendi Masculinity and Subject Formation in Colonial Modernity, 1870–1940*. Durham, NC: Duke University Press, 2011.

James, C. L. R. *Beyond a Boundary*. London: Hutchinson, 1963.

Jankowsky, Richard. *Ambient Sufism: Ritual Niches and the Social Work of Musical Form*. Chicago: University of Chicago Press, 2021.

———. *Stambeli: Music, Trance, and Alterity in Tunisia*. Chicago: University of Chicago Press, 2010.

Joffé, George. "The Moroccan Nationalist Movement: Istiqlal, the Sultan, and the Country." *Journal of African History* 26, no. 4 (1985): 289–307.

Jones, Alyson E. "Playing Out: Women Instrumentalists and Women's Ensembles in Contemporary Tunisia." PhD diss., University of Michigan, 2010.

Jones, Andrew F. *Yellow Music: Media Culture and Colonial Modernity in the Chinese Jazz Age*. Durham, NC: Duke University Press, 2001.

Jones, L. Jafran. "A Sociohistorical Perspective on Tunisian Women as Professional Musicians." In *Women and Music in Cross-Cultural Perspective*, ed. Ellen Koskoff, 69–83. New York: Greenwood, 1987.

Journo, Raoul. *Ma vie; Propos recueillis par ma fille Flavie*. Paris: Biblieurope, 2002.

Julien, Charles-André. "Colons français et jeunes Tunisiens (1892–1912)." *Revue française d'histoire d'outre-mer* 54 (1967): 87–150.

———. *Histoire de l'Algérie contemporaine. Vol. 1: La conquête et les débuts de la colonisation (1827–1871)*. Paris: Presses Universitaires de France, 1964.

———. *L'Afrique du nord en marche: Nationalismes musulmans et souveraineté française*. Paris: Éditions René Julliard, 1952.

Kably, Mohamed. *Histoire du Maroc: Réactualisation et synthèse*. Rabat: Ed. de l'Institut royal pour la recherche sur l'histoire du Maroc, 2012.

Kafadar, Cemal. "Between Past and Present, Part 2," episode 474. *Ottoman History Podcast*, September 1, 2020; http://www.ottomanhistorypodcast.com/2020/08/kafadar-2.html.

Kapchan, Deborah. *Gender on the Market: Moroccan Women and the Revoicing of Tradition*. Philadelphia: University of Pennsylvania Press, 1996.

Katz, Ethan. *Burdens of Brotherhood: Jews and Muslims from North Africa to France*. Cambridge, MA: Harvard University Press, 2015.

———. "Did the Paris Mosque Save Jews? A Mystery and Its Memory." *Jewish Quarterly Review* 102, no. 2 (Spring 2012): 256–87.

———. "Who Were the Jewish Underground of Algiers? A Sectorial Analysis of the Paths to Resistance." In *Ha-historiyah ha-arukah shel ha-mizrahim: Kivunim hadashim be-heker yehude aratsot ha-islam*, ed. Aviad Moreno et al. Be'er Sheva: The Ben-Gurion Institute for the Study of Israel and Zionism, Ben-Gurion University of the Negev, 2021.

Katz, Israel. *Henry George Farmer and the First International Congress of Arab Music (Cairo 1932)*. Leiden: Brill, 2015.

Katz, Jacob. *The Darker Side of Genius: Richard Wagner's Anti-Semitism*. Hanover, NH: Brandeis University Press, 1986.

Kazdaghli, Habib, ed. *Mémoire de femmes: Tunisiennes dans la vie publique, 1920–1960*. Tunis: Imprimerie Principale, Édition média com, 1993.

Kelly, Alan, ed. *Gramophone Company Matrix Series 1898–1932*. Computer file. York, UK: 2009.

Kenbib, Mohammed. *Juifs et musulmans au Maroc, 1859–1948*. Rabat: Université Mohammed V, Faculté des Lettres et des Sciences Humaines, 1994.

———. *Juifs et musulmans au Maroc: Des origines à nos jours*. Paris: Tallandier, 2016.

———. "Moroccan Jews and the Vichy Regime, 1940–42." *Journal of North African Studies* 19, no. 4 (2014): 540–53.

Kerr, Malcolm H. *The Arab Cold War, 1958–1964: A Study of Ideology in Politics*. Oxford: Oxford University Press, 1965.

Khuri-Makdisi, Ilham. *The Eastern Mediterranean and the Making of Global Radicalism, 1860–1914*. Berkeley: University of California Press, 2010.

Klarsfeld, Serge. *Memorial to the Jews Deported from France, 1942–1944: Documentation of the Deportation of the Victims of the Final Solution in France*. New York: Beate Klarsfeld Foundation, 1983.

Lagrange, Frédéric. "Musiciens et poètes en Égypte au temps de la nahda." PhD diss., Université de Paris à Saint-Denis, 1994.

———. "Women in the Singing Business, Women in Songs." *History Compass* 7, no. 1 (2009): 226–50.

Laloum, Jean. "Cinéma et histoire. La mosquée de Paris et les Juifs sous l'Occupation," *Archives Juives* 45, no. 1 (2012): 116–28.

———."Des juifs d'afrique du nord au Pletzl? Une presence méconnue et des épreuves oubliées (1920–1945)." *Archives Juives, revue d'histoire des Juifs de Frances*, Les Belles lettres 38 (2005): 47–83.

Langlois, Tony. "Music and Politics in North Africa." In *Music and the Play of Power in the Middle East, North Africa and Central Asia*, ed. Laudan Nooshin, 207–27. Farnham, UK: Ashgate, 2009.

Laroui, Abdallah. *L'Histoire du Maghreb: Un essai de synthèse*. Paris: Librairie François Maspero, 1980.

Laskier, Michael M. *The Alliance Israélite Universelle and the Jewish Communities of Morocco, 1862–1962*. Albany: State University of New York Press, 1983.

———. *North African Jewry in the Twentieth Century: The Jews of Morocco, Tunisia, and Algeria*. New York: New York University Press, 1997.

Leff, Lisa Moses. *Sacred Bonds of Solidarity: Jewish Internationalism in Nineteenth-Century France*. Stanford, CA: Stanford University Press, 2006.

Le Foll-Luciani, Pierre-Jean. *Les juifs algériens dans la lute anticoloniale: Trajectoire dissidents (1934–1965)*. Rennes: Presses Universitaires de Rennes, 2015.

"Lettre de Constantine." *Droits et Liberté*. May 1961, no. 200, 5; http://archives.mrap .fr/images/6/69/Dl61_200opt.pdf.

Levy, André. "A Community That Is Both a Center and a Diaspora: Jews in Late Twentieth-Century Morocco." In *Homelands and Diasporas: Holy Lands and Other Places*, ed. André Levy and Alex Weingrod, 68–96. Stanford, CA: Stanford University Press, 2005.

———. *Return to Casablanca: Jews, Muslims, and an Israeli Anthropologist*. Chicago: University of Chicago Press, 2015.

Lewis, Mary Dewhurst. *Divided Rule: Sovereignty and Empire in French Tunisia, 1881–1938*. Berkeley: University of California Press, 2014.

Loeffler, James. "Richard Wagner's 'Jewish Music': Antisemitism and Aesthetics in Modern Jewish Culture." *Jewish Social Studies* 15, no. 2 (Winter 2009): 2–36.

L. V. "Le théâtre arabe à Tunis." *Revue des Études Islamiques*, book 4. Paris: P. Geuthner, 1932.

MacDonald, Callum A. "Radio Bari: Italian Wireless Propaganda in the Middle East and British Countermeasures 1934–38." *Middle Eastern Studies* 13, no. 2 (May 1977): 195–207.

Machado, Margarida Maria da Mota Ferreira. "Habiba Messika: Uma biografia (im) possível." MA thesis, Faculdade de Letras da Universidade do Porto, 2006.

Macias, Enrico, with Florence Assouline. *Mon Algérie*. Paris: Plon, 2001.

Mac Orlan, Pierre. *Le Bataillon de la mauvaise chance: Un civil chez les "Joyeux."* Paris: Les Éditions de France, 1933.

Maghraoui, Driss. "The *Goumiers* in the Second World War: History and Colonial Representation." *Journal of North African Studies* 19, no. 4 (2014): 571–86.

Mahfoufi, Mehenna. *Chants kabyles de la guerre d'indépendence. Algérie 1954–1962.* Paris: Séguier, 2002.

Mahjoubi, Ali. *Les origines du mouvement national en Tunisie (1904–1934).* Tunis: Publications de l'Université de Tunis, 1982.

Mahjoubi, Ali, and Hachemi Karoui. *Quand le soleil s'est levé à l'ouest. Tunisie 1881–impérialisme et résistance.* Tunis: Centre d'Etudes et de Recherches Economiques et Sociales, 1983.

Mamelouk, Nadia. "Anxiety in the Border Zone: Transgressing Boundaries." In *Leila: Revue Illustrée de la Femme* (Tunis, 1936–1940) and in *Leila: Hebdomadaire Tunisien Independent* (Tunis, 1940–1941). PhD diss., University of Virginia, 2008.

Mandel, Arnold. "Algeria." *American Jewish Year Book* 64 (1963): 403–11.

Mandel, Maud. *Muslims and Jews in France: History of a Conflict.* Princeton, NJ: Princeton University Press, 2014.

Manela, Erez. *The Wilsonian Moment: Self Determination and the International Origins of Anticolonial Nationalism.* Oxford: Oxford University Press, 2007.

Marcus, Sharon. *The Drama of Celebrity.* Princeton, NJ: Princeton University Press, 2019.

Marglin, Jessica M. *Across Legal Lines: Jews and Muslims in Modern Morocco.* New Haven, CT: Yale University Press, 2016.

———. "Modernizing Moroccan Jews: The AIU Alumni Association in Tangier, 1893–1913," *Jewish Quarterly Review* 101, no. 4 (Fall 2011): 574–603.

Margueritte, Victor. *La garçonne.* Paris: Ernest Flammarion, Éditeur, 1922.

Marolle, Emmanuel. "Enrico Macias: Enfant de deux pays." *Le Parisien,* June 23, 2019; https://www.leparisien.fr/culture-loisirs/musique/enrico-macias-enfant-de-deux-pays-23-06-2019-8100543.php.

Marouf, Nadir, ed. *Le chant arabo-andalou.* Paris: L'Harmattan, 1995.

Marrus, Michael R., and Robert O. Paxton. *Vichy France and the Jews.* New York: Basic Books, 1981.

Marzano, Arturo. *Onde fasciste: La propaganda araba di Radio Bari (1934–43).* Rome: Carocci editore, 2015.

Marzouki, Ilhem. *Le mouvement des femmes en Tunisie au XXème siècle: Feminisme et politique.* Paris: Maisonneuve et Larose, 1993.

Massad, Joseph. "Zionism's Internal Others: Israel and the Oriental Jews." *Journal of Palestine Studies* 25, no. 4 (2007): 53–68.

McDougall, James. *A History of Algeria.* Cambridge: Cambridge University Press, 2017.

Memmi, Albert. *The Colonizer and the Colonized.* Boston: Beacon Press, 1991.

Merdaçi, Abdelmadjid. "Cheikh Raymond, the 'Hseïni' (1912–1961)." In *A History of Jewish-Muslim Relations: From the Origins to the Present Day,* ed. Abdelwahab

Meddeb and Benjamin Stora, 982–83. Princeton, NJ: Princeton University Press, 2013.

———. *Dictionnaire des musiques et des musiciens de Constantine*. Constantine: Simoun, 2002.

Mernissi, Fatima. *Dreams of Trespass: Tales of a Harem Girlhood*. New York: Basic Books, 1994.

Mestyan, Adam. "Arabic Theatre in Early Khedivial Culture, 1868–1872: James Sanua Revisited." *International Journal of Middle East Studies* 46, no. 1 (2014): 117–37.

———. "Upgrade? Power and Sound during Ramadan and ʿId al-Fitr in the Nineteenth-Century Ottoman Arab Provinces." *Comparative Studies of South Asia, Africa and the Middle East* 37, no. 2 (2017): 262–79.

Michman, Dan, and Haïm Saadoun, eds. *Les Juifs d'Afrique du nord face à l'allemagne Nazie*. Paris: Perrin, 2018.

Miliani, Hadj. "Crosscurrents: Trajectories of Algerian Jewish Artists and Men of Culture since the End of the Nineteenth Century." In *Jewish Culture and Society in North Africa*, ed. Emily Benichou Gottreich and Daniel J. Schroeter, 177–87. Bloomington: Indiana University Press, 2010.

———. "Déplorations, polémiques et strategies patrimoniales. Á propos des musiques citadines en Algérie en régime colonial," *Insaniyat* 79 (January–March 2018): 27–41.

———. "Diasporas musiciennes et migrations maghrébines en situation coloniale," *Volume!* 12, no. 1 (2010): 155–69.

———. "Le cheikh et le phonographe: Notes de recherche pour un corpus des phonogrammes et des vidéogrammes des musiques et des chansons algériennes," *Les cahiers du CRASC* no. 8, *Turath* no. 4 (2004): 43–67.

Miliani, Hadj, and Samuel Sami Everett. "Marie Soussan: A Singular Trajectory." In *Jewish-Muslim Interactions: Performing Cultures between North Africa and France*, ed. Samuel Sami Everett and Rebekah Vince, 81–100. Liverpool: Liverpool University Press, 2020.

Miller, Susan Gilson. "Filling a Historical Parenthesis: An Introduction to 'Morocco from World War II to Independence,'" *Journal of North African Studies* 19, no. 4 (2014): 461–74.

———. *A History of Modern Morocco*. New York: Cambridge University Press, 2013.

———. *Years of Glory: Nelly Benatar and the Pursuit of Justice in Wartime North Africa*. Stanford, CA: Stanford University Press, 2021.

Mitchell, Allan. *Nazi Paris: The History of an Occupation, 1940–1944*. New York: Berghahn Books, 2008.

Moreno, Aviad. "Beyond the Nation-State: A Network Analysis of Jewish Emigration from Northern Morocco to Israel." *International Journal of Middle East Studies* 52, no. 1 (2020): 1–21.

Morton, David. *Sound Recording: The Life Story of a Technology.* Baltimore, MD: Johns Hopkins University Press, 2006.

Moussali, Bernard. "Les premiers enregistrements de musique tunisienne par les compagnies discographiques," presented at "Liens et interactions entre les musiques arabes et méditerranéennes," Le Centre des musiques arabes et méditerranéennes (CMAM), Tunis, Tunisia, 1992.

Nelson, Carolyn Christensen, ed. *A New Woman Reader: Fiction, Articles, and Drama of the 1890s.* Peterborough, ON: Broadview Press, 2001.

Ockman, Carol, and Kenneth E. Silver, eds. *Sarah Bernhardt: The Art of High Drama.* New York: Jewish Museum, New York, under the auspices of the Jewish Theological Seminary of America; New Haven, CT: Yale University Press, 2005.

Ouijjani, Hinda. "Le fonds de disques 78 tours Pathé de musique arabe et orientale donné aux Archives de la Parole et au Musée de la Parole et du Geste de l'Université de Paris: 1911–1930," parts 1 and 2, *Bulletin de l'AFAS* 38 and 39, Spring–Summer 2012 and Fall–Winter 2013; https://journals.openedition.org/afas/2835 and https://journals.openedition.org/afas/2903.

Ounnoughene, Mouloud. *Mohamed Iguerbouchène: Un oeuvre intemporelle.* Algiers: Dar Khettab, 2015.

Pasler, Jann. "Teaching Andalousian Music at Rabat's *Conservatoire de musique marocaine.*" In *Music and Encounter at the Mediterranean Crossroads: A Sea of Voices,* ed. Ruth Davis and Brian Oberlander, 124–50. New York: Routledge Press, 2022.

Perkins, Kenneth. *A History of Modern Tunisia.* New York: Cambridge University Press, 2014.

Poché, Christian. *La musique arabo-andalouse.* Paris: Cité de la Musique/Actes Sud, 1995.

Raccagni, Michelle. "Origins of Feminism in Egypt and Tunisia." PhD diss., New York University, 1982.

Racy, Ali Jihad. "Historical Worldviews of Early Ethnomusicologists: An East-West Encounter in Cairo, 1932." In *Ethnomusicology and Modern Music History,* ed. Stephen Blum, Philip V. Bohlman, and Daniel M. Neuman, 68–94. Urbana: University of Illinois Press, 1991.

———. *Making Music in the Arab World: The Culture and Artistry of Tarab.* Cambridge: Cambridge University Press, 2003.

———. "Record Industry and Egyptian Traditional Music: 1904–1932," *Ethnomusicology* 20, no. 1 (January 1976): 23–48.

Rahnama, Sara. "Hijabs and Hats in Interwar Algeria." *Gender & History* 32, no. 2 (July 2020): 429–46.

Rath, Richard Cullen. "Hearing American History." *Journal of American History* 95, no. 2 (September 2008): 417–31.

Razlogova, Elena. *The Listener's Voice: Early Radio and the American Public*. Philadelphia: University of Pennsylvania Press, 2011.

Read, Oliver, and Walter L. Welch. *From Tin Foil to Stereo: Evolution of the Phonograph*. Indianapolis, IN: Howard W. Sams, 1977.

Regev, Motti, and Edwin Seroussi. *Popular Music and National Culture in Israel*. Berkeley: University of California Press, 2004.

Reynolds, Dwight F. "Al-Maqqarī's Ziryab: The Making of a Myth." *Middle Eastern Literatures* 11, no. 2 (2008): 155–68.

———. "Musical 'Membrances of Medieval Muslim Spain." In *Charting Memory: Recalling Medieval Spain*, ed. Stacy N. Beckwith, 229–62. New York: Garland, 2000.

Reynolds, Nancy Y. *A City Consumed: Urban Commerce, the Cairo Fire, and the Politics of Decolonization in Egypt*. Stanford, CA: Stanford University Press, 2012.

Rézette, Robert. *Les partis politiques marocains*. Paris: A. Colin, 1955.

Rizqi, al-Sadiq. *Al-Aghani al-tunisiyya*. Tunis: Al-Dar al-tunisiyya lil-nashr, 1967.

Roberts, Mary Louise. *Disruptive Acts: The New Woman in Fin-de-Siècle France*. Chicago: University of Chicago Press, 2002.

Roberts, Sophie B. *Citizenship and Antisemitism in French Colonial Algeria, 1870–1962*. New York: Cambridge University Press, 2017.

———. "Jews, Vichy, and the Algiers Insurrection of 1942." *Holocaust Studies* 12, no. 3 (2006): 63–88.

Roby, Bryan K. *The Mizrahi Era of Rebellion: Israel's Forgotten Civil Rights Struggle 1948–1966*. Syracuse, NY: Syracuse University Press, 2015.

Roda, Jessica, and Stephanie Tara Schwartz. "Home beyond Borders and the Sound of Al-Andalus: *Jewishness in Arabic; The Odyssey of Samy Elmaghribi*." *Religions* 11, no. 11 (2020): 609.

Rodrigue, Aron. *French Jews, Turkish Jews: The Alliance Israélite Universelle and the Politics of Jewish Schooling in Turkey, 1860–1925*. Bloomington: Indiana University Press, 1990.

Rosen, Lawrence. *The Culture of Islam*. Chicago: University of Chicago Press, 2002.

Rosenberg, Clifford. *Policing Paris: The Origins of Modern Immigration Control between the Wars*. Ithaca, NY: Cornell University Press, 2006.

Ross, Alex. *The Rest Is Noise: Listening to the Twentieth Century*. New York: Picador, 2007.

———. *Wagnerism: Art and Politics in the Shadow of Music*. New York: Farrar, Straus, and Giroux, 2020.

Roth, Arlette. *Le théâtre algérien de langue dialectale, 1926–1954*. Paris: François Maspero, 1967.

Rouget, Gilbert. *Musique et transe chez les arabes*. Paris: Éditions Gallimard, 1980.

Russell, Mona L. *Creating the New Egyptian Woman: Consumerism, Education, and National Identity, 1863–1922.* New York: Palgrave Macmillan, 2004.

Saidani, Maya. *La musique du constantinois: Contexte, nature, transmission et définition.* Algiers: Casbah Editions, 2006.

Sakli, Mourad. "La chanson tunisienne: Analyse technique et approche sociologique." PhD diss., Université de Paris IV-La Sorbonne, 1994.

Salamon, Hagar, and Esther Juhasz. "'Goddesses of Flesh and Metal': Gazes on the Tradition of Fattening Jewish Brides in Tunisia." *Journal of Middle East Women's Studies* 7, no. 1 (Winter 2011): 1–38.

Saraf, Michal. *The Hitler Scroll of North Africa: Moroccan and Tunisian Jewish Literature on the Fall of the Nazis.* Lod: Haberman Institute, 1988.

Sarfatti, Michele. *The Jews in Mussolini's Italy: From Equality to Persecution.* Madison: University of Wisconsin Press, 2006.

Sater, James N. *Morocco: Challenges to Tradition and Modernity.* London: Routledge, 2016.

Scales, Rebecca P. "Subversive Sound: Transnational Radio, Arabic Recordings, and the Dangers of Listening in French Colonial Algeria, 1934–1939." *Comparative Studies in Society and History* 52, no. 2 (April 1, 2010), 384–417.

Schade-Poulsen, Marc. *Men and Popular Music in Algeria: The Social Significance of Raï.* Austin: University of Texas Press, 1999.

Schafer, R. Murray. *The Soundscape: The Tuning of the World.* Rochester, VT: Destiny Books, 1994.

Schreier, Joshua. *Arabs of the Jewish Faith: The Civilizing Mission in Colonial Algeria.* New Brunswick, NJ: Rutgers University Press, 2010.

Schroeter, Daniel J. *Merchants of Essaouira: Urban Society and Imperialism in Southwestern Morocco, 1844–1886.* Cambridge: Cambridge University Press, 2009.

———. "Vichy in Morocco, the Residency, Muhammad V and His Indigenous Jewish Subjects." In *Colonialism and the Jews*, ed. Ethan B. Katz, Lisa Moses Leff, and Maud S. Mandel, 215–50. Bloomington: Indiana University Press, 2017.

Schuyler, Philip D. "Moroccan Andalusian Music." *World of Music* 20, no. 1 (1978): 33–43.

Sebag, Paul. *Histoire des Juifs de Tunisie: Des origins à nos jours.* Paris: L'Harmattan, 1991.

Segalla, Spencer. "Natural Disaster, Globalization, and Decolonization: The Case of the 1960 Agadir Earthquake." *In French Mediterraneans: Transnational and Imperial Histories, ed. Patricia M. E. Lorcin and Todd Shepard*, 101–28. *Lincoln: University of Nebraska Press, 2016.*

Seroussi, Edwin. "Elmaghribi, Samy (Amzallag)." In *Encyclopedia of Jews in the Islamic World*, ed. Norman A. Stillman, 165–66. Leiden: Brill, 2010.

———. "Music: The 'Jew' of Jewish Studies." *Yearbook of the World Union of Jewish Studies* 46 (2009): 3–84.

———. "Music: Muslim-Jewish Sonic Encounters." In *The Routledge Handbook of Muslim-Jewish Relations*, ed. Josef Meri, 429–48. London: Routledge, 2016.

———. "Sanctity and Celebrity: The Musical Journey of Rabbi David Buzaglo from Casablanca to Kiryat Yam." Forthcoming.

Serri, Sid Ahmed. *Chants andalous. Recueil de poèmes des noubate de la musique SANÂA: Musique classique algérienne*. Algiers: Editions ENAG, 2006.

Shannon, Jonathan H. *Performing al-Andalus: Music and Nostalgia across the Mediterranean*. Bloomington: Indiana University Press, 2015.

Shepard, Todd. *The Invention of Decolonization: The Algerian War and the Remaking of France*. Ithaca, NY: Cornell University Press, 2008.

Shiloah, Amnon. "Al-Manṣūr al-Yahūdī." In *Encyclopaedia Judaica*, ed. Michael Berenbaum and Fred Skolnik, vol. 1, 2nd ed., 679. Detroit: Macmillan Reference, 2007.

———. *Music in the World of Islam: A Socio-Cultural Study*. Detroit: Wayne State University Press, 1995.

Shin, Gi-Wook, and Michael Edson Robinson, eds. *Colonial Modernity in Korea*. Cambridge, MA: Harvard University Press, 2001.

Shohat, Ella. "The Invention of Judeo-Arabic." *Interventions* 19, no. 2 (2017): 153–200.

———. "Sephardim in Israel: Zionism from the Standpoint of Its Jewish Victims." *Social Text* 19–20 (1988): 1–35.

Silver, Christopher. "The Life and Death of North Africa's First Superstar." *History Today*, April 24, 2018; https://www.historytoday.com/miscellanies/life-and-death -north-africas-first-superstar.

———. "Listening to the Past: Music as a Source for the Study of North African Jews." In "Jews of Morocco and the Maghreb: History and Historiography," ed. Aomar Boum, Jessica Marglin, Khalid Ben-Srhir, and Mohammed Kenbib, special issue of *Hespéris-Tamuda* LI (2016): 243–55.

———. "Nationalist Records: Jews, Muslims, and Music in Interwar North Africa." In *Jewish-Muslim Interactions: Performing Cultures between North Africa and France*, ed. Samuel Sami Everett and Rebekah Vince, 61–80. Liverpool: Liverpool University Press, 2020.

———. "Radio Tunis' Hebrew Hour (1939–1956): A Microhistory." Forthcoming.

———. "Sonic Geniza: Finding Zohra El Fassia in Los Angeles." In *100 Years of Sephardic Los Angeles*, ed. Sarah Abrevaya Stein and Caroline Luce. Los Angeles: UCLA Leve Center for Jewish Studies, 2020; http://www.sephardiclosangeles .org/portfolios/sonic-geniza/.

———. "The Sounds of Nationalism: Music, Moroccanism, and the Making of Samy Elmaghribi." *International Journal of Middle East Studies* 52, no. 1 (2020): 23–47.

Simon, Reeva S. *The Jews of the Middle East and North Africa: The Impact of World War II*. London: Routledge, 2019.

Slyomovics, Susan. *How to Accept German Reparations*. Philadelphia: University of Pennsylvania Press, 2014.

———. "'Other Places of Confinement,' Bedeau Internment Camp for Algerian Jewish Soldiers." In *The Holocaust and North Africa*, ed. Aomar Boum and Sarah Abrevaya Stein, 95–112. Stanford, CA: Stanford University Press, 2018.

Sraieb, Noureddine. "L'idéologie de l'école en Tunisie coloniale (1881–1945)." *Revue de l'Occident Musulman et de la Méditerranée* 68–9 (1993): 239–54.

Stanton, Andrea. *"This Is Jerusalem Calling": State Radio in Mandate Palestine*. Austin: University of Texas Press, 2014.

Starr, Deborah A. *Togo Mizrahi and the Making of Egyptian Cinema*. Oakland: University of California Press, 2020.

Stein, Sarah Abrevaya. "The Field of In-Between." *International Journal of Middle East Studies* 46, no. 3 (2014): 581–83.

———. *Saharan Jews and the Fate of French Algeria*. Chicago: University of Chicago Press, 2014.

Stenner, David. *Globalizing Morocco: Transnational Activism and the Postcolonial State*. Stanford, CA: Stanford University Press, 2019.

Sterne, Jonathan. *The Audible Past: Cultural Origins of Sound Reproduction*. Durham, NC: Duke University Press, 2003.

Sternfeld, Lior. *Between Iran and Zion: Jewish Histories of Twentieth-Century Iran*. Stanford, CA: Stanford University Press, 2018.

Stora, Benjamin. *Les clés retrouvées: Une enfance juive à Constantine*. Paris: Stock, 2015.

———. *Les trois exils juifs d'Algérie*. Paris: Stock, 2006.

———. "Une enfance à Constantine." In *La Méditerranée des Juifs: Exodes et enracinements*, ed. Paul Balta, Catherine Dana, and Régine Dhoquois-Cohen, 235–50. Paris: L'Harmattan, 2003.

Swedenburg, Ted. "Against Hybridity: The Case of Enrico Macias/Gaston Ghrenassia." In *Palestine, Israel, and the Politics of Popular Culture*, ed. Rebecca L. Stein and Ted Swedenburg, 238–39. Durham, NC: Duke University Press, 2005.

———. "On the Origins of Pop Rai." *Middle East Journal of Culture and Communication* 12 (2019): 7–34.

Tamzali, Haydée. *Images retrouvées*. Tunis: Maison tunisienne de l'édition, 1992.

Théoleyre, Malcolm. "Musique arabe, folklore de France? Musique, politique et communautés musiciennes en contact à Alger durant la période coloniale (1862–1962)." PhD diss., Sciences-Po, 2016.

Tlili, Bechir. "Socialistes et Jeunes-Tunisiens à la veille de la grande guerre (1911–1913)." *Cahiers de Tunisie* 22, nos. 85–86 (1974): 49–134.

Tobi, Yosef, and Tsivia Tobi. *Judeo-Arabic Literature in Tunisia, 1850–1950*. Detroit: Wayne State University Press, 2014.

Trabelsy, Allouche. "Ughniyyat al-madhlumin." Tunis, n.p., n.d.

Trevisan Semi, Emanuela. "Double Trauma and Manifold Narratives: Jews' and Muslims' Representations of the Departure of Moroccan Jews in the 1950s and 1960s." *Journal of Modern Jewish Studies* 9, no. 1 (2010): 107–25.

Trevisan Semi, Emanuela, and Hanane Sekkat Hatimi. *Mémoire et représentations des Juifs au Maroc: Les voisins absents de Meknès*. Paris: Publisud, 2011.

Turki, Mohamed. *Abdelaziz Laroui: Témoin de son temps*. Tunis: Éditions Turki, 1988.

Turner, Tamara. "The 'Right' Kind of Ḥāl: Feeling and Foregrounding Atmospheric Identity in an Algerian Music Ritual." In *Music as Atmosphere: Affective Sounds and Collective Feelings*, ed. Friedlind Riedel and Juha Torvinen, 113–30. London: Routledge, 2020.

Valensi, Lucette. "Une conversation entre Raoul Journo, Jacques Taïeb et Lucette Valensi (juin 1999)." In *Juifs au Maghreb: Mélanges à la mémoire de Jacques Taïeb*, ed. Ariel Danan and Claude Nataf, 211–18. Paris: Éditions de l'Éclat, 2013.

Virolle, Marie. *La chanson raï. De l'Algérie profonde à la scène internationale*. Paris: Éditions Karthala, 1995.

Walters, Keith. "Education for Jewish Girls in Late Nineteenth- and Early Twentieth-Century Tunis and the Spread of French in Tunisia." In *Jewish Culture and Society in North Africa*, ed. Emily Benichou Gottreich and Daniel J. Schroeter, 257–81. Bloomington: Indiana University Press, 2011.

Walters, Vernon A. *Silent Missions*. New York: Doubleday, 1978.

Waterbury, John. *The Commander of the Faithful: The Moroccan Political Elite—a Study in Segmented Politics*. New York: Columbia University Press, 1970.

*Watha'iq*, no. 24–25, Institut supérieur d'Histoire du Mouvement National. Tunis: Université de Tunis, 1998–99.

Weideman, Julian. "Tahar Haddad after Bourguiba and Bin Ali: A Reformist between Secularist Islamists." *International Journal of Middle East Studies* 48 (2016): 47–65.

Weinbaum, A. E., L. M. Thomas, P. Ramamurthy, U. G. Poiger, M. Y. Dong, and T. E. Barlow, eds. *The Modern Girl around the World: Consumption, Modernity, and Globalization*. Durham, NC: Duke University Press, 2008.

Weiss, Yfaat. *A Confiscated Memory: Wadi Salib and Haifa's Lost Heritage*. New York: Columbia University Press, 2011.

Wertheim, Uri. "Ha-khanut ba-kikar ha-shaʿon." In *Zemer boded hu ha-lev: Muzikah mizrahit ba-yisrael*, ed. Eran Litvin, 80–97. Ashdod: Ashdod Art Museum, 2017.

White, Luise. *Speaking with Vampires: Rumor and History in Colonial Africa*. Berkeley: University of California Press, 2008.

Wildangel, René. "More than the Mufti: Other Arab-Palestinian Voices on Nazi Germany, 1933–1945, and Their Postwar Narrations." In *Arab Responses to Fascism and Nazism: Attraction and Repulsion*, ed. Israel Gershoni, 101–25. Austin: University of Texas Press, 2014.

Williams, Manuela. *Mussolini's Propaganda Abroad: Subversion in the Mediterranean and the Middle East, 1935–1940*. London: Routledge, 2006.

Wurtzler, Steve J. *Electric Sounds: Technological Change and the Rise of Corporate Mass Media*. New York: Columbia University Press, 2008.

Wyrtzen, Jonathan. *Making Morocco: Colonial Intervention and the Politics of Identity*. Ithaca, NY: Cornell University Press, 2016.

Yafil, Edmond Nathan. *Diwan al-aghani min kalam al-andalus*. Algiers: Imprimerie Express Sauveur Solal, 1904.

———. *Majmu' al-aghani wa-l-alhan min kalam al-Andalus*. Algiers: Imprimerie Administrative Gojosso, 1904.

———. *Répertoire de musique arabe et maure: Collection de mélodies, ouvertures, noubet, chansons, préludes, etc.* In *Collection Yafil*, collected by Edmond Nathan Yafil under the direction of Jules Rouanet. Algiers: E. N. Yafil, n.d.

Yahi, Naïma, Driss El Yazami, and Yvan Gastaut, eds. *Générations: Un siècle d'histoire culturelle des Maghrébins en France*. Paris: Gallimard, 2009.

Y. B. "Qinat Hitler." Tunis: Imprimerie Castro, ca. 1943.

Yehoshua, Yaacov. *Yaldut bi-Yerushalayim ha-yeshanah pirke hayai mi-yamim avaru*. Jerusalem: R. Mas, 1965.

Zaki, M'Barek. *Le mouvement de libération marocain et l'indépendance inachevée, 1948–1958*. Rabat: Éditions & Impressions Bouregreg, 2009.

Zayzafoon, Lamia Ben Youssef. *The Production of the Muslim Woman: Negotiating Text, History, and Ideology*. Lanham, MD: Lexington Books, 2005.

Zisenwine, Daniel. *The Emergence of Nationalist Politics in Morocco: The Rise of the Independence Party and the Struggle against Colonialism after World War II*. London: Tauris Academic Studies, 2010.

Zuhur, Sherifa. *Asmahan's Secrets: Woman, War, and Song*. Austin: Center for Middle Eastern Studies, University of Texas at Austin, 2000.

# INDEX

Page numbers in *italics* indicate illustrations.

CPSIA information can be obtained
at www.ICGtesting.com
Printed in the USA
JSHW050310140522
25829JS00002B/3